R Blayt

The Humanities

LIBRARY SCIENCE TEXT SERIES

Introduction to Public Services for Library Technicians. By Marty Bloomberg.

Introduction to Technical Services for Library Technicians. 2nd ed. By Marty Bloomberg and G. Edward Evans.

A Guide to the Library of Congress Classification. 2nd ed. By J. Phillip Immroth.

Science and Engineering Reference Sources: A Guide for Students and Librarians. By Harold Robert Malinowsky.

The Vertical File and Its Satellites: A Handbook of Acquisition, Processing and Organization. By Shirley Miller.

The School Library Media Center. By Emanuel T. Prostano and Joyce S. Prostano.

The School Library and Educational Change. By Martin Rossoff.

Introduction to Cataloging and Classification. 4th rev. ed. By Bohdan S. Wynar.

LIBRARY SCIENCE TEXT SERIES

The Humanities

A Selective Guide to Information Sources

A. Robert Rogers

Professor of Library Science
Kent State University

1974

LIBRARIES UNLIMITED, INC., LITTLETON, COLO.

Library of Congress Card Number 74-78393
International Standard Book Number 0-87287-091-X

LIBRARIES UNLIMITED, INC.
P.O. Box 263
Littleton, Colorado 80120

ACKNOWLEDGMENTS

Because this book is planned as a text rather than a research treatise, with a minimum of footnotes and other scholarly apparatus, it is appropriate to indicate here the sources most frequently consulted but not otherwise noted.

The Encyclopedia Americana (New York: Americana Corporation, 1973) has been used for general information on individuals, schools, movements, and national trends, and *The Encyclopedia of Associations* (8th ed. Detroit: Gale Research Co., 1973) has been invaluable.

In philosophy, *The Encyclopedia of Philosophy*, edited by Paul Edwards (New York: Macmillan & Free Press, 1967), and *Sarva-Darsana-Sangraha: A Bibliographical Guide to the Global History of Philosophy*, by John C. Plott and Paul D. Mays (Leiden: E. J. Brill, 1969), have been most useful.

In religion, the *New Catholic Encyclopedia* (New York: McGraw-Hill, 1967), the *Encyclopaedia Judaica* (New York: Macmillan, 1972), *A Dictionary of Comparative Religion*, edited by S. G. F. Brandon (New York: Scribner's, 1970), and *Religion*, edited by Paul Ramsey (Englewood Cliffs, N.J.: Prentice-Hall, 1965) have proved valuable.

In the visual arts, *A History of Art from Prehistoric Times to the Present*, by Germain Bazin (New York: Bonanza Books, 1959), and *History of Art*, by Jean Anne Vincent (2nd ed. New York: Barnes & Noble, 1967), have been used frequently. "The Use of Art Reference Sources in Museum Libraries," by John C. Larsen (*Special Libraries*, November 1971, pp. 481-86) has been extremely valuable.

Other works that have been very helpful are Hugh Miller's *History of Music* (3rd ed. New York: Barnes & Noble, 1960) and Donald W. Heiney's *Essentials of Contemporary Literature* (Woodbury, N.Y.: Barron's Educational Series, Inc., 1954).

Finally, I must express warm appreciation to many people who have helped with this project. Guy A. Marco, Dean of the School of Library Science at Kent State University, not only offered encouragement but also arranged for a reduced teaching load in the Winter Quarter of 1973. Cynthia McLaughlin, of the State Library of Ohio, very graciously gave permission to use a portion of her Master's research paper on "The Computer and the Humanities." Two graduate assistants, Marsha Koelliker and Roger Hecht, labored many hours on the typing. Most of all, however, I am grateful to my wife, Rhoda, who typed substantial portions of the manuscript in two drafts, assisted with the index, and patiently endured the trials and tribulations associated with writing a book.

Any errors of omission or commission are, of course, entirely my own. I would appreciate suggestions as to how this book can be improved to meet the needs of library science classes, reference librarians, and other users of information in the humanities.

December 1973   *A. Robert Rogers*

TABLE OF CONTENTS

PHILOSOPHY

RELIGION

LANGUAGE AND LITERATURE

Of making many books there
is no end; and much study is
a weariness of the flesh.
(Ecclesiastes 12:12)

1 INTRODUCTION

In our media-saturated time when men must take refuge from the stimuli which daily bombard the senses, how dare a writer put pen to paper and start yet another book? The accusation is the more devastating when one reflects that the words quoted above were written nearly two millenia before the invention of printing. Like Eliot's Prufrock, one must indeed ask, "And should I then presume? And how should I begin?"

Through more than 3,000 years of civilization, the humanities have nourished the spirit of man. They have a message for our own time as well—if we can find our way through the contemporary clutter. Our problem is not scarcity, but overabundance. Librarians and other users of libraries need road maps to guide the search for that knowledge which is of most value. The need for some additional mapmaking is perhaps greater in the humanities than in the natural and social sciences, which are already somewhat better charted.

The Humanities and the Library, by Lester Asheim (Chicago: American Library Association, 1957), represented a seminal approach, refreshing in its holistic concepts of librarianship. The marriage of classification, cataloging, and subject content continues to be fruitful. Nevertheless, time has rendered obsolescent the bibliographic portions of Asheim; the present writer prefers to treat classification, cataloging, and subject headings as subordinate to the process of identifying, locating, retrieving, and using information.

Information Sources in the Humanities, compiled by Thomas Slavens (Ann Arbor, Mich.: Campus Publishers, 1968), is an annotated bibliography of a few of the major sources of information in each of the five disciplines (philosophy, religion, art, music, literature) commonly included in humanities courses. There are test questions to assist the student in consolidating his knowledge, and the annotations are excellent. Nevertheless, the book does not contain background information on trends, landmark works, or major divisions of each field. Coverage is limited to a few commonly used reference works. No particular attention is paid to selection aids. There is nothing on subject headings or indexing systems. And the book is now out of print.

Reference Books in the Humanities and Social Sciences, by Rolland E. Stevens (3rd ed. Champaign, Ill.: Illini Union Bookstore, 1971), is not sufficiently extensive in its coverage of the humanities, while Barbara Hale's *The Subject Bibliography of the Social Sciences and Humanities* (New York: Pergamon Press, 1970) is excellent in its coverage of such topics as bibliographic theory and information flow but less helpful on the matter of individual reference titles.

It was hoped that the rearrangement of Constance Winchell's *Guide to Reference Books* (8th ed. Chicago: American Library Association, 1967) might facilitate its use as a text, but the sheer bulk and the need to consult several supplements now render it less useful than formerly expected. A. J. Walford's *Guide to Reference Material* (London: Library Association, 1966-70. 3 vols.) offers valuable supplementation to Winchell but hardly serves as a basic text. *American Reference Books Annual* (Littleton, Colo.: Libraries Unlimited, 1970–), edited by Bohdan S. Wynar, provides comprehensive coverage of reference books published or distributed in this country. The first volume of ARBA, covering 1969 imprints, was published in 1970. About 9,000 titles are covered in the first five volumes (through ARBA 74), and 2,368 of these titles are in the humanities. A cumulative index to the first five volumes will be published in 1974, facilitating the use of this tool. Despite its scope and demonstrated usefulness, however, ARBA makes no claim to be a textbook. Paul A. Winckler's *Humanities: Outline and Bibliography* (Palmer Graduate Library School, Long Island University, 1971) is marvellous in its range and comprehensiveness but is perhaps so comprehensive as to be intimidating and, in any event, it lacks annotations except for a few titles.

We are left, then, with a situation in which there is no single work today that will serve the needs of the humanities in a fashion comparable to Carl M. White's *Sources of Information in the Social Sciences: A Guide to the Literature* (2nd ed. Chicago: American Library Association, 1973).

What, then, is the need? The need is for a moderately priced text which students of library science can use for courses in the bibliography and/or literature of the humanities. Ideally, such a book should also meet the needs of reference librarians engaged in knowledge broadening or collection building and should be of help to scholars in pursuit of information outside their immediate areas of specialization.

The heart of this book is the bibliographical chapters, which deal with information sources in philosophy, religion, the visual arts, the performing arts, and literature. Some closely related areas (e.g., history and archaeology) are excluded as belonging more properly to the social sciences. Each bibliographical chapter is preceded by a chapter on historical trends (including major figures and landmark works) and a chapter on accessing information in that discipline.

The arrangement of each bibliographical chapter betrays the author's eclectic bias—a firm commitment to the "types and titles" approach. The rather formidable number of titles has, it is hoped, been rendered somewhat more manageable by this arrangement and by the device of mentioning lesser or older titles rather briefly in annotations for major works.

The book has evolved from the author's teaching of a particular course at a particular university. A description of that course may assist others in determining the extent to which the book is likely to meet their particular needs and the extent to which they will probably need to depart from it. The course is entitled "Literature of the Humanities," but a more descriptive title might be "Bibliography and Literature of the Humanities" or even "Information Sources in the Humanities." The course lasts for one quarter and carries three hours of graduate credit. Students come to the course after completing two prerequisites: basic and intermediate reference. In addition to bi-weekly assignments of 20 to

25 reference questions to be answered from the books covered in each unit and two lab quizzes in which questions are answered from the library's reference collection under time constraints, each member of the class completes the following projects: 1) a "pathfinder" in philosophy (see "Teaching Reference and Bibliography: The Pathfinder Approach," by Eloise Harbeson, *Journal of Education for Librarianship* 13: 111-15, Fall 1972); 2) a comparison of the treatment of any topic in three major religious encyclopedias; 3) a comparison of reproductions of any famous painting in at least three art books; 4) selection of a small, basic record collection; 5) a review of trends since 1960 in some area of world literature.

For those library schools that draw a sharp distinction between the "literature" and the "bibliography" of the humanities and that offer separate courses in each, this book will be most useful for teaching the "bibliography" of the humanities.

An attempt has been made to find a middle ground between general guides like Frances Neel Cheney's *Fundamental Reference Sources* (Chicago: American Library Association, 1971) or *Introduction to Reference Work*, by William Katz (2nd ed. New York: McGraw-Hill, 1974. 2 vols.) and specialized works like Vincent Duckles' *Music Reference and Research Materials* (3rd ed. New York: Free Press, 1974). Attention has been given to such studies as John Larsen's "Titles Currently Studied in Humanities Courses" (*Journal of Education for Librarianship* 10: 120-28, Fall 1969) and his "Art Reference Sources in Museum Libraries" (*Special Libraries* 62: 481-86, November 1971), but no fresh research along those lines has been undertaken. Comments from users concerning suggested inclusions and exclusions will be welcomed.

The remainder of this introductory chapter will be devoted to the nature of scholarship in the humanities and the types of literature available to the librarian seeking to meet user requests for information, inspiration, and enlightenment.

At the outset it should be remarked that humanistic research is differentiated most sharply from research in the natural sciences by the constant intrusion of questions of value. To the scientist *qua* scientist, such considerations are, indeed, intrusions. They interfere with and damage the quality of research concerned with objective, empirically verifiable data and with experimental results that can be replicated by other researchers. "Informed judgment" might play a part in deciding what experiments to conduct, but "refined sensibility" would have no impact on the outcome. Yet these are the "bread of life" for the humanistic scholar, whether he is dealing with a poem, a piece of music, a painting, a religious doctrine, or a philosophical theory. Thus, humanistic scholarship has traditionally been intimately intertwined with considerations of value.

One consequence of this connection between scholarship and value systems is the peculiarly personal and individualistic nature of humanistic research. Unlike colleagues in the natural sciences or even, to a lesser degree, in the social sciences, the humanist finds research to be such an intimately personal matter that it is more difficult than in other diciplines to function effectively as a member of a team. The results of team effort are more likely to be compromise and mediocrity than productive division of labor. Collaborative efforts are, of course, possible. But they require special planning and are not nearly as "normal" as in the natural sciences.

A further result of this state of affairs is the general lack of ability on the part of the humanistic scholar to delegate bibliographic searching to others. The interconnections within the researcher's mind are so subtle and complex that it is necessary to examine personally the index entry or abstract to identify an item of potential relevance and the original book or article to determine its actual relevance. The problem is, of course, compounded by the lack of standardized and controlled vocabularies of the sort that have become increasingly common in the pure and applied sciences. Yet the humanistic scholar needs help in the form of access to a wide variety of finding aids.

Part of the problem faced by the humanistic scholar also relates to the nature of "knowledge" in the humanities. It is not likely to consist of hard, identifiable facts like formulas in chemistry, or population and income statistics from census data. Facts there are, aplenty, but their sum total is considerably less than what the humanist is looking for. To know the number of times Shakespeare uses the word "mince" in *Hamlet* is to tell us very little of importance about *Hamlet*. Yet the patient accumulation and analysis of factual data (often with the aid of the computer) can lay the foundation for knowledge of a higher order.

Closely related to the nature of "knowledge" is the question of "progress." In the natural sciences, knowledge tends to be "progressive." Each significant experiment either confirms, modifies, or overturns some piece of existing "knowledge." This is true whether the item in question is a new virus that has been detected through more sophisticated laboratory equipment or a far-ranging perception of relationships, such as the replacement of Newtonian physics with Einsteinian. In the humanities, no such "progress" is observable. Sophocles' *Antigone*, the "Bhagavad-Gita," Michelangelo's "Pieta," or Mozart's *The Magic Flute* are not superseded as was the "phlogiston" theory in chemistry. Perception of beauty, insight into the human condition, and artistic creativity are not cumulative, though patterns of influence can be traced. Indeed, there is often a tendency for a work of artistic genius to be followed by a host of inferior imitations—not by new works that refine and improve it!

The factors noted in the preceding paragraphs have their impact on patterns of use of library materials. For the humanist and the social scientist, the library is the heart of the research enterprise. For the natural scientist, the laboratory is at the center, with the library in a supporting role. In this respect, the position of the creative artist (as distinct from the researcher) in the humanities may more nearly resemble that of the scientist—as anyone who has witnessed "dialogue" between a sculptor and an art historian can testify!

The centrality of the library for the humanistic researcher is still accompanied by the centrality of the monograph as distinct from the periodical article. Although there have been fewer use studies in the humanities than in other fields, the pattern of preference for books and pamphlets continues to emerge—in sharp contrast to the preference of the natural scientist for journal articles, reprints, and preprints.

Another characteristic reported in such few user studies as we have is the greater spread of individual titles used by researchers in the humanities.

Whereas a relatively small number of journals contain a high proportion of the frequently cited articles in fields like chemistry and mathematics, the same high degree of concentration in journal or monographic titles has not been observed in the humanities. This is not to deny that critical studies tend to cluster around certain landmark works like Milton's *Paradise Lost* or Kant's *Critique of Pure Reason*, but the spread of titles is greater and the concentration much less intense.

A third use pattern which distinguishes humanistic from scientific researchers is a much greater time spread. Whereas publications of the last five years are crucial to scientific research, with usage dropping off rapidly after that, the humanist is likely to be equally interested in publications of 20, 40, or 50 years ago. Indeed, if one considers the "classics" in each field (as distinct from modern editions or reproductions), the range of interest may readily extend to items two or three thousand years old.

The working scholar in a humanistic discipline tends to perceive the materials with which he works as falling into three broad categories: 1) original texts or artifacts; 2) critical literature; 3) literature designed for specific groups or purposes. Each of these categories requires further elaboration.

The heart of all humanistic study is the original creative work, whether this is an epic poem, a piece of sculpture, a symphony, a devotional psalm, or a discourse on the nature of the good life. Without the outpourings of creative genius and the lesser efforts at creativity, there would be no enduring contribution to the illumination of the human condition—and nothing for humanistic scholars to analyze and interpret.

The second major category, utterly dependent upon the first, is critical literature. Normally, this takes the form of analysis, interpretation, or commentary on a particular creative work, on a group of creative works, or on the output of a given historical period. It may also include efforts to develop general theories of criticism and even histories of critical theories.

The literature designed for specific groups or purposes may be further subdivided into popularizations, access tools, and professional literature.

Popularizations have been common in the field of religion for centuries. In other disciplines, their advent is more recent. The rise of the art museum movement in the nineteenth century, for example, and the twentieth century addition of an educational role to the curatorial function have created demand for inexpensive books with reproductions of acknowledged masterpieces and simple commentary. Books on music appreciation now reach wide audiences. Ironically, philosophy and literature, once scarcely in need of popularization, became increasingly narrow and technical in the early years of the twentieth century, necessitating special efforts to bridge the gap. A good popularization should simplify without distortion or misinformation.

Access tools cover most of the items commonly thought of by reference librarians: bibliographies, indexes, abstracts, encyclopedias, dictionaries, handbooks, atlases, etc. The exponential growth of knowedge in the twentieth century has been in no small measure dependent on the increasing availability and sophistication of these access tools.

The professional literature is designed by the practitioners within each discipline for their mutual enlightenment and the advancement of knowledge.

Typically, it is created through the efforts of one or more major professional societies at the national level in each country and a host of specialized, regional, or local groups. Journals, indexes, and abstracts are the most typical outputs, although conference proceedings and current awareness (tables of contents) services are also common. In recent years, international cooperation has become increasingly widespread, often with the aid of subventions from Unesco.

2 THE COMPUTER AND THE HUMANITIES*

Since World War II, great emphasis has been placed upon science and technology. Military establishments and industrial organizations have carried out many research and development programs. Because of this emphasis on science, the humanities have been somewhat ignored. Scholars believe that there is still a need for the humanities in society. William Cornog states that it is because of the "seeking of these deeper illuminations of human values and the human spirit that the humanities have special power to inform the mind and refresh the soul of man."[1] Humanistic disciplines are seen as "the medium through which man's belief in himself will be restored."[2] A third statement, by John Fisher, defines the humanities as offering "unparalleled methods and materials by which the mind can contemplate and examine the universal implications of both science and art."[3]

If the humanities are to fulfill any of the above purposes, they must stay abreast of research and maintain control over the printed material in their fields. Modern technology must be used to achieve these ends. Until recently, humanists have tended to avoid the use of the computer for fear of dehumanizing the humanities. This fear is unjustified; automatic data processing machines do not take over the human aspect of research but instead "assist us in remembering and organizing external stimuli in coordinating the tools which give us power over our environment, and in probing more deeply into the foundations of the sciences. The import of computers is far more than technological. These machines are serving an ever increasing function in the rational organization of social effort."[4]

The computer's major contribution to the humanities is its ability to store large amounts of information and to arrange it systematically, so that it can be retrieved at a later date. This enables researchers to spend more time gathering more information. Because of the great increase in material available, the scholar needs as much time as possible to be able to control this material.

Although the computer has had a limited use in relation to the humanities for the past 20 years, the most significant advancements have come about only in the last seven years. The literature concerning computer research in the humanities includes more than three thousand items published since 1945. With this recent increase in interest came the support for computer-oriented studies. Studies done by the American Council of Learned Societies have helped to solve a problem that previously separated the humanities and the computer.

*This chapter was contributed by Cynthia McLaughlin, State Library of Ohio

Because most humanists had no knowledge of mathematics, it was necessary to create computer program languages that non-mathematicians could use. This has now been accomplished. In addition, several universities have designed courses that explain these languages, and courses are also being offered in computer techniques relating to specific fields. Herbert S. Donow at Southern Illinois University conducts a course of studies in literature and the computer, while Stanford University offers courses in computing in the social sciences and humanities in which the language ALGOL W is taught.

In view of the increasing involvement of the humanities with computers, there has developed a feeling that far more needs to be done to aid computer-oriented researchers. Computer scientists now regard the humanities as a new frontier. However, a basic essential is still lacking—namely, "an organization or human mechanism to make known and available to scholars and their professional organizations the capabilities of the computer in the field of bibliographical control."[5] One of the existing projects of this nature is the ACLS Bibliographic Data-Processing Center.

Another aid is the creation of new journals covering computer applications in the various fields of the humanities. *Computer and the Humanities*, which covers the whole scope of the humanities, was begun in 1967 and is published five times a year by Queens College of the City University of New York, Flushing, New York. Its articles, covering all phases of computer technology and humanities research, include reports of conferences, lists of scholars active in research, annual bibliographies, book reviews, abstracts of related articles and writings found elsewhere, lists of available programs in the humanities, and notice of new courses being offered in computer applications to the humanities. A more recently created journal is *Hephaistos*, published quarterly by St. Joseph's College, Philadelphia, Pennsylvania. It, too, covers the entire area. The *Newsletter* of the ICRH (Institute for Computer Research in the Humanities), published regularly since 1964 by New York University, includes the same type of material as the previously mentioned journals. *Calculi* is the newsletter for computer-oriented classicists, and *Computer Studies in the Humanities and Verbal Behavior* covers research in language and literature.

Although other fields may not have specific journals covering computer application, many articles covering individual projects are found in the recent issues of prominent journals for specific fields. *English Studies*, for example, includes descriptions of computer-produced concordances as well as data bases and translations. The material in these journals must also be bibliographically controlled so that the researcher will be aware of other projects being done in his field and related areas. The computer's ability to store and manipulate large quantities of data in a very short time assists in maintaining this control. The scholar is free to cover broader areas in greater depth than ever before; this extended research will result in the creation of a great variety of data bases in all fields.

A data base is a set of characters, objects, qualities, or values that represents information on a specific topic. The information is collected, coded, and stored in the computer for retrieval at a later time, and the arrangement of this information within the computer and the programming of the computer produce various results. The researchers in the humanities see great potential for computer application and realize that this application is only in the primary stages, although some disciplines have experimented with these applications more than others.

Few architecturally oriented computer applications are available; computer applications to architecture did not begin until about 1960. Because of the complexity of design problems, architects had not utilized the computer to any appreciable degree in the design process. This is no longer true, since the computer can now be programmed to manipulate total design problems and various aspects of these problems. One such project is operation GREAT (Graphics Research with Ellerbe Architects Technology), constructed by Ellerbe architects to develop software required for very elementary interactive manipulation of simple architectural space components used during the initial design stage.[6] The computer's ability to deal simultaneously with a vast number of factors has made possible the storage of an entire building description. The principal justification for taking the effort to maintain a current description of a building in a computer throughout the design process is the fact that the computer can be used as a means of communication among all those concerned with design decisions. It is now being realized that the computer can perhaps actually enhance the architect's capabilities to determine aesthetic qualities by assisting him in or relieving him from many of the other design tasks that consume a great deal of his talent and time. The time saved by architects in the design process offsets the costs generated by computer equipment and software expenses. These types of programs, however, are used only within an individual organization, due to the high degree of competition among architectural firms.

The field of art includes several very different computer applications. One application is that of computer graphics, which gained attention in the early 1960s. Computer graphics can be made in one of three ways: a computer-driven graphic plotter that follows instructions from a magnetic tape; a cathode ray tube display or television tube on which designs can be drawn; and various printers that produce patterns composed of letters or symbols. The two primary applications of computer graphics are the utilitarian and the aesthetic. The utilitarian function had its beginnings with William Fetter, of the Boeing Company, who used computer graphics to simulate landings on the runway and determine possible movement of a pilot sitting in the cockpit. The greatest development in the aesthetic function has come about in large universities where artists have had access to a computer. One such artist is Charles Csuri, of Ohio State University at Columbus, Ohio, who is primarily responsible for work in computer graphics. Other artists are also becoming involved in this art form and are exhibiting their creations. The yearly computer art contest held by *Computers and Automation* provides a gallery for their work. The August issue has published the results of this contest each year since 1962.[7] The number of entries each year has grown, therefore proving the advancing interest and development taking place in the field.

The attraction of artists to computerized art forms proves that the computer can be used to enhance man's creative abilities rather than to destroy them. "Besides the challenge of breaking new ground, one might be able to learn something significant about pattern and design, about order and disorder, about general laws of aesthetics."[8] Grace C. Hertlein states that "computer-aided graphics is a valid art form. Personal style can be achieved by an artist who uses this technical tool as an aid in creation."[9] Miss Hertlein goes on to say that "the computer has become the symbol of man's creative, affirmative use of science and technology for constructive, creative purposes,"[10] and is limited only to "the artist's imagination and the degree to which the artist accepts the computer as an aid in creation."[11]

The computer is also used in the creation of oil paintings and sculpture. Completely automatically-produced paintings were shown at the formal opening of the Chicago office for the Univac Division of Sperry Rand Corporation in 1968. Those paintings were produced from programs recorded on magnetic tapes by UNIVAC 1107 at the University of Notre Dame. Don Mittleman, Director of the Computing Center at Notre Dame, developed the software system, which used the FORTRAN IV language, to process the instructions. Mittleman, who is a pioneer in the field, uses a variety of materials such as inks, water and vegetable colors.[12] An example of computer-aided sculpture is Alfred Duca's spheroid sculpture,[13] which he created by using a numerically-controlled flame-cutting machine. His product is a sphere seven feet in diameter, with 80 layers of one-inch thick steel. The computer program was developed and written by Andrew Wales, President of Brown-Wales, a steel distributing company in Cambridge, Massachusetts.

In addition, the computer is used in a variety of applications to cinematography. An electronic microfilm recorder can be used to create computer-generated films. This technique was used in the 1960s by Bell Telephone Laboratories to create a series of computer-produced movies. An IBM 7094 computer and a Stromberg-Carlson 4020 microfilm were used, with the FORTRAN language. Kenneth C. Knowlton has devised a mosaic picture system to produce films;[14] he and Stan Vanderbeek have used this technique in making films for pleasure, one of which is "Man and His World." An example of an educational film using Knowlton's method is "Force, Mass, and Motion," developed by F. W. Siden. Motion picture animation by computer is also possible. The computer generates visual displays that correspond to single frames of film. There are at least two organizations that use computers to produce animated films of professional quality: one is located in New York for commercials on an off-line operation and the other is an on-line system in Canada. Full descriptions and explanations of these computer applications are given in Jasia Reichardt's *The Computer in Art.*[15] It is the most up-to-date and comprehensive coverage of the field.

Computers are used not only to aid man's creativity, but also to retrieve information. Most of the information retrieval in art is done by art museums. It is becoming more difficult for museums to maintain control of their holdings and at the same time to make the material available to their patrons. The Metropolitan Museum of Art is studying ways of adapting the computer's capabilities to its work. Its first project involves pottery typography with the use of the cathode ray tube. The development of the CRT attachment has extended the computer's abilities to include the visual. This is a great advantage to the fields in which so much depends upon sight rather than words. The Metropolitan Museum of Art sponsored a conference in April of 1968 to discuss the computer's potential in museums, including the possibility of replacing the traditional catalog with computerized data banks, and the linking of these data banks to create an international network. This would save both space and clerical man hours and would unify the available knowledge. Other topics of the conference included organization of bibliographical materials, data analysis, and solving problems of graphic design. The United States Museum Computer Network, established in 1967 by the National Gallery of Art and 15 art museums in New York City, is another example of efforts to incorporate the computer in museum work. The Network set up a trial data bank in relation to compiling a combined catalog. This project also considered the capabilities of the GRIPHOS macro language, existing museum records, and information needs of museums and their patrons.[16]

Other examples of the work being done in this area include the assembling of computerized data banks that cover distinct classes of museum information, the listing, by the International Council of Museums, of the records of single museums, and the development of automated documentation. The work in computer-oriented documentation falls primarily into three main categories: creation of comprehensive data bases, reduction of museum collections to machine-readable form, and analysis of discrete bodies of data pertinent to a particular and narrowly defined problem.[17] The shift in recent years from philology to interpretation presents a clearer picture of the museum's educational function.

The use of the computer in the control of music research allows the researcher to broaden his data base to include all pertinent material. The major result of information retrieval in music is thematic indexing, which is a common tool for musicological research. Use of the computer for this indexing can decrease the amount of time necessary for its production while increasing its efficiency. Examples of thematic indexing include the development of a thematic locator for Mozart's works as contained in Köchel's *Werkverzeichnis*,[18] developed by a research group in the Department of Music at New York University. Also, Barry S. Brook and Murry Gould have developed "Plaine and Easie Code System for Musicke," described as a "Computer-oriented language for symphonic scores in print, in manuscripts, in libraries and in private hands collated where possible with available disc and tape recordings."[19]

The second major area of computer applications in music is stylistic analysis. Here the computer not only retrieves information but identifies, locates, counts, and codes the information to present an analysis of it. Projects in this area include a study of the stylistic properties of the Masses of Josquin (by Arthur Mendel and Lewis Lockwood at Princeton) and an analysis of Haydn's symphonies by Jan La Rue, at New York University. Closely related to stylistic analysis are analyses of theory and harmony. Examples include the theoretical possibilities of equally tempered musical systems done by William Stoney in 1966 and 1967, and Robert M. Mason's encoding algorithm to provide each harmony with an individual designation.[20]

Like the visual arts, music has faced the problem of the conversion of information to machine-readable form. This conversion can be either the sound of music or the printed musical score. In 1964, a programming language, MIR (Machine Information Retrieval), was developed at Princeton as part of a pilot project in the use of the digital computer for music research. Two other languages used with specific types of problems are ALMA (Alphameric Language for Music Analysis) and DARMS (Digital Alternate Representation of Music Symbols).

Although special languages have been developed for music research, a general-purpose system for the analysis of music has not. Such a program would require

> "principles for encoding, means of detecting and correcting errors, a translator to convert input data to the internally stored form most efficient for information retrieval purposes, and musical analysis procedures properly speaking. It would also include the following special features: not built around a specific encoding language, written in high-level programming language PL/1 for relative machine independence and generated output tables whose form is easily changed to suit the requirements of different problems."[21]

The computer has changed the dimension of academic research within the field of music. Instead of individuals working alone with isolated data, teams of people are now working together. Total bibliographic control of all scholarly information about music past and present is the purpose of RILM (Répertoire International de la Littérature Musicale). Sponsored by the International Association of Music Libraries and the International Musicological Society, RILM is an international center in the United States where literature and computers are available. Its publication, an abstracted-computer-indexed bibliography of scholarly literature on music, includes current literature and retrospective material. With this project, the scholar is able to accomplish much more than was possible before the implementation of the computer.

The various fields of the humanities previously discussed are isolated in their computer applications. However, the limited research done with computers in religion and philosophy overlaps that done in language and literature. The Testaments are being studied for omissions from the standard text; substitution of one word or words for another; additions to the text; inversions of word order; spelling of proper names; itacisms; differences caused by case and tense endings which made meaningful variations in the sentence; and nonsense spelling errors.[22] J. W. Ellison, at the Harvard Computation Laboratory, carried out the first of these studies with a Mark IV computer. Another use of the computer is for production of a complete concordance to the Revised Standard Version, produced on a Remington Rand UNIVAC. A computer program for indexing the words in the Dead Sea Scrolls has been developed by Paul Tasman and Robert Busa.[23] Joseph G. Devine and Joseph Seberz developed a program in 1964 for processing the works of the early Christian writers. The steps involved are preparation of the texts in machine-readable form; production of "Text Tape" by a program called PROOFREADER; and production of the concordance by a program called CONCORDER. The text is prepared for the computer by key-punching and key-verifying. After verification the cards are read onto magnetic tape. This is the "Text Tape." PROOFREADER, the next step, checks and corrects possible errors. The "Text Tape" is then processed by the concordance-generated CONCORDER program. The format of the concordance is the IBM Key Word in Context indexing system. This type of product, which would mean hours of tedious work for the researcher, can be accomplished in a small amount of time with much less possibility of error.

Savings in time and reduction of error are also the prime reason for computer-generated concordances for the classics. Much of the work done has been involved with the preparation of basic philological tools such as concordances. Two well-noted examples are Louis Robert's *A Concordance to Lucretius*, and Alva Walter Bennett's *Index Verborum Sallustianus*. Three methods of publishing can be used for these concordance productions—normal typesetting methods, photo-offset directly from computer print-out, or photocomposition—but it is also hoped that these productions will be distributed on microfilm or magnetic tape. The advancement of computer design and programming has broadened the area of computer application in the classics. Another use of the computer has been for statistical analysis, such as the work done by Michael Levison, A. Q. Morton, and A. D. Winspean[24] to support their theory that the Seventh Letter of Plato was written by someone else. Other applications that do not depend on the counting and sorting abilities of the computer include Louis Delatte's project to determine mental attitudes of Roman lyric poets through location and restoration of papyrological fragments, and the use of familial relationships of the Greek pantheon to test programs for kinship structures. In order to enhance the awareness of computer applications in the classics, the American Philological Association has established a regular Advisory Committee for Computer Archives. One development has been the idea of a library of classical texts, accessed by teletype or computer, to serve as a distribution center for magnetic tape copies of the texts.

Similar centers have been set up for the distribution of machine-readable material in language and literature. Details may be found in "Verbal Materials in Machine-Readable Form," which appears sporadically in *Computers and the Humanities*. The greatest number of experiments and advancements in computer application to the humanities have been made in these areas. Data processing in the field of literature had its first general use when Stephen Parrish at Cornell used an IBM 704 computer to develop automatic indexing techniques in 1957. The first product of this development was a concordance to Matthew Arnold's poetry. Since that time, computer-produced concordances have become commonplace. Another area of study in which the computer has been applied is stylistic analysis. The result of this type of application is described by Sally Y. Sedelow of the University of North Carolina as "a sequentially multidimensional view of the test."[25] Stylistic analysis consists of the "study patterns formed in the process of the linguistic encoding of information,"[26] but the term "stylistic analysis" encompasses the whole range of literary research and involves other types of analysis, including syntactic analysis, qualitative analysis, factor analysis, and content analysis. Any one of these analyses can be used either to help determine stylistic analysis or as an end result in itself. For example, factor analysis has been used by Hanan C. Selvin of the University of Rochester to determine poetic style of certain seventeenth century poets.[27] The two main end results of stylistic analysis are attributive stylistics and interpretive stylistics. Attributive stylistics is the identification of a given work as the product of a given writer through the style of the work. Interpretive stylistics is used to gain a deeper understanding of the writer, his mind, and his personality.[28] A fairly well-known study in attributive stylistics is Frederick Mosteller and David L. Wallace's attempt to determine the authorship of the disputed *Federalist Papers*;[28] statistical analysis of various words is used to determine whether the style of the writings is that of Alexander Hamilton or James Madison. An example of interpretive stylistics is Louis T. Milic's project to determine the personality of Jonathan Swift,[30] in which he uses syntactic analysis to determine the author's style.

Conferences on the use of computers in literary research are now held biennially; the first was held at Cambridge in 1970, the second at Edinburgh University in 1972, and a third is planned for 1974. The audience at the Edinburgh Conference consisted of approximately one hundred scholars, about equally divided among North Americans, British, and Continental Europeans. A selective and edited version of the 36 papers presented has been prepared by W. J. Aitken, R. W. Bailey, and N. Hamilton-Smith under the title *The Computer and Literary Studies* (Edinburgh: Edinburgh University Press, 1973).

Automation of Shakespearean studies covers the entire range of computer applications. Concordances have been developed, analyses of various types have been taken, and authorship has been disputed. These projects are now listed and described in issues of *The Shakespearean Newsletter*.

There are several other computer applications in language and literature. Thematic analysis has been used in the study of folk tales, but as yet this sytem lacks methodology. The computer's ability to isolate words has resulted in automatic textual editing, such as Vinton Dearing's editing of volumes of Dryden with the use of an IBM 7090 computer (UCLA).[31] A final application is the computer's manipulation of individual words to produce poetry. Computer-produced poetry has been described as being similar to computer-produced art; however, it has not received as much attention and the results have not encouraged others to pursue the area.

In linguistics, information retrieval is primarily used for machine translation, which has been the object of study for a number of years. The many programs developed for its use include the production of foreign language textbooks. Nevertheless, other linguistics research, such as phonological typology, has also incorporated the computer. All computer-oriented linguistics studies have been aided greatly by the development of COMIT, a program designed for natural language process. A problem still remains, however, since this language has not been standardized; the only area in which an attempt at standardization has been made is Old English studies. Interchangeable programs have been developed in order that all workers will use compatible programs.

The problem of standardization is one that plagues all fields of the humanities. Until recently the closest thing to a programming language was FORTRAN, now one of the more common computer languages. Languages have been developed within specific fields to satisfy the needs of that particular discipline, such as MIR for music. IBM has developed a new language, PL/1, which contains a set of characters large enough to make it applicable to fields other than language and literature. Another new programming language, primarily used to process text material mechanically, is SNAP, developed by Michael P. Barnett and used in a course of information processing at

Columbia.[32] The program runs on computers made by several manufacturers and its procedure consists of simple English sentences.

Until recently each field in the humanities required a different language, and each type of computer required a different program. This resulted in the isolation not only of each field but also of individual data bases within these fields. The problem has now been recognized and attempts are being made to solve it. With the development of languages common to all fields and programs applicable to various computers, data bases will be available to anyone interested in their contents.

In order that the humanities may maintain their place in our society, they need extensive research and development. This can be accomplished through the interrelated use of data bases, but the availability of these data bases must be made known. Directories of these data bases must be made accessible and, until the time when all data bases use a common language and common equipment, individual differences must be noted.

In addition to the numerous articles on specific projects already cited, some general surveys, or state-of-the-art reviews, are beginning to appear in such places as the *Annual Review of Information Science and Technology.*[33] The student or reference librarian will find such surveys to be of increasing value as the number of computer applications in the humanities continues to rise.

FOOTNOTES

1. William H. Cornog, "Teaching Humanities in the Space Age," *School Review* LXXII (Autumn 1964), 393.
2. Sister Frances Tinucci, "A Rationale for a Humanities-Centered Curriculum in a Cybernetic-Centered Society," *Catholic Educational Review* LXVI (January 1969), 634.
3. John Hurt Fisher, "The Humanities in an Age of Science," *Journal of General Education* XVIII (October 1966), 190.
4. William H. Desmonde, *Computers and Their Use* (Englewood Cliffs, N.J.: Prentice-Hall, 1964), p. 1.
5. Theodore Stern, "Computers, Traditional Scholarship, and the ACLS," *Journal of Asian Studies* XXVII (February 1968), 330.
6. Sheldon Anonsen, "Interactive Computer Graphics in Architecture," *Computers and Automation* XIX (August 1970), 28.
7. Edmund C. Berkeley, "Computer Art: Turning Point," *Computers and Automation* XVI (August 1967), 7.
8. L. Mezei, "Artistic Design by Computer," *Computers and Automation* XVI (August 1964), 12.
9. Grace C. Hertlein, "An Artist Views Discovery Through Computer-Aided Graphics," *Computers and Automation* XIX (August 1970), 26.
10. *Ibid.*, 25.
11. *Ibid.*, 26.
12. Edmund C. Berkeley, "Oil Paintings Produced with the Aid of Computer," *Computers and Automation* XVII (September 1968), 56.

13. Roger Ives, "Computer-Aided Sculpture," *Computers and Automation* XVIII (August 1969), 33.

14. Jasia Reichardt, *The Computer in Art* (New York: Van Nostrand Reinhold, 1971), p. 77.

15. *Ibid.*

16. David Vance, "A Data Bank of Museum Holdings," *ICRH Newsletter* IV (March 1969), 3.

17. Everett Ellin, "An International Survey of Museum Computer Activity," *Computers and the Humanities* III (November 1968), 65.

18. George Hill, "The Thematic Index to the Köchel Catalog," *ICRH Newsletter* IV (March 1969), 8.

19. Barry S. Brook and Harold Heckman, "Utilization of Data Processing Techniques in Musical Documentation," *Fontes Artis Musicae* XII (May-December 1965), 115.

20. Robert M. Mason, "An Encoding Algorithm and Tables for the Digital Analysis of Harmony (I)," *Journal of Research in Music Education* XVII (Fall 1969), 286.

21. Raymond Erickson, "A General System for the Analysis of Music: Some Projected Applications," *ICRH Newsletter* IV (March 1969), 9.

22. J. W. Ellison, "Computers and the Testaments," in *Computers and Humanistic Research*, ed. by Edmund A. Bowles (Englewood Cliffs, N.J.: Prentice-Hall, 1967), p. 163.

23. Edmund A. Bowles, *Computers and Humanistic Research* (Englewood Cliffs, N.J.: Prentice-Hall, 1967), p. 119.

24. Stephen V. F. Waite, "Computers and the Classics," *Computers and the Humanities* V (September 1970), 49.

25. Edmund A. Bowles, *Computers and Humanistic Research* (Englewood Cliffs, N.J.: Prentice-Hall, 1967), p. 120.

26. Sally Yeates Sedelow and Walter A. Sedelow, Jr., "A Preface to Computational Stylistics," in *The Computer and Literary Style*, ed. by Jacob Leed (Kent, Ohio: Kent State University Press, 1966), p. 1.

27. Josephine Miles and Hanan C. Selvin, "A Factor Analysis of the Vocabulary of Poetry in the Seventeenth Century," in *The Computer and Literary Style*, ed. by Jacob Leed (Kent, Ohio: Kent State University Press, 1966), p. 116.

28. Louis T. Milic, "Unconscious Ordering in the Prose of Swift," in *The Computer and Literary Style*, ed. by Jacob Leed (Kent, Ohio: Kent State University Press, 1966), p. 82.

29. Ivor S. Francis, "An Exposition of the Statistical Approach to the *Federalist* Dispute," in *The Computer and Literary Style*, ed. by Jacob Leed (Kent, Ohio: Kent State University Press, 1966), p. 83.

30. Louis T. Milic, "Unconscious Ordering in the Prose of Swift," in *The Computer and Literary Style*, ed. by Jacob Leed (Kent, Ohio: Kent State University Press, 1966), p. 83.

31. Edmund A. Bowles, *Computers and Humanistic Research* (Englewood Cliffs, N.J.: Prentice-Hall, 1967), p. 121.

32. Michael P. Barnett, "SNAP—A Programming Language for Humanists," *Computer and the Humanities* IV (1969-70), 225.

33. Joseph Raben and R. L. Widman, "Information Systems Applications in the Humanities," *Annual Review of Information Science and Technology* VII (Washington, D.C.: American Society for Information Science, 1972), 439-69.

PHILOSOPHY

3 TRENDS IN PHILOSOPHY

In the period before 600 B.C., philosophy was still enmeshed in poetry (Hesiod, Homer), religion (Moses, Zoroaster, Vedas, Brahmanas), or politics (pre-Confucian classics and law code). The next three centuries witnessed a remarkable outpouring of creative philosophical speculation in Greece, India, and China.

EARLY PHILOSOPHY (ca. 600 B.C. to 300 B.C.)

Early Greek philosophers took the natural world as their starting point and viewed matter as the ultimate reality whether it took the form of water (Thales), air (Anaximenes), fire (Heraclitus), or some small imperishable substance (Anaximander). Parmenides turned from material things to the one unchanging reality beneath changing appearances, while Pythagoras believed that numbers and the relationships between them constituted reality. Socrates (470?–399 B.C.) broke with his predecessors and focused his attention upon man and the nature of the good life. Plato (427?–347 B.C.) continued this emphasis but borrowed elements from Pythagoras and Parmenides. He is the first philosopher whose writings have survived in any substantial way. A literary artist as well as an original speculator, Plato developed his philosophical doctrines in a series of dialogues in which opposing viewpoints were stated, definitions clarified, and arguments developed in the form of conversations among friends. Between 30 and 40 such works have survived, of which about 25 were probably written by Plato. Among the most famous are the *Apology*, *Crito*, and *Phaedo*, which deal with the trial and death of Socrates; the *Republic*, which is concerned with the nature of the ideal state; and the *Parmenides*, a tribute to an influential predecessor. Aristotle (384-322 B.C.) was more of a naturalist and logician than Plato. Of the 400 works attributed to him, only 50 have survived and only half of these are genuine. It is customary to divide these last into five groups. The first group, which deals with logic, is collectively known as the *Organon*; its best-known works are the *Categories*, *Prior Analytics*, and *Posterior Analytics*. The second group deals with such questions as matter, space, and time and includes *Physics* and *Metaphysics*. In the third group are such biological and psychological works as *Historia Animalium* and *De Anima*. The fourth group consists of the *Nicomachean Ethics*, *Eudemian Ethics*, and *Politics*. The last group is made up of the *Rhetoric* and *Poetics*.

During this same period, the Indian scriptures were becoming finalized and certain elements of philosophical speculation were emerging from the religious matrix. The *Upanishads*, written at various times from the seventh century B.C. until the early years of the Christian era, embody many of these ideas. Among the 30 major works in this group, the *Mahabharata* is the best known, especially the section called *Bhagavad-Gita*. A major philosophic and religious innovator of this period was Siddhartha Gautama (566-486 B.C.), founder of Buddhism. Although he left no writings, his teachings were later gathered by his disciples into a three-part compilation known as the *Tripitaka* (or "three baskets"). The first and oldest part, called *Vinaya-Pitaka* ("basket of discipline"), deals with the rules of the community of followers. The second part, called *Sutra-Pitaka* ("basket of sutras"), consists of dialogues between the Buddha and his disciples, while the third (and latest), entitled *Abhidharma-Pitaka* ("basket of scholastic elaboration"), consists of commentary on the sutras.

In sharp contrast with the situation in India, philosophy in China emerged with such vigor from the womb of religion that it soon came to dominate the intellectual landscape. The most influential school was founded by Confucius (551-479 B.C.), who placed great emphasis on the role of the virtuous man in a well-ordered society. His teachings are recorded in the *Analects* and augmented by the *Great Learning* and the *Doctrine of the Mean*, attributed to his disciples. In sharp contrast with this social and political emphasis was Taoism, which, with its stress on humility and quietude, was more appealing to recluses. Founded by Lao Tzu (c.604-531 B.C.), whose teachings are contained in the *Tao Te Ching*, and augmented by Chuang Tzu (369-286 B.C.), whose principal work bears his own name, it was a strong philosophical rival in this period and only later became more of a popular religion. In contrast to the humanistic ethics of Confucianism, the Moist school, founded by Mo Tzu (c.468-376 B.C.), placed ethics on a religious basis and taught universal love as the law of Heaven. A school of logicians, whose most outstanding scholars were Hui Shih (c.380-305 B.C.) and Kung-sun Lung (born 380 B.C.), also flourished but had little permanent influence. More influential was the Yin Yang school, based on the notion of tension between the two opposing cosmic forces of Yin (negative, passive, weak, disintegrative) and Yang (positive, active, strong, integrative). This concept was developed by Tsou Yen (305-240 B.C.) from ideas in a much earlier work called the *Classic of Changes*, then combined by him with the notion of the five elements (metal, wood, water, fire, earth) drawn from the *Classic of History* into a complex process philosophy in which the five elements became forces or change agents rather than material elements. Legalism, embodying a belief that man should be subordinate to the state, was taught by Han Fei Tzu (c.280-233 B.C.), whose followers helped establish the dictatorial Ch'in dynasty in 221 B.C. The overthrow of this oppressive regime by the Han dynasty in 206 B.C. marked the end of legalism as a philosophical influence.

TRENDS FROM 300 B.C. TO 300 A.D.

Three movements dominated Western philosophy in the next five or six centuries: Stoicism, Epicureanism, and Neo-Platonism. Founded by Zeno, of Citium (c.334-262 B.C.), the Stoic school emphasized virtuous behavior in conformity to the law of nature and reason, called the logos. It held great appeal for practical Romans like Cicero (106-43 B.C.), Seneca (4 B.C.–65 A.D.), Epictetus (c.50-130 A.D.) and the Emperor Marcus Aurelius (121-180 A.D.). Much Stoic doctrine is preserved in Cicero's philosophical writings—like *On Duties*, *On the Laws*, *On the Republic*, *On the Nature of the Gods*, and *On Limits*—and in such works of Epictetus as *Moral Discourses*, *Golden Sayings*, and *Enchiridion*, as well as in the famous *Meditations* of Marcus Aurelius. Epicureanism was founded by Epicurus (341-270 B.C.), who taught that enduring pleasure might be found through a rational understanding of man and his place in the universe. Most of our knowledge of this movement comes from a long poem *On the Nature of Things* by Lucretius (c.94-55 B.C.). Neo-Platonism took one aspect of Plato's teaching (the unity behind appearances) and developed it along mystical lines. The best-known exponent of the movement was Plotinus (205-270 A.D.), whose writings were collected and published after his death by one of his pupils in a compilation known as the *Enneads*.

In Indian philosophy, the period under review corresponds very roughly to the time in which a series of Hindu texts known as the "sutras" evolved, along with an extensive series of commentaries, and in which the six orthodox systems of philosophy, known as "darsanas" (or "views"), were developed: 1) "Nyaya," the logical approach to knowledge, which involved consideration of intuition, inference, comparison, and verbal testimony; 2) "Vaisheshika," which found reality in particulars and stressed methods of differentiation; 3) "Sankhya," which also reacted against monism and stressed the infinite plurality of individual souls; 4) "Yoga," which was essentially a system of physical and mental discipline to prepare for illumination; 5) "Purva Mimamsa," which concentrated on the determination of duty; 6) "Vedanta," which attempted to interpret the teachings of the Upanishads in a consistent way.

Although Confucianism became the official Chinese ideology in 136 B.C. and then dominated government, society, education, and literature for the next two millenia, its purity as a philosophical movement was being rapidly undermined by the incorporation of Yin and Yang in *I Ching* ("The Book of Changes") and the philosophical teaching of Tung Chung-shu (176-104 B.C.). The collapse of the Han dynasty stimulated the rise of Neo-Taoism, under the leadership of its most brilliant expositor, Wang Pi (226-249 A.D.). Buddhism as a philosophical movement rose to prominence in China during this period, though it was modified by contact with Confucianism.

FROM SAINT AUGUSTINE TO GALILEO

During these centuries, Confucian influences spread to Japan, while Central and Southeast Asia continued to be dominated by religions. In Europe, Christianity rose to prominence. Heavily influenced by Neo-Platonism, St. Augustine (354-430) sought a philosophical foundation for faith in an analysis of human consciousness as recorded in his *Confessions*. In *The City of God*, he grappled with the meaning of history. His counterpart in the East was Buddhaghosa (fl.412-434), who set the pattern for Hinayana Buddhism in Ceylon and Burma for the next millennium. In China, the interaction of Buddhism with Confucianism and Taoism produced a school of philosophy known as Ch'an Buddhism, which was predominant from the fifth to the tenth centuries. Among the Arab people a new religious movement, Islam, developed from the teachings of the prophet Mohammed (570-632) as contained in the *Koran*. Debates with Christians in centers like Damascus led to increasing translation of Greek philosophical works and use of Greek analytical tools to defend the faith. Islamic philosophy combined Aristotelian and Neo-Platonic elements. The latter were emphasized by Al-Kindi (801-873) and the former by Al-Farabi (875-950).

The next three centuries were rich in philosophical speculation. Avicenna (979-1037), the most original of the Islamic philosophers, summarized ancient knowledge and commented on logic, physics, mathematics, and metaphysics in the *Shifa* ("Healing of the Soul"), which was later translated into Latin and influenced Christian philosophers. Averroës (1126-1198) defended the claims of philosophy against Islamic religious conservatives in *Fasl al-Maqal* ("The Decisive Treatise") and wrote commentaries on Aristotle. After 1230, his works were available in Latin and Hebrew translations. St. Thomas Aquinas (1227-1274) wrote *Summa Contra Gentiles* to defend Christianity against its Islamic adversaries. A synthesis of Christianity and Aristotelian philosophy was achieved by Aquinas in *Summa Theologica*, which has had a permanent influence. Indian philosophy was revived by Abhinava Gupta (fl.990-1015), whose *Paramartha Sara* was a major treatise in metaphysics. In China, Neo-Confucianism was the dominant movement during the Sung dynasty (979-1279). The pioneer leader was Chou Tun-yi (1017-1073), but soon two divisions were in evidence: a rationalistic wing, with Ch'eng Yi (1033-1107) and Chu Hsi (1130-1200) as its leading exponents, and an idealistic group led by Lu Chiu-yuan (1139-1193) and Wang Shou-jen (1472-1529).

FROM GALILEO TO THE NINETEENTH CENTURY

Although the modern spirit in European philosophy had its forerunners in Roger Bacon (1214?-1294) and William of Ockham (1285?-1349), the decisive shift came with Galileo Galilei (1564-1642) and Francis Bacon (1561-1626), who stressed empirical observation rather than intuition and logical deduction. René Descartes (1596-1650) was most thorough-going in his attempt to establish philosophy on a new basis. The concept of methodological doubt pervades his *Discourse on Method* and *Meditations on the First Philosophy*. Baruch Spinoza (1632-1677) built on Descartes's mathematical foundations but also drew heavily on his own Jewish heritage in his *Ethics*. Gottfried Wilhelm von Leibniz (1646-1716) was a rationalist who tried to reconcile theology and science in such works as *Discourse on Metaphysics*, *New Essays Concerning Human Understanding*, and *The Monadology*. Meanwhile, John Locke (1632-1704), taking a more empirical approach in *An Essay Concerning Human Understanding*, found his ideas attacked by Bishop George Berkeley (1685-1753) in *A Treatise of Human Nature*. Immanuel Kant (1724-1804) was stimulated by Hume's writings to search for a more solid theoretical foundation for human knowledge, which he endeavored to provide in his *Critique of Pure Reason*. Kant developed his ethical theories in the *Critique of Practical Reason* and his ideas about aesthetics in the *Critique of Judgment*. Unlike Kant, Wilhelm Friedrich Hegel (1770-1831) concentrated on the meaning of history in such works as *The Phenomenology of the Spirit*, *Philosophy of Right and Law*, and *Philosophy of History*. In these, and in *The Science of Logic*, Hegel developed the notion of the dialectic (progress through conflict of opposites), which exercised such a powerful influence on Karl Marx (1818-1883) even though he rejected Hegel's idealism in favor of the dialectical materialism expounded in *Economic and Philosophic Manuscripts of 1844*, the *Communist Manifesto*, and *Capital*. A leading British philosopher of the nineteenth century was John Stuart Mill (1806-1873), noted for such works as *Utilitarianism*, *On Liberty*, and *A System of Logic*.

During these centuries, Indian philosophy continued to be dominated by the religious traditions. A major thinker was Ram Mohan Roy (1772-1833). Even more influential was the Bengali saint Ramakrishna (1834-1886). Chinese philosophy shifted from idealism to a form of materialism with Wang Ch'uan-shan (1619-1692) and Tai Chen (1723-1777), but then reverted to Neo-Confucianism in the time of K'ang Yu-wei (1858-1927).

In this period, Slavic—and particularly Russian—philosophy emerged from the domination of the Church, stimulated by the Western contacts initiated by Peter the Great (1672-1725). The first philosopher of note was a Ukrainian, Gregory Skovoroda (1722-1794), whose works were in dialogue form. A theorist of natural law was A. N. Radischev (1749-1802), whose most original work, *O Cheloveke, o Yevo Smertnosti i Bessmertii* ("On Man, His Mortality and Immortality"), was written in exile in Siberia and not published until after his death. As a result of the Decembrist uprising of 1825, the teaching of philosophy was forbidden in Russian universities from 1826 to 1863. The influence of Hegel was noticeable in the works of A. I. Herzen (1812-1870) and that of Mill in the thought of N. G. Chernyshevski (1828-1889). Much philosophic speculation also occurred in the works of such noted literary figures as F. M. Dostoyevsky (1821-1881) and L. N. Tolstoy (1828-1910). One of the most original and systematic thinkers was Vladimir Solovyov (1853-1900), whose major work, *Osnovy Teoreticheskoi Filosofii* ("Foundation of Theoretical Philosophy"), was unfinished at the time of his death.

TWENTIETH CENTURY TRENDS

Philosophy in the twentieth century evolved gradually from trends that had been evident much earlier. Treatment of the subject, however, will be facilitated by discussion of schools of thought instead of a chronological arrangement. The major trends may be identified as follows: idealism; realism; analytical philosophy; phenomenology; existentialism; pragmatism; Oriental philosophies; and Marxism.

Idealism is the notion that ultimate reality consists of mind or ideas. It is opposed to materialism, naturalism, and, sometimes, to realism. It has been a persistent strand in the history of philosophy from Plato to Descartes, Berkeley, and Kant. In the nineteenth century it drew great impetus from the writings of Hegel. F. H. Bradley (1846-1924) attacked empiricism and utilitarianism in

Ethical Studies and *The Principles of Logic*. His major work on metaphysics was *Appearance and Reality*. Bernard Bosanquet (1848-1923) differed with Bradley in *Knowledge and Reality* and *Logic or the Morphology of Knowledge*. Other major works were *History of Aesthetics, The Principle of Individuality and Value*, and *The Value and Destiny of the Individual*. Josiah Royce (1855-1916) discussed problems of knowledge and reality in *The World and the Individual*. His ethical thought was best expressed in *Philosophy of Loyalty* and his religious views in *The Religious Aspect of Philosophy* and *The Problem of Christianity*. John E. McTaggart (1866-1925) published several studies on Hegel as well as *Some Dogmas of Religion* and *The Nature of Existence*. Brand Blanshard (1892-) explored a variety of problems common to philosophy and psychology in *The Nature of Thought*. His ethical concerns were expressed in *Reason and Goodness*, while his disagreements with analytical philosophy were set forth in *Reason and Analysis*.

Realism in ancient and medieval philosophy meant belief in the objective existence of ideas, or universals, as opposed to nominalism, which stressed that only individual objects are real. In the twentieth century, however, the term has taken on quite another meaning: the view that natural objects exist independently of us and our perception of them. It is thus opposed to idealism, which dominated the philosophic scene at the end of the nineteenth century and the beginning of the twentieth. G. E. Moore (1873-1958) was one of the early critics in such articles as "The Refutation of Idealism," which later appeared with other papers by him in *Philosophical Studies*. His ethical theories were expounded in *Principia Ethica* and *Ethics*, while *Philosophical Papers* and *Some Main Problems in Philosophy* dealt with metaphysics and epistemology. *The Philosophy of G. E. Moore*, edited by P. A. Schilpp, contained articles about his theories and their influence as well as a "Reply" by Moore. Bertrand Russell (1872-1970) began as an idealist but was influenced by G. E. Moore toward realism. His position underwent changes during his long life. Among his major philosophical works are: *Principia Mathematica* (with Alfred North Whitehead); *Problems of Philosophy*; *Our Knowledge of the External World*; *The Analysis of Mind*; *The Analysis of Matter*; *An Inquiry into Meaning and Truth*; *Human Knowledge: Its Scope and Limits*; and *My Philosophical Development*. *The Philosophy of Bertrand Russell*, edited by P. A. Schilpp, is valuable for commentaries and Russell's reply. Samuel Alexander (1859-1938) was another member of the realist school who began as an idealist in *Moral Order and Progress* but had shifted position entirely by the time his major work, *Space, Time and Deity*, appeared. E. B. Holt (1873-1946), both a philosopher and a psychologist, edited *The New Realism*, a collection of writings by six American philosophers.

The realistic movement led gradually and almost imperceptibly into a later development known as philosophical analysis, concern with clarifying the meanings of words. Bertrand Russell and G. E. Moore were among the first to employ the analytical method. Ludwig Wittgenstein (1889-1951) developed, and then modified, these approaches in his *Tractatus Logico-Philosophicus, Philosophical Investigations*, and *Remarks on the Foundations of Mathematics*. John Wisdom (1904-) has been closely associated with Wittgenstein. Among his major works are *Interpretation and Analysis, Problems of Mind and Matter, Other*

Minds, *Philosophy and Psycho-Analysis*, and *Paradox and Discovery*. Gilbert Ryle (1900-) has emphasized the importance of philosophical method not only in books like *Philosophical Arguments* and *Dilemmas* but also in *The Concept of Mind* and in numerous short articles.

An offshoot of philosophical analysis was "logical positivism," which was a radical departure based on the belief that only empirically verifiable statements could be meaningful and that much of traditional philosophy (especially metaphysics) was nonsense. The period of its greatest prominence was from the 1920s to about 1950, beginning with the so-called "Vienna Circle" (Otto Neurath, Moritz Schlick, Herbert Feigl, Rudolf Carnap, etc.) and ending with gradual reabsorption into the broader analytical movement. The height of logical positivism in the 1930s was represented in its most articulate and persuasive formulations in Rudolf Carnap's (1891-) *The Logical Syntax of Language* and *Philosophy of Logical Syntax* and in the first edition of A. J. Ayer's *Language, Truth and Logic*. *Logical Positivism*, edited by A. J. Ayer, contains an anthology of writings pro and con as well as an extensive bibliography. In the later works of Wittgenstein, Wisdom, and Ryle, major changes have occurred in the concept of what language is and how it functions. These changes are also reflected in such works by John Austin (1911-) as *Philosophical Papers*, *Sense and Sensibilia*, and *How to Do Things with Words*. Meanwhile, Carnap's thought has continued to evolve in works like *Meaning and Necessity: A Study in Semantics and Modal Logic*, *Logical Foundations of Probability*, and *The Continuum of Inductive Methods*. Ayer's most important book since 1936 is *The Problem of Knowledge*, but other major titles include *The Foundation of Empirical Knowledge*, *Thinking and Meaning*, *Philosophical Essays*, and *The Concept of a Person*.

Phenomenology was another philosophical movement of the twentieth century with roots in the nineteenth. Led by Edmund Husserl (1859-1938), it stressed direct investigation and description of phenomena as consciously experienced, without theories of causal explanation. English translations are now appearing for most of Husserl's works, including *Cartesian Meditations*, *The Crisis of European Sciences and Transcendental Phenomenology*, *Formal and Transcendental Logic*, *Ideas*, *Logical Investigations*, and *Phenomenology and the Crisis of Philosophy*. Maurice Merleau-Ponty (1908-1961) gave attention to definition and clarification but defined phenomenology in a way that differed substantially from that of Husserl and his followers. Among his major works available in English translation are *Phenomenology of Perception*, *The Primacy of Perception*, and *Signs*. Alden L. Fisher has edited a volume entitled *The Essential Writings of Merleau-Ponty*.

Existentialism also had its precursors in the nineteenth century (such as Søren Kierkegaard), but it did not emerge into prominence until after World War II. As a philosophical movement it has enjoyed greater esteem in Europe and Latin America than in English-speaking countries, where philosophical analysis has tended to predominate. It has, however, enjoyed wide appeal outside the field of professional philosophy, especially among literary figures and the general public. Embracing both atheistic and religious wings, the movement is man-centered, stressing that the goal of philosophy is not simply clear thought but a total way of life and that man's values have not been predetermined but must be invented. Freedom of choice is crucial. Shunning abstractions, existentialists stress that, first of all, man *is*, and that *what* he is, is settled in the course of his existence. Karl Jaspers (1883-1969) is perhaps best known for *The Perennial Scope of Philosophy*, but other works in English translation include *Nietzsche and Christianity, Truth and Symbol, The Origin and Goal of History, The Way to Wisdom, Myth and Christianity, The Future of Mankind*, and *The Great Philosophers*. Martin Heidegger (1889-) is often considered the key figure of the movement. His most influential work is *Being and Time*, but other books translated from German include *Introduction to Metaphysics, Kant and the Problems of Metaphysics, What Is Philosophy?*, and *Essays in Metaphysics: Identity and Difference*. Gabriel Marcel (1889-) was converted to Catholicism in 1929. Among his works translated from French are *The Mystery of Being, Philosophy of Existentialism, Man Against Mass Society*, and *The Existential Background of Human Dignity*. Jean-Paul Sartre (1905-), by contrast, represents both the atheistic wing of existentialism and its literary arm. Among his major philosophical works available in English are *Being and Nothingness, Existentialism and Humanism, The Problem of Method, The Psychology of Imagination, Sketch for a Theory of the Emotions*, and *The Transcendence of the Ego*. Among his most famous literary works are *No Exit, The Flies, Nausea, Lucifer and the Lord*, and *Saint Genet: Actor and Martyr*. Albert Camus (1913-1960) was essentially a novelist and essayist. His most famous works include *The Stranger, The Myth of Sisyphus, The Plague, The Rebel*, and *The Fall*.

A philosopher of great literary skill who is not readily classifiable was George Santayana (1863-1952); his major works include *The Sense of Beauty, The Life of Reason, Scepticism and Animal Faith*, and *The Realms of Being*.

Although "process philosophy" may serve as a convenient umbrella for linking Henri Bergson (1859-1941) and Alfred North Whitehead (1861-1947), their approaches to the problems of change differed substantially. Bergson was heavily influenced by the Darwinian theory of evolution and other biological concepts, whereas Whitehead was a mathematician. Among Bergson's best-known works are *Creative Evolution, Time and Free Will, Matter and Memory, Introduction to Metaphysics, The Creative Mind*, and *The Two Sources of Morality and Religion*. Whitehead collaborated with Bertrand Russell in writing *Principia Mathematica*, but thereafter their philosophic paths diverged. Among his many books, *Science and the Modern World, Adventures of Ideas*, and *Modes of Thought* are most accessible to the average reader, while *Process and Reality*, which sets forth the heart of his system, is the most difficult. *The Philosophy of Alfred North Whitehead*, edited by P. A. Schilpp, is an excellent source of critical commentary.

Pragmatism is a distinctly American philosophical movement. The root word means "deed" or "act." The emphasis is on what works in the long run, on testing the truth of an idea through examining its value as a predictor. The pragmatist is concerned with the contribution that the sciences (especially the social sciences) can make to human affairs, but he is more concerned with method than with content. The logic of pragmatism is "instrumentalism," which treats ideas as tools for solving problems. C. S. Peirce (1839-1914) is commonly regarded as the founder of pragmatism. His thought, which evolved from

Kantian idealism in four stages, is expounded in the eight-volume set entitled *The Collected Papers of Charles Sanders Peirce*. William James (1842-1910) was a philosopher, psychologist, and gifted writer; he was the brother of the novelist, Henry James. His most famous works were *Varieties of Religious Experience*, *Pragmatism*, and *A Pluralistic Universe*, but other books of fundamental importance include *Principles of Psychology*, *The Will to Believe*, *The Meaning of Truth*, *Some Problems of Philosophy*, and *Essays in Radical Empiricism*. John Dewey (1859-1952) was better known as an educator, but he made major contributions to philosophy in such books as *Art as Experience*, *Experience and Nature*, *Reconstruction in Philosophy*, *Logic: The Theory of Inquiry*, and *Human Nature and Conduct*. Good critical evaluations may be found in *The Philosophy of John Dewey*, edited by P. A. Schilpp, and a very comprehensive bibliography in *John Dewey: A Centennial Bibliography*, by M. H. Thomas. George Herbert Mead (1863-1931) was a friend and colleague of Dewey whose major works included *Mind, Self and Society*, *The Philosophy of the Present*, and *The Philosophy of the Act*. C. I. Lewis (1883-1964) wrote *A Survey of Symbolic Logic*, *Mind and the World-Order*, *An Analysis of Knowledge and Valuation*, *The Ground and Nature of the Right*, and *Our Social Inheritance*. Sidney Hook (1902-) emphasized social philosophy in books like *From Hegel to Marx*, *Reason, Social Myths and Democracy*, *The Paradoxes of Freedom*, *In Defense of Academic Freedom*, and *Common Sense and the Fifth Amendment*.

Twentieth century Indian philosophy has exhibited both religious and secular tendencies. Among thinkers in the former group, Sir Sarvepalli Radhakrishnan (1888-) is best known in the West. Among his major works are *Indian Philosophy*, *The Hindu View of Life*, and *Eastern Religions and Western Thought*. He has also prepared translations into English and commentaries on *The Bhagavadgita*, *The Principal Upanishads*, and *The Brahma Sutra*. P. A. Schilpp has edited a volume of commentary entitled *The Philosophy of Sarvepalli Radhakrishnan*. A noted religious philosopher in what is now Pakistan was Muhammad Iqbal (1877?-1938), whose works included *The Development of Metaphysics in Persia* and *Reconstruction of Religious Thought in Islam*. More concerned with strictly philosophical issues was K. C. Bhattacharya (1875-1949), whose books include *Studies in Philosophy*. On the other hand, Aurobindo Ghose (1872-1950) was both a philosopher and founder of a religious community. His principal work is *The Life Divine*. A five-volume work entitled *A History of Indian Philosophy*, by Surendranath Dasgupta (1885-1952), should also be mentioned, as well as *The Central Philosophy of Buddhism*, by T. R. V. Murti, and *Early Buddhist Theory of Knowledge*, by K. N. Jayatilleke.

Chinese philosophers in the twentieth century at first showed receptivity to Western ideas, especially pragmatism, then revived both Buddhism and Confucianism, and finally remained silent or adopted Marxism. Confucianism was revived by Fung Yu-lan (1895-), whose most noted works available in English are *The Spirit of Chinese Philosophy*, *A Short History of Chinese Philosophy*, and *A History of Chinese Philosophy*. Other major thinkers of this school were Hsiung Shih-li (1885-) and Chang Tung-sun (1886-). Marxism became the official state philosophy with the establishment of the People's Republic of China in 1949.

Marxism became an influential philosophy in Russia in the 1890s. One of the leading early exponents was G. V. Plekhanov (1856-1918), whose translated works include *The Development of the Monist View of History*, *Essays in the History of Materialism*, *The Materialist Conception of History*, *The Role of the Individual in History*, and *Fundamental Problems of Marxism*. V. I. Lenin (1870-1924) dealt with philosophical issues in *Materialism and Empirio-Criticism* and *Philosophical Notebooks* (Vol. 38 of his *Collected Works*). Joseph Stalin (1879-1953) wrote a short pamphlet entitled *Dialectical and Historical Materialism*. During Stalin's time, the leading official philosopher was M. B. Mitin, whose *Dialekticheski Materializm* appeared in 1933. A more original philosopher was P. Dosev, whose *Teoriya Otrazheniya* ("The Copy Theory") appeared in 1936. Soviet philosophers under Stalin were subject to rigid political control, as A. M. Deborin discovered in 1931 when he was accused of idealist distortions, and G. F. Aleksandrov in 1947 when his *Istoriya Zapadno-Europeiskoi Filosofii* ("The History of Western European Philosophy") was condemned for "bourgeois objectivism." The period since the death of Stalin has been one of modest liberalization, as shown in the reinterpretations by E. Kolman and A. A. Zinoviev. Marxist philosophers in other Communist countries are also at work on adaptations and new interpretations. Georg Lukacs and György Tamas in Hungary are examples from Eastern Europe. In China, there were Marxist philosophers of some standing as early as the 1920s: Ch'ien Tu-hsia, Li Ta-chao, and Yeh Ch'ing. Mao Tse-tung wrote a pamphlet "On Practice" in 1937. In the People's Republic of China, most philosophy has been the result of collective effort. Some philosophers from the earlier period, like Fung Yu-lan, have accepted Marxism and have continued to write for publication.

4 ACCESSING INFORMATION IN PHILOSOPHY

MAJOR DIVISIONS OF THE FIELD

Although the term "philosophy" is derived from two Greek words usually translated as "love of wisdom," there is reason to believe that the original usage of the term was somewhat broader, connoting free play of the intellect over a wide range of human problems and even including such qualities as curiosity, shrewdness, and practicality. A gradual narrowing of meaning began in antiquity and has proceeded in stages until modern times. Socrates differentiated his activity from that of the sophists by stressing the raising of questions for clarification in the course of discussion, as distinct from giving authoritative answers, or by teaching techniques for winning arguments. This emphasis on critical examination of issues remained central to philosophic method in succeeding centuries. Encyclopedic concepts of philosophy were finally shattered by the rise of modern science in the seventeenth century. First, the natural sciences emerged as separate disciplines. Somewhat later, the social and behavioral sciences also effected their separation from philosophy.

What, then, is left? First, there are questions about the nature of ultimate reality. Then there is the matter of knowledge as a whole as well as interrelationships of the various specialized branches. Also, there are questions about the methodology and presuppositions of individual disciplines. The term "philosophy of . . ." is frequently assigned to this type of endeavor. Finally, there are certain normative issues for which no scientifically verifiable answers are available.

Philosophy today is customarily divided into five areas: metaphysics, epistemology, logic, ethics, and aesthetics.

Metaphysics may be further subdivided into ontology and cosmology. Ontology is concerned with the nature of ultimate reality, or sometimes referred to as "being." It includes consideration of whether reality has one basic component (monism), two (dualism), or many (pluralism). Monistic philosophies discuss whether reality is ultimately mental or spiritual (idealism), or physical (materialism). Dualistic philosophies commonly regard both matter and mind as irreducible ultimate components. Cosmology is concerned with questions about origins and processes. The nature of causality has been a frequent topic for debate. Although a few have argued for pure chance, more philosophers have emphasized either antecedent causes (i.e., preceding events which cause the event under consideration to happen) or final causes (ends, or purposes, which exert an influence on the outcome of events). Many of the former persuasion are convinced that there is no room for either chance or freedom in the chain of causality. These determinists are called mechanists if they also believe that reality is ultimately physical. Philosophers who emphasize final causes are known as teleologists.

Epistemology is concerned with the scope and limits of human knowledge. What can we know? With what degree of certainty? Rationalists stress the role of human reason. Empiricists emphasize the importance of data derived from experience. It is generally agreed that there are two types of knowledge: *a priori*, which is knowable without reference to experience and which alone possesses theoretical certainty (e.g., the principles of logic and mathematics); and *a posteriori*, which is derived from experience, and possesses only approximate certainty (e.g., the findings of the sciences).

Logic deals with the principles of correct reasoning, or valid inference. It differs from psychology in that it does not describe how people actually think but prescribes certain canons to be followed if they would think correctly. Deductive logic (sometimes known as Aristotelian or traditional logic) arose in antiquity and is concerned with the process by which correct conclusions can be drawn from sets of axioms known or believed to be true. Its most familiar form is the syllogism, which consists of three parts: a major premise, a minor premise, and a conclusion:

> All men are mortal.
> Socrates is a man.
> Therefore, Socrates is mortal.

Inductive logic is a result of the development of modern scientific methods. It deals with the canons of valid inference, but is concerned with probabilities rather than certainties and frequently involves the use of statistics. It is, in a sense, the opposite of deductive logic (which proceeds from the general to the particular) in that it attempts to reach valid generalizations from an enumeration of particulars.

In ethics, the questions relate to matters of conduct. Can certain actions be considered morally right or wrong? If so, on what basis? Should the interests of the self have priority (egoism)? Or the interests of others (altruism)? Or is there some greater good (*summum bonum*) to which both should be subordinate? Ethical theories may be classified by the manner in which criteria for right actions are discovered or by the nature of the highest good. In the first group, authoritarians stress submission to the will of God or some other external authority. Rationalists stress the free activity of the mind in examining all aspects of a question. Intuitionists stress the importance of obedience to conscience. Emotive theorists stress feeling as the proper ground for ethical decision-making. In the second classification, hedonists regard pleasure as the highest good. Eudaemonists pursue happiness. Perfectionists seek the ideal fulfillment of human life. Kantians stress purity of motive and universalizability of individual ethical decisions.

The nature of beauty is the subject matter of aesthetics. The concerns of the philosopher may be differentiated from those of the psychologist and those of the critic. The psychologist concentrates on human reactions to aesthetic objects. The critic focuses on individual works of art or on general principles of criticism, usually within the confines of a particular discipline. The philosopher is broadly concerned with beauty, *per se*, whether in art or nature. Does beauty inhere in the beautiful object? Are there objective criteria by which it may be determined? Or is beauty a subjective experience, with no universally valid norms? Classical theories tend to stress objectivity. Romantic theories emphasize individualism and subjectivity.

MAJOR CLASSIFICATION SCHEMES

Utilization of shelf arrangement as a tool for philosophic information retrieval must be considered secondary to other approaches, but some knowledge of the major library classification schemes will be advantageous. In order of approximate frequency of use, these are: the Dewey Decimal Classification (DDC) and the Library of Congress Classification (LC).

From the standpoint of user needs, there are three principal approaches to the arrangement of philosophic writings: 1) By individual philosophers. This approach is particularly helpful for those who wish to study either the total thought system of a philosopher or a particular work. It is doubly helpful if secondary works (commentaries, criticism, etc.) are also shelved with the primary sources. 2) By specialized branches of the discipline (metaphysics, epistemology, logic, ethics, aesthetics). 3) By interrelationships and influences (periods, schools of thought, language and nationality groupings, etc.). Most classification systems attempt to achieve some balance among these differing (and somewhat conflicting) approaches.

First devised by Melvil Dewey in 1876, the Decimal Classification (DDC) has been frequently updated and expanded. The section on philosophy (100-199) is the least successful; the latest edition (18th), by its inclusion of psychology, still reflects a late nineteenth century view of the world. It is frequently criticized for its separation of philosophical viewpoints from the sections on ancient, medieval and modern philosophy, and for its failure to include a section on aesthetics (which DDC places with the arts in the 700s). Nevertheless, it is the most commonly used library classification system. Examples illustrating the major divisions and selected subdivisions are shown below.

100	PHILOSOPHY AND RELATED DISCIPLINES	110	METAPHYSICS
101	Theory of philosophy	111	Ontology
103	Dictionaries of philosophy	112	Classification of knowledge
105	Serials on philosophy	113	Cosmology
107	Study and teaching of philosophy	114	Space
109	Historical treatment of philosophy	115	Time
		117	Matter

120 KNOWLEDGE, CAUSE, PURPOSE,
MAN
121 Epistemology
122 Cause and effect
123 Freedom and necessity

130 POPULAR AND PARAPSYCHOLOGY,
OCCULTISM

140 SPECIFIC PHILOSOPHICAL
VIEWPOINTS
141 Idealism and related systems and
doctrines
142 Critical philosophy
143 Intuitionism and Bergsonism
144 Humanism and related systems
145 Sensationalism and ideology
146 Naturalism and related systems
147 Pantheism and related systems
148 Liberalism and other systems
149 Other systems and doctrines

150 PSYCHOLOGY

160 LOGIC
161 Induction
162 Deduction
166 Syllogisms
167 Hypotheses

170 ETHICS
171 Systems and doctrines
172 Ethics of political relationships
173 Ethics of family relationships
174 Professional and occupational ethics
174 Ethics of recreation
176 Sexual ethics
177 Ethics of social relations
178 Ethics of temperance and
intemperance
179 Other applications of ethics

180 ANCIENT, MEDIEVAL, ORIENTAL
PHILOSOPHY
181 Oriental
182 Pre-Socratic Greek
183 Sophistic, Socratic and related Greek
184 Platonic
185 Aristotelian
186 Skeptic and Neoplatonic
187 Epicurean
188 Stoic
189 Medieval Western

190 MODERN WESTERN PHILOSOPHY
191 United States and Canada
192 British Isles
193 Germany and Austria
194 France
195 Italy
196 Spain and Portugal
197 Russia and Finland
198 Scandinavia
199 Other countries

The Library of Congress (LC) schedule for philosophy was first published in 1910 and revised in 1950. LC includes psychology, but otherwise is generally superior to DDC. Subclass B is designed to keep the works of individual philosophers together and to place philosophers in relation to periods, countries, and schools of thought. The general pattern for individual philosophers is 1) collected works; 2) separate works; 3) biography and criticism. LC also has sections for the major divisions of the field (including aesthetics). The principal divisions are shown in the synopsis below:

B   PHILOSOPHY (GENERAL)
     Serials, Collections, etc.
     History and systems
BC   LOGIC
BD   SPECULATIVE PHILOSOPHY
     General philosophical works
     Metaphysics
     Epistemology
     Methodology
     Ontology
     Cosmology

BF PSYCHOLOGY
     Parapsychology
     Occult sciences
BH AESTHETICS
BJ ETHICS
     Social usages, Etiquette

Although some special philosophy classifications have been developed, their use appears to have been confined to the arrangement of certain bibliographies.

SUBJECT HEADINGS FREQUENTLY USED

Searching library catalogs (whether in card, book or computer form) continues to play an important role in the retrieval of philosophical information. Although many subject indexes in recent years have been constructed on the basis of key words from document titles, or from text, most library subject catalogs use a controlled or standardized vocabulary embodied in a list of subject headings. Such lists usually include guidance on choice of main headings, methods of subdividing major topics, and cross references to lead the user to the headings chosen or to related topics.

The overwhelming majority of large American libraries today follow the *Subject Headings Used in the Dictionary Catalogs of the Library of Congress* (7th ed. Washington, D.C.: Library of Congress, Card Division, 1966). These headings enable the reader looking for a specific topic in philosophy to go directly to that heading. The disadvantage is that philosophic topics are scattered throughout an entire alphabetical sequence. This is true whether the library uses a "dictionary" catalog (in which entries for authors, titles and subjects are interfiled in one alphabetical sequence) or a "divided" catalog (in which author and title entries are separated from the alphabetical subject portion).

This chapter will include some discussion of the general principles governing the choice and arrangement of Library of Congress subject headings. Examples will be chosen, insofar as possible, from philosophy. In later chapters dealing with other disciplines, the general discussion will not be repeated but attention will be paid to examples from each discipline. In each field, the main cluster of subject headings will be reproduced from the seventh edition of *Subject Headings Used in the Dictionary Catalogs of the Library of Congress*. In disciplines in which there has been widespread library use of some alternative system of subject headings, this fact will be noted and major deviations from LC will be indicated. The general principles discussed here are extracted from *Subject Headings: A Practical Guide*, by David Judson Haykin (Washington, D.C.: U.S. Government Printing Office, 1951). As Chief of the Subject Cataloging Division of LC, Haykin helped to shape the system he described.

The main cluster of "philosophy" is outlined on the following pages.

LIBRARY OF CONGRESS SUBJECT HEADINGS IN PHILOSOPHY*

Philosophers
   x Philosophy—Biography
  —Correspondence, reminiscences, etc.
Philosophers, American, [French, German,
     etc.]
   x American [French, German, etc.]
     philosophers
  —Correspondence, reminiscences, etc.
Philosophers, Ancient *(B108-708)*
Philosophers, Medieval *(B720-785)*
Philosophers, Modern
   x Modern philosophers
Philosophers' egg
  See Alchemy
Philosophers' stone
  See Alchemy
Philosophical analysis
  See Analysis (Philosophy)
Philosophical anthropology *(BD450)*
  sa Humanism
     Man—Animal nature
     Mind and body
     Persons
  x Anthropology, Philosophical
     Man (Philosophy)
  xx Civilization—Philosophy
     Humanism
     Life
     Man
     Ontology
     Persons
Philosophical grammar
  See Grammar, Comparative and
     general
Philosophical theology *(BT40)*
  x Theology, Philosophical
  xx Christianity—Philosophy
     Natural theology
     Philosophy
     Philosophy and religion
     Religion—Philosophy
     Theology, Doctrinal
Philosophy *(B-BJ)*
  sa Aesthetics
     Analysis (Philosophy)
     Atomism
     Axioms
     Belief and doubt
     Causation
     Consciousness
     Cosmology
     Creation
     Criticism (Philosophy)
     Dualism
     Egoism

Epiphanism
Ethics
Evidence
Experience
Fate and fatalism
Free will and determinism
Gnosticism
God
Good and evil
Hedonism
Humanism
Hylozoism
Idealism
Ideology
Individuation
Intuition
Knowledge, Theory of
Logic
Materialism
Mechanism (Philosophy)
Metaphysics
Mind and body
Monadology
Monism
Mysticism
Naturalism
Neoplatonism
Nihilism (Philosophy)
Nominalism
Ontology
Opposition, Theory of
Optimism
Panpsychism
Pantheism
Perception
Personalism
Pessimism
Phenomenalism
Philosophical theology
Platonists
Pluralism
Polarity (Philosophy)
Positivism
Power (Philosophy)
Pragmatism
Psychology
Rationalism
Realism
Reality
Scholasticism
Situation (Philosophy)
Skepticism
Soul
Space and time
Sufficient reason

Teleology
Theism
Thought and thinking
Transcendentalism
Truth
Universals (Philosophy)
Utilitarianism
Whole and parts (Philosophy)
Will
x Mental philosophy
xx Cosmology
Ontology
−Authorship
−Biography
  See Philosophers
−Historiography *(B51.4-6)*
−History *(Indirect) (B69-4695)*
  −Methodology *(B53)*
−Introductions *(BD10-28)*
−Methodology
  See Methodology
−Miscellanea *(B68)*
−Pictures, illustrations, etc. *(B51.8)*
−Study and teaching *(Direct) (B52)*
−Terminology *(B49-50)*
Philosophy, American, [Arabic, Chinese. etc.]
Philosophy, American *(B851-945)*
  sa Mercersburg theology
Philosophy, Analytical
  See Analysis (Philosophy)
Philosophy, Ancient *(B108-708)*
  Here are entered works dealing with ancient philosophy in general and with Greek and Roman philosophy in particular.
  sa Atomism
    Eleatics
    Gnosticism
    Manichaeism
    Neoplatonism
    Peripatetics
    Platonists
    Pythagoras and Pythagorean school
    Science, Ancient
    Skeptics (Greek philosophy)
    Sophists (Greek philosophy)
    Stoics
  x Greek philosophy
    Philosophy, Greek
    Philosophy, Roman
    Roman philosophy
Philosophy, Arabic
  sa Fate and fatalism (Mohammedanism)
    Mohammedanism and philosophy
  xx Philosophy, Mohammedan

Philosophy, Buddhist *(B123)*
  sa Abhidharma
    Buddhist logic
    Philosophy, Indic
  x Buddhist philosophy
  xx Buddha and Buddhism
    Philosophy, Hindu
    Philosophy, Indic
Philosophy, Chinese
  sa Neo-Confucianism
Philosophy, Comparative *(B799)*
  Here are entered works on the comparison of the philosophies of the East and the West.
  x Comparative philosophy
  xx East and West
    Oriental studies
    Philosophy, Oriental
Philosophy, Doctor of
  See Doctor of philosophy degree
Philosophy, East Indian
  See Philosophy, Indic
Philosophy, English
  xx Philosophy, Modern
Philosophy, French
  sa Libertines (French philosophers)
  xx Philosophy, Modern
  −16th century
  −17th century *(B1815-1818)*
  −18th century *(B1911-1925)*
  −19 century *(B2185-8)*
  −20th century *(B2421-4)*
Philosophy, German
  xx Philosophy, Modern
Philosophy, Greek
  See Philosophy, Ancient
Philosophy, Hindu
  sa Advaita
    Dharma
    Dvaita (Vedanta)
    Lokāyata
    Mandala
    Maya (Hinduism)
    Nyaya
    Philosophy, Buddhist
    Philosophy, Indic
    Vaisesika
    Yoga
  xx Philosophy, Indic
Philosophy, Indic *(BP130-133)*
  sa Philosophy, Buddhist
    Philosophy, Hindu
  x East Indian philosophy
    Indic philosophy
    Philosophy, East Indian
  xx Philosophy, Buddhist
    Philosophy, Hindu
Philosophy, Jaina *(B162.5)*

sa Jaina logic
x Jaina philosophy
Philosophy, Japanese
sa Mitogaku
Philosophy, Jewish
sa Hasidism—Philosophy
x Jewish philosophy
Jews—Philosophy
Philosophy, Mechanistic
See Mechanism (Philosophy)
Philosophy, Medieval (B720-785)
sa Scholasticism
Summists
xx Scholasticism
Philosophy, Modern (B790-4695)
sa Evolution
Existentialism
Humanism—20th century
Humanism, Religious
Neo-Scholasticism
Phenomenology
Positivism
Pragmatism
Semantics (Philosophy)
Transcendentalism
also Philosophy, English, [French,
German, etc.]
x Modern philosophy
—16th century
See Philosophy, Renaissance
—17th century (B801)
—18th century (B802)
sa Enlightenment
—19th century (B803)
—20th century (B804)
Philosophy, Mohammedan
Here are entered works on modern
Mohammedan philosophy not lim-
ited to the historic Mohammedan
philosophy in Arabic or Persian.
sa Mohammedanism and philosophy
Philosophy, Arabic
Philosophy, Persian
x Mohammedan philosophy
Philosophy, Moral
See Ethics
Philosophy, Natural
See Physics
Philosophy, Oriental (B121)
sa Philosophy, Comparative
x Oriental philosophy
Philosophy, Patristic
See Fathers of the church
Philosophy, Persian
xx Philosophy, Mohammedan
Philosophy, Polish
sa Messianism, Polish
Philosophy, Primitive (GN470)

Philosophy, Renaissance (B770-785)
x Philosophy, Modern—16th century
xx Renaissance
Philosophy, Roman
See Philosophy, Ancient
Philosophy and astronomy
See Astronomy—Philosophy
Philosophy and Mohammedanism
See Mohammedanism and philosophy
Philosophy and religion
sa Faith and reason
Mohammedanism and philosophy
Personalism
Philosophical theology
Religion—Philosophy
x Christianity and philosophy
Religion and philosophy
xx Religion—Philosophy
Note under Faith and reason
Philosophy and science
See Science—Philosophy
Philosophy in literature (PN49)
sa Existentialism in literature
Philosophy of history
See History—Philosophy
Philosophy of international law
See International law—Philosophy
Philosophy of language
See Languages—Philosophy
Philosophy of law
See Law—Philosophy
Philosophy of literature
See Literature—Philosophy
Philosophy of medicine
See Medicine—Philosophy
Philosophy of nature (BD581)
sa Cosmology
Natural theology
Nature—Religious interpretations
x Nature—Philosophy
Nature, Philosophy of
xx Natural theology
Philosophy of psychiatry
See Psychiatry—Philosophy
Philosophy of teaching
See Education—Philosophy

*From *Subject Headings Used in the
Dictionary Catalogs of the Library of
Congress* (7th ed. Washington, D.C.:
Library of Congress, Card Division,
1966), pp. 971-72.

To use these headings as a guide in the formulation of search strategy, it is helpful to understand the basic forms that main headings may take:

1. **Simple nouns as headings.** This form is the most direct, immediate, and uncomplicated. If adequate to the task, it is normally preferred. The most obvious example, in this context, is "Philosophy."

2. **Adjectival headings.** These may be in natural or inverted form. An example of the natural form would be "Philosophical anthropology"; an example of the inverted form would be "Philosophy, American." The choice is determined by the need to emphasize those search words of greatest importance to the intended user. In the first example, the word "philosophical" is more significant to the philosophy student than the word "anthropology." In the second example, the word "American" would be of significance to the person seeking information on American philosophy but the natural order would bury the topic among dozens (perhaps hundreds) of other entries beginning with "American." Since the prime topic is philosophy, with American philosophy as one variety, the inverted form is chosen.

3. **Phrase headings.** These usually consist of nouns connected by a preposition. An example would be "Philosophy in literature." Sometimes, it is necessary to invert the natural word order to emphasize a key search term. There is no ready example from the philosophy list, but an example from another field would be "Plants, Protection of." Another type of phrase heading is the so-called "compound heading," made up of two or more coordinate elements connected by "and." An example would be "Philosophy and religion."

It frequently happens that the approaches described above do not result in headings that are sufficiently specific, so that further division of the topic is required. The techniques most frequently used for division are as follows:

1. **By form.** This plan of division is not based on the content of a work but on its manner of arrangement or the purpose it is intended to serve. Examples would include:

> Philosophy–Bibliography
> Philosophy–Dictionaries
> Philosophy–Directories
> Philosophy–Outlines, Syllabi, etc.
> Philosophy–Study and teaching.

2. **By political or geographic area.** There are two principal methods of local division: direct and indirect. If the direct method is used, the name of a specific place occurs immediately after the dash, indicating a division of the main heading. If the indirect approach is chosen, the name of a country or larger unit will be inserted between the main heading and the specific place. Places likely to be familiar to American users will probably be entered directly. Places less likely to be familiar will be entered indirectly. Philosophy is not the best subject to choose for examples, since the need for geographic subdivision in philosophy is largely achieved in another way–namely, by use of the inverted form of adjectival headings, such as "Philosophy, English," or "Philosophy, French." There is one area of philosophy, however, in which the principle of local or geographic division can be illustrated. From the list above, we note that "Philosophy–History" is to be further subdivided by using the indirect method.

Thus, a book dealing with the history of philosophy in Padua would appear under the subject heading "Philosophy–History–Italy–Padua."

3. **By period.** This represents a departure from the customary alphabetical approach in that headings for generally accepted historical periods are arranged *chronologically*. In philosophy, this technique is used to subdivide under the different countries. Thus, we find that "Philosophy, French–17th century" precedes "Philosophy, French–18th century" although an alphabetical arrangement would have reversed that order. It should be noted, however, that very broad periods for philosophy as a whole are filed in *alphabetical* sequence. Thus, "Philosophy, Ancient" precedes "Philosophy, Arabic," and "Philosophy, Medieval" follows "Philosophy, Jewish," while "Philosophy, Modern" precedes "Philosophy, Mohammedan" in the 1966 list.

It should also be noted that any formal list of subject headings will not include one very large category of subject entries–individual names as subjects. These may be personal (e.g., "James, William") or corporate (e.g., "American Philosophical Association"). In the case of very prominent or prolific writers, the entries may be further subdivided–e.g., "Dewey, John–Addresses, essays, lectures."

A subject heading system must make provision for the user who may choose as his initial search term a word or phrase other than the one used in the system. Usually this will be a synonym for the term chosen. The necessary connections are provided by means of "see" references, which direct the reader from headings not used to those which are used. In the list of LC subject headings provided above, the chosen terms are given in bold type and other terms in lighter type. The cross reference "Philosophy–Biography. *See* Philosophers" is given in light type. The heading "Philosophers" appears in bold type. Under this heading in bold type is the following entry in light type: "*x* Philosophy–Biography." The symbol "*x*" is used to indicate that a "see" reference has been made from "Philosophy–Biography" to "Philosophers."

A subject heading system also provides the user with access to other headings that might lead to relevant information. This is done by means of "see also" references. These may direct the user to other topics of equal breadth and scope or they may direct him to more specific subjects. A good example of the latter type is the list of more than 75 specific "see also" references under "Philosophy." (The symbol "*sa*" preceding this list indicates that these are "see also" references.) It is customary to enumerate all of these specific headings, which will be found elsewhere in the catalog. Sometimes, a more generalized kind of "see also" reference occurs, illustrated by only a few examples. Such generalized "see also" references are given after the full enumeration of specific "see also" references. An example of this type of heading from the philosophy list occurs under "Philosophy, Modern." After an enumeration of 10 specific "see also" references, this general "see also" reference is given: "Philosophy, English [French, German, etc.] ."

The symbol "*xx*" is used to indicate the reverse pattern of "see also" references and is sometimes defined as "see also from." Thus, under "Philosophy" there occurs "*xx* Cosmology." This means that there will be a cross reference "Cosmology. *See also* Philosophy" in the catalog.

To remove doubt or confusion about what may or may not be covered by certain subject headings, scope notes are provided. These are relatively infrequent, usually noting limitations and sometimes referring to other entries. Examples from the 1966 list may be found under "Philosophy, Ancient" and "Philosophy, Mohammedan."

Comparison of the list reproduced above with the subject catalog of a medium-sized or larger library will make it apparent that many more headings are used in practice than are enumerated in the list. Most of these headings are formed in accordance with the principles already discussed and can readily be anticipated by the searcher who understands these principles. Checking the philosophy section of a recent volume of *Library of Congress Catalog: Books: Subjects* will reveal examples. It should be noted, however, that new terms are constantly coming into use and older terms are being revised or deleted. Even in a relatively stable field like philosophy half a dozen to a dozen changes will typically be reported in each new supplement to *Subject Headings Used in the Dictionary Catalogs of the Library of Congress*. One such change has been the cancellation of the heading "Philosophy, Mohammedan" and the substitution of the more modern "Philosophy, Islamic."

Ease and precision in philosophic information retrieval will be greatly facilitated by an understanding of the filing system used in a particular library. The dictionary catalog or the subject portion of a divided catalog will normally follow an alphabetical arrangement, but a chronological arrangement is used wherever a division by date seems more logical than a strictly alphabetical sequence.

Alphabetical arrangements usually follow one of two patterns. The first is the so-called "letter by letter" method used in many reference tools, including several indexes and encyclopedias. With this method, all the words in the heading are treated as parts of one unit. Filing proceeds strictly on the basis of the order of the letters in the unit as a whole, regardless of whether they are in separate short words or in a single long word. Thus, "Newark" would precede "New York." Libraries have not favored this method because it tends to scatter closely related topics. Instead, most libraries have adopted the "word by word" or "nothing before something" approach, in which each word is treated as a separate unit for filing purposes. Using this method, "New York" would precede "Newark" in the catalog. Within this general framework of "word by word" filing, the Library of Congress has developed the following sequence for subject headings:

1. Main heading alone—e.g., "Philosophy";
2. Main heading plus form divisions (indicated by a dash)—e.g., "Philosophy—Terminology";
3. Main heading plus time divisions;
4. Main heading plus geographic divisions;
5. Inversions (indicated by a comma)—e.g., "Philosophy, American";
6. Phrases—e.g., "Philosophy of nature."

As noted above, a chronological arrangement is used whenever a division by date seems more logical than a strictly alphabetical sequence. In philosophy, the practice is not altogether consistent. Broad periods, with definitely assignable names, are filed in alphabetical sequence with other inverted headings (e.g., "Philosophy, Ancient," "Philosophy, Medieval," and "Philosophy, Modern"). But the last-named is then subdivided chronologically (e.g., "Philosophy, Modern—16th century," "Philosophy, Modern—17th century," etc.). Period subdivisions are also used under the headings for philosophy in different countries (e.g., "Philosophy, French—20th century").

MAJOR PHILOSOPHICAL SOCIETIES, INFORMATION CENTERS AND SPECIAL COLLECTIONS

It has become a truism to say that the competent reference librarian will utilize information sources beyond the collections of one library. The role of bibliographies, indexes, and union catalogs in this process is already familiar and need not be elaborated here. What may be of assistance, however, is some discussion of supplementary information sources. In philosophy, these may be roughly grouped into three categories: philosophical societies; information centers; and special collections. Each of these will be examined. No attempt at completeness will be made; rather, a sampling of major sources will be offered, together with some suggestions about where additional information may be found.

Unesco has supported international philosophical activities in a variety of ways. In 1946, it recognized the International Council of Scientific Unions (The Hague) as a coordinating body. One of its branches is the International Union of the History and Philosophy of Science (Paris), which in turn has national committees in over 25 countries and which maintains affiliations with a variety of national and international organizations. Another organization recognized by Unesco is the International Council for Philosophy and Humanistic Studies (Paris). This Council is composed of many international non-governmental organizations, such as the International Union of Academies (Brussels) and the International Federation of Societies of Philosophy (Brussels). The latter, composed of approximately 90 philosophical societies in more than 35 countries, sponsors international congresses every five years. Unesco also provides grants for the activities of some of these groups and for certain philosophical documentation centers.

Further details concerning international philosophical societies and leading national philosophical groups outside North America may be found in *International Directory of Philosophy and Philosophers 1972/73*. Current information concerning philosophical congresses can be found in the "Chroniques" section of *Revue philosophique de Louvain*.

The most comprehensive philosophical society in the United States is the American Philosophical Association, founded in 1900 to promote not only the exchange of ideas among philosophers but also creative and scholarly activity in philosophy. Its membership (about 3,800) is restricted to those qualified to teach philosophy at the college or university level. In addition to the national officers (chairman and secretary), there are officers for three regional divisions (Eastern, Western, and Pacific), each of which sponsors an annual conference. Publications include *Proceedings and Addresses of the American Philosophical Association*, *Jobs in Philosophy*, and *APA Bulletin*.

The organization with the largest membership (over 7,500) is Phi Sigma Tau, founded in 1930 to promote ties nationally between philosophy students and departments of philosophy. It publishes *Dialogue* and a *Newsletter*.

Another major organization is the American Catholic Philosophical Association, founded in 1926, with a current membership of over 1,600. Its publications include *The New Scholasticism* and *Proceedings of the American Catholic Philosophical Association*.

There are also many specialized societies. Sometimes, the interest centers around a particular philosopher (e.g., Hegel, or Dewey); sometimes, it is focused on a particular topic (like phenomenology and existential philosophy).

A number of local, state, or regional groups complete the picture. Further details may be found in the "Societies" section of the *Directory of American Philosophers 1972/73* or in subsequent issues of this biennial publication.

There are several information centers actively at work in philosophy. In a number of cases, advanced computerized techniques are used for information retrieval and/or production of publications.

The Philosophy Documentation Center (Bowling Green State University, Bowling Green, Ohio 43404) exists to collect, store, and disseminate bibliographic data in philosophy. It issues a quarterly publication (cumulated annually) entitled *The Philosopher's Index*, which is a subject and author index with abstracts. Computerized searches of the data base are also possible.

The Philosophy Information Center (Philosophy Institute, University of Düsseldorf, Düsseldorf, West Germany) cooperates in the production of *The Philosopher's Index* by providing subject headings and abstracts of articles published in all German journals. The Center also makes use of a Siemens computer to produce its own series of bibliographies and indexes, such as *Gesamtregister zur Zeitschrift für Philosophische Forschung 1-21 (1946-1967)* and *Gesamtregister der Kant-Studien* (Vol. 1, 1897-1925; Vol. 2, 1926-1969).

Le Centre Nationale de la Recherche Scientifique, through its Centre de Documentation, Sciences Humaines (54, Boulevard Raspail, Paris VIe, France), lists or abstracts periodical articles in its *Bulletin signalétique—Section Philosophie*, a quarterly publication with annual cumulative indexes. The Director of this center, Mrs. L. Cadoux, also supervises the Cercle Internationale de Recherches Philosophiques par Ordinateur (CIRPHO), a new organization to promote philosophical research which arose out of the Montreal Congress (1971) of the Congrès des Sociétés de Philosophie de Langue Française.

Over 25 national centers participate in the work of L'Institut International de Philosophie (173, Boulevard Saint-Germain, 75-Paris-06, France), which publishes a quarterly bulletin entitled *Bibliographie de la philosophie* with the aid of a grant from Unesco and which cooperates with L'Institut Supérieure de Philosophie de l'Université Catholique de Louvain in publication of *Répertoire bibliographique de la philosophie*, which is also subsidized by Unesco.

Although not concerned solely with philosophy, the Institute of East European Studies (University of Fribourg, Switzerland) is a major source of information on Marxist philosophy.

Another major source of such information is Zentralstelle für die philosophischen Information und Dokumentation (GRD-108 Berlin, Tauben-strasse 19/23), which tries to cover all Marxist philosophical literature in *Bibliographie Philosophie* (1967-).

More detailed coverage of philosophical research and publication projects (especially those making use of computers) is contained in "L'informatique au service de la philosophie; réalisations et projects," by Christian Wenin [*Revue philosophique de Louvain* 6 (May 1972): 177-211].

Special collections in philosophy may attempt to cover the discipline as a whole, some period in the history of philosophy, some special topic, or the works of an individual philosopher.

The Hoose Library of Philosophy at the University of Southern California contains more than 40,000 volumes and covers virtually every period from medieval manuscripts to the latest contemporary publications. A catalog of this collection was published in 1968 by G. K. Hall.

The Professor Don C. Allen Collection at the University of California, San Diego, concentrates on the Renaissance period.

The General Library of the University of Michigan has a large collection dealing with Arabic philosophy.

The Weston College Library (Massachusetts) attempts to be comprehensive in Catholic philosophy, while the Dominican College Library (Washington, D.C.) specializes in Thomist works and attempts to collect all works by Dominican authors.

The Van Pelt Library of the University of Pennsylvania has a collection of nearly 3,000 manuscripts from the fifteenth to the nineteenth centuries dealing mainly with Hindu philosophy, religion, and grammar.

The Special Collections Department of the Columbia University Libraries and the Jewish Institute of Religion Library of Hebrew Union College (Cincinnati) have distinguished Spinoza collections.

In 1968, McMaster University Library (Hamilton, Ontario, Canada) acquired the papers of Bertrand Russell—more than 250,000 items. Information is now being disseminated in *Russell: The Journal of the Bertrand Russell Archives*.

The foregoing examples are cited merely to show the range of specialized information available. These, and many more, will be found under "Philosophy" and related headings or under the names of individual philosophers in *Subject Collections*, by Lee Ash and Denis Lorenz (4th ed. New York: Bowker, 1974).

Subject Collections in European Libraries, by Richard C. Lewanski (New York: Bowker, 1965), is arranged first by Dewey Decimal Classification and then by country. A series of useful appendices in the back cover such topics as British regional schemes, German plans, and the Scandia Plan.

5 PRINCIPAL INFORMATION SOURCES IN PHILOSOPHY

INTRODUCTORY WORKS AND BIBLIOGRAPHIC GUIDES

1.   Borchardt, Dietrich Hans. **How to Find Out in Philosophy and Psychology**. New York: Pergamon Press, 1968. 97p.
An extended bibliographical essay by a noted Australian librarian. Designed for the intelligent layman and the undergraduate student, it contains evaluative as well as descriptive comments. Borchardt has provided an update: "Recent International Documentation in Philosophy: A Survey of Select Reference Works," *International Library Review* 4 (April 1972): 199-212.

2.   Carritt, Edgar Frederick. **The Theory of Beauty**. New York: Barnes and Noble, 1962. 244p.
A good general introduction.

3.   Croce, Benedetto. **Aesthetic as Science of Expression and General Linguistic**. 2nd ed. New York: Macmillan, 1922. 503p.
First published in 1909, later reprinted by Peter Smith. Somewhat technical, but now a classic work by one of the greatest philosophers of the twentieth century.

4.   DeGeorge, Richard T. **A Guide to Philosophical Bibliography and Research**. New York: Appleton-Century-Crofts, 1971. 141p.
Compiled by the Chairman of the Department of Philosophy, University of Kansas, and published in the Century Philosophy Series, edited by Justus Buchler, this classified, annotated bibliography is the best single volume

currently available. It is much more comprehensive than *The Bibliography of Philosophy*, by Charles L. Higgins (Ann Arbor, Mich.: Campus Publishers, 1965), though Higgins has more detail on basic bibliographies and bibliographic patterns up to the time of compilation.

5. Dewey, John. **Art as Experience**. New York: Minton, 1934. (Reprinted New York: Putnam, 1958). 355p.
An introduction from the perspective of American pragmatism.

6. Greene, Theodore Meyer. **The Arts and the Art of Criticism**. 2nd ed. New York: Gordian Press, 1947.
Still a useful overview.

7. Koren, Henry J. **Research in Philosophy: A Bibliographical Introduction to Philosophy and a Few Suggestions for Dissertations**. Pittsburgh: Duquesne University Press, 1966. 203p.
Intended for graduate students in philosophy, this book is less crisply professional than DeGeorge and more prone to "fatherly advice," but it is supplementary in its approach and coverage.

8. Lachs, John. **Marxist Philosophy: A Bibliographical Guide**. Chapel Hill: University of North Carolina Press, 1967. 166p.
Compiled by a professional philosopher whose prime concern is substantive issues rather than niceties of bibliography, and limited to works in English, French, and German (with emphasis on English), this guidebook is divided into 38 chapters, mostly representing various aspects of Marxist and Marxist-Leninist thought. Each chapter begins with a short, critical essay. About 1,500 items are listed. There are chapters on documents, journals of special relevance, bibliographies, and reference works. This is still the best work available in English, although *Guide to Marxist Philosophy: An Introductory Bibliography*, edited by I. M. Bochenski (Chicago: Alan Swallow, 1972), is more recent and serves as a useful supplement. Bochenski is Director of the Institute of East European Studies, Fribourg, Switzerland. His annotations (and selections) are regarded by some American reviewers as rather biased.

9. Langer, Susanne Katherina (Knauth). **Philosophy in a New Key**. 3rd ed. Cambridge: Harvard University Press, 1957. 313p.
Highly regarded as a creative approach to the field of aesthetics. Other works by the same author include *Feeling and Form* (New York: Scribner's, 1953), and *Problems of Art* (New York: Scribner's, 1957). She has also edited *Reflections on Art: A Source Book of Writings by Artists, Critics, and Philosophers* (Baltimore: Johns Hopkins University Press, 1958. Reprinted New York: Oxford University Press, 1961).

10. Magill, Frank N. **Masterpieces of World Philosophy in Summary Form**. New York: Harper and Row, 1961. 1166p.
Summarizes 200 major works from ancient times to the middle of the twentieth century. Chronological arrangement is supplemented by an alphabetical list of

titles (front) and authors (back). Also includes "Glossary of Common Philosophical Terms" (pp. xvii-xxx).

11.   Malraux, André. **The Voices of Silence**. Garden City, N.Y.: Doubleday, 1953. 661p.
Reflections on aesthetics by a distinguished French critic.

12.   **Philosophy**. By Roderick M. Chisholm and others. Englewood Cliffs, N.J.: Prentice-Hall, 1964. (The Princeton Studies: Humanistic Scholarship in America). 560p.
A general survey of trends in American philosophical scholarship from 1930 to 1960 is followed by chapters on metaphysics, theory of knowledge, ethical theory, and philosophy of science.

13.   Plott, John C., and Paul D. Mays. **Sarva−Darsana−Sangraha: A Bibliographical Guide to the Global History of Philosophy**. Leiden: E. J. Brill, 1969. 305p.
Attempts worldwide coverage as a corrective to the traditional emphasis on Western philosophy. Intended for upper level undergraduates and graduate students. Also useful for area studies. Classified and annotated. Items of special importance are starred or double-starred. Introduction explains spelling and alphabetizing. Tends to slight the analytic tradition. Cites works in foreign languages selectively. Appendix I is "A Syllabus Outline to the Global History of Philosophy"; Appendix II (folded in back) is "A Synchronological Chart to the Global History of Philosophy." Name index (pp.293-305) includes cross references.

14.   Richards, Ivor A., C. K. Ogden, and James Wood. **Foundations of Aesthetics**. 2nd ed. New York: Lear, 1925. 92p.
Consideration of this topic by noted literary critics.

BIBLIOGRAPHIES

15.   Albert, Ethel M., Clyde Kluckhohn, and others. **A Selected Bibliography on Values, Ethics, and Esthetics in the Behavioral Sciences and Philosophy, 1920-1958**. Glencoe, Ill.: Free Press, 1959. 342p.
A listing of some 2,000 books and articles, classified by discipline. A detailed guide (pp. 3-41) assists the user in locating pertinent references through a topical approach. There is also an alphabetical index of authors. A more recent work which attempts to promote an interdisciplinary approach to the study of ethical questions is Sebastian A. Matczak's *Philosophy: A Select, Classified Bibliography of Ethics, Economics, Law, Politics, Sociology* (Louvain: Nauwelaerts, 1970).

16.   **Bibliographie de la philosophie, 1937-1953**. Paris: Vrin, 1937-1953.
This polylingual quarterly did not appear during World War II (1940-45). It was compiled by the staff of the Institut Internationale de Philosophie, which often translated titles from little-known languages and tried to cover philosophy

exhaustively. In the post-war years, 730 journals (100 of them French) were scanned. The arrangement is complex, with two general divisions. In the first division are 1) geographical arrangement of publishers; 2) directory of periodicals, reviews, newspapers, etc., under country of origin; 3) alphabetical arrangement under author of all books and periodical articles published in the period covered. The second division includes: 1) alphabetical index of philosophers who are the subject of books and articles in the first part; 2) systematic classification of materials in the first part; 3) alphabetical arrangement of philosophic terms and concepts with applicable book and periodical articles under each. Superseded by *Bibliographie de la philosophie, bulletin trimestriel*, 1954– .

17.   **Bibliographie de la philosophie, bulletin trimestriel, 1954–** . Paris: Vrin, 1954– . Quarterly.
The revised editorial policy of the successor publication is to list books only and to annotate each entry with an objective description of the content and the aspect under which each book deserves attention. Summaries of English, French, German, Italian, and Spanish books appear in languages in which books are written. Other languages are summarized in French or English. Arrangement is classified. Annual author and title index.

18.   **Bibliographie der sowjetischen Philosophie.** Dordrecht, Holland: D. Reidel Publishing Company, 1957-68. 7 vols.
Includes Soviet books and articles in philosophy from 1947 through 1966. Continued by bibliographies in *Studies in Soviet Thought*.

19.   **Bibliographie Philosophie mit Autoren und Sach Register**, Vol. 1, No. 1, 1967– . Berlin: Zentrallstelle für die Philosophische Information und Dokumentation, 1967– . Bimonthly.
Attempts to cover Marxist philosophy comprehensively.

20.   Brie, G. A. de. **Bibliographia philosophica, 1934-1945.** Bruxelles: Editiones Spectrum, 1950-1954. 2 vols.
A major effort, subsidized by Unesco, containing 48,000 entries (both books and periodical articles) gleaned from 400 journals. Vol. I covers history of philosophy in five major sections: General; Greek and Roman; Patristic and Medieval; Recent; Oriental. Each is further subdivided by period, area, or individual. Material by and about individual philosophers is grouped first by birth date of the philosopher and then by date of publication. Vol. II is a systematic survey: General; Logic; Theories of Knowledge; Psychology; etc. The literature of cognate fields is well represented. A critical study of a specific work will be found in Vol. II; a biography or an evaluation of a philosopher will be found under the individual's name in Vol. I.

21.   Chan, Wing-tsit. **An Outline and an Annotated Bibliography of Chinese Philosophy.** New Haven: Yale University Press, 1969. 220p.
The "Outline" is arranged chronologically by four main periods: Ancient; Middle; Modern; Contemporary. Items of essential reading are triple-starred. The

second part is an annotated bibliography arranged alphabetically by author. There is a list of Chinese characters and a subject index. Chan has also compiled *Chinese Philosophy, 1949-1963: An Annotated Bibliography of Mainland China Publications* (Honolulu: East-West Center Press, 1967).

22. Dennison, A. T. "Philosophy Periodicals: An Annotated Select World List of Current Serial Publications." **International Library Review** 2 (July 1970): 355-86.

Notes on about 100 serials. Also, a country-by-country list (title only) of 269 journals. More recent than *Philosophie: Liste mondiale des périodiques spécialisés*. *Philosophy: World List of Specialized Periodicals* ('s-Gravenhage, Netherlands: Mouton, 1967).

23. *Répertoire bibliographique de la philosophie*, 1949– . Louvain: Editions de l'Institut Superiéure de Philosophie, 1949– . Quarterly.

From 1934 to 1948, its predecessor appeared as an appendix to *Revue néo-scholastique de philosophie*. From 1939, it also appeared as a supplement of the Dutch *Tijdschrift voor Philosophie* entitled *Bibliographisch Repertorium*. As such, it appeared even during World War II when *Revue néo-scholastique* was suspended. Since 1949 it has been an independent supplement to *Revue philosophique de Louvain*, assisted by grants from Unesco. Koren classes it as "perhaps the most important single tool for assembling a bibliography on a particular subject." Tries to cover all books in Catalan, Dutch, English, French, German, Italian, Latin, Portuguese, and Spanish as well as philosophical articles from more than 300 periodicals. Entries are arranged in classified order and each entry is assigned a number. There are cross references by number and topic from the thematic part to works listed in the historical part. The first three issues each year cover books and periodicals. The final one (November) lists book reviews and also contains an index of names (authors of books, articles, and reviews, editors, translators, etc.). Complete instructions for use (in French, English, German, Spanish, and Italian) appear in the February issue.

24. Totok, W., and H. Schroer. **Handbuch der Geschichte der Philosophie**. Frankfurt am Main: Klosterman, Vol. 1, 1964– .

Title misleading. Actually, a major bibliography. Vol. 1 covers ancient philosophy as well as Indian and Chinese. Arranged by periods. Author index has about 5,000 entries. Over 10,000 references in all. Brief subject index and list of journals cited. Vol. 2 is to cover the Middle Ages; Vol. 3 will cover modern times.

25. Varet, Gilbert. **Manuel de bibliographie philosophique**. Paris: Presses Universitaires de France, 1956. 2 vols.

A selective bibliography which covers the entire field of philosophy with special emphasis on 1914-1934, providing a foundation for Brie's *Bibliographia philosophica*. Vol. I treats the subject historically beginning with Oriental philosophy and coming to the present. There are subdivisions by period and by individual. Works in all languages are included. For prolific authors, the most important editions are mentioned. Vol. II is concerned with the development of systematic thinking. One section covers philosophy of art, religion, and history; another, philosophy of the sciences; a third, political philosophy, educational philosophy, etc. There are many brief annotations. A general index of names is given at the end of Vol. II. Retrospective coverage of some 60,000 books and periodical articles up to 1902 will be found in Benjamin Rand's *Bibliography of Philosophy, Psychology and Cognate Subjects* (New York: Macmillan, 1905. Reprinted 1949), which originally appeared as Vol. 3 of Baldwin's *Dictionary of Philosophy and Psychology*.

INDEXES, ABSTRACTS, AND CURRENT AWARENESS SERVICES

26.   France. Centre Nationale de la Recherche Scientifique. *Bulletin signalétique. Sciences humaines: philosophie*, 1947–60. Quarterly.
Has remained a quarterly through several title changes. Attempts to be exhaustive in coverage of serial literature of philosophy proper as well as such areas as theology and religion, psychology, sociology, linguistics, etc. Worldwide indexing coverage: 4,400 serials, 24,000 entries. Does *not* list books. Is an *abstracting* journal. Abstracts explain scope, viewpoint, argumentation, nad conclusion. Classified arrangement. Indexes book reviews and also gives digests of reviews.

27.   **The Philosopher's Index: An International Index to Philosophical Periodicals**, Vol. 1, No. 1, 1967– . Bowling Green, Ohio: Philosophy Documentation Center, Bowling Green State University, 1967– .
A quarterly index (with annual cumulations) to 235 philosophy periodicals, including all the major ones in the United States and Britain, with more selective coverage of other countries. Assisted by the Philosophy Information Center, Düsseldorf, West Germany. Each issue contains four parts: Subject Index; Bibliographic Data and Abstracts; Book Review Index; and Translations in Progress. Instructions precede each part.

28.   **Philosophic Abstracts**, 1939-54. Vols. 1-16. New York: Russell F. Moore Co., 1939-54.
Index to volumes 1 to 12 comprised author, title, and subject indexes to supplement basic arrangement of main work by country of publication.

DICTIONARIES AND ENCYCLOPEDIAS

29.   Baldwin, James Mark, ed. **Dictionary of Philosophy and Psychology, Including Many of the Principal Conceptions of Ethics, Logic, Aesthetics, Philosophy of Religion, Mental Pathology, Anthropology, Biology, Neurology, Physiology, Economics, Political Science and Social Philosophy, Philology, Physical Science and Education, and Giving a Terminology in English, French, German, and Italian.** New York: Macmillan, 1901-1905. 3 v. in 4. New ed. with corrections, 1925. Reprinted New York: Peter Smith, 1960.

Long preeminent in the field, but now largely superseded by *The Encyclopedia of Philosophy*, except for historical treatment and biographies.

29a.   **Dictionary of the History of Ideas: Studies of Selected Pivotal Ideas.**
Ed. by Philip P. Wiener. New York: Scribner's, 1973. 4 vols.
Compiled by the editor of *Journal of the History of Ideas*, this interdisciplinary work contains over 300 articles of some length, arranged alphabetically, supplemented by an analytical table of contents and an alphabetical list of article titles. Articles are written by noted scholars and contain bibliographies. There are many cross references. An index volume is planned for 1974.

30.   **Enciclopedia filosofica**. 2nd ed. Firenze: Sansoni, 1968-69. 6 vols.
Arrangement is dictionary-style, with individuals, places, ideas, schools, and movements in one alphabet. Articles are signed and accompanied by reading lists. Books, monographs, and periodical articles are listed. Greatest prominence is given to Continental European languages. Works are often listed in Italian translations. Suitable for the advanced student. The new edition is a complete revision of this scholarly work. The index is in Vol. 6.

31.   **The Encyclopedia of Philosophy**. Paul Edwards, Editor in Chief. New
York: Macmillan, 1967. 8 vols.
Tries to cover the whole of philosophy (East and West) and points of contact with other disciplines. Contains nearly 1,500 articles, some the length of small books and most with copious bibliographies. There are excellent articles on philosophical movements (both ancient and modern), major ideas (e.g., progress), the philosophy of various subject fields (e.g., history, law, religion, science), the history of philosophy in different countries (e.g., Indian philosophy, Russian philosophy), and biographies of major philosophers. Coverage of ancient, medieval and early modern philosophers is generally good. Coverage of contemporary philosophers is better for Western Europe, North America, and India than for the Soviet bloc and the People's Republic of China. Reference librarians will find the articles on philosophical bibliographies, dictionaries and encyclopedias, and journals of particular value. The editor has tried to minimize editorial bias. His own outlook is influenced by the Anglo-Saxon empirical and analytic approach. Thus, some topics that a Hegelian or an existentialist would omit may be discussed, and vice versa. Articles are long. The integrated approach has been preferred to a series of short articles. Smaller topics can be located by means of a detailed index in Vol. 8 (pp. 387-543). More than 500 philosophers from all over the world contributed; their names and brief credentials (including major publications) occupy over 30 pages. Over 150 scholars from the United States, Britain, and Europe served on the Editorial Board. This is likely to remain the definitive encyclopedia of philosophy for many years to come.

32.   **Filosofskaya Entsiklopediya**. Ed. by F. V. Konstantinov. Moscow:
Sovetskaya Entsiklopediya, 1960-70. 5 vols.
A general encyclopedia of philosophy written from a Marxist standpoint. The major articles carry lengthy bibliographies. It is especially valuable for the theoretical basis of communism and for biographical material.

33.   Foulquié, Paul. **Dictionnaire de la langue philosophique** . . . Paris: Presses Universitaires de France, 1962. 776p.

Lists words in groups under the main root word, with cross references from the derivative forms. Each entry gives etymology and definitions, indicating various areas of usage; synonyms; and illustrative quotes from literature, with brief references from sources. No bibliographies.

34.   Lalande, André. **Vocabulaire technique et critique de la philosophie.** 10th ed. rev. and enl. Paris: Presses Universitaires de France, 1968. 1324p.

Defines current philosophical meanings of terms and gives history of usage as well as German, English, and Italian equivalents.

35.   Peters, F. E. **Greek Philosophical Terms: A Historical Lexicon.** New York: New York University Press, 1967. 234p.

Designed for the "intermediate" student rather than the beginner or the mature philosopher. The basic arrangement is alphabetical in the main part. English words, with references to appropriate Greek terms in the main section, are given in the index at the end. Liberal references are made to passages in books of the Greek philosophers to clarify and illustrate usage and aid further study.

36.   Ritter, Joachim, ed. **Historisches Wörterbuch der Philosophie.** Vollig neubearb. Ausg. Basel, Schwabe; Darmstadt, Wissenschafliche Buchgesellschaft, 1971– . Vol. 1– .

Volume 1, A–C. Over 700 scholars have contributed to this revision of Rudolf Eisler's *Wörterbuch der Philosophischen Begriffe.* Some subjects covered in the earlier work (e.g., psychology) have been dropped and new material added. Other topics are revised and updated. "The articles, ranging in length from a few sentences to several pages, treat the historical development of philosophical terms and concepts in a very scholarly manner. Documentation is abundant and up to date. An index and list of abbreviations is to be included in each volume. It should be noted that articles on individual philosophers are not within the scope of this dictionary, although schools of thought based on the teachings of a single man are discussed" [*College and Research Libraries* 33 (January 1972): 42]. Also reviewed in *Australian Journal of Philosophy* 50 (May 1972): 100-101; *Archives de philosophie* 34 (July-September 1971): 503-506; and *Revue philosophique de France* 97 (January-March 1972): 114-16.

37.   Urmson, James Opie. **The Concise Encyclopedia of Western Philosophy and Philosophers.** Rev. ed. New York: Hawthorn, 1968.

Articles by about 50 scholars, mostly British. Written for "intelligent laymen." Coverage is selective. Biographies, general descriptions of trends, and definitions. No bibliography. More specialized in focus is Bernard Wuellner's *A Dictionary of Scholastic Philosophy* (2nd ed. Milwaukee: Bruce, 1966).

SOURCES OF DIRECTORY AND BIOGRAPHICAL INFORMATION

38. **Directory of American Philosophers**, Vol. 1– , 1962/63– . Bowling Green, Ohio: Philosophy Documentation Center, 1972– .
This biennial was formerly published by University of New Mexico Press. Edited by Archie J. Bahm (6th ed., 1972/73). Covers both the United States and Canada: 9,300 philosophers with addresses; fellowships and assistantships; 2,900 colleges and universities; 98 philosophy journals; 125 publishers of philosophy books; 55 philosophical societies; and professional statistics.

39. **International Directory of Philosophy and Philosophers 1972/73**. 2nd ed. Ed. by Ramona Cormier, Paul Kurtz, Richard H. Lineback, and Gilbert Varet. Bowling Green, Ohio: Philosophy Documentation Center, 1972.
Information on 91 countries excluding the United States and Canada: 5,000 philosophers with addresses; 700 colleges and universities; 240 institutes of philosophy; 175 philosophical societies; 450 philosophy journals; 690 publishers of philosophy books.

40. Ziegenfuss, Werner. **Philosophen-lexicon: Handwörterbuch der Philosophie nach Personnen**. Berlin: DeGruyter, 1949/50. 2 vols.
Useful biographical dictionary of philosophers, with emphasis on nineteenth and twentieth centuries. Gives under each name: biographical data; critical and descriptive digest of author's contribution to field; catalog of philosopher's principal published works; and a section which cites books and periodical articles that evaluate the philosopher's works.

HISTORIES OF PHILOSOPHY

41. Armstrong, Arthur Hilary, ed. **The Cambridge History of Later Greek and Early Medieval Philosophy**. London: Cambridge University Press, 1967. 711p.
Despite some unevenness of treatment, this has become a standard work in the field. Reference features include an excellent bibliography, an index of ancient and medieval works referred to in the text, a general index, and an index of Greek terms.

42. Beck, Lily (Moresby) Adams. **The Story of Oriental Philosophy**. New York: Farrar and Rinehart, 1928. 429p.
Though criticized by professional philosophers, this book has a useful role to play in arousing interest on the part of a lay person or beginning student.

43. Bosanquet, Bernard. **A History of Aesthetics**. 2nd ed. London, New York: Macmillan, 1904. (Reprinted New York: Humanities Press, 1966).
A classic work by a leading British philosopher of the idealist school.

44.   Bréhier, Emile. **The History of Philosophy**. Chicago: University of Chicago Press, 1963-1969. 7 vols.

The author is Professor of Philosophy at the Sorbonne and the set was published earlier in France. Translation is by Joseph Thomas and Wade Baskin. Useful bibliographies. Contents: Vol. 1, *The Hellenic Age*; Vol. 2, *The Hellenistic and Roman Age*; Vol. 3, *The Middle Ages and the Renaissance*; Vol. 4, *The Seventeenth Century*; Vol. 5, *The Eighteenth Century*; Vol. 6, *The Nineteenth Century: Period of Systems, 1800-1850*; Vol. 7, *Contemporary Philosophy: Since 1850*.

45.   Brinton, Clarence Crane. **A History of Western Morals**. New York: Harcourt, Brace & Co., 1959. 502p.

Generally praised for its informal style and balanced common sense. A successful popularization rather than a profound work of scholarship, yet written by a major scholar in the field.

46.   Brinton, Clarence Crane. **Ideas and Men: The Story of Western Thought**. 2nd ed. Englewood Cliffs, N.J.: Prentice-Hall, 1963. 484p.

Highly regarded for its coherent plan of organization and for the lucidity with which complex ideas are discussed. Useful for the lay reader or as an introductory college text.

47.   **Contemporary Philosophic Thought: Papers Delivered at the International Philosophy Year Conference at Brockport, 1967-68**. Ed. by Howard E. Kiefer and Milton K. Munitz. Albany: State University of New York Press, 1970. 4 vols.

Contents: Vol. 1, *Language, Belief and Metaphysics*; Vol. 2, *Mind, Science and History*; Vol. 3, *Perspectives in Education*; Vol. 4, *Ethics and Social Justice*.

48.   **Contemporary Philosophy: A Survey**. Ed. by Raymond Klibansky. Montreal: Mario Casalini, 1968-71. 4 vols.

Klibansky, of McGill University, is President of the Institut Internationale de Philosophie, and this set was sponsored by that body in cooperation with La Nuova Italia Editrice, Firenze. Contents: Vol. 1, *Logic and Foundations of Mathematics*; Vol. 2, *Philosophy of Science*; Vol. 3, *Metaphysics, Phenomenology, Language and Structure*; Vol. 4, *Ethics, Aesthetics, Law, Religion, Politics, Historical and Dialectical Materialism, Philosophy in Eastern Europe, Asia and Latin America*.

49.   Copleston, Frederick Charles. **A History of Philosophy**. London: Burns and Oates, 1947-66. 8 vols.

Covers the entire period from ancient times to the twentieth century. Written from "the standpoint of the scholastic philosopher." Each volume has an extensive bibliography and an analytical index.

50.   Durant, William James. **The Story of Philosophy**. New York: Simon and Schuster, 1926. 577p.

A popularization, often criticized by philosophers, but useful to stimulate interest. The most serious weakness is the omission of medieval philosophy.

51.   Feng, Yu-lan. **A History of Chinese Philosophy**. Princeton, Princeton University Press, 1952-53. 2 vols.
Contents: Vol. 1, *The Period of Philosophers* (from beginning to 100 B.C.); Vol. 2, *The Period of Classical Learning* (to 20th century A.D.).

52.   Gilson, Etienne Henry. **History of Christian Philosophy in the Middle Ages**. New York: Random House, 1955. 829p.
A major scholarly work by a leading Catholic philosopher.

53.   Gilson, Etienne Henry, ed. **A History of Philosophy**. New York: Random House, 1962– . 4 vols.
Contents: Vol. 1, *Ancient Philosophy*, by Anton Pegis (in preparation); Vol. 2, *Medieval Philosophy*, by Armand Augustine Maurer; Vol. 3, *Philosophy: Descartes to Kant*, by Etienne Gilson and Thomas Langan; Vol. 4, *Recent Philosophy: Hegel to the Present*, by Etienne Gilson and Thomas Langan. LC classifies and catalogs these separately.

54.   Guthrie, William Keith Chambers. **A History of Greek Philosophy**. Cambridge: Cambridge University Press, 1962– . 5 vols.
Reviewers of the first three volumes agree that this work is erudite, technical, and detailed, yet remarkably lucid. Some regard it as the best work available in English.

55.   Prosch, Harry. **The Genesis of Twentieth Century Philosophy: The Evolution of Thought from Copernicus to the Present**. Garden City, N.Y.: Doubleday, 1964. 418p.
Emphasizes the role of Sir Isaac Newton. Views major twentieth century schools (Marxism, pragmatism, analysis, existentialism) as revolts against Hegel. Well done, but difficult in parts for the layman.

56.   Raju, Poolla Tirupati. **The Philosophical Traditions of India**. Pittsburgh: University of Pittsburgh Press, 1972. 256p.
An introduction for beginning students by a teacher who has devoted more than 40 years to the subject. Reference features include a glossary of Sanskrit terms, a selective bibliography, and an index.

57.   Russell, Bertrand. **A History of Western Philosophy**. New York: Simon & Schuster, 1945. 895p.
Written in the lively, opinionated style for which Russell was famous. Unusual for its emphasis on social, economic, and political conditions, and for the inclusion of some thinkers not ordinarily regarded as philosophers.

58.   Russell, Bertrand. **Wisdom of the West: A Historical Survey of Western Philosophy in Its Social and Political Setting**. New York: Doubleday, 1959. 320p.

59.   Schilpp, Paul A., ed. **The Library of Living Philosophers**. Evanston,
        Ill.: Northwestern University Press, 1939-1949 (Vols. 1-7); La Salle,
        Ill.: Open Court Pub. Co., 1952– (Vol. 8–).
A major series in contemporary philosophy. Each volume is devoted to a single
twentieth century philosopher. In addition to biographical and bibliographical
information, there are critiques by other philosophers and a reply by the subject
of the book. Several volumes have been updated or reprinted. Some 15 volumes
are available from the current publisher. LC catalogs and classifies separately.

60.   Schneider, Herbert Wallace. **A History of American Philosophy**. 2nd
        ed. New York: Columbia University Press, 1963. 590p.
First edition published in 1946. This is a standard work in the field.

61.   Ueberweg, Friedrich. **Grundriss der Geschichte der Philosophie**. 12th
        ed. Basel: Benn Schwabe & Co., 1965– .
Excellent bibliographies to supplement encyclopedic treatments by eminent
scholars. Now in process of being published in a new edition. Last edition
(1923-28, in five volumes) was a landmark.

PHILOSOPHY PERIODICALS

62.   American Catholic Philosophical Association. **Proceedings**. 1926– .
        Baltimore. Annual. Catholic University of America, Washington, D.C.
        20017.
Indexed in: *Philosopher's Index*. Valuable for scholarly papers and for activities
of the Association.

63.   American Philosophical Association. **Proceedings and Addresses**.
        Vol. 1, 1927– . Annual. The Antioch Press, Yellow Springs, Ohio
        45387.
Indexed in: *Philosopher's Index*. Major professional association in the United
States. Valuable for information about activities and for scholarly papers
presented at conferences.

64.   **American Philosophical Quarterly**, 1964– . Quarterly. Department of
        Philosophy, University of Pittsburgh, Pittsburgh, Pennsylvania 15213.
Indexed in: *Philosopher's Index, Répertoire bibliographique de la philosophie*.
Lengthy articles, concentrating on logic and linguistic analysis. No book reviews
or news items.

65.   **Analysis**, 1933– . 6 times per year. Basil Blackwell & Mott, Ltd., 49
        Broad Street, Oxford, England.
Indexed in: *Philosopher's Index, Répertoire bibliographique de la philosophie,
British Humanities Index*. As the name implies, this journal concentrates on very
detailed, specialized articles by philosophers associated with the analytical
movement. Many articles require a knowledge of mathematical logic.

66.   **Archives de philosophie: recherches et documentation**, 1923– .
Quarterly. Beauchesne et ses Fils, 117, rue de Rennes, Paris 6e,
France.
Indexed in: *Philosopher's Index, Répertoire bibliographique de la philosophie.*
Original articles, historical surveys, book reviews, bibliography.

67.   **Archiv für Geschichte der Philosophie**, 1918– . 3 per year. U.S.
distributors: Walter de Gruyter, Inc., 162 Fifth Ave., New York, N.Y.
10010.
Indexed in: *Philosopher's Index, Répertoire bibliographique de la philosophie.*
Contains articles on history of philosophy and book reviews.

68.   **British Journal for the Philosophy of Science**, 1950– . Quarterly.
Cambridge University Press, 32 East 57th Street, New York, N.Y.
10022.
Indexed in: *Philosopher's Index, British Humanities Index, Psychological
Abstracts, Répertoire bibliographique de la philosophie.* Official publication of
the British Society for the Philosophy of Science. Lengthy, technical papers. A
major journal in this field. Contains book reviews.

69.   **British Journal of Aesthetics**, 1960– . Ed. by Harold Osborne for
British Society of Aesthetics. Thames & Hudson, Ltd., 30 Bloomsbury
St., London, W.C. 1, England.
Indexed in: *Philosopher's Index, British Humanities Index, Art Index, Réper-
toire bibliographique de la philosophie.* Official publication of the British
Society of Aesthetics. Most articles are by philosophers, though some are by
practitioners in the arts. Includes book reviews.

70.   **Chinese Studies in Philosophy: A Quarterly Journal of Translations**,
1969– . International Arts and Sciences Press, 901 North Broadway,
White Plains, N.Y. 10603.
Indexed in: *Philosopher's Index.* Unabridged translations from journals published in the People's Republic of China. Maoist thought predominates.
Individual articles are often lengthy. There appears to be about an eight-year
time lag between original publication and translation.

71.   **Dialectica: International Review of Philosophy of Knowledge**,
1947– . Quarterly. W. Roesch & Co., Manbijoustrasse 9, 3000 Berne,
Switzerland.
Indexed in: *Philosopher's Index, Répertoire bibliographique de la philosophie.*

72.   **Dialogue (Canada): Canadian Philosophical Review/Revue Canadienne
de Philosophie**, 1962– . Quarterly. Canadian Philosophical Associa-
tion, Department of Philosophy, Queen's University, Kingston,
Ontario, Canada.
Indexed in: *Philosopher's Index, Répertoire bibliographique de la philosophie.*
Covers all aspects and periods of philosophy. Articles in English and French.
Book reviews.

73.   **Ethics: An International Journal of Social, Political and Legal Philosophy**, 1890– . Quarterly. University of Chicago Press, 5750 Ellis Ave., Chicago, Illinois 60637.
Indexed in: *Philosopher's Index, Social Sciences and Humanities Index, Répertoire bibliographique de la philosophie.* Articles by social scientists as well as philosophers. Book reviews.

74.   **History and Theory: Studies in the Philosophy of History**, 1960– . 3 per year. Wesleyan University Press, 190 Riverview Center, Middletown, Conn. 06457.
Indexed in: *Philosopher's Index, Historical Abstracts, Social Sciences and Humanities Index, Répertoire bibliographique de la philosophie.* Long scholarly articles and book reviews. Some special bibliographical issues.

75.   **Indian Philosophy and Culture.** 1956– . Quarterly. Institute of Oriental Philosophy, Vrindaban (Mathura), U.P., India.
Indexed in: *Philosopher's Index.*

76.   **International Philosophical Quarterly**, 1961– . Foundation for International Philosophical Exchange, Fordham University Press, Bronx, N.Y. 10458.
Indexed in: *Philosopher's Index, Catholic Periodical and Literature Index, Social Sciences and Humanities Index, Répertoire bibliographique de la philosophie.* Encourages contemporary exchange of ideas across national boundaries and among different schools of thought. Theistic and humanistic in general orientation. Long scholarly articles, book reviews, and short selections on recent trends.

77.   **Journal of Aesthetics and Art Criticism**, 1941– . Quarterly. Cleveland Museum of Art, University Circle, Cleveland, Ohio 44106.
Indexed in: *Art Index, Music Index, Psychological Abstracts, Philosopher's Index.* Published by the American Society for Aesthetics. In the Summer 1973 issue, the new editor, John Fisher, described the purpose in these words: "There are other journals of art history, of literature, of philosophy, and of music. We will not try to do what they do. If there is any justification for this publication it is solely as a journal of aesthetics." Scholarly articles, replies, and book reviews.

78.   **Journal Of Philosophy**, 1904– . Fortnightly. Philosophy Hall, Columbia University, New York, N.Y. 10027.
Indexed in: *Philosopher's Index, Social Sciences and Humanities Index, Répertoire bibliographique de la philosophie.* Wide circulation among philosophers. Stresses analytical philosophy and philosophy of science. Some book reviews.

79.   **Journal of the History of Philosophy**, 1963– . Quarterly. Philosophy Department, University of California, La Jolla, California 92037.
Indexed in: *Philosopher's Index, Répertoire bibliographique de la philosophie.*

International coverage, though articles are mostly in English. Descriptions of movements and trends rather than original philosphic speculation. Also includes book reviews and notes.

80.   **Journal of Symbolic Logic**, 1936– . Quarterly. Association for Symbolic Logic, Inc., Box 6248, Providence, R.I. 02904.

Indexed in: *Philosopher's Index, Social Sciences and Humanities Index, Répertoire bibliographique de la philosophie.* Specializes in original, technical papers. Extensive section on reviews, including articles as well as books.

81.   **Mind: A Quarterly Review of Philosophy and Psychology**, 1876– . Quarterly. Basil Blackwell, 49 Broad Street, Oxford, England.

Indexed in: *Philosopher's Index, British Humanities Index, Répertoire bibliographique de la philosphie.* Throughout most of its long history, this journal has included broad coverage of virtually all aspects of philosophy. The present editor is Gilbert Ryle, and articles reflect his interest in problems of language and logic. Book reviews.

82.   **Philosophical Books**, 1960– . 3 per year. Leicester University Press, England.

Has signed reviews, each about 1,000 words. Covers about 20 books per issue. English language books only.

83.   **Philosophical Review**, 1892– . Quarterly. Sage School of Philosophy, 218 Goldwyn Smith Hall, Cornell University, Ithaca, N.Y. 14850.

Indexed in: *Philosopher's Index, Social Sciences and Humanities Index, Répertoire bibliographique de la philosophie.* Emphasis on linguistic philosophy and logical analysis. Book reviews.

84.   **Philosophische Rundschau: Zeitschrift für Philosophische Kritik**, 1953– . Quarterly. J. C. B. Mohr (Paul Siebeck), 7400 Tübingen, Postfach 2040, West Germany.

Indexed in: *Philosopher's Index, Répertoire bibliographique de la philosophie.*

85.   **Philosophy**, 1931– . Quarterly. Macmillan (Journals), Ltd., Brunel Road, Basingstoke, Hants, England.

Indexed in: *Philosopher's Index, British Humanities Index, Psychological Abstracts, Répertoire bibliographique de la philosophie.* Broad coverage of all phases and schools of philosophy. Book reviews.

86.   **Philosophy and Phenomenological Research**, 1940– . Quarterly. Department of Philosophy, State University of New York at Buffalo, Buffalo, N.Y. 14226.

Indexed in: *Philosopher's Index. Répertoire bibliographique de la philosophie.* Published for the International Phenomenological Society. Articles appeal to the educated lay person as well as to the professional philosopher. Variety of philosophical topics. Numerous book reviews.

87.   **Philosophy, East and West**, 1951– . Quarterly. University of Hawaii Press, 535 Ward Avenue, Honolulu, Hawaii 96814.

Indexed in: *Philosopher's Index, Répertoire bibliographique de la philosophie*. Covers a wide range of philosophical topics, with emphasis on comparative approach. This is a major source in English for information on Asian philosophy. Book reviews.

88.   **Philosophy of Science**, 1934– . Quarterly. Department of Philosophy, Michigan State University, East Lansing, Michigan 48823.

Indexed in: *Philosopher's Index, Social Sciences and Humanities Index, Répertoire bibliographique de la philosophie, Science Citation Index*. Contains both original articles and historical surveys, plus some book reviews. Official publication of the Philosophy of Science Association.

89.   **Revue internationale de philosophie**, 1938– . Quarterly. 99 Avenue de l'Université, 1050 Bruxelles, Belgium.

Indexed in: *Philosopher's Index, Répertoire bibliographique de la philosophie*. Text in English, French, German, Italian, and Spanish.

90.   **Revue philosophique de Louvain**, 1894– . Quarterly. E. Nauwelaerts, Mgr Ladeuzeplein, 2, 13-3000 Louvain, Belgium.

Indexed in: *Philosopher's Index, Répertoire bibliographique de la philosophie, Catholic Periodical and Literature Index*. Original papers (mainly by Catholic philosophers) and historical surveys. Book reviews. A quarterly supplement, also available separately, is *Répertoire bibliographique de la philosophie*.

91.   **Société Internationale pour l'Etude de la Philosophie Médiévale. Bulletin**. Louvain: Secrétariat de la S.I.E.P.M., Vol. 1– , 1959– . Annual.

92.   **Soviet Studies in Philosophy: A Journal of Translations from Soviet Sources**, 1962– . Quarterly. 901 North Broadway, White Plains, N.Y. 10601.

Indexed in: *Philosopher's Index, Répertoire bibliographique de la philosophie*. Prompt, unabridged translations. Marxist emphasis.

93.   **Studies in Soviet Thought**, 1961– . Quarterly. D. Reidel Pub. Co., P.O. Box 17, Dordrecht, Holland.

Indexed in: *Philosopher's Index, Répertoire bibliographique de la philosophie*. Jointly published by the Institute of East European Studies, University of Fribourg (Switzerland), the Russian Philosophical Studies Program at Boston College, and the Seminar for Political Theory and Philosophy at the University of Munich. Includes *Bibliographie der Sovjetischen Philosophie*, which was published separately before 1967.

RELIGION

6   TRENDS IN RELIGION

What is religion? Traditional and familiar definitions tend to concentrate on man's relation to God, a group of gods, and/or other supernatural beings. More recently, definitions have been broadened in scope. A typical one is that provided by Clyde A. Holbrook in *Religion, A Humanistic Discipline* (Englewood Cliffs, N.J.: Prentice-Hall, 1963, p. 36):

> Stated in comprehensive terms, religion embraces the study of those forms of conviction, belief and behavior and those systems of thought in which men express their concerned responses to whatever they hold to be worthy of lasting and universal commitment. Religion takes for its province of study not only the normative beliefs, practices and literatures of the world, but also manifestations of religious attitudes which impinge upon cultural contexts—political, economic or artistic—often considered foreign to religious aims.

Although the origins of religion are lost in the mists of antiquity, surviving cave art provides evidence of religious beliefs in the upper Paleolithic age (about 30,000 B.C.). It was not until the period between 3,000 and 1,000 B.C. that sacred scriptures that have survived until modern times began coming into existence.

Among the earliest of these scriptures were the so-called "Pyramid Texts" (c.2300-2100 B.C.), from which the Egyptian *Book of the Dead* (c.1500 B.C.) was largely derived.

HINDUISM

Among the world's living religions, Hinduism is probably the oldest. Its basic scriptures were written between 3,000 and 1,500 B.C. These consist of three collections of songs and ritual formulas known as the *Rig Veda*, the *Sama Veda*, and the *Yajur Veda*, together with a book of priestly instructions entitled *Atharva Veda*. The *Rig Veda* is the oldest and best known. It includes more than 1,000 hymns arranged in ten books. The *Sama Veda* provides musical notations for many of the hymns in the *Rig Veda*. In time, each of the Vedas was explicated by one or more priestly commentaries known as the Brahamanas and some esoteric commentaries called the Aranyakas.

More philosophical in their orientation are the Upanishads, although these are correlated with the Vedas. The Sutras represented an attempt to popularize religion and extend the range of application of the Vedas. The *Mahabharata* is a major religious epic in which the *Bhagavad-Gita* ("Song of the Blessed One") occurs. The latter is probably the most influential piece of Indian devotional literature. During the first dozen centuries of the Christian era, a series of sectarian commentaries known as the Puranas came into existence.

In modern times, the teachings of Ramakrishna (1834-1886) have been very influential. His disciple, Vivekananda (1863-1902), expanded the work, founding the Ramakrishna Mission in India and the Vedanta Society in the United States. *The Complete Works of Swami Vivekananda* were published in seven volumes (1924-1932).

Rabindranath Tagore (1861-1941) has expressed the spirit of modern Hinduism eloquently in *Gitanjali* ("Song Offerings," 1912), *The Religion of Man* (1931) and *Collected Poems and Plays* (1958). Unfortunately, most of his work has not yet been translated into English.

BUDDHISM

Buddhism arose as a reform movement within Hinduism, led by Siddhartha Gautama (566-486 B.C.). He left nothing in writing. The canon of Buddhist scriptures took several centuries to develop and was finally completed in the first century A.D. It consists of the *Ti-Pitaka* (or "three baskets") already mentioned: *Vinaya-Pitaka*, *Sutra-Pitaka*, and *Abhidhamma-Pitaka*. These have bene preserved in two major languages: Pali (closest to that spoken by the Buddha) and Sanskrit (the ancient language of most Hindu scriptures). The Pali texts are now regarded as most authentic. A concise account of English translations will be found on page 619 of S. G. F. Brandon's *Dictionary of Comparative Religion*.

In addition to these texts, there are many non-canonized works, which fall broadly into three categories: chronicles, commentaries, and original compositions inspired by the canonical texts. Several have been translated into English. One of special interest is *Milinda's Questions* (1963-64, 2 vols.), which purports to be a dialogue between a Greek king of Bactria and a Buddhist philosopher.

Among the variety of schools of thought that developed, the two major ones are the Theravada and the Mahayana. The Theravada (or "School of the Elders") appears to be closest to traditional Buddhism. It is sometimes called Hinayana (or "Small Vehicle") because of the belief that relatively few people will attain perfect deliverance from reincarnation. The Theravada Buddhists convened the "Sixth Great Buddhist Council" in Rangoon, Burma (1954-1956) to celebrate the 2,500th anniversary of Buddha's career and to stimulate further study and research.

A more liberal school, with its scriptures in Sanskrit, sought to reinterpret Buddhist doctrine and became known as Mahayana (or "Great

Vehicle") because of the belief that large numbers of people will attain final salvation. Mahayana Buddhism has been intensively studied in Japan since the establishment of the Chair of Science of Religion at Tokyo University in 1905. Japanese scholars participate in the International Congress for the History of Religions; they hosted the 1958 Congress in Tokyo.

OTHER EASTERN RELIGIONS

Zoroastrianism arose in Persia at about the same time as Buddhism in India. Led by Zoroaster or Zarathustra (c.570 B.C.), it stressed the struggle between forces of good and evil in the world. It was largely obliterated in the seventh century A.D. with the rise of Islam. The teachings of the founder have been preserved in the Gathas, translated into English as *The Hymns of Zarathustra* (1952). These form a part of the larger body of sacred scriptures known as the *Avesta*, or *Zend-Avesta*. An English translation was included in *Sacred Books of the East* (1880-1887) and has since been reprinted several times.

Confucius (c.551-479 B.C.) was, in many ways, more of a philosopher than a religious leader, but elements of religious veneration later emerged and Confucianism was even made the official state religion for a time. Major texts in the Confucian tradition include the Five Classics and the Four Books. Of the Five Classics, Confucius is believed to have written the *Ch'un-ch'iu* ("Spring and Autumn Annals") and to have edited the rest: *Shih Ching* ("Classic of Poetry"); *Shu Ching* ("Classic of History"); *I Ching* ("Classic of Changes"); and *Li Chi* ("Classic of Ceremonials"). The Four Books (*Analects, Mencius, Great Learning,* and *Doctrine of the Mean*) are most readily available in English translations.

Taoism is a philosophical and religious movement second in importance to Confucianism in its influence on Chinese life and thought. The word "Tao" has both an ethical meaning ("the Way," or path to virtue) and a metaphysical one (the first principle whereby all things are created). The founder of the movement was Lao Tzu (c.604-531 B.C.). Its classic work is a short treatise entitled *Tao Te Ching* ("Classic of the Way and Its Virtue") traditionally ascribed to Lao Tzu, but now believed to be a later document reflecting his teaching. It has inspired many commentaries, of which about 350 still survive. There are over 40 English translations.

Shintoism, the national religion of Japan for many centuries, does not have a clear historic founder or canon of sacred scriptures. The most authoritative writings are the *Kojiki* ("Records of Ancient Events") and the *Nihongi* ("Chronicles of Japan"), both completed early in the eighth century A.D.

Sikhism originated in northern India as an attempt to combine the best elements of Hinduism and Islam. Its principal founder was the Guru Nanak (1469-1539). The sacred scriptures, known as the *Adi Granth* (sometimes called the *Guru Granth*), contain about 6,000 hymns and prayers and are available in G. S. Dardi's *Translation of the Adi Granth* (1960, 4 vols.).

ISLAM

Islam originated in Arabia with the preaching of Muhammad (570-632), who stressed submission to the will of Allah, the only true God. The sacred book is the −Qur'an (or Koran), which orthodox Muslims believe was revealed to Muhammad by the angel Gabriel. For a selected list of English translations, see page 526 of S. G. F. Brandon's Dictionary of Comparative Religion. The Koran has been the subject of numerous commentaries, of which the best known is a 30-volume work by al-Tabari (died 923). Traditional sayings attributed to Muhammad were collected by the ninth century into the Six Sacred Books, second in authority only to the Koran itself.

An outstanding feature of Islam for the several centuries has been a mystical and ascetic movement known as Sufism, with various organized orders or brotherhoods. The greatest scholar of this movement was Abu Hamid al-Ghazali (1058-1111), whose major work, The Revivification of Religious Sciences, has been compared with the achievements of St. Augustine and St. Thomas Aquinas. In the twentieth century there has been a revival within Islam and a growth in size and vigor that contrast with the declines reported for other religions.

JUDAISM

The traditional faith of the Hebrew people, now known as Judaism, probably arose in the period between the twentieth and seventeenth centuries B.C. Its origin is associated with the patriarch Abraham. The Hebrews entered Egypt in the seventeenth century B.C. and left, under the leadership of Moses, in the thirteenth. After a period of unsettled conditions in Palestine, they were unified under the kings around 1,000 B.C. The construction of the Temple in Jerusalem by Solomon (965-925 B.C.) marked the high point. After his death, the nation was split into two kingdoms: Judah and Israel.

The earliest oral traditions and laws were put into writing during this time—the beginning of the Law or Torah. The evolution of religious thought continued with such prophets as Amos (760 B.C.) and Jeremiah (c.626-586 B.C.). A crisis occurred with the fall of the Temple in 586 B.C. and the exile in Babylon. There was a return to the homeland, accompanied by a rebuilding of the Temple, and then a religious revival under Ezra, who reinstated the Torah (first five books of the Bible) late in the fifth century B.C. National independence was at an end, and eventually the Temple in Jerusalem was destroyed by the Romans (70 A.D.).

During this period, the Sadducees clung to a strict interpretation of the Written Torah while the Pharisees gave equal weight to liberal rabbinic interpretations known as the Oral Torah. These commentaries were compiled into the Mishnah in the second century A.D. and became a part of normative Judaism. The Mishnah, in turn, generated its own commentary called the Gemara, and together they make up the Talmud. Meanwhile, final decisions on Jewish sacred scriptures were taken, probably at the Council of Jamnia in 100 A.D. In addition to the Torah, groups of books known as the Prophets and the *Writings* were included as authoritative. (Although the order is different, these are the works included in the King James Version of the *Old Testament*.)

The process of interpretation has continued through the centuries. Moses Maimonides (1135-1204) was an outstanding scholar, responsible for *Mishne Torah*, a compilation of rabbinic law up to his period, and a famous treatise entitled *Guide for the Perplexed*. Mysticism found wide appeal, whether of the personal, ethical variety expressed in *Sefer Hasidim* or the more speculative kind expressed in the *Kabbala*. In more recent times, the mystical approach has found expression in a movement known as Hasidism.

Modern Judaism represents a rich admixture of approaches to the traditional faith and the contemporary world. Orthodox Judaism represents the strictly traditional approach. Basic beliefs include: acceptance of the revelation at Sinai as described in the *Torah*; acceptance of Divine Law, in both written and oral forms, as binding for all times; acknowledgement of the authority of duly qualified rabbis to interpret and administer the Law; and adherence to Jewish beliefs as outlined in the *Thirteen Articles of Faith* by Maimonides.

Conservative Judaism is a religious movement, particularly strong in the United States, which stresses commitment to scientific scholarship but reaffirmation of such traditional Jewish values as the Hebrew language and the land of Israel (with some Zionist influences). A coalition that stresses unity in diversity, its intellectual leadership is centered in the Jewish Theological Seminary, New York.

The Reform movement advocates numerous changes to conform to modern needs. Organizationally, it is represented by the Union of Hebrew Congregations (1873) and Hebrew Union College, Cincinnati (1875). Prophetic ideals are emphasized, and some Mosaic laws (e.g., dietary laws) are relaxed.

Reconstructionism represents an effort to relate philosophic naturalism to the Jewish faith. Organizationally, it is represented by the Society for the Advancement of Judaism; it has a publishing program. Adherents range in persuasion from Conservative through Reform to secularist. It sees religion as essentially a human undertaking and views Judaism as an outgrowth of the Jewish struggle for survival.

Among the leaders of the Orthodox school in the twentieth century were A. K. Kuk (1865-1935), one of whose works is translated into English as *Rabbi Kuk's Philosophy of Repentance*, and Isaac Breuer (1883-1946), represented in English by *People of the Torah*. In the United States, the Orthodox school is ably led by Joseph Dov Soloveitchik (1903–), whose essays "The Man of Law" and "The Man of Faith" have been influential.

Existentialism exerted an influence on Leo Baeck (1873-1956), a leader of Progressive Judaism, who is represented in English by *The Essence of Judaism*, *The Pharisees and Other Essays*, and *This People Israel*. Best known among the theologians influenced by existentialism is Martin Buber (1878-1965), noted for such books as *I and Thou*, *The Prophetic Faith*, *Hasidism and Modern Man*, *The Origin and Meaning of Hasidism*, and *Kingship of God*.

Conservative Judaism is represented in the works of an American rabbi, Milton Steinberg (1903-1950): *The Making of the Modern Jew, Basic Judaism, A Believing Jew*, and *Anatomy of Faith*. Widely read by Christian as well as Jewish thinkers, the works of Abraham Joshua Heschel (1907-1972) include such titles as *Man Is Not Alone*, *God in Search of Man*, *The Prophets*, and *Israel: An Echo of Eternity*. A major source of bibliographical and other information on Heschel is *Between God and Man: An Interpretation of Judaism from the Writings of Abraham J. Heschel*, edited by Fritz A. Rothschild.

Will Herberg (1909–) is best known for *Protestant, Catholic, Jew: An Essay in American Religious Sociology*. Louis Jacobs (1920–) is an English rabbi who has created controversy in Orthodox circles by acceptance of some of the methods of biblical higher criticism and denial of the literal inspiration of the Pentateuch. Among his books are: *We Have Reason to Believe*, *Jewish Values*, *Principles of the Jewish Faith*, and *Faith*. Mordecai Kaplan (1881–) is an American rabbi and the founder of the Reconstructionist movement. Among his major works are such titles as *Judaism as a Civilization*, *Judaism without Supernaturalism*, and *The Religion of Ethical Nationhood*.

Three anthologies of contemporary Jewish theology should be mentioned: *Rediscovering Judaism: Reflections on a New Jewish Theology*, edited by A. J. Wolf; *Varieties of Jewish Belief*, edited by I. Eisenstein; and *The Condition of Jewish Belief*, originally published in the August 1966 issue of *Commentary*. Periodicals that frequently contain articles on the subject include *Judaism*, *Conservative Judaism*, *Tradition*, and *CCAR Journal*.

CHRISTIANITY

Christianity originated in the life and teachings of Jesus of Nazareth (4 B.C.–30 A.D.). The earliest accounts of his ministry were transmitted orally. It was not until nearly a generation after his death that written documents began to appear. By the end of the second century, the Christian Church had, by and large, determined which of these writings (known as the *New Testament*) should be added to the Hebrew scriptures (henceforth known as the *Old Testament*) to constitute the *Holy Bible*. These decisions were formalized in the West with a Latin translation (called the *Vulgate*) by St. Jerome in 404. The major versions of the English Bible are described in Chapter 8, and the discussion need not be repeated here. Instead, the balance of the present chapter will be devoted to highlighting the principal works of major Christian thinkers in the three main branches of the Church: Roman Catholicism, Eastern Orthodoxy, and Protestantism.

Roman Catholicism

Among the early leaders of the Church, St. Augustine (354-430) was probably most influential in later centuries. His *Confessions*, which recount his spiritual pilgrimage, continue to exercise wide appeal. *The City of God* sets forth his philosophy of history and *On the Trinity* is commonly regarded as his greatest theological work. Influential historians of the early period included Eusebius (260-340), noted for his *Ecclesiastical History*, and the Venerable Bede (673-735), whose *Ecclesiastical History of the English People* illuminates what would otherwise be a period of historical darkness. Although influenced by

St. Augustine, St. Anselm (1033-1109) was a creative and original thinker who is famous for the so-called "ontological proof" of the existence of God; his most noted theological work is *Why God Became Man*.

The great systematizer of the medieval period was St. Thomas Aquinas (1225-1274), whose synthesis of Aristotelian philosophy and Christian theology is still influential in the twentieth century. His greatest works were *Summa contra Gentiles* and *Summa theologica*. The decline of speculative theology in the next two centuries was accompanied by the rise of mysticism and the appearance of works of devotion like the *Imitation of Christ*, usually attributed to Thomas à Kempis (1380-1471).

In response to Renaissance humanists and Protestant reformers, the Roman Catholic Church convened the Council of Trent (1545-1563) to define its doctrinal position, and the next century was one of great theological vigor. One of the leaders in this revival was St. Robert Bellarmine (1542-1621), whose *Disputations on the Controversies of the Christian Faith* proved very effective against the Protestants. The most prolific writer of the time was Francisco Suarez (1548-1617), whose efforts ranged from commentaries on Aquinas to the divine right of kings (which he opposed), and whose *Metaphysical Disputations* appeared in 18 editions in less than a century. Though not a theologian *per se*, Blaise Pascal (1623-1662) produced a set of notes published after his death as *Pensées*, and this work has gained the stature of a religious classic.

The late seventeenth and eighteenth centuries witnessed a decline in theological writing, but this was followed by a revival in the nineteenth and twentieth centuries. A leading figure was John Henry Cardinal Newman (1801-1890), whose *Collected Works* (1874-1921) fill some 40 volumes but who is best remembered for *The Idea of a University* and for his spiritual autobiography, *Apologia pro vita sua*. Pope Leo XIII (1810-1903) fostered a revival of Thomism.

In the twentieth century, there has been a resurgence of interest in biblical studies and in the early Fathers of the Church. Pope John XXIII (1858-1963) convened Vatican Council II (1962-1965) to review the total situation of the Church. The result was Council action on 16 documents. The first four were constitutions: *Dogmatic Constitution of the Church*; *Dogmatic Constitution on Divine Revelation*; *Constitution on the Sacred Liturgy*; and *Pastoral Constitution on the Church in the World Today*. There were nine decrees on subjects ranging from the office of the bishops to the media of social communication. Finally, there were three declarations: *Declaration on Religious Freedom*; *Declaration on the Church's Attitude toward Non-Christian Religions*; and *Declaration on Christian Education*. An overview of the extensive documentation and commentary may be obtained from Charles J. Dollen's *Vatican II: A Bibliography* (Metuchen, N.J.: Scarecrow Press, 1969).

Among the noted Catholic thinkers of the twentieth century, Maurice Blondel (1861-1949) is especially remembered for his Great Trilogy (*La Pensée*, *Etre et les êtres*, and *L'Action*) and for *La philosophie et l'esprit chrétien*. Yves Marie Joseph Congar (1904–) has greatly influenced reform movements in Europe by such works as *Vraie et fausse réforme dans l'Eglise* and has contributed to the worldwide ecumenical movement through such works as *Divided Christendom*, *Dialogue between Christians*, and *Ecumenism and the*

Future of the Church. These same themes are reflected in the writings of Hans Küng (1938–), whose book *The Council, Reform, and Reunion* was one of the most influential documents in the preparation for Vatican II.

Karl Rahner (1904–) has exercised an immense influence over contemporary Catholic theology through more than 2,000 books and articles. Among those translated into English are *Theological Investigations* and *Spirit in the World*. Etienne Gilson (1884–) is best known as a philosopher, but the relation between philosophy and theology is such that mention should be made of works like *The Christian Philosophy of St. Thomas Aquinas* and *History of Christian Philosophy in the Middle Ages*. The situation is similar with Jacques Maritain (1882–); mention should be made of his *Prayer and Intelligence, Religion and Culture*, and *On the Grace and Humanity of Jesus*. Pierre Teilhard de Chardin (1881-1955) sought to integrate the Christian faith with modern evolutionary concepts from science in such works as *The Phenomenon of Man* and *The Divine Milieu*. A more popular writer was Thomas Merton (1915-1968), whose autobiography *The Seven Storey Mountain* was followed by such works as *Seeds of Contemplation*, *Mystics and Zen Masters*, and *Contemplation in a World of Action*.

A few Catholic periodicals should be noted. The oldest is *Theologische Quartalschrift*, edited at the University of Tübingen. In the United States, English translations of papal statements may be found in *The Pope Speaks*. The leading journal in this country is *Theological Studies*, edited by the Jesuits. Both philosophy and theology are included in *The Thomist*.

Eastern Orthodoxy

Next in size to Roman Catholicism is the Orthodox Eastern Church, with some 150 million members, primarily in Greece and the U.S.S.R. Separation from the Western Church occurred in stages; the final schism took place in 1054. One of the leaders at a crucial period was Photius (820-891), Patriarch of Constantinople, whose *Mystogogia* was a key work in the theological controversy with the West and whose *Letters* have also been preserved. Another major figure was Theodore Romanov Philaret (1553-1633), Patriarch of Moscow and founder of the Romanov dynasty, whose *Catechism* has been a document of lasting importance. A leading Russian theologian of the nineteenth century was A. S. Khomiakov (1804-1860), whose teachings about *Sobornost* (community) exerted wide influence. Vladimir Soloviev (1853-1900) is remembered for *Russia and the Universal Church*.

After the Revolution of 1917 a number of leading thinkers fled to Paris, where Sergei Bulgakov (1871-1944) established the St. Sergius Institute. George Florovsky (1893–) taught there and later in the United States; *Bible, Church, Tradition: An Eastern Orthodox View* is the first volume of his *Collected Works* now in process of appearing in English. Another exile was Nicolai Berdyaev (1874-1948), whose fundamental ideas were expounded in *Freedom and the Spirit*, *The Meaning of History*, and *The Destiny of Man*.

Protestantism

Protestantism is a general descriptive term for a great variety of Christian movements which stem, directly or indirectly, from the sixteenth century religious upheaval known as the Reformation. Among the early leaders, Martin Luther (1483-1546) commanded first place. His work that had the most immediate impact—next to his famous 95 theses nailed to the door of Wittenberg Castle on October 31, 1517—was perhaps *An Appeal to the Nobility of the German Nation* (1520). He was a prolific writer of tracts, sermons, and hymns. One of his most notable accomplishments was the first German translation of the entire Bible (1534). A multi-volume set of *Luther's Works* is appearing in English under the editorship of Jaroslav Pelikan and H. P. Lehmann.

Among the reformers, John Calvin (1508-1564) was the great organizer and systematizer. His most famous work, *Institutes of the Christian Religion*, was revised and enlarged on several occasions during his lifetime. His collected works run to some 60 volumes. A major translation was done by the Calvin Translation Society (Edinburgh, 1843-1855) and a more recent translation is being done by T. H. L. Parker and others. Richard Hooker (1554-1600) wrote a classic exposition of the faith and practice of the Church of England entitled *Of the Lawes of Ecclesiastical Politie*. The prodigious activities of John Wesley (1703-1791) are recorded in his *Journal* and his *Letters*.

The nineteenth century was dominated by liberalism stemming from two major sources: increasing application of the methods of higher criticism (authorship, historical setting, etc.) and lower criticism (accuracy of transmission of text) to the Bible; and reinterpretation of doctrine under the leadership of thinkers like Friedrich Schleiermacher (1768-1834), whose *On Religion: Speeches to Its Cultured Despisers* and *The Christian Faith* were very influential. These two strands were combined in monumental works like *A History of Dogma* by Adolf von Harnack (1851-1930) and *Outlines of a Philosophy of Religion*, by Louis Auguste Sabatier (1839-1901). A later outgrowth was the rise of interest in relating Christianity to the social order, as exemplified in *The Social Teachings of the Christian Churches*, by Ernest Troeltsch (1865-1923), and *A Theology for the Social Gospel*, by Walter Rauschenbusch (1861-1918).

Twentieth century theology has included not only continuation of these trends but also sharp reaction against them. *The Idea of the Holy*, by Rudolph Otto (1869-1937), was influential among liberal theologians. In the United States, some representative thinkers and works included Albert C. Knudson (*The Doctrine of God* and *The Doctrine of Redemption*); D. C. Macintosh (*Theology as an Empirical Science* and *The Reasonableness of Christianity*); Henry Nelson Wierman (*The Wrestle of Religion with Truth*); and John Dewey (*A Common Faith*).

The first American reaction against liberalism came in a series of tracts called *The Fundamentals*, which began to appear in 1910. One of the more scholarly leaders of the movement was J. Gresham Machen (*Christianity and Liberalism* and *The Virgin Birth of Christ*). More recent fundamentalists have included Louis Berkhof (*Reformed Dogmatics*), H. Orton Wiley (*Christian Theology*), Cornelius Van Til (*The New Modernism* and *The Defense of the Faith*) and E. J. Carnell (*An Introduction to Christian Apologetics*).

European reaction emerged most clearly in the "neo-orthodox" or "dialectical" theology of Karl Barth (*Commentary on the Epistle to the Romans, Church Dogmatics*, etc.). Paul Tillich (*Systematic Theology, The Courage to Be*, and *Dynamics of Faith*) led a liberal reaction while Anders Nygren (*Agape and Eros*) and Gustaf Aulen (*Christus Victor*) responded from the perspective of Scandinavian Lutheranism, and Emil Brunner (*Dogmatics, The Divine Imperative*, and *Justice and the Social Order*) adopted a position appreciative of Barth but more moderate.

In the United States, Reinhold Niebuhr combined a reassessment of Reformation theology with social concern (*The Nature and Destiny of Man, The Children of Light and the Children of Darkness*, and *The Irony of American History*). Charles Hartshorne (*Man's Vision of God, The Divine Relativity*, and *Reality as Social Process*) and Nels F. S. Ferré (*Christian Understanding of God*) were influenced by Whitehead's process philosophy. H. Richard Niebuhr (*Radical Monotheism and Western Civilization* and *Christ and Culture*) reappropriated traditional Christian themes.

In the 1960s, a radical type of theology sometimes described as the "Death of God" movement rose to brief prominence. Some of its leaders claimed to be influenced by Dietrich Bonhoeffer (*The Cost of Discipleship* and *Letters and Papers from Prison*), but influences from other sources (such as Friedrich Nietzsche and William Blake) were also evident. William Hamilton (*New Essence of Christianity*) collaborated with Thomas J. J. Altizer to write *Radical Theology and the Death of God*, while Altizer also wrote *The Gospel of Christian Atheism*. Paul Van Buren (*The Secular Meaning of the Gospel*) was influenced by the analytical movement in philosophy. Gabriel Vahanian (*Death of God* and *Wait without Idols*) and John A. T. Robinson (*Honest to God*) were more moderate in approach.

In Europe, the "demythologizing" movement associated with Rudolf Bultmann (*Jesus Christ and Mythology* and *The Presence of Eternity: History and Eschatology*) is now undergoing revision. Meanwhile, the work of Oscar Cullmann (*Christ and Time*) continues to be influential, and a strong new movement centered around Jurgen Moltmann (*Theology of Hope, Religion, Revolution and the Future, Hope and Planning*, and *Theology of Play*) has spread to the United States as well. Harvey Cox (*The Secular City*) and Joseph Fletcher (*Situation Ethics*) represent other strands of the American theological debate. The distinguished Church historian Martin Marty (*The New Shape of American Religion* and *Righteous Empire: The Protestant Experience in America*) continues to write on a variety of themes. Eschatology is one of the major concerns of Carl Braaten (*The Future of God: The Revolutionary Dynamics of Hope*), while the use of religious language has been studied by Langdon Gilkey (*Naming the Whirlwind: The Revival of God-Language*, and *Religion and the Scientific Future: Reflections on Myth, Science and Theology*), and the relationship between theology and process philosophy has been explored further by Schubert Ogden (*The Reality of God, and Other Essays*).

7 ACCESSING INFORMATION IN RELIGION

MAJOR DIVISIONS OF THE FIELD

Religions are commonly classified as being predominantly sacramental, prophetic, or mystical. Sacramental religions place great emphasis on the observance of ritual and on the sacredness of certain objects. Eastern Orthodoxy and Roman Catholicism are familiar examples. Prophetic religions emphasize communication of the Divine Will in verbal form, often with a strong moralistic emphasis. Islam and Protestantism reflect this approach. Mystical religions stress direct encounter with God and view words, rituals, and sacred objects as auxiliary aids at best, or hindrances at worst, to that full communion which is seen as the ultimate goal of all religious striving. Certain branches of Hinduism and Buddhism are examples of this type.

The literature generated by the religions of the world may be conveniently analyzed under the following headings: 1) Personal religion; 2) Theology; 3) Philosophy of religion; 4) Science of religion.

Personal religion is the primary and most direct source of religious writing. It is intimately related to the experiences of the individual and reflections about their significance. A major class of documents in this category would be the sacred scriptures of the world's great religions. Closely related to the sacred writings are those documents of explication and interpretation commonly known as commentaries. Finally, there is a much larger body of literature that does not have the same authoritative standing as the sacred scriptures and their commentaries. Works in this category may be devotional, autobiographical, or biographical. In this group also would be included a large number of popularizations.

Theology is an attempt to express in intellectually coherent form the principal doctrines of a religion. It is the product of reflection upon the primary sources of religion. It differs from philosophy in that the basic truth of the religious position is accepted and attention is given to its systematic and thoughtful exposition. The field has many subdivisions. Within the Christian tradition, systematic (or topic-oriented) theology and Biblical theology have been especially important, but there is also a substantial body of literature on moral, ascetic, mystical, symbolic, pastoral, philosophical, liturgical, and natural theology as well.

The philosophy of religion is an attempt to relate the religious experience to other spheres of experience. It differs from theology in that it makes fewer assumptions about the truth of a religious position, at least in the beginning. It differs from philosophy in its selection of religion as the area for speculative investigation. Perhaps it could best be described as a bridge between philosophy and theology.

The science of religion has also generated a substantial body of literature. Here, emphasis is placed on a comparative and historical approach, with no presuppositions about (and possibly no interest in) the truth or falsity of the religions being examined. Whereas the locus of interest in the first three categories is usually one of the world's living religions, this is not usually the case in the scientific study of religion, where a purely objective approach to the description and comparison of religious phenomena represents the ideal.

MAJOR CLASSIFICATION SCHEMES

The Dewey Decimal Classification and the Library of Congress Classification are the two schemes most widely used for the classification of materials in religion, despite numerous deficiencies. Many theological libraries have adopted the classification system developed for the Library of Union Theological Seminary, New York City. The treatment of religion in these three systems will be described briefly in the paragraphs that follow.

The Second Summary of Dewey gives the following overview of the subject:

200	Religion
210	Natural religion
220	Bible
230	Christian doctrinal theology
240	Christian moral and devotional theology
250	Local church and religious orders
260	Social and ecclesiastical theology
270	History and geography of church
280	Christian denominations and sects
290	Other religions and comparative religion

The general section (200-209) is not, in fact, concerned with religion in general but with an application of the conventional form divisions (e.g., 203-Dictionaries) to the general literature of Christianity. The "Natural religion" section (210-219) is arranged by topics or problems (e.g., 215–Science and religion; 216–Good and evil). The treatment of the Bible (220-229) follows a conventional Protestant approach in its divisions and concludes (229) with "Apocrypha and pseudepigrapha." "Christian doctrinal theology" (230-239) includes such topics as "God, Trinity, Godhead" (231) and "Creeds and confessions of faith" (238). In addition to the expected topics, "Christian moral and devotional theology" (240-249) also includes "Art in Christianity" (246) and "Church furnishings and related articles" (247). In addition to Church governance and parochial activities, "Local church and religious orders" (250-259) includes "Preaching (Homiletics)" (251) and "Texts of sermons" (252). "Social and ecclesiastical theology" (260-269) includes "Missions" (266) and "Religious training and instruction" (268). The greater part of "History and geography of church" (270-279) is arranged by continents, but the beginning portion of the section includes "Religious congregations and orders" (271), "Persecutions" (272), and "Doctrinal controversies and heresies" (273). "Christian denominations and sects" (280-289) has places for the various denominations while "Other religions and comparative religion" (290-299) is divided as follows:

291	Comparative religion
292	Classical (Greek and Roman) religion
293	Germanic religion
294	Religions of Indic origin
295	Zoroastrianism
296	Judaism
297	Islam and religions derived from it
298	
299	Other religions

The outline of the Library of Congress Classification is as follows:

BL	Religions, Mythology. Rationalism.
BM	Judaism
BP	Islam, Bahaism, Theosophy, etc.
BR	Christianity
BS	Bible
BT	Doctrinal theology
BV	Practical theology
BX	Denominations and sects

BL proceeds from "Religion (General)" to "Natural theology," "The myth," and "Classification of religions." These are followed by brief sections on the relations of religions to one another and their relations with science, art, etc. The BL section of LC then proceeds to "Religious doctrines (General)" and "Worship" before reaching a lengthy section on "History and principles of religions." The latter includes the following subdivisions:

Indo-European. Aryan
Ural-Altaic
European. Occidental
    Classical (Etruscan, Greek, Roman)
    Germanic and Norse
    Other European
Asian. Oriental
    General
    By region
    By religion
African
Oceanian (Australian and Pacific)

Native American religions are covered in classes E and F. BL concludes with a section on "Rationalism. Free thought." As can be seen from the outline at the beginning of this paragraph, LC deals first with religion in general, then with most of the other world religions, and finally with Christianity, which is clearly separated from the others and treated in much greater depth and detail.

Although Dewey and LC are widely used in libraries of theological seminaries, a substantial number of these libraries are using classification systems that attempt to bring the entire universe of knowledge into focus from a theological perspective and to provide more adequate coverage of religion itself than is possible in a general classification scheme. One of the best-known and most widely used systems is the *Classification of the Library of Union Theological Seminary* (Rev. ed. New York: Union Theological Seminary, 1967). An abbreviated synopsis of the Union Classification is given below:

General and Introductory Group	AA –AZ	General Works (Including bibliography, libraries and reference works)
Literature Group	BA –BZ	Philogy and Literature
	CB –FY	Bible
	GA –GZ	Christian Literature Patristics
Historical	HA –HZ	History (General)
	IA –KZ	Church History, General, More than One Country
	LA –MZ	History by Country, Both Church History and Political History
	N	Missions, General and Comprehensive Works, Theory of Missions
	OA –OZ	Comparative Religion
Group of the Sciences	PA –PX	Sciences
	PZ	Mathematics
Philosophical and Systematic Group	QA –QZ	Philosophy
	R	Systematic Christian Theology
Practical Group	SA –SZ	Sociology, Social Sciences
	TA –TX	Education
	UA	The Church, Its Constitution, Orders, and Ministry

UB −UF	Church Law
UG −UU	Church Worship
V	Music, Hymnology
WA −WW	Practical Church Work
XA −XW	Culture and Care of the Individual Religions and Moral Life, Devotional Literature
Y	Fine Arts, Practical Arts, Medicine
Z	Reserved for Polygraphy and Miscellaneous Special Collections

SUBJECT HEADINGS FREQUENTLY USED

The situation with respect to subject headings in religion has been ably summarized by Edwin B. York:

> General guidelines for determining appropriate subject headings for theological librarianship were provided in the 1965 *Report of the Committee on Cataloging and Classification, American Theological Library Association*. That report offered statistical evidence that theological libraries relied heavily upon Library of Congress headings and also reported general dissatisfaction with these headings both on the basis of currency and general accuracy. The general acceptance of the Library of Congress as the functioning standardizing agency for determining and publishing subject headings for theological libraries was further underlined by the suggestion that new theological subject headings be recommended by the staff of *The Index of Religious Periodical Literature* to the Library of Congress.[1]

Evidence of continued use of Library of Congress headings and of cooperation between the American Theological Library Association and the Library of Congress is contained in the following report by Margaret Whitelock:

> Mr. Warren S. Kissinger, who is a subject cataloger in religion at the Library of Congress, has volunteered to supply the new religious subject headings as they are available to him. The first installment (for the Period January 1–August 17, 1972) was

mailed to institutional members of the ATLA in September . . .[2]

Since the principles underlying the Library of Congress subject headings have already been explained and illustrated with numerous examples from the field of philosophy, only selected examples of subject headings in the field of religion are given below:

Religion
  sa Agnosticism
      Atheism
      Belief and doubt . . .
  also subdivision Religion *or* Religion and mythology *under names of countries, races, people, etc. e.g.*
      France–Religion; Germanic tribes–Religion;
      Indians–Religion and mythology;
      Indians of North America–Religion and mythology;
  and headings beginning with the word Religious.
  xx God
      Religious
      Theology . . .
  –Exhibitions and museums
      sa subdivision Exhibitions and museums *under name of denominations, e.g.* Catholic Church–Exhibitions and museums . . .
  –Study and teaching
      Here are entered works treating the study and teaching of religion and religions as a science. Works dealing with religious instruction in schools and in private life are entered under Religious education. Works dealing with the scientific and professional study of the Christian religion are entered under "Theology–Study and teaching."
Religion, Assyro-Babylonian
  See Assyro-Babylonian religion
Religion, Comparative
  See Religions . . .
Religion and art
  See Art and religion . . .
Religion and education
  See Church and education
Religion and ethics
  See Buddhist ethics
      Christian ethics
      Ethics, Jewish . . .

Religion and science
      This heading is used only with subdivisions . . .
Religion and society
      See Religion and sociology
Religion and Sociology
      Here are entered general and comparative works *not* limited to the Christian religion. Works so limited are entered under the heading Sociology, Christian, and related subjects referred to under that heading.
      sa Buddhism and social problems . . .
Religion in literature
      sa Bible in literature
          Fiction–Moral and religious aspects
          God in literature
          Gods in literature
          Jesus Christ–Drama
          Jesus Christ–Fiction
          Jesus Christ–Poetry
          Judaism in literature
          Literature and morals . . .
Religion in the public schools (*Direct***) . . .**
Religions
      sa . . . Buddha and Buddhism
          Christianity
          Confucius and Confucianism . . .
          Hinduism
          Humanism, Religious
          Jains
          Judaism . . .
Religious biography
      sa Christian biography
      xx Biography . . .
Religious denominations
      See Religions
          Sects
          and particular denominations and sects . . .
Religious education (*Indirect***)**
      Here are entered works dealing with instruction in religion in schools and private life. Cf. note under Church and education . . .

Religious life
  See Monastic and religious life
    Monastic and religious life of women
    and subdivision Religious life
    underclasses of persons
    for works descriptive of their
    general religious life], e.g.,
    Children—Religious life; *and*
    subdivision
    Religious life and customs
    under names of countries, cities,
    etc. . . .
Religious literature, English [French,
    German, etc.] . . .

Religious newspapers and periodicals
    (*Direct*)
    sa Journalism, Religious . . .
Religious thought (*Indirect*)
    This heading is used only with
    subdivisions.
    —Ancient period. . .
    —Middle ages. . .
    —Modern period. . .
    —16th century. . .
    —17th century. . .
    —18th century. . .
    —19th century. . .
    —20th century. . .

MAJOR RELIGIOUS ORGANIZATIONS, INFORMATION CENTERS, AND SPECIAL COLLECTIONS

Religious organizations are major sources of information. These may be denominational, ecumenical, or academic. The number of denominational organizations (especially in the United States) is immense. Certain useful generalizations can be made about the larger religious groups. Generally, they maintain national offices and have extensive publishing programs. Much of the publishing is designed to serve the needs of local congregations for devotional and educational materials, but a number of denominations maintain research staffs at the national level and nearly all of them gather such basic statistics as size of church membership and Sunday school attendance. Most also issue a variety of directories as well as reports of national, regional or state conferences and other activities. Most support theological seminaries and some have parochial schools and colleges as well. Many maintain collections of historical and other materials pertaining to the denomination. Some are active in promoting church libraries among their local congregations. Although the Lutherans, Southern Baptists and United Methodists have such organizations, the Catholic Library Association (461 West Lancaster Ave., Haverford, Pa. 19041) probably has the widest range of activities, including publication of *Catholic Library World* and *Catholic Periodical and Literature Index*.

Ecumenical cooperation is exemplified by the work of the National Council of Churches of Christ in the U.S.A. (475 Riverside Drive, New York, N.Y. 10027), which includes publication of the *Yearbook of American and Canadian Churches*, and by the activities of the Church and Synagogue Library Association (P.O. Box 530, Bryn Mawr, Pa. 19010), which publishes *Church and Synagogue Libraries*.

The oldest of the academic organizations in this country is the Association for the Sociology of Religion (formerly the American Catholic Sociological Society), which was founded prior to World War II and which publishes a journal entitled *Sociological Analysis*. The largest of the academic groups is the Society for the Scientific Study of Religion, which publishes *Journal for the Scientific Study of Religion*. Smaller and more recent are the

Religious Research Association (which publishes *Review of Religious Research*) and the American Society of Christian Ethics. The role of special congresses, such as the International Congress of Learned Societies in the Field of Religion held in 1972 in Los Angeles, should not be overlooked.

In response to a need for greater coordination of research and improved dissemination of religious information, an organization known as the Association for the Development of Religious Information Systems (ADRIS) came into existence. Major publications to date include *International Directory of Religious Information Systems* (Milwaukee: Marquette University Department of Sociology and Anthropology, 1971) and the *ADRIS Newsletter.*

In Europe, a major source of coordination is the International Federation of Institutes for Social and Socio-Religious Research, with headquarters in Louvain, Belgium. This organization published a *Directory of Centers for Religious Research and Study* in 1968.

Only a few of the major information centers can be mentioned. The Office of Research, Evaluation and Planning of the National Council of Churches is noteworthy for its extensive research efforts and for its computerized inventory of more than 2,000 documents in the H. Paul Douglass Collection of research reports. The American Theological Library Association (McCormick Seminary Library, 800 West Belden Ave., Chicago, Ill. 60614) publishes *Index to Religious Periodical Literature* and a *Newsletter.* A major Catholic research effort is conducted by the Center for Applied Research in the Apostolate (1717 Massachusetts Ave., N.W., Washington, D.C. 20036). The Centre Protestant d'Etudes et de Documentation (8, Villa du Parc Montsouris, Paris 14e, France) publishes a *Bulletin* and cooperates closely with a similar research center in Strasbourg.

The number of special collections in the field of religion is immense. The best starting point for a search is under "Religion" in *Subject Collections*, by Lee Ash. Related headings cited by Ash and the names of individual religions (e.g., "Buddha and Buddhism"), denominations (e.g., "Baptists") and religious leaders (e.g., "Wesley, John") will prove fruitful for more specialized inquiries. G. K. Hall & Co. have published catalogs of some of the more outstanding collections, such as the American Jewish Archives (Cincinnati), the Klau Library of Hebrew Union College–Jewish Institute of Religion (Cincinnati), the Pontifical Institute of Medieval Studies (Toronto), Union Theological Seminary (New York), Dr. Williams' Library (London) and Institut des Etudes Augustiniennes (Paris).

Some local or regional surveys of special collections in religion as well as descriptions of individual collections have appeared in the library press. The most useful headings in *Library Literature* are "Special collections–Special subjects–Religion" and "Special collections–Special subjects–Religious literature."

In the event that informational needs cannot be met within the United States, an extremely useful compilation of British sources will be found in Volume 2 of the *ASLIB Directory* (3rd ed. London: ASLIB, 1970). The basic arrangement is alphabetical by names of cities, but this is supplemented by a very helpful subject index, which has not only numerous entries under religion but entries on such specialized topics as "Rabbinic literature," "Quakers," or "Church–plate–Lincolnshire."

Lewanski's *Subject Collections in European Libraries* has already been mentioned and need not receive further description here, except for notation of the fact that the section on religion is much more extensive than the section on philosophy.

FOOTNOTES

1. Edwin G. York, "Subject Headings for Theological Librarianship," *Drexel Library Quarterly* 6 (January 1970): 53.
2. Margaret Whitelock, "Theological Subject Headings," *American Theological Library Association Newsletter* 20 (February 17, 1973): 54.

8 PRINCIPAL INFORMATION SOURCES IN RELIGION AND MYTHOLOGY

CHAPTER OUTLINE

INTRODUCTORY WORKS AND BIBLIOGRAPHIC GUIDES

94.   Adams, Charles J., ed. **A Reader's Guide to the Great Religions**. New York: Free Press, 1965. 364p.

Consists of eight scholarly bibliographical essays on: primitive religion; religions of China; Hinduism; Buddhism; religions of Japan; Judaism; Christianity; Islam. Has both name and subject indexes.

95.   Burtt, Edwin A. **Types of Religious Philosophy**. Rev. ed. New York: Harper and Row, 1951. 468p.

Widely praised for its scope, clarity, and fairness. The revised edition is significantly different from the original, published in 1939. Part I describes the historical background, with chapters on Hebrew and Greek influence and the formation of orthodox theology. Part II surveys the major Western philosophies of religion, with chapters on Catholicism, Protestant fundamentalism, the religion of science, agnosticism, ethical idealism, Protestant liberalism, modernism versus humanism, and the new supernaturalism. Part III deals with basic issues in religious philosophy, with chapters on religious knowledge, structure of the universe, etc. Select bibliographies at ends of chapters. Name and subject index at end of book.

96. Finegan, Jack. **The Archaeology of World Religions: The Background of Primitivism, Zoroastrianism, Hinduism, Jainism, Buddhism, Confucianism, Taoism, Shinto, Islam, and Sikhism**. Princeton, N.J.: Princeton University Press, 1965 (c.1952). 3 vols.

Widely acclaimed as an excellent treatment of the subject. The paperback reprint of 1965 has retained the page numbering of the hardcover edition and has included a *complete* index in each volume. Scholarly, comprehensive treatment, with 260 black and white photographs. Excludes Judaism and Christianity, which are covered in Finegan's *Light from the Ancient Past*.

97. Finegan, Jack. **Light from the Ancient Past: The Archeological Background of Judaism and Christianity**. 2nd ed. Princeton, N.J.: Princeton University Press, 1959. 638p.

Sound, scholarly treatment, in readable language. Supplemented and updated by Finegan's *Archeology of the New Testament: The Life of Jesus and the Beginning of the Early Church* (Princeton University Press, 1969).

98. **Great Religions of Modern Man**. Ed. by Richard A. Gard. New York: George Braziller, 1961. 6 vols.

Each volume contains a brief introduction and a selection of sacred texts or authoritative writings. Useful for introductory or comparative courses, or for the educated lay person. Most libraries (including LC) classify and catalog separately. Contents: *Judaism*, Arthur Hertzberg; *Catholicism*, George Brantl; *Protestantism*, J. Leslie Dunstan; *Buddhism*, Richard A. Gard; *Hinduism*, Louis Renou; *Islam*, John Alden Williams.

99. James, William. **The Varieties of Religious Experience**. New York: Modern Library, 1936. 526p.

Reflections on the nature of religion by one of America's foremost philosophers. Originally delivered as the Gifford Lectures at Edinburgh University in 1901-1902. Reprinted many times.

100. Parrinder, Edward Geoffrey, ed. **Religions of the World, from Primitive Beliefs to Modern Faiths**. New York: Madison Square/Grosset, 1971. 440p.

The compiler has assembled a collection of concise, accurate essays on the world's major religions. Illustrations (some in color) have been well chosen and are of excellent quality. Bibliography. Index. A popular presentation, noted for its excellent pictures, is *The World's Great Religions* (New York: Time, 1957). A recent work with excellent color illustrations and concise commentary is *Great Religions of the World* (Washington, D.C.: National Geographic Society, 1971).

101.   **Religion**. Ed. by Paul Ramsey. Englewood Cliffs, N.J.: Prentice-Hall, 1965. 468p.

Covers historical, philosophical, philological, and theological studies in biblical religions.

102.   Smith, James Ward, and A. Leland Jamison. *Religion in American Life*. Princeton, N.J.: Princeton University Press, 1961– . 4 vols.

Contents: Vol. 1, *The Shaping of American Religion* (1961); Vol. 2, *Religious Perspectives in American Culture* (1961); Vol. 3, *Religious Thought and Economic Society: The European Background*, by J. Viner (this has apparently never been published); Vol. 4, *Critical Bibliography of Religion in America*, by Nelson R. Burr (2 vols. 1961). Vol. 4 is often cited separately. It is a very comprehensive bibliography in classified order with running commentary, tables of contents, and an author index, but no subject index. Useful updating can be found in *Religions and Spiritual Groups in Modern America*, by Robert S. Ellwood (Englewood Cliffs, N.J.: Prentice-Hall, 1973).

103.   **The Study of Judaism: Bibliographical Essays**. Contribs. by Richard Bavier and others. Introd. by Jacob Neusner. Publ. for the Anti-Defamation League of B'nai B'rith, by Ktav, 1972. 229p.

"This collection fills a long-felt need for an authoritative and functional bibliography of Judaism for students and scholars" [Charles Berlin, Harvard College Library (*Library Journal*, Oct. 15, 1972, p. 3303)].

BIBLIOGRAPHIES

104.   Barrow, John Graves. **A Bibliography of Bibliographies in Religion**. Ann Arbor, Mich.: Edwards Brothers, 1955. 489p.

A valuable research tool. Basic arrangement is by subject, subarranged by dates of publication. Gives evaluations and, for many items, locations. Author, title, and subject index.

105.   Berkovitz, Morris I., and J. Edmund Johnson. **Social Scientific Studies of Religion: A Bibliography**. Pittsburgh: University of Pittsburgh Press, 1967. 258p.

A selective bibliography of some 6,000 items in English, representing American and European scholarship. Classification scheme (six main divisions and 132 subdivisions) shows relation of religion to society and culture. No annotations. Alphabetical author index. Supplementary coverage is given in *Religions: A Select, Classified Bibliography*, by Joseph F. Mitros (Jamaica, N.Y.: Learned Publications, 1972).

106.   **Bibliographie bouddhique**. Paris: Librairie d'Amérique et d'Orient, 1930– . Vol. 1– .

Coverage begins with 1928/29. Each volume covers one year. Publication is irregular and often late. Classified, annotated bibliography which covers books and articles in 200 periodicals. The period before 1928 is covered in Shinsho

Hanayama's *Bibliography on Buddhism* (Tokyo: Hokuseido Press, 1961), which contains over 15,000 numbered entries, arranged alphabetically by author with a subject index.

107.   **A Bibliography of the Catholic Church, Representing Holdings of American Libraries Reported to the National Union Catalog in the Library of Congress.** London: Mansell, 1970. 572p.

Taken from volumes 99-100 of *National Union Catalog, Pre-1956 Imprints*. Includes main and added entries with all organizational and form headings (16,000 entries).

108.   **CLA Booklist**, 1942-45— . Haverford, Pa.: Catholic Library Association, 1942–45.

Formerly *Catholic Booklist*. Three basic parts: adult section; elementary school section; and high school section. Adult section is a classified annotated bibliography with an author and title index. Elementary and high school sections are divided into fiction and non-fiction, with a combined index (author and title) for these two sections.

109.   Case, Shirley Jackson, ed. **A Bibliographical Guide to the History of Christianity**. Chicago: University of Chicago Press, 1931. (Reprinted New York: Peter Smith, 1951). 265p.

A selective, classified bibliography, with an author and subject index. Journal articles are included as well as books.

110.   Dollen, Charles, comp. **Vatican II: A Bibliography**. Metuchen, N.J.: Scarecrow Press, 1969. 208p.

Covers more than 2,500 books and articles on Vatican II published between 1959 and 1968. Easy to use. Main entries under author. Subject index.

111.   Hebrew Union College–Jewish Institute of Religion. Library. **Dictionary Catalog of the Klau Library, Cincinnati**. Boston: G. K. Hall, 1964. 32 vols.

Photographic reproduction of nearly half a million cards, including entries for periodical articles.

112.   **International Bibliography of the History of Religions. Bibliographie internationale de l'histoire des religions** . . . 1952— . Leiden: E. J. Brill, 1954— .

Subsidized by Unesco and published under the auspices of the International Council for Philosophy and Humanistic Studies by the International Association for the History of Religions. Classified annual lists of books and journal articles. Author indexes since 1958/59. Book reviews noted. No annotations. About 2,000 items per year. Five-year cumulations.

113.   McCabe, James Patrick. **Critical Guide to Catholic Reference Books**. Littleton, Colo.: Libraries Unlimited, 1971. 287p.

A classified, annotated bibliography of some 900 titles, with an author, subject, and title index which refers to item numbers rather than page numbers. Emphasis is on works available in the United States.

114. New York (City). Union Theological Seminary. Library. **The Shelf List of the Union Theological Seminary Library in New York City: In Classification Order**. Boston: G. K. Hall, 1960. 10 vols. **Alphabetical Arrangement of the Main Entries from the "Shelf List"** . . . Boston: G. K. Hall, 1960 (1965). 10 vols.

These sets provide access to more than 350,000 items.

115. **Scripta Recenter Edita: International Current Bibliography of Books Published in the Fields of Philosophical and Theological Sciences**. Nijmegen, Netherlands: World Library Service, 1959– . 10 issues per year.

116. Sharma, Umesh, and John Arndt. **Mysticism: A Select Bibliography**. Waterloo, Ontario, Canada: Waterloo Lutheran University, 1973. 109p.

Includes both Eastern and Western religions. Lists 1,540 books and periodical articles in English since 1900. Alphabetical by author with name and subject index. No annotations.

117. Starr, Edward Caryl, ed. **A Baptist Bibliography: Being a Register of Printed Material by and about Baptists; Including Works Written against the Baptists**. Rochester, N.Y.: American Baptist Historical Society, 1947– .

Since 1947, over 17 volumes (more than half-way through the alphabet) have been published. Basic arrangement is alphabetical by author, with an index in each volume to joint authors, translators, Baptist publishers, distinctive titles, and subjects. Gives locations. Although more comprehensive than most, this work should be regarded as one example of the kind of bibliographical activity encouraged by many denominations.

118. Streit, P. **Biblioteca Missionum**. Begonnen von P. Streit; fortgefuhrt von P. J. Didinger; hrsg. von P. J. Rommerskrichen und P. N. Kowalsky. Freiburg: Herder, 1916– .

To be published in 24 volumes. Most have appeared and some are in second editions. Each volume covers a particular area of the world and has about 2,000 entries, arranged chronologically.

119. Williams, Ethel L., and Clifton L. Brown, comps. **Afro-American Religious Studies: A Comprehensive Bibliography with Locations in American Libraries**. Metuchen, N.J.: Scarecrow Press, 1972. 454p.

Classified bibliography of about 6,000 items with a very detailed table of contents which serves in lieu of a subject index. Appendices: periodical titles; manuscript collections; sources consulted. Author index.

INDEXES, ABSTRACTS, AND CURRENT AWARENESS SERVICES

120.   American Theological Library Association. **Index to Religious Periodical Literature: An Author and Subject Index to Periodical Literature, 1949/52– , Including an Author Index to Book Reviews**. Chicago: McCormick Seminary Library, 1952– . Includes major religious and archaeological journals in the United States and Europe. Protestant emphasis, but some Catholic and Jewish periodicals also included. Supplementary coverage may be obtained from *Christian Periodical Index* (Buffalo: Christian Librarians' Fellowship, 1958–), *Religious Periodicals Index* (New York: Jarrow Press, 1970–), and *Theological and Religious Index* (Harrogate, England, 1972–).

121.   **The Catholic Periodical and Literature Index**. Haverford, Pa.: Catholic Library Association, 1968– .
Annotated author-title-subject bibliography of adult books by Catholics, with a selection of Catholic-interest books by other authors published during or before the calendar year, and a cumulative author and subject index to a selected list of Catholic periodicals. Book reviews are entered under "Book Reviews," subarranged by author. Absorbed *Catholic Periodical Index* (1930-1968) and *The Guide to Catholic Literature* (1888-1968).

122.   Diehl, Katharine Smith. **Hymns and Tunes–An Index**. New York: Scarecrow Press, 1966. 1185p.
Coverage includes 78 hymnals used for public worship in the twentieth century, chiefly in English. Prefatory matter includes detailed instructions on use, and an essay on hymns and tunes. Part I deals with the hymns: Index I–first lines and variants, with citations; Index IV–composers and tune names; Index V–melodies, a systematic index. Appendixes include "The Scales," "Piano Keyboard," etc. More specialized are *Early English Hymns: An Index*, by Edna D. Parks (Metuchen, N.J.: Scarecrow Press, 1972), which covers some 900 hymns written before the time of Isaac Watts (1674-1748), and *Organ Preludes: An Index to Compositions on Hymn Tunes, Chorales, Plainsong, Melodies, Gregorian Tunes, and Carols*, by Jean Slater Edson (Metuchen, N.J.: Scarecrow Press, 1970), which covers 3,000 tunes by composer (Vol. I) and tune name (Vol. II).

123.   France. Centre National de la Recherche Scientifique. **Bulletin signalétique. 19. Sciences religieuses**. Paris, 1961– . Quarterly.
Part of sections 19-24, *Sciences humaines. Philosophie*, but published separately. About 4,000 abstracts per year. Four main parts: philosophy of religion; history of religion; exegesis and biblical criticism; and theology.

124.   London. University. School of Oriental and African Studies. Library. **Index Islamicus, 1906-1955: A Catalogue of Articles on Islamic Subjects in Periodicals and Other Collective Publications**. Comp. by J. D. Pearson and Julia F. Ashton. Cambridge: Heffer, 1958. Suppl. 1956-60, 1962. 2nd suppl. 1961-65, 1967. 3rd supp. 1965-70 (London: Mansell, 1972).

Tries to cover the entire field of Islamic studies, with over 26,000 entries in the main work. Classified arrangement with author index.

125.   Metzger, Bruce Manning, comp. **Index to Periodical Literature on Christ and the Gospels**. Leiden: E. J. Brill, 1966. 602p.
A classified bibliography of more than 10,000 items from 160 periodicals. Author index. No annotations.

126.   **Religious and Theological Abstracts**, 1958– . Quarterly. Religious and Theological Abstracts, Inc., 301 South College St., Myerstown, Pa. 17067.
A non-sectarian abstracting service that covers 150 journals. Abstracts are initialed unless done by editorial staff, and abstractors are listed in each issue. Arrangement is classified into four major categories: Biblical; Theological; Historical; Practical. The abstracts, which are in English, average around 100 words in length and give language of original article if other than English.

127.   **Religious and Theological Resources**, Vol. 1, 1970– .
Monthly publication from Office of the Librarian of the Boston Theological Institute. Concentrates on providing information about the library resources of a group of cooperating seminaries in the Boston area.

DICTIONARIES AND ENCYCLOPEDIAS

128.   **A Catholic Dictionary of Theology: A Work Projected with the Approval of the Catholic Hierarchy of England and Wales**. New York: Thomas Nelson & Sons, 1962– .
Planned as a four-volume set to provide a coherent exposition of Catholic theology through well-written, scholarly articles with bibliographies. *A Catholic Dictionary*, edited by Donald Attwater (3rd ed. New York: Macmillan, 1958), gives briefer definitions in philosophy, theology, canon law, liturgy, etc. It omits biography except for saints in the calendar of the Church.

129.   Davies, John Gordon, ed. **A Dictionary of Liturgy and Worship**. New York: Macmillan, 1972. 385p.
Concentrates mainly on Christian worship, with some information on other religions. Articles are signed. Information on denominational practices. Not indexed; the system of cross references could be improved.

130.   **A Dictionary of Comparative Religion**. Gen. ed., S. G. F. Brandon. New York: Scribner's, 1970. 704p.
The general editor, whose specialties are Judaism and Christianity, is Professor of Comparative Religion, University of Manchester, England. There are sectional editors for Buddhism, Hinduism, Islam, China, and the Far East. Short, signed articles (with bibliographies) by British scholars. Topics include beliefs, rituals, important figures, schools, councils, and sacred books. Very compact. Many abbreviations. Arrows designate cross references. There is a general index of

names and subjects not given separate articles, and a synoptic index, which groups under the name of each religion all entries about that religion. Brief explanation of pronunciation of names in non-European language. Good starting point for most religious questions. One major segment has been extracted and published separately as *A Dictionary of Buddhism*, with an introduction by T. O. Ling (New York: Scribner's, 1972).

131.   **Encyclopaedia Judaica**. New York: Macmillan, 1972. 16 vols.
Comprehensive and authoritative treatment of all aspects of Jewish life. Over 25,000 articles (mostly signed) by 1,800 contributors and 300 editors. Index has been placed in Volume I to emphasize its importance. This volume also includes transliteration tables and lists of Israeli place names and Hebrew newspapers and periodicals. Does not entirely supersede older works like *The Jewish Encyclopedia* (New York: Funk & Wagnalls, 1901-1906. 12 vols.), which was designed to interpret Jewish religion and life to a Christian audience, or *The Universal Jewish Encyclopedia* (New York: U.J.E., Inc., 1939-43. 10 vols.), which was designed to acquaint Jews with their own heritage. Recent shorter general works like *The New Standard Jewish Encyclopedia* (Garden City, N.Y.: Doubleday, 1970) and *Gateway to Judaism: Encyclopedia Home Reference* (New York: Yoseloff, 1972) may occasionally be useful, as may specialized works like Werblowsky's *The Encyclopedia of the Jewish Religion* (New York: Holt, 1966).

132.   **Encyclopaedia of Buddhism**. Ed. by G. P. Malalasekera. Colombo: Government of Ceylon, 1961– .
Issued in separate fascicles over a period of years under the auspices of the International Association for the History of Religions. Comprehensive coverage of religion, culture, and history. Signed, scholarly articles (often lengthy) have bibliographies and are arranged in alphabetical order.

133.   **Encyclopaedia of Islam**. New edition, prepared by a number of leading Orientalists under the patronage of the International Union of Academies. Leyden: E. J. Brill; London: Luzac, 1954– .
The most authoritative work available in English. Signed articles, with bibliographies, cover an extremely wide range of topics. Published first in separate fascicles, which later become parts of a bound volume (e.g., fasc. 1-22 became Vol. 1 in 1960 and fasc. 23-40 became Vol. 2 in 1965). Basic arrangement is alphabetical. An Arabic term may be used instead of the more familiar English one (e.g., "Masdjid" for "mosque"), but the new edition includes more cross references in English and French. Until the second edition is complete, libraries will need to retain and use the first (1911-1938, 4 vols. plus suppl.).

134.   **Encyclopaedia of Religion and Ethics**. Ed. by A. J. Hastings, with the assistance of J. A. Selbie and other scholars. New York: Scribner's, 1910-27. 13 vols. Reprinted 1961.
Still the most comprehensive work available in English. Long, scholarly articles are frequently subdivided in a systematic fashion. Articles are signed and have bibliographies. Final volume has an analytical index, an index to foreign words,

an index to scripture passages, and an index to authors of articles. An important recent work is *A Dictionary of Christian Ethics*, edited by John Macquarrie (Philadelphia: Westminster, 1967).

135. **Encyclopédie des sciences ecclésiastiques, rédigée par les savants catholiques les plus éminents de France et de l'étranger.** Paris: Letouzey, 1907– .

Most extensive modern work in theology. Parts are: 1) *Dictionnaire de la Bible*, by F. G. Vigouroux and L. Pirot (5 vols. 1907-12; Suppl., Vol. 1, 1928–); 2) *Dictionnaire de théologie catholique*, by A. Vacant and others (15 vols. 1909-1950; Tables générales, 1951–); 3) *Dictionnaire d'archéologie chrétienne et de liturgie*, by F. Cabrol and H. Leclercq (15 vols. in 30. 1907-53); 4) *Dictionnaire d'histoire et de géographie ecclésiastiques*, by A. Baudrillart (Vol. 1, 1912–); 5) *Dictionnaire de droit canonique* (Vol. 1, 1935–).

136. **Evangelisches Kirchen Lexikon. Kirchlichtheologisches Handwörterbuch.** Hrsg. von Heinz Brunotte und Otto Weber. Gottingen: Vanderhoeck & Ruprecht, 1956-61. 4 vols.

Signed articles, often lengthy and with bibliographies. Table of church history in Vol. 2 (pp. 663-730). Vol. 4 has a subject index and a biographical supplement which covers briefly about 15,000 persons and also serves as a name index to Vols. 1-3. Viewpoint is German Protestant.

137. Ferm, Vergilius Ture Anselm. **An Encyclopedia of Religion.** New York: Philosophical Library, 1945. 844p.

Protestant standpoint. Wide range of articles with bibliographies. Many cross references, plus entries for variant spellings of terms. Supplemented in one aspect by Ferm's *A Protestant Dictionary* (New York: Philosophical Library, 1951).

138. Julian, John. **A Dictionary of Hymnology Setting Forth the Origin and History of Christian Hymns of All Ages and Nations.** Rev. ed. with new suppl. New York: Scribner's, 1907. Reprinted New York: Dover Publications, 1957. 2 vols.

Still the standard work on the subject. The novice can easily miss information because of the way in which supplements and revisions were handled. Contents: 1) Dictionary; 2) Cross reference index to first lines; 3) Index of authors, translators, etc.; 4) Appendix A-Z, late articles; 5) Appendix A-Z, additions and corrections to articles in main part; 6) New supplement; 7) Index to appendices and supplement. Additional information may sometimes be found in *The Gospel in Hymns: Backgrounds and Interpretations*, by A. E. Bailey (New York: Scribner's, 1950) and in *Companion to the Hymnal*, by Fred D. Gealy (Nashville: Abingdon Press, 1970). The latter is based on the 1964 Methodist hymnal.

139. Lockyer, Herbert. **The All Series.** Grand Rapids, Mich.: Zondervan, 1958-71. 13 vols.

LC catalogs each volume separately: Bk. 1, *All the Apostles of the Bible*; Bk. 2,

All the Books and Chapters of the Bible; Bk. 3, *All the Doctrines of the Bible*; Bk. 4, *All the Children of the Bible*; Bk. 5, *All the Holy Days and Holidays*; Bk. 6, *All the Kings and Queens*; Bk. 7, *All the Men of the Bible*; Bk. 8, *All the Women of the Bible*; Bk. 9, *All the Miracles of the Bible*; Bk. 10, *All the Parables of the Bible*; Bk. 11, *All the Prayers of the Bible*; Bk. 12, *All the Promises of the Bible*; Bk. 13, *All the Trades and Occupations of the Bible*.

140.　Mead, Frank Spencer, ed. **The Encyclopedia of Religious Quotations.** Westwood, N.J.: Revell, 1965. 534p.

About 10,000 quotations are arranged under alphabetical headings from "Adversity" to "Zeal." Selections are from both Christian and non-Christian sources. There are no cross references, but there is an author index in the back as well as a subject index; the latter not only refers to the main topics but also serves as a kind of concordance to other quotations that contain the index term but that were placed under another main topic. (For example, "selfishness makes Christmas a great burden . . ." appears with other quotations about "Christmas" but can also be located under "Selfishness" in the subject index.) *The World Treasury of Religious Quotations*, edited by R. L. Woods (New York: Hawthorn, 1966) has about 10,000 quotations under 1,500 subject headings, with many cross references and an author index, but no subject index.

141.　Negev, Avraham, ed. **Archaeological Encyclopedia of the Holy Land.** New York: Putnam, 1972. 354p.

Some 20 Israeli and American scholars have prepared concise, unsigned articles on places in the Holy Land and nearby countries, peoples who inhabited the area, and related topics. There are nine maps and numerous other black and white illustrations, placed on the same pages as the articles to which they refer and captioned clearly to relate to the articles. Cross references are indicated by asterisks. A glossary and a chronological chart are provided at the end.

142.　Neill, Stephen Charles, Gerald H. Anderson, and John Goodwin, eds. **Concise Dictionary of the Christian World Mission.** Nashville: Abingdon Press, 1971. 682p.

Covers the entire period from 1492 to the present. Over 200 contributors. Viewpoint is international, ecumenical, and liberal. Countries, leaders, and subjects are given concise articles in one alphabet with many cross references. Leaders still living are omitted, as are those lacking strong connections with missionary movements. Coverage is supplemented by *The Encyclopedia of Modern Christian Missions: The Agencies* (Camden, N.J.: T. Nelson, 1967).

143.　**New Catholic Encyclopedia.** New York: McGraw-Hill, 1967. 15 vols.

Subtitled "an international work of reference on the teachings, history, organization and activities of the Catholic Church, and on all institutions, religions, philosophies and scientific and cultural developments affecting the Catholic Church from its beginning to the present." Prepared under the Editorial Staff of Catholic University of America. Not a revision of *The Catholic Encyclopedia* (1907-1922) but a completely new work, with about 17,000 articles by about 4,800 contributors. Vol. 15 is the index, which has 300,000 entries. Articles are signed and have select bibliographies. Especially valuable on scholastic philosophy and theological writers. Well produced and illustrated. A major special encyclopedia. Quite different in purpose is the 12-volume *Catholic Encyclopedia for School and Home* (New York: McGraw-Hill, 1965), which presents Catholic teaching on a great variety of topics (both secular and religious) for students.

144.   **Oxford Dictionary of the Christian Church**. New York: Oxford University Press, 1958. 1492p.

Over 6,000 entries from 94 contributors. Especially strong on biographies, definitions, theologies and heresies. Good bibliographies. Entries are unsigned, but coverage is generally balanced. Asterisks indicate cross references. Supplementary coverage may be found in *Corpus Dictionary of Eastern Churches*, edited by Thomas C. O'Brien (Washington, D.C.: Corpus Publications, 1970).

145.   **Die Religion in Geschichte und Gegenwart: Handwörterbuch für Theologie und Religionswissenschaft**. 3. vollig. new bearb. Aufl. in Gemeinschaft mit Hans Freihern v. Campenhausen; hrsg. von Kurt Galligan. Tübingen: Mohr, 1957-65. 7 vols.

A scholarly work, with lengthy signed articles and bibliographies. Vol. 7 has biographical notes on the contributors (over 3,000) and an extensive subject index. Viewpoint is German Protestant.

146.   Richardson, Alan, ed. **A Dictionary of Christian Theology**. Philadelphia: Westminster Press, 1969. 364p.

Editor and 36 contributors have defined about 500 words, phrases, and ideas in the context of current theological debate. Articles are signed and vary in length; the longest is 7,500 words. Numerous cross references, citations, and separate bibliographies. Some biographical articles about leading theologians of all periods. Does not duplicate Richardson's *Theological Word Book of the Bible* (London: SCM Press, 1950). At a more elementary level is *A Christian's Dictionary: A Popular Guide to 1600 Names*, by James Kerr and Charles Lutz (Philadelphia: Fortress Press, 1969).

147.   **Sacramentum Mundi: An Encyclopedia of Theology**. Ed. by Karl Rahner and others. New York: Herder and Herder, 1968– .

A major work of modern Catholic scholarship, reflecting the outlook since Vatican II. The level is somewhat too erudite and technical for the average lay person, but the work is valuable for the priest, minister, or serious student. Topics covered range over the whole spectrum of knowledge and society. Articles have bibliographies. Published simultaneously in English, Dutch, French, German, Italian, and Spanish. To be completed in six volumes (of which four have appeared). A detailed index is planned for the final volume.

148.   Schaff-Herzog Encyclopedia. **The New Schaff-Herzog Encyclopedia of Religious Knowledge** . . . New York: Funk & Wagnalls, 1908-1912. (Reprinted Grand Rapids, Mich.: Baker House, 1949-50. 13 vols.)

Based on the third edition of the Herzog-Hauch *Realencyclopädie*. Protestant in tone. More than a translation; some new material. Some German articles condensed. Describes all religions and religious leaders. Extensive coverage of theology, sects, denominations, doctrines, controversies, biographies, etc., to the early twentieth century. Updated and supplemented by *Twentieth Century Encyclopedia of Religious Knowledge . . .* (Grand Rapids, Mich.: Baker Book House, 1955. 2 vols.), which may be used either with the basic set or independently.

149. **Twentieth Century Encyclopedia of Catholicism**. Ed. by Henri Daniel-Rops. New York: Hawthorn Books, 1958-68. 150 vols.

Call numbers vary. LC made an entry for the set, but also for each book separately because each is an independent treatise by a major scholar. For a list, see *Titles in Series*, by Eleanora A. Baer (2nd ed. Metuchen, N.J.: Scarecrow Press, 1964), and supplement. Now out of print.

150. Walker, George Benjamin. **The Hindu World: An Encyclopedic Survey of Hinduism**. New York: Praeger, 1968. 2 vols.

Brings together in one alphabetical sequence brief articles with appended bibliographies on all aspects of Hinduism. First of its kind. The author is a diplomatic officer in the Indian Foreign Service. Included in the 700 articles are biographical sketches, descriptions of symbols, and commentary on Indian life. Recommended as a popular source for general collections.

151. **Word Book of Religious Terms**. Ed. by Clara A. McCartt. New York: World Publishing, 1969. 320p.

Over 25,000 terms most used by churchmen are defined, given syllabification, and accented, with variant spellings and inflected forms. Another useful work is *The Vocabulary of the Church: A Pronunciation Guide*, by Richard White (New York: Macmillan, 1960), which concentrates on proper nouns and words from the Bible.

DIRECTORIES AND ANNUALS

152. Mead, Frank S. **Handbook of Denominations of the United States**. 5th ed. Nashville: Abingdon Press, 1970. 265p.

Information on more than 250 groups. Includes brief accounts of history and doctrines and fairly recent information on membership. Well indexed. Appended list of addresses of headquarters, glossary of terms, and bibliography arranged by denomination.

153. **Official Catholic Directory**, 1886– . New York: Kenedy, 1886– . Annual.

Superseded some earlier (nineteenth century) publications. Some variations in title over the years. Large amounts of directory, institutional, and statistical information about the Catholic Church in the United States, Canada, Britain, Mexico, etc. Clergy, missions, schools, churches, religious orders, etc., are covered in detail.

154. **World Christian Handbook**. Ed. by H. Wakelin Coxill and Kenneth Grubb. 5th ed. Nashville: Abingdon Press, 1968.
First published in 1949. Three main parts: articles; statistics; directory. Coverage generally is worldwide and ecumenical. The statistics section also includes non-Christian religions.

155. **Yearbook of American and Canadian Churches**. New York: National Council of Churches, 1916– . Annual.
Some changes of title and some irregularity in publication in earlier years. Canadian coverage was substantially increased in 1972. There are four main parts: 1) A Calendar for Church Use; 2) Directories (classified into several categories and alphabetical within each category); 3) Statistical and Historical Section (also classified, then alphabetical); 4) Index. The index supplements the directory section by grouping denominations under generic headings, such as "Baptist Bodies (U.S.)," thus making it easier to locate groups separated in the directory by the strictly alphabetical arrangement. Care has been taken to gather current statistics and to indicate when information is not current.

HISTORIES

156. Burrows, Millar. **The Dead Sea Scrolls**. New York: Viking, 1955. 435p.
Author was Director of the American School of Oriental Research in Jerusalem when the first scrolls were discovered in 1947. A successful effort at popularization by a noted scholar. The sequel, *More Light on the Dead Sea Scrolls* (New York: Viking, 1958), was equally successful.

157. Gaustad, Edwin Scott. **Historical Atlas of Religion in America**. New York: Harper and Row, 1962. 179p.
By maps, charts, tables, and text, shows expansion of denominations in the United States from 1650 to 1960. Gaustad has also written *Dissent in American Religion* (Chicago: University of Chicago Press, 1973), which is part of the Chicago History of American Religion series, edited by Martin Marty. Further information may be found in other titles in this series and also in *Religion in America: An Historical Account of the Development of American Religious Life*, by Winthrop S. Hudson (2nd ed. New York: Scribner's, 1973).

158. Jedin, Hubert, and John Dolan, eds. **Handbook of Church History**. New York: Herder & Herder, 1965) .
Translated from the third revised German edition. Vol. I covers period down to Constantine. Includes bibliographies.

159. Latourette, Kenneth Scott. **Christianity in a Revolutionary Age: A History of Christianity in the Nineteenth and Twentieth Centuries**. New York: Harper & Row, 1958-62. 5 vols.
Well-documented work by a noted scholar. Each volume has extensive bibliographies and footnotes. There is an analytical index.

160. Latourette, Kenneth Scott. **A History of Christianity**. New York: Harper, 1953. 1516p.
Author was Stirling Professor of Missions and Oriental History at Yale University. This excellent book is *not* a condensation of *A History of the Expansion of Christianity* but a new work. It has selective chapter bibliographies, 20 maps, and a good index.

161. Latourette, Kenneth Scott. **A History of the Expansion of Christianity**. New York: Harper, 1937-45. 7 vols.
Major scholarly study of missions from the earliest times to the twentieth century. Each volume has maps, an extensive bibliography, and an index. Balanced and fair treatment of Roman Catholic, Orthodox, and Protestant missions. Likely to remain the standard work in this field for many years to come.

162. **The Sacred Books of the East**. Tr. by various Oriental scholars and ed. by F. Max Muller. Oxford: Clarendon Press, 1879-1910. (Reprinted Mystic, Conn.: Lawrence Verry, Inc., 1965-66). 50 vols.
A massive collection of translated sacred literature. Despite the fact that Vol. 50 is an index to the series, most libraries (including LC) catalog each volume separately and assign separate call numbers. A list is given on page 205 of *Guide to Reference Books*, by Constance M. Winchell (8th ed. Chicago: American Library Association, 1967).

BIOGRAPHIES

163. **American Catholic Who's Who**, 1934/5– . Washington, D.C.: NC Publications, Inc., 1934– .
Biennial. An earlier edition, edited by G. P. Curtis, was published in St. Louis in 1911. The 1972/3 volume has concise biographical articles on well-known Catholics, a list of members of the National Conference of Catholic Bishops, a geographical index, and a list of persons who have died since the previous volume was published.

164. Butler, Alban. **Lives of the Saints**. Ed., rev., and suppl. by Herbert Thurston and Donald Attwater. New York: Kenedy, 1956. 4 vols.
This work is a condensation of Thurston's earlier 12-volume edition (1925-38). Many sketches have been included without change, some short ones have been omitted, and some sketches of recently canonized saints have been added. The homilies originally included have been omitted.

165. Delaney, John J., and James Edward Tobin. **Dictionary of Catholic Biography**. Garden City, N.Y.: Doubleday, 1961. 1245p.
Biographies of 13,000 clergy and laity from earliest times to the present. Cross references and bibliographies. Appendices: saints as patrons of vocations; saints as patrons of places; symbols of saints in art; chart correlating papal and secular reigns.

166.   Moyer, Elgin Sylvester, ed. **Who Was Who in Church History**. Rev. ed.
       Chicago: Moody Press, 1968. 466p.
Includes 1,700 people from apostolic times to the early twentieth century. Does
not include persons still living. Chronological index (by death date).

167.   Peerman, Dean G., and Martin E. Marty, eds. **A Handbook of Christian
       Theologians**. Cleveland: World Publishing, 1965. 506p.
Includes articles on 25 Protestant theologians and one Orthodox theologian. The
authoritative essays by major scholars are 15 to 20 pages long; they include brief
biographical data but concentrate on key ideas of the theologians. Editors regret
omission of Catholic thinkers and also of several major liberal Protestants.

168.   **Who's Who in the Catholic World**. Ed. 1– , 1967/68– . Montreal:
       Intercontinental Book and Publishing Co.; Düsseldorf: L. Schwann,
       1967– .
Vol. 1, Europe, contains over 5,000 brief biographies of people prominent in
European Catholicism, including clergy and laymen. Part I is alphabetical by
name. Part II is a survey of the hierarchical organization of the Roman Catholic
Church.

169.   Williams, Ethel L. **Biographical Directory of Negro Ministers**. 2nd ed.
       Metuchen, N.J.: Scarecrow Press, 1970. 605p.
Only directory of living black clergymen in the United States. Most of the
information on the 1,700 ministers covered is not available from any other
source.

THE BIBLE

Versions and Editions

The books of the Old Testament were written in Hebrew at various
times between 1200 and 100 B.C. Final decisions about which ones should be
included in the Jewish Canon (list of divinely inspired books) appear to have
been taken around 100 A.D. A notable translation into Greek, known as the
Septuagint, was made in the third and second centuries B.C. It included some
books not officially accepted as part of the Jewish Canon. The books of the New
Testament were written in Greek, mainly in the last half of the first
century A.D. Final decisions concerning the New Testament Canon were not
made until 692 A.D. A major translation of the Bible into Latin (known as the
Vulgate) was completed by St. Jerome in 404 A.D. Articles in general
encyclopedias give further details. The article in the 1973 edition of *The
Encyclopedia Americana* has a very useful chart (Vol. 3, pp. 652-53) comparing
books included in the Hebrew, Greek, Latin, and English versions. Discussion of
various versions and editions will also be found in the chapter on Bibles in Vol. 2
of *The Reader's Adviser*, by Winifred Courtenay (11th ed. New York: R. R.
Bowker, 1969). A few of the major English versions are listed below:

170a.   **King James** or **Authorized Version** (1611).
Because of the majestic beauty of its language, this version is still a favorite among Protestants. Numerous editions are in print.

170b.   **Douay Bible** (1635, rev. by Challoner in 1749-50).
Translated from the *Vulgate*, this version has been for Roman Catholics what the *King James* has been for Protestants.

170c.   **Revised Standard Version**. New York: T. Nelson, 1952.
A translation into modern English by a group of American scholars from many denominations. Attempts to follow the style of the *King James Version*.

170d.   **The New English Bible**. New York: Oxford University Press, 1970.
The result of more than 20 years of work by a group of British scholars to translate the Bible into clear, modern English. Differs from the *Revised Standard Version* in that no effort is made to follow the style of the *King James Version*.

170e.   **The Holy Scriptures According to the Masoretic Text**. Philadelphia: Jewish Publication Society of America, 1917.
Kept in print in a variety of bindings.

170f.   **The New American Bible**. Chicago: Catholic Press, 1971.
Sponsored by the Bishops' Committee of the Confraternity of Christian Doctrine, this is a modern translation for American Catholics.

N.B.: Various disputed books, commonly known as the Apocrypha, are included in several of the versions listed above and have also been published separately.

Reference Works

Bibliographies

171.   British and Foreign Bible Society. **Historical Catalogue of the Printed Editions of Holy Scripture in the Library ... of the Society**. Comp. by T. H. Darlow and H. F. Moule. London: Bible House, 1903-1911. (Reprinted New York: Kraus Reprint, 1964). 2 vols. in 4.
One of the most comprehensive bibliographies. Vol. 1 covers English Bibles and the remaining volumes cover polyglot and foreign languages. Over 10,000 items.

172.   British Museum. **General Catalogue of Printed Books**. Photographic ed. to 1955. Vols. 17-19, Bible. London, 1965.
An extremely comprehensive bibliography of the Bible in a wide range of languages (Vols. 17, 18), plus an appendix (Vol. 19) covering works about the Bible and an index. The arrangement is somewhat complex, and the instructions at the beginning of Vol. 17 are worth careful study.

173.   Herbert, Arthur Sumner. **Historical Catalogue of Printed Editions of the English Bible, 1525-1961**. New York: American Bible Society, 1968. 549p.

Revised and expanded from the 1903 *Catalogue*. Arranged by year of publication. Entries include complete bibliographical description and often annotations with historical data. Indexes of translators, revisers and editors; of printers and publishers; of places of printing and publication; also, a general index.

174.   Hills, Margaret Thorndike. **The English Bible in America: A Bibliography of Editions of the Bible and the New Testament Published in America, 1777-1957**. New York: American Bible Society, 1961. 477p.
Chronological list of U.S. and Canadian publications, with locations of known copies. Indexes to places of origin, printers and publishers, translators and revisors, editors and commentators, and titles, plus a general index.

175.   **New Testament Abstracts: A Record of Current Periodical Literature Issued by the Theological Faculty of Weston College, Weston, Mass., 1956– . Vol. 1– . 3 per year.**
Abstracts in English of pertinent articles in many languages from Catholic, Protestant, and Jewish periodicals. Indexes of Scripture texts and authors in each volume.

176.   San Francisco Theological Seminary. **Bibliography of New Testament Literature, 1900-50**. San Anselmo: Seminary Cooperative Bookstore, 1953. 312p.
About 2,400 items (mostly books) are included in this classified, annotated bibliography.

Concordances and Indexes

177.   Cruden, Alexander. **Cruden's Complete Concordance to the Old and New Testaments . . . with . . . a Concordance to the Apocrypha**. Grand Rapids, Mich.: Zondervan, 1949. 783p.
First published in 1737. Long a classic. Frequently reprinted. Has about 250,000 English entries in alphabetical order. Appendices of proper names and concordance to Apocrypha.

178.   Ellison, John William. **Nelson's Complete Concordance of the Revised Standard Version of the Bible**. New York: Nelson, 1957. 2157p.
Includes all the words of the *Revised Standard Version* except a few non-significant terms. Computer-produced. Does not give Hebrew or Greek originals.

179.   Garland, George Frederick, comp. **Subject Guide to Bible Stories**. New York: Greenwood Publishing, 1969. 365p.
Part I is an alphabetical subject index. Part II lists characters from the Bible.

180.   Joy, Charles Rhind. **Harper's Topical Concordance**. Rev. ed. New York: Harper & Row, 1962. 628p.
Approximately 25,000 texts are grouped under 2,100 subject headings. Cross references.

181. **The New World Idea Index to the Holy Bible**. Ed. by Harvey K. Griffith. New York: World, 1972. 907p.

Not a concordance. More like a syntopicon. It includes 147 key ideas, with explanations and subheadings.

182. Stevenson, Burton Egbert. **The Home Book of Bible Quotations**. New York: Harper, 1949. 645p.

Arranged in alphabetical order by subjects, with a concordance-type index. Based chiefly on the *King James Version*. Includes the Apocrypha.

183. Thompson, Newton Wayland, and Raymond Stock. **Complete Concordance to the Bible (Douay Version)**. St. Louis: Herder, 1945. 1914p.

First published under the title *Concordance to the Bible (Douay Version)* in 1942.

184. Young, Robert. **Analytical Concordance to the Bible: About 311,000 References, Subdivided under the Hebrew and Greek Originals, with the Literal Meaning and Pronunciations of Each**. Rev. ed. Grand Rapids, Mich.: W. B. Eerdmans, 1955. 1000p.

Includes names of people and places. The revised edition has a supplement, "Recent Discoveries in Bible Lands," by Maxwell Albright.

Dictionaries and Encyclopedias

185. Bauer, Johannes Baptist, ed. **Sacramentum Verbi: An Encyclopedia of Biblical Theology**. New York: Herder & Herder, 1970. 3 vols.

A major work of modern Catholic biblical scholarship which gives in-depth treatment to about 200 terms. Bibliographies include works in many languages. A more elementary book, written from a Protestant viewpoint, is H. H. Rowley's *Short Dictionary of Bible Themes* (New York: Basic Books, 1968). More advanced than Rowley and ecumenical in outlook is *A Theological Word Book of the Bible*, edited by Alan Richardson (London: SCM Press, 1950).

186. Gehman, Henry Snyder, ed. **The New Westminster Dictionary of the Bible**. Philadelphia: Westminster Press, 1970. 1027p.

Based originally on J. D. Davis's *Dictionary of the Bible* (4th rev. ed. 1924. Reprinted Grand Rapids, Mich.: Baker, 1972), this work has evolved through the 1944 and 1970 revisions in a much more liberal direction, with major changes in the latest edition to incorporate recent scholarship. Includes short biographies, outlines of books of the Bible, pronunciations of proper names, and descriptions of things and places.

187. Hastings, James, ed. **Dictionary of the Bible**. New York: Scribner's, 1898-1904. 5 vols.

Still regarded by many as the standard work on this subject, despite its age and the appearance of newer dictionaries. The main sequence is alphabetical in Vols. 1-4, with Vol. 5 treated as an "extra," containing indexes, maps, and some additional articles. A one-volume independent work of the same title was published in 1909, and was thoroughly revised and updated by Frederick C. Grand and H. H. Rowley (New York: Scribner's, 1963). Less comprehensive, but also very useful, is *Harper's Bible Dictionary*, by M. S. Miller and J. L. Miller (7th ed. New York: Harper & Row, 1961).

188.   **Interpreter's Dictionary of the Bible**. Nashville: Abingdon Press, 1962. 4 vols.

Subtitled "an illustrated encyclopedia identifying and explaining all proper names and significant terms and subjects in the Holy Scriptures, including the Apocrypha with attention to archaeological discoveries and researches into the life and faith of ancient times." Many libraries will also need *Young Reader's Dictionary of the Bible* (Nashville: Abingdon Press, 1969).

189.   Kittel, Gerhard. **Bible Key Words**. New York: Harper, 1951-64. 2 vols. in 6 parts.

The 1951 volume (four parts) is translated by J. R. Coates from Kittel's *Theologisches Wörterbuch zum neuen Testament*. The four parts are: 1) Love, by Gottfried Quell and Ethelbert Stauffer; 2) The Church, by Karl Ludwig Schmidt; 3) Sin, by Gottfried Quell and others; 4) Righteousness, by Gottfried Quell and Gottlob Schrank. The 1964 volume (two parts) is translated by Dorothea M. Barton and P. R. Ackroyd: 1) Law, by Hermann Kleinknecht and W. Gutbrod; 2) Wrath, by Hermann Kleinknecht and others.

190.   Kittel, Gerhard. **Theological Dictionary of the New Testament**. Tr. and ed. by George W. Bromiley. Grand Rapids, Mich.: W. B. Eerdmans, 1964-72. 8 vols.

A major scholarly work, the result of the collaboration of many specialists. Arranged by letters of the Greek alphabet. Defines Christian meanings of Greek terms. Many articles of monographic length.

191.   Moller-Christensen, Vilhelm, and Karl Edmund Jorat Jorgensen. **Encyclopedia of Bible Creatures**. Tr. by Arne Unjem. Philadelphia: Fortress Press, 1965. 302p.

Both scientific and popular names are included, as well as definitions and general information about animals, insects, etc.

Commentaries

192.   **Anchor Bible**. Garden City, N.Y.: Doubleday, 1964– . Vol. 1– .

Prepared under editorial supervision of William Foxwell Albright and David Noel Freedman, with about 40 volumes planned. As of 1973, approximately half had been published. Catholic, Protestant, and Jewish scholars are cooperating to produce new translations of the books of the Bible and commentaries to accompany them. LC catalogs individual volumes separately but provides a series entry and common call number.

193.   Brown, Raymond E., Joseph A. Fitzmyer, and Roland E. Murphy, eds. **The Jerome Biblical Commentary**. Englewood Cliffs, N.J.: Prentice-Hall, 1968. 2 vols. in 1.

Has 80 articles, written by eminent Catholic scholars at American universities, on individual books of the Bible, the Pentateuch, wisdom literature, Old Testament and New Testament criticism, biblical geography, archaeology, Pauline and Johannine theology, bibliographies.

194.   **Cambridge Bible Commentary: New English Bible**. New York: Cambridge University Press, 1961(?)– .

As of 1973, over 25 volumes were available in this series. Most libraries (including LC) catalog them separately. For a list, see the publisher's catalog.

195.   **International Critical Commentary on the Holy Scriptures of the Old and New Testaments**. Ed. by S. R. Driver, A. Plummer, and C. A. Briggs. New York: Scribner's, 1896-1937. 40 vols.

In 1956, the firm of Alec R. Allenson, of Naperville, Illinois, began to reprint this set. By 1973, most of the volumes had been reprinted. See Allenson catalog for list of authors and titles. LC catalogs the volumes separately with no series entry.

196.   **The Interpreter's Bible: The Holy Scriptures in the King James and Revised Standard Versions with General Articles and Introduction, Exegesis, Exposition for Each Book of the Bible**. New York: Abingdon-Cokesbury Press, 1952-57. 12 vols.

Eminent theologians and biblical scholars from virtually all Christian churches contributed, with consulting editors from most large Protestant denominations. Vol. 1 has general articles on the Bible and Old Testament and commentary on Genesis and Exodus. Other volumes follow the order of books in the Bible. A typical page will have both King James and Revised Standard versions at the top, then a section of exegesis, and finally a section of exposition. Vol. 7 has general articles on the New Testament plus Matthew and Mark. Vol. 12 has James to Revelation, more general articles (including one on the Dead Sea scrolls), and indexes. Smaller libraries may prefer *The Interpreter's One Volume Commentary on the Bible*, edited by Charles M. Laymon (Nashville: Abingdon Press, 1971).

197.   **New International Commentary on the New Testament**. Ed. by F. F. Bruce. Grand Rapids, Mich.: W. B. Eerdmans, 1951– . 17 vols. planned.

For a list of volumes available (12 in 1972), see publisher's catalog.

198.   Tamissier, Robert, ed. **The Bible in History: A Contemporary Companion to the Bible**. New York: Hastings House, 1968– .

To be published in 12 volumes, translated from the French. The purpose is to present the historical context in which biblical writings developed. Not a scholar's guide on the latest research, but a clear, helpful, and authoritative presentation for the general reader. Recommended both for general reading and for reference.

Handbooks

199. Baly, Denis. **Geographical Companion to the Bible**. New York: McGraw-Hill, 1963. 196p.
Designed to help the layman and the college student visualize the setting in which biblical events occurred. Part I, "Land of the Bible," is predominantly text but has 31 figures (sketched diagrams and maps). Part II, "Cartography of the Bible," contains 10 colored maps. Part III, "Camera and the Bible," includes 28 black and white photographs keyed to Bible verses. Part IV, "Place Names of the Bible," is followed by an index to biblical references and a general index. Does not supersede author's earlier book entitled *Geography of the Bible* (New York: Harper, 1957).

200. Bruce, Frederick Fyvie. **The English Bible: A History of Translations from the Earliest Versions to the New English Bible**. New rev. ed. New York: Oxford University Press, 1970. 262p.
First published in 1961. Author is Rylands Professor of Biblical Criticism and Exegesis at the University of Manchester, England. A very readable book. Reference value is enhanced by explicit table of contents and by name and title index. An older but much lengthier work is *English Versions of the Bible*, by Hugh Pope (rev. and ampl. by Sebastian Bullough. St. Louis: Herder, 1952).

201. **The Cambridge History of the Bible**. New York: Cambridge University Press, 1963-70. 3 vols.
Vol. 1, *From the Beginnings to Jerome*, edited by P. R. Ackroyd and C. F. Evans (1970); Vol. 2, *The West, from the Fathers to the Reformation*, edited by G. W. H. Lampe (1969); Vol. 3, *The West, from the Reformation to the Present Day*, edited by S. L. Greenslade (1963).

202. Child, Heather, and Dorothy Colles. **Christian Symbols Ancient and Modern: A Handbook for Students**. New York: Scribner's, 1973. 270p.
Designed both for continuous reading and for reference. Topically arranged (e.g., the Cross) with a detailed table of contents and a good index. Has 33 plates and 114 line drawings.

203. Deen, Edith. **All of the Women of the Bible**. New York: Harper & Row, 1955. 410p.
Three parts: studies of women; alphabetical list of named women; chronological list of unnamed women.

204. Dennett, Herbert. **A Guide to Modern Versions of the New Testament: How to Understand and Use Them**. Chicago: Moody Press, 1966. 142p.
Describes and evaluates from a conservative Protestant viewpoint. Also includes a guide to concordances.

205. Finegan, Jack. **Handbook of Biblical Chronology: Principles of Time Reckoning in the Ancient World and Problems of Chronology in the Bible**. Princeton, N.J.: Princeton University Press, 1964. 338p.

Includes descriptions of Egyptian, Babylonian, Jewish, and other ancient calendars.

206.   Harvey, Anthony Ernest. **The New English Bible, Companion to the New Testament**. New York: Oxford University Press, 1970. 850p.
Intended for the general reader. Reflects careful research of biblical scholars but is written in a clear, straightforward way. Recommended for home use as well as public libraries. There is an index that is useful, though it is not as comprehensive as a concordance.

207.   Rowley, Harold H., and T. W. Manson, eds. **A Companion to the Bible**. 2nd ed. Naperville, Ill.: Alec R. Allenson, 1963. 628p.
Has 18 chapters with bibliographies, maps, and plans. Four indexes: scripture references; author; general; Latin, Greek, and Oriental words. Another work, edited by a noted scholar but planned for the general reader, is William Neil's **The Bible Companion: A Complete Pictorial and Reference Guide to the People, Places, Events, Background and Faith of the Bible** (London: Skeffington, 1959).

208.   Wright, George Ernest. **Biblical Archaeology**. Rev. ed. Philadelphia: Westminster Press, 1962. 291p.
Text consists of 14 chapters with bibliographies and over 200 illustrations. Indexes for modern names, biblical names, biblical places, subjects and biblical references.

Atlases

209.   Aharoni, Jochanan, and Michael Avi-Yonah. **The Macmillan Bible Atlas**. New York: Macmillan, 1968. 184p.
Contains 262 well-indexed maps of high quality on religious, political, military, and economic events of the Old and New Testaments. Sound scholarship. Skilled cartographers. Appendices give key to maps by books of Bible and by chronological order. Authors are professors at Hebrew University in Jerusalem.

210.   Grollenberg, Lucas H. **Atlas of the Bible**. Tr. and ed. by J. M. H. Reid and H. H. Rowley. Camden, N.J.: Nelson, 1965 (c.1956). 165p.
A scholarly work that follows the historical development of the Bible from the beginning through New Testament times. Has 37 excellent maps in color and over 400 black and white photographs. The index (pp. 140-65) is unusually thorough. Substantial explanatory matter in text. Useful for the general reader is the **Rand McNally Bible Atlas**, by E. G. H. Kraeling (2nd ed. Chicago: Rand McNally, 1962).

211.   Negenman, Jan H. **New Atlas of the Bible**. Ed. by Harold H. Rowley. Tr. from the Dutch by Hubert Hoskins and Richard Beckley, with a Foreword by Harold H. Rowley and an Epilogue by Lucas H. Grollenberg. Garden City, N.Y.: Doubleday, 1969. 208p.
This is a new work, rather than a revision of Grollenberg. The text (which traces the Bible from its beginnings through the New Testament) is more prominent

than the 34 maps (21 in color). Of the 200 maps and pictures, many are in full color and were taken in Lebanon, Jordan, and Israel, with the advice of Grollenberg. The index (pp. 201-208) appears somewhat skimpy.

212.   Wright, George Ernest, and Floyd V. Filson, eds. **Westminster Historical Atlas to the Bible**. With an introductory article by William Foxwell Albright. Rev. ed. Philadelphia: Westminster, 1956. 130p.

An authoritative work. Arrangement plainly set forth in detailed table of contents. Three indexes: 1) Index to the Text; 2) Index to Maps, Including a Topographical Concordance to the Bible; 3) Index of Arabic Names Identified with Biblical Places in Syria and Palestine. There are 18 colored plates containing 33 maps and 88 black and white illustrations (mainly photographs).

MYTHOLOGY AND FOLKLORE

213.   **Abstracts of Folklore Studies**, 1963– . Quarterly. American Folklore Society, c/o University of Texas Press, Austin, Texas 78712.

Over 1,000 abstracts per year. International coverage of all areas of folklore, though English language periodicals are preponderant. Detailed indexes in individual issues are cumulated annually in the fourth issue. Also includes annual bibliography formerly carried (1954-63) in *Journal of American Folklore*.

214.   Briggs, Katharine M. **A Dictionary of British Folk-Tales. Part A. Folk Narratives**. Bloomington: Indiana University Press, 1970– . 4 vols.(?).

Will be issued in two parts—A and B. Contains full tales and summaries as well as citations to original sources and classification by type or motif. Five main categories: fables, fairy tales, jocular tales, novelles, and nursery tales. Within these categories, arrangement is alphabetical by title. Part B will cover folk legends. Part A is in two volumes.

215.   Bulfinch, Thomas. **Bulfinch's Mythology: The Age of Fable; The Age of Chivalry; Legends of Charlemagne**. New York: Crowell, 1970. 957p.

The original nineteenth century text has been retained but is supplemented by 50 photographs of famous art works and a new appendix describing archaeological finds made at about 60 sites mentioned in the myths and legends. The dictionary-index, retained from the original, is good for quick reference. Another popular work is E. C. Brewer's *Dictionary of Phrase and Fable* (9th ed. New York: Harper & Row, 1965). Charles Gayley's *The Classic Myths in English Literature and Art* (Boston: Ginn, 1939) was based originally on Bulfinch's *The Age of Fable*.

216.   Diehl, Katharine Smith. **Religions, Mythologies, Folklores: An Annotated Bibliography**. 2nd ed. Metuchen, N.J.: Scarecrow Press, 1962. 573p.

Includes over 2,300 numbered items in a classified arrangement with author and title (but *not* subject) index.

217.   Frazer, Sir James George. **The Golden Bough: A Study in Magic and Religion.** 3rd ed. New York: St. Martin's Press, 1955. 13 vols.

Vols. 1 through 12 of the third edition were published between 1911 and 1915. They have been kept in print but not revised. Contents: Vols. 1 and 2, *Magic Art and the Evolution of Kings*; Vol. 3, *Taboo and the Perils of the Soul*; Vol. 4, *The Dying God*; Vols. 5 and 6, *Adonis, Attis, Osiris: Studies in the History of Oriental Religion*; Vols. 7 and 8, *Spirits of the Corn and of the Wild*; Vol. 9, *Scapegoat*; Vols. 10 and 11, *Balder the Beautiful: Fire Festivals of Europe, and Doctrine of the External Soul*; Vol. 12, *Bibliography and General Index*; Vol. 13, *Aftermath*. Supplement, 1936.

218.   **Funk and Wagnall's Standard Dictionary of Folklore, Mythology and Legend.** Maria Leach, ed.; Jerome Fried, assoc. ed. New York: Funk & Wagnalls, 1949-50. 2 vols.

In addition to authoritative survey articles (signed, and with bibliographies) on regions and major topics, this work has shorter articles on gods, heroes, tales, motifs, customs, beliefs, songs, dances, proverbs, games, etc. Arrangement is alphabetical.

219.   Hamilton, Edith. **Mythology.** Boston: Little, Brown, 1950 (c.1942). 497p.

Includes both classical and Norse myths. Comparisons of original and later versions. Family charts are on pages 457 to 473. Illustrations by Steele Savage. A somewhat more subjective treatment is given by Robert Graves in *The Greek Myths* (Baltimore: Penguin Books, 1955) and *The White Goddess: A Historical Grammar of Poetic Myth* (Rev. ed. New York: Vintage Press, 1958).

220.   Haywood, Charles. **A Bibliography of North American Folklore and Folksong.** 2nd ed. rev. New York: Dover, 1961. 2 vols.

About 40,000 items are included in this extensive, classified bibliography, which covers printed music and recordings as well as books and articles. There are some descriptive and evaluative annotations. Some reviewers consider the close classification and detailed tables of contents of great value. The reference librarian is likely to be grateful for the very full index in Vol. 2 and for the index supplement of composers, arrangers, and performers.

221.   **Larousse Encyclopedia of Mythology.** With an Introduction by Robert Graves. New York: Prometheus Press, 1959. 500p.

Articles on mythologies of various countries from prehistory to the present. Material is presented in essay form. It is not easy to get to specific points. Folklore, legend and religious customs are covered.

222.   **The Mythology of All Races . . .** Louis Herbert Gray, ed.; George Foote Moore, assoc. ed. Boston: Marshall Jones, 1916-32. 13 vols.

Contents: Vol. 1, *Greek and Roman*; Vol. 2, *Eddic*; Vol. 3, *Celtic and Slavic*; Vol. 4, *Finno-Ugric and Siberian*; Vol. 5, *Semitic*; Vol. 6, *Indian and Iranian*; Vol. 7, *Armenian and African*; Vol. 8, *Chinese and Japanese*; Vol. 9, *Oceanic*; Vol. 10, *North American*; Vol. 11, *Latin American*; Vol. 12, *Egyptian*; Vol. 13,

Index. Besides being the most useful reference work in English, it is also valuable for its illustrations.

223.   Thompson, Stith. **Motif-Index of Folk Literature**. Rev. ed. Bloomington: Indiana University Press, 1955-58. 6 vols.
Subtitle: "a classification of narrative elements in folktales, ballads, myths, fables, medieval romances, exempla, fabliaux, jest-books and local legends." A rather intricate decimal classification scheme is used for Vols. 1-5, with Vol. 6 serving as an alphabetical index.

224.   Tripp, Edward. **Crowell's Handbook of Classical Mythology**. New York: Crowell, 1970. 631p.
Alphabetical arrangement. Articles, which vary in length from brief notes to 20 pages, cover both characters and events. The text is interestingly written, designed for the educated layman rather than the specialist. There is a pronouncing index in the back. There are five maps of the classical world as well as genealogical charts.

PERIODICALS

225.   **America: National Catholic Weekly Review**, 1909– . Weekly. America Press, Inc., 106 W. 56th St., New York, N.Y. 10010.
Indexed in: *Reader's Guide, Abridged Reader's Guide, Catholic Periodical and Literature Index*. Published by the Jesuits of the United States and Canada. Liberal viewpoint. Book reviews, film reviews, music reviews, play reviews. Indexed semi-annually.

226.   **Canadian Journal of Theology: A Quarterly of Christian Thought**, 1955– . Quarterly. University of Toronto Press, Toronto 5, Canada.
Indexed in: *Religious Periodicals Index, Religious and Theological Abstracts*. Contains book reviews.

227.   **Christian Century: An Ecumenical Weekly**, 1884– . Weekly. Christian Century Foundation, 407 S. Dearborn St., Chicago, Ill. 60605.
Indexed in *Reader's Guide*. Book reviews. Liberal Protestant views on religion, social and political problems, the arts, etc.

228.   **Christianity and Crisis: A Christian Journal of Opinion**, 1941– . Fortnightly. Christianity and Crisis, Inc., 537 W. 121st St., New York, N.Y. 10027.
Indexed in: *Public Affairs Information Service, Religious Periodicals Index*. Book reviews, film reviews, play reviews. Somewhat radical political views.

229.   **Christianity Today**, 1956– . Fortnightly. Ed., Carl F. Henry. Washington Building, Washington, D.C. 20005.
Indexed in: *Religious Periodicals Index, Religious and Theological Abstracts, Reader's Guide*. Conservative Protestant viewpoint.

230.   **Church History**, 1932– . Quarterly. American Society of Church History, 305 E. Country Club Lane, Wallingford, Pa. 19086.
Indexed in: *Religious and Theological Abstracts, Social Sciences and Humanities Index*. Scholarly and interdenominational. Book reviews and abstracts of dissertations.

231.   **Commentary (U.S.): Journal of Significant Thought and Opinion on Jewish Affairs and Contemporary Issues**, 1945– . Monthly. American Jewish Committee, 165 E. 56th St., New York, N.Y. 10022.
Indexed in: *Public Affairs Information Service, Reader's Guide*. Book reviews. Articles on a wide range of contemporary issues. No longer "New Left" in viewpoint. Index.

232.   **Commonweal**, 1924– . Weekly. Commonweal Publishing Co., Inc., 232 Madison Ave., New York, N.Y. 10016.
Indexed in: *Reader's Guide, Catholic Periodical and Literature Index*. Book reviews, film reviews, play reviews. Index. Liberal Catholic viewpoint on religion and current affairs.

233.   **Concordia Theological Monthly**, 1930– . Monthly. Concordia Publishing House, 3358 S. Jefferson Ave., St. Louis, Mo. 36118.
Indexed in: *Religious Periodicals Index, Religious and Theological Abstracts*. Book reviews. Index. Conservative Lutheran viewpoint.

234.   **Ecumenical Review**, 1948– . Quarterly. World Council of Churches, 150 Route de Ferney, 1211 Geneva, Switzerland.
Indexed in: *Social Sciences and Humanities Index*. Available in microfilm. Book reviews. Index. Articles on interchurch cooperation, Christianity and social issues, etc.

235.   **Evangelical Quarterly**, 1929– . Quarterly. Paternoster Press, Paternoster House, 3 Mount Radford Crescent, Exeter, Devon, England.
Indexed in: *Religious Periodicals Index*. Book reviews. Index.

236.   **Harvard Theological Review**, 1908– . Quarterly. Harvard University Press, 79 Garden St., Cambridge, Mass. 02138.
Indexed in: *Religious and Theological Abstracts, Social Sciences and Humanities Index*. Scholarly. Nondenominational.

237.   **Interpretation: A Journal of Bible and Theology**, 1947– . Quarterly. Union Theological Seminary, 3401 Brook Rd., Richmond, Va. 23227.
Indexed in: *Religious Periodicals Index, Religious and Theological Abstracts, Social Sciences and Humanities Index*. Bibliographies. Book reviews. Index (cumulative, Vols. 1-10).

238.   **Journal for the Scientific Study of Religion**, 1961– . Quarterly. Executive Office, Society for the Scientific Study of Religion, Box U 68 A, University of Connecticut, Storrs, Conn. 06268.

Indexed in: *Religious Periodicals Index*. Concerned with theories, research findings, and methodological problems encountered in the study of religion. Scholarly articles. Book reviews. News notes. Available on microfilm.

239.   **Journal of Biblical Literature**, 1882– . Quarterly. Maurice Jacobs, Inc., 1010 Arch St., Philadelphia, Pa. 19107.
Indexed in: *Religious Periodicals Index, Religious and Theological Abstracts, Social Sciences and Humanities Index*. Book reviews. Index.

240.   **Journal of Church and State**, 1959– . 3 per year. Ed. by James E. Wood, Jr., J. M. Dawson. Studies in Church and State, Box 380, Baylor University, Waco, Texas 76703.
Indexed in: *Education Administration Abstracts, Historical Abstracts, Religious Periodicals Index, Religious and Theological Abstracts*. Book reviews.

241.   **Journal of Ecclesiastical History**, 1950– . Quarterly. Cambridge University Press, Bentley House, 200 Euston Rd., London, N.W.1, England.
Indexed in: *British Humanities Index, Religious Periodicals Index, Religious and Theological Abstracts, Historical Abstracts*.

242.   **Journal of Pastoral Care**, 1948– . Quarterly. Association for Clinical Pastoral Education, 475 Riverside Drive, New York, N.Y. 10027.
Indexed in: *Psychological Abstracts, Religious Periodicals Index, Religious and Theological Abstracts*. Bibliographies. Book reviews. Index.

243.   **Journal of Religion**, 1882– . Quarterly. University of Chicago Press, 5750 Ellis Ave., Chicago, Ill. 60637.
Indexed in: *Social Sciences and Humanities Index*. Book reviews. Index. Scholarly. Non-denominational. All aspects of religion. Of special interest for students and teachers of theology.

244.   **Journal of Semitic Studies**, 1956– . Semi-annual. Manchester University Press, 316 Oxford Road, Manchester 13, England.
Indexed in: *Religious Periodicals Index*. Bibliographies. Book reviews. Index.

245.   **Journal of the American Academy of Religion**, 1967– . Quarterly. Ray L. Hart, Wilson College, Chambersburg, Pa. 17201.
Indexed in: *Religious and Theological Abstracts, Religious Periodicals Index*. Cumulative index of *Journal of Bible and Religion*, 1933-57. Supersedes *Journal of Bible and Religion* (1933-66). Book reviews.

246.   **Journal of Theological Studies**, 1899– . Semi-annual. Oxford University Press, Press Road, London, N.W. 10, England.
Indexed in: *British Humanities Index, Religious Periodicals Index, Religious and Theological Abstracts*. Bibliographies. Book reviews. Index.

247.   **Judaism: A Quarterly Journal of Jewish Life and Thought**, 1952– . American Jewish Congress, 15 E. 84th St., New York, N.Y. 10028.
Indexed in: *Religious Periodicals Index*. Book reviews. Index.

248. **The Month: A Review of Christian Thought and World Affairs**, 1969– .
       Peter Hibblethwaite, 114 Mount St., London, W1Y 6AH, England.
Indexed in: *British Humanities Index*, *Catholic Periodical and Literature Index*.
The result of the merger of *IDOC–International* (a North American edition of
an ecumenical documentation service on the renewal movement) with *Herder
Correspondence* and *The Dublin Review Incorporated*. Book reviews. Index
every six months.

249. **Muslim World: A Quarterly Journal of Islamic Study and of Christian
       Interpretation Among Muslims**, 1911– . Hartford Seminary Founda-
       tion, Hartford, Conn., 06105.
Indexed in: *Religious Periodicals Index*, *Religious and Theological Abstracts*.
Abstracts, bibliographies, book reviews, and index. Cumulative index: Vols. 1-25
(1911-35), Vols. 26-50 (1936-60).

250. **New Testament Studies**, 1954– . Quarterly. Cambridge University
       Press, 200 Euston Road, London, N.W. 1, England.
Indexed in: *Religious Periodicals Index*, *Religious and Theological Abstracts*.
Book reviews.

251. **Religious Education: A Platform for the Free Discussion of Issues in
       the Field of Religion and Their Bearing on Education**, 1906– .
       Bi-monthly. Religious Education Association, 545 W. 111th St., New
       York, N.Y. 10025.
Indexed in: *Catholic Periodical and Literature Index*, *Education Index*,
Psychological Abstracts, *Religious and Theological Abstracts*. Book reviews.
Abstracts of doctoral dissertations. Index. Available on microform.

252. **Review of Religious Research**, 1959/60– . 3 per year. Religious
       Research Association, Box 228, Cathedral Station, New York,
       N.Y. 10025.
Indexed in: *Religious and Theological Abstracts*. Book reviews. Index. Charts.
Cumulative index in preparation. Available in microform. Articles by sociolo-
gists, psychologists, political scientists, etc., as well as professionals in the field
of religion.

253. **Sociological Analysis: A Journal of the Sociology of Religion**, 1940– .
       Quarterly. Association for the Sociology of Religion, Loyola Univer-
       sity, Los Angeles, Calif. 90045.
Indexed in: *Catholic Periodical and Literature Index*, *Sociological Abstracts*.
Formerly entitled *American Catholic Sociological Review* and published by the
American Catholic Sociological Society, both the periodical and its parent
organization have changed names and been broadened in scope. Scholarly and
research articles. Book reviews.

254. **Soundings: An Interdisciplinary Journal**, 1968– . Quarterly. Society
       for Religion in Higher Education, New Haven, Conn.
Indexed in: *Education Index*, *Religious and Theological Abstracts*. Supersedes

Christian Scholar: A Journal of Christian Higher Education, 1917-68. Book reviews.

255. **Spectrum** (formerly **International Journal of Religious Education**). 1924– . 6 per year. National Council of Churches, 475 Riverside Drive, New York, N.Y. 10027.

Indexed in: *Education Index*, *Current Contents*. Book reviews. Index.

256. **Thomist: A Speculative Quarterly Review of Theology and Philosophy**, 1939– . Quarterly. Thomist Press, 487 Michigan Ave., N.E., Washington, D.C. 20017.

Indexed in: *Catholic Periodical and Literature Index*. Bibliographies. Book reviews. Index. Cumulative index, Vols. 1-15 (1939-52).

257. **Zygon: Journal of Religion and Science**, 1966– . Quarterly. University of Chicago Press, 5750 Ellis Ave., Chicago, Ill. 60637.

Indexed in: *Religious Periodicals Index*. Scholarly. Non-denominational.

VISUAL ARTS

9 TRENDS IN THE VISUAL ARTS

Cave paintings of bison and bulls found in Lascaux, France, and Altamira, Spain, appear to be the earliest examples of human art. These, along with stone carvings of female fertility goddesses, date from the period between 15,000 and 10,000 B.C. and depict a concern with the elements necessary for survival.

EARLY FORMS

In Mesopotamia, the Sumerians had begun to erect ziggurats (large terraced earthen structures with temples at the top) as early as 3500 B.C. In Egypt, the characteristic surviving structure was the pyramid, designed to insure for the ruler and his retinue a comfortable life in the afterworld. Interior walls were decorated with scenes from Egyptian life and with statues of the pharaohs and their queens. The art was highly stylized in the period of the Old Kingdom (2780-2280 B.C.) and the Middle Kingdom (2133-1786 B.C.). The most famous and largest pyramids are those of Khufu (Cheops), Khafre, and Menkure, located at Giza. Also at Giza is the Great Sphinx, a piece of sculpture of architectural proportions, with the body of a lion and the head of a king in royal headdress, symbolizing power and majesty. By the time of the New Kingdom (1574-1085 B.C.), more personalization was evident, as is shown in the portrait bust of Queen Nefertiti.

In Crete, a style of art known as the Minoan began to develop about 2000 B.C. In the early period, the most characteristic art was pottery decorated with geometric forms. Later, painting on walls (as in the famous palace at Knossos) and vases became more naturalistic.

The early period of Greek art (1100-700 B.C.) was devoted to geometric forms. Around 650 B.C., sculptors and painters began to concentrate on accurate depiction of the human body. The classical style of sculpture and architecture reached its height in the Parthenon, built in Athens between 448 and 432 B.C. and characterized by great harmony of form, motion, and proportion. Among the outstanding sculptors of the period were Myron and Phidias. In the later, or Hellenistic, period (338-146 B.C.) all of the arts became more ornate and emotional.

Roman architecture was characterized by practicality in the construction of civic centers (forums), administrative buildings (basilicas), and water conduits (aqueducts). Roman sculpture tended to be realistic, although there was an appreciation of Greek, and especially Hellenistic, efforts. Roman pictorial arts included fresco, mosaic, and encaustic. Vaulted architecture, enclosing large interior spaces, was a major Roman innovation.

Meanwhile, civilizations with high levels of artistic achievement had developed in the Far East, most notably in India and China. Because these cultures tended to exhibit greater continuity over a long period of time than was evident in the West, it may be useful to review developments there from ancient to modern times and then return to the art of Europe.

INDIAN ARTS

Indian architecture, sculpture, and painting reflect the major religions: Hinduism, Buddhism, Jainism, and (later) Islam. The Hindu influence has been most extensive—from the fifth century B.C. to the present. Hindu gods and goddesses are represented in a warmly human (sometimes erotic) fashion. The columns of the palace at Patna as remodeled by Asoka (274-237 B.C.), with their inverted lotus shape, symbolized cosmic pillars separating heaven and earth. Also from this period is the front half of an elephant carved from the living rock at Dhauli. Another characteristic structure was the stupa, originally a cairn of stones over the body of a dead leader and later an egg-shaped dome on a circular, block-like base.

By the first century A.D., free-standing temples to serve Buddhist worshippers were becoming common. A notable example was the sanctuary at Bodh-Gaya, Bihar, which enclosed the Bo tree under which the Buddha found enlightenment. Rock-cut monasteries were common. About 1,200 such caves were in use by the fifth century.

Sculpture in this period normally served a narrative purpose, often illustrating previous lives of the Buddha. Wall paintings in the monastic cave at Ajanta are done in warm colors. *The Story of the Six-Tusked Elephant* (2nd century A.D.) is done as a frieze. A treatise on painting from the sixth century has survived. From about the seventh century, the development of Indian sculpture and architecture centers on the Hindu temples built of stone or brick. The leading type, known as the Nagara, is found all over India. Sculpture continued to reflect religious meanings.

Muslim influence began to affect Indian art as early as the eighth century but did not become strong until the thirteenth. The characteristic Muslim building, the mosque, came into prominence. One of the finest examples of Muslim architecture is the Taj Mahal, at Agra, completed in 1648.

Paintings continued to adorn temples and caves. By the twelfth century, illustrations of Jain and Buddhist texts were being produced on palm leaves and paper. The painted scrolls of the fourteenth and fifteenth centuries were especially beautiful, but the sixteenth century was particularly important in Indian painting because full-page illustrations replaced the small ones heretofore in use. An outstanding example from the period is *The Ancient Lore of Lord Krishna*. Persian and European Renaissance influences later became evident and a cosmopolitan style has developed in the twentieth century.

CHINESE ARTS

Chinese architecture constituted the matrix from which painting and sculpture emerged as separate arts. Because many of the buildings were made of timber, not much has survived before the eighth century A.D. Some idea of early periods can be gained from paintings in cave temples. Because Chinese buildings have been without load-bearing walls, interior partitioning has been very flexible. The oldest surviving wooden structure is the Buddhist temple Fo-Kwang Ssu, Watai, Shansi, completed in 857. It houses examples of calligraphy, sculpture, and a fresco from this period.

A major architectural achievement is the massive and complex Forbidden City in Peking, which includes palaces, audience halls, temples, and apartments; it dates largely from the seventeenth century. A characteristic Chinese structure is the pagoda, similar in some respects to the Indian stupa, and usually marking a Buddhist shrine. Some fairly early examples of brick and stone pagodas have survived. Other major architectural achievements are the Great Wall of China, begun in the third century B.C. and extended or repaired on many subsequent occasions (notably during the Ming dynasty, 1368-1644), and the Great Stone Bridge, Chaohsien, Hopeh, constructed during the Sui dynasty, 581-618.

The earliest surviving Chinese painting, a scroll attributed to Ku K'ai-chih (344?–406?) entitled *Admonitions of the Instructress to the Court Ladies*, is preserved in the British Museum. Painting in the T'ang dynasty (618-906) enjoyed a particularly brilliant period. One of the noteworthy early works is a scroll entitled *Portraits of Emperors and Kings*, attributed to Yen Li-pen (c.600-673) and now in the Boston Museum of Fine Arts. The most famous painter was Wu Tao-tzu (c.689-760), who is credited with more than three hundred paintings, most of which have been destroyed. Landscape painting came into prominence in the eighth century, under the leadership of Li Ssu-hsun and his son, Li Chao-tao. The twelfth and thirteenth centuries saw a revival of landscape painting.

By contrast with the honor that the Chinese accorded to painters, sculptors were virtually unrecognized as individuals. Human and animal figures began to appear around 500 B.C. Sculpture gained greater importance in the Han dynasty. In later centuries Buddhism exercised a profound influence until the fall of the T'ang dynasty, which coincided with a decline in the quality of Chinese sculpture.

WESTERN ARTS

After the conversion of Constantine to Christianity in 312, Roman art was changed to reflect religious purposes; the fall of Rome in 476 meant that the leadership passed to Constantinople. Under Justinian, the Byzantine style matured and was exemplified in the church of Hagia Sophia (532-537). Succeeding centuries saw a refinement of this highly spiritualized art until the capture of Constantinople by the Turks in 1453. In the meantime, schools of illumination arose in England and Ireland around 700. The most noteworthy survival from this period is *The Book of Kells*.

On the Continent, the arts enjoyed a revival under Charlemagne, who was crowned emperor in 800. In the eleventh century, the Roman system of vaulting was revived and the plain, dimly-lit, fortress-like churches with rounded arches, which are called Romanesque, became common. In the twelfth century, the Gothic style emerged, with its emphasis on height and on stained glass windows, first in the Church of St. Denis, near Paris, and later in Notre Dame and great cathedrals at Chartres, Reims, and Amiens. Sculpture moved away from abstraction and idealization toward a warm and lively realism. Manuscript illumination reached great heights of excellence in such works as *Très riches heures du duc de Berry*.

In the early fourteenth century, Giotto revived monumental painting and in the next century other Florentine artists, such as the sculptors Ghiberti and Donatello, the architect Brunelleschi, and the painter Masaccio, brought the Italian Renaissance into being. Around 1480, Leonardo da Vinci synthesized in his work the discoveries of his predecessors in anatomy and perspective and added fresh discoveries in the use of light and shade to give three-dimensional effects. In Flanders, Jan van Eyck and others were making effective use of painting in oil. In Italy, Leonardo's genius paved the way for the painter Raphael. In this same period Donato Bramante prepared the plans for St. Peter's in Rome. Michelangelo's major achievements were the paintings of the creation of the world on the ceiling of the Sistine Chapel in the Vatican, and the dome for St. Peter's. Venetian painters of the period included Bellini, Carpaccio, and Giorgione.

The Renaissance style was followed by a movement known as mannerism, which abandoned formal balance. One of the mannerists was Giorgio Vasari, who also wrote *Lives of the Painters*.

The baroque style was a reaction against mannerist excesses. Annibale tried to revive the style of Michelangelo while Caravaggio painted the common people. After studying for a time in Italy, Peter Paul Rubens returned to Antwerp to develop a vibrant, colorful style of oil painting. Other trends were evident in the works of Rembrandt van Rijn and Jan Vermeer.

By the eighteenth century, Paris was the setting for pacemakers in the arts. A delicate rococo style evolved at the French court in the paintings of Watteau and Fragonard. Toward the middle of the century, there was a neo-classical revival with political overtones, as exemplified in the work of Jacques Louis David, painter of the French Revolution. In Spain, his contemporary, Francisco Goya, painted social commentary in a satirical manner.

Nineteenth and Twentieth Centuries

The developments of the nineteenth and twentieth centuries in Europe and America will be treated in somewhat greater detail in the paragraphs that follow. Trends in criticism will also be indicated.

In reaction to the neo-classicism of the late eighteenth century and its new orthodoxy of artistic taste, many artists in the early nineteenth century began to flaunt artistic conventions in an emotional and highly individualistic fashion. The romantic movement in the visual arts, like its counterparts in literature and music, preferred medieval or Oriental subject matter to that of

Greece and Rome. There was a revival of Gothic architecture. As the nineteenth century progressed, there was a rising emphasis on realism—facts, scientific observation of details. Sometimes this led to rather unimaginative copying of nature. The subject matter shifted from lords and ladies of the age of chivalry to scenes from everyday life, in factories, homes, and mines. The leading architects concentrated on meeting the demands of the industrial revolution. A leading realist painter was Gustave Corbet.

Later in the century, a new artistic movement, known as impressionism, began to emerge. Among the changes were: increased interest in local color, including variations in light at different times of day or in different kinds of weather; and viewing ordinary objects from unfamiliar angles in an attempt to reproduce the image on the retina of the eye without interpretation. The impressionists did not try to blend colors, but left the brush strokes in evidence. Primary colors were applied directly to the canvas. There were connections with the music of the period; Whistler, for example, used musical terms as titles for his paintings. The forerunner of the movement was Edouard Manet, while representative painters at the height of the movement were Claude Monet, Edgar Dégas, Camille Pisarro, Auguste Renoir, and Henri de Toulouse-Lautrec. A variant of the movement, known as pointillism, was represented by Georges Seurat.

A reaction against impressionism took place at the end of the century. Leaders in the revolt were Paul Cézanne, Paul Gauguin, and Vincent Van Gogh. Cézanne emphasized a return to formal structural problems, concern for surface design, and use of color; he was also the first to use deliberate distortion to achieve certain effects. He believed that all nature could be reduced to certain basic forms: cube, cone, and cylinder. By contrast, Gauguin and Van Gogh were decorative, emotional, and individualistic. Van Gogh was noted for his frenzied brush strokes, which conveyed a high state of emotional agitation. The two main trends of the twentieth century art stem from the work of these three. Abstract art draws inspiration from Cézanne, while the expressionist movement derives much from Gauguin and Van Gogh.

In abstract art, the subject tends to disappear in geometric forms of representation. Sometimes, there is no subject and the work is entirely nonobjective. The styles used by these artists are generally rational, geometrical, structural, austere, and logical. They may be regarded as classic and formalist, adhering strictly to rules of intellectual decision-making. Cubism began with the facet and space analysis of Georges Braque and Pablo Picasso, in which several sides of an object were shown at the same time. Later, synthetic textures were added to produce collage. Futurism used the geometric discoveries of cubism to represent modern ideas such as speed.

In expressionist art, the style is decorative, colorful, emotional, spontaneous, mystical, and romantic. Henri Matisse was one of the leaders. Sometimes the movement was called "Fauvism" from the French word meaning "wild." Paul Klee and Emil Nolde were German painters of this school, which has been marked by a sense of urgency and conflict. It has also encouraged the revival of national schools. There has been a sharp break with naturalism. Shock effect is often achieved by sheer color and brush work. Georges Rouault expressed Christian anguish in his paintings. Maurice Utrillo interpreted the disillusionment of the suburbs. The paintings of Marc Chagall reveal both uneasiness and supernaturalism. Dadaism was a nihilistic movement, emphasizing nonsense and incongruity, which gained prominence after World War I. Surrealism was influenced by psychological theories and tried to portray the inspiration drawn from the subconscious. Artists of this school included Max Ernst, Yves Tanguy, André Masson, and Salvador Dali.

Recent trends in the United States have included abstract expressionism, with its emphasis on large size and bright colors (as exemplified in the work of Jackson Pollock, Franz Kline, and Robert Motherwell); pop art, with its satirical use of motifs chosen from the most blatant forms of advertising; and op art, based on certain optical principles and similar to nonobjective art.

American architecture began to make a distinctive contribution with the Romanesque buildings of H. H. Richardson in the 1880s, as in the Marshall Field Wholesale Store in Chicago. Louis Sullivan, who designed the first skyscraper (the Wainwright Building in St. Louis) was famous for his dictum "form follows function." His pupil, Frank Lloyd Wright, discarded all traditional forms. Wright's work stimulated a number of architects in Europe to make more creative use of modern structural components like steel and reinforced concrete. Walter Gropius and Ludwig Mies van der Rohe made extensive use of glass. This "international style" was challenged by the French architect, Le Corbusier, in such buildings as the church at Ronchamp.

Sculpture in the twentieth century has included some noted efforts to move away from literal representation and toward the barest formal essentials, as in Sebastian Brancusi's *Bird in Flight* or, more recently, in the work of the American sculptor David Smith.

Various schools of art criticism have flourished in the nineteenth and twentieth centuries. The environmentalists have stressed the total setting in which an artist lives. Leading works by members of this school include Hippolyte Taine's *Philosophy of Art* (1865-67) and Jacob Burckhardt's *Civilization of the Renaissance* (1860). Racial theorists included Josef Strzygowski, whose book *Orient oder Rom* (1901) emphasized the difference between southern European art, with its academic tendencies, and northern European art, which he regarded as more creative because of the greater imaginative capacity of the Nordic peoples. At the end of the nineteenth century, Heinrich Wölfflin defined "classical" and "baroque" for the first time. An elaborate theory of artistic cycles was developed by Elie Faure (*Esprit des formes*, 1927) and Henri Focillon (*Vie des formes*, 1934). The urge to play has been given due weight in *Homo Ludens* (1938) by Johan Huizinga. In recent years, art critics have paid considerable attention to the findings of psychologists. André Malraux's *Psychologie de l'art* (1947-50) is a major contribution to psychologically-oriented criticism. The view that art offers significant clues to the spiritual outlook of a period has been expressed by Emile Mâle in *Religious Art from the Twelfth to the Eighteenth Century* (1949).

10 ACCESSING INFORMATION IN THE VISUAL ARTS

MAJOR DIVISIONS OF THE FIELD

The term "art" is derived from the Latin word "ars," which means skill or ability. At the time of the Italian Renaissance, the craft guilds were known as "arti" and the word "arte" denoted craftsmanship, skill, mastery of form, or inventiveness. The phrase "visual arts" serves to differentiate a group of arts that are non-verbal in character and that communicate by means of symbols and the juxtaposition of formal elements. This communication takes place through the creation of emotional moods and through expansion of the range of aesthetic experience. "Beauty," as such, is not an integral part of art, but more a matter of subjective judgment. Nevertheless, certain concepts of harmony, balance, and contrast have become a part of our way of thinking about art as a result of Greek speculation about the nature of beauty. "Style" normally refers to the whole body of work produced at a given time in history; however, there may be regional and national styles as well as one basic style for the period. In modern times, attention has even been given to the "styles" of individual artists. "Iconography" is the use of symbols by artists to express universal ideas; the Gothic style of architecture, for example, symbolized man's reaching out toward God.

The visual arts may be divided into four main groups: 1) pictorial arts; 2) plastic arts; 3) building arts; 4) minor arts.

The pictorial arts employ flat, or two-dimensional, surfaces. The term is most frequently applied to painting, but can also include drawing, graphic arts, photography (including motion pictures), and mosaics. Painting may be done with oil, tempera, water color, or other media. Drawing is usually with pencil, pen and ink, wash, crayon, pastel, or charcoal. The graphic arts are produced by the printing process, with three basic methods employed: 1) intaglio, in which the design is hollowed out of a flat surface (as in engravings and etchings) and the ink is gathered in the hollows for transmission to the paper; 2) cameo, or relief, in which the design is on a raised surface (as in woodcuts, mezzotint, aquatint, or drypoint) and only the raised surface is inked; 3) planographic, in which a completely flat surface is used and the design created by using substances that will either attract or repel ink. This process is often known as lithography because the flat surface was frequently made of stone. The pictorial arts employ one or more of three basic forms: 1) murals, in which the pictures are on the walls of buildings, either painted directly on the walls or painted on canvases and permanently attached to the walls; 2) panels, which are generally painted on canvas or wood and are sometimes known as easel paintings; 3) pages, which may be illuminated manuscripts or produced as a result of the printing process. The basic problems with which the pictorial artist must cope include surface, design, movement, space, and form. These are commonly solved by use of line, color, values (light and dark), and perspective.

In the plastic arts (of which sculpture is the outstanding example), ideas are expressed by means of three-dimensional objects. The materials used include stone, metal, wood, clay, plaster, or synthetics (such as plastic). The techniques used, which are determined by the materials, might include carving, casting, modeling, or welding. The finished product may be free-standing or bas-relief (part of a wall or surface). In sculpture, the human figure has traditionally provided the most common subject matter, although the twentieth century has seen increased use of abstractions.

In the building arts (architecture), spaces are enclosed in such a way as to meet certain practical needs (as in homes, factories, schools, or office buildings) and to make some kind of symbolic statement of basic values. These values may be utilitarian and the symbolic statement very pedestrian, or they may be related to the highest aspirations of the human spirit. Factories and gasoline stations are frequently examples of the former and Gothic cathedrals are often cited as examples of the latter. Architects design buildings of three basic types: 1) trabeated, in which a lintel (or beam) is supported by two posts; 2) arcuated, in which arches are created capable of supporting rounded vaults and domes; 3) cantilevered, in which only one post is required to support a lintel. The materials used in construction will determine which type is used. Wood is useful for trabeated construction, but brick and stone can be better adapted to the requirements of arcuated construction. Large-scale cantilevered construction became possible only with the advent of structural steel and reinforced concrete.

The minor arts are a special group, often classified on the basis of materials used: ceramics, glass, metals, textiles, ivory, precious gems, woods, reeds, synthetics, etc. Ordinarily, they follow the same styles as the major art forms. The end products may be useful everyday objects like coins, baskets, utensils, furniture, clothing, weapons and harness, or they may be ornamental items like jewelry, stained-glass windows, and much interior decoration.

MAJOR CLASSIFICATION SCHEMES

The needs of art libraries and their users are not comfortably accommodated by Dewey or LC. Some art librarians have developed their own schemes, as in the libraries of the Metropolitan Museum of Art and the Museum of Modern Art in New York City. Others, like Peter F. Broxis in *Organising the Arts* (Hamden, Conn.: Archon Books, 1968), have recommended faceted classification schemes. In 1968, the *Fine and Applied Arts* section of the English

Full Edition of the Universal Decimal Classification was published by the British Standards Institution. Because of the economics of cataloging and classification, however, most librarians continue to use Dewey or LC.

"The Arts" portion (700-799) of Dewey includes a wide range of topics, from aesthetics to outdoor recreation. The bulk of the notation, however, is assigned to the visual arts. Those portions most pertinent for our purposes are:

700	The Arts
708	Galleries, museums, art collections
720	Architecture
730	Plastic arts. Sculpture
740	Drawing, decorative and minor arts
750	Painting and paintings
751	Processes and forms
759	Historical and geographical treatment
750	Graphic arts. Prints
761	Relief processes
763	Lithographic processes
765	Metal engraving
769	Prints
770	Photography and photographs

The Library of Congress published the fourth edition of Class N (Fine Arts) in 1970. Pertinent highlights of the LC Classification are:

N	Visual Arts	
	1-55	General
	61-79	Theory. Philosophy. Aesthetics.
	81-390	Study and teaching
	400-4040	Art museums, galleries, etc. . . .
	4390-5098	Exhibitions . . .
	5300-7418	History . . .
	8510-8553	Art studios, materials, etc. . . .
NA	Architecture	
	1-60	General
	4100-8480	Special classes of buildings
	4100-4145	Classed by material
	4150-4160	Classed by form
	4170-8480	Classed by use
	9000-9425	Aesthetics of cities. City planning.
NB	Sculpture	
NC	Drawing. Design, Illustration.	
ND	Painting	
	25-47	General
	49-1113	History
	1115-1120	Study and teaching
	1130-1156	General works
		Special subjects . . .
	1300-1337	Portraits
	1340-1367	Landscape painting . . .
	1470-1660	Technique and materials
	1700-2495	Watercolor painting
	2550-2888	Mural painting
	2890-3416	Illumination of manuscripts and books

NE   Print Media

NK   Decorative Arts. Applied Arts. Decoration and Ornament

NX   Arts in General

SUBJECT HEADINGS FREQUENTLY USED

Most libraries have elected to use LC. Searching for information on the visual arts in general may be accomplished through the use of the generic heading "art." It will be found, however, that much searching will be done directly under the headings for the major arts (architecture, painting, sculpture) and the minor arts (interior decoration, jewelry, pottery, etc.). A few examples will illustrate these points:

Art
sa Aesthetics . . .
   Archeology
   Architecture
   Architecture, Domestic, in art . . .
   Art nouveau
   Art objects . . .
   Ballet in art . . .
   Books in art . . .
   Christian art and symbolism . . .
   Cubism . . .
   Etching . . .
   Expressionism (Art) . . .
   Illumination of books and manuscripts
   Illustration of books . . .
   Interior decoration
   Jewelry . . .
   Lithography
   Mannerism (Art) . . .
   Painting . . .
   Pottery . . .
   Sculpture . . .
   Symbolism in art . . .
also subdivision Art *under special headings*, e.g. Saints—Art
x Arts, Fine
   Fine arts
   Iconography
xx Aesthetics . . .
—Analysis, interpretation, appreciation
   See Aesthetics
      Art—Philosophy
      Art—Study and teaching
      Art criticism
      Painting
      Pictures
      and similar headings . . .

—Catalogs
   Here are entered dealers' and general sales catalogs. For catalogs of exhibitions, use Art—Exhibitions; for catalogs of private collections use Art—Private collections. Catalogs of the art galleries of a city are entered under Art—[city]—Catalogs, e.g., Art—London—Catalogs.
   Art—Prices
   Drawings—Prices . . .
—Conservation and restoration
   See Art objects—Conservation and restoration
—Education
   See Art—Study and teaching . . .
—Galleries and museums
   This heading is used for the general subject only, not for particular galleries nor for the galleries of a particular country or city. For the latter use Art—[country or city]—Galleries and museums. References are made from Art—[City]—Galleries and museums to invidivual galleries, e.g. Washington, D.C.—Galleries and museums *see also* Corcoran Gallery of Art, Washington D.C.; Art—Boston—Galleries and museums *see also* Boston. Museum of Fine Arts . . .
—History
   —17th-18th centuries
   —19th century
   —20th century . . .
—Therapeutic use
   see Art therapy

Art, Abstract
  sa Modernism (Art) . . .
Art, Ancient
  sa Art, Greco–Roman
      Art, Primitive
      Classical antiquities . . .
  also Art, Greek; Art, Roman; *and*
      similar headings . . .
Art, Rococo
  sa Sculpture, Rococo
  x Rococo art . . .
Art, African, [Italian, Spanish, etc.]
      The references indicated here are
      general in application. Exceptions to
      this pattern and examples of
      additional references required in
      specific cases are shown under the
      headings below.

  sa Art–Africa, [Italy, Spain, etc.]
  x African [Italian, Spanish, etc.] art
  xx Art–Africa, [Italy, Spain, etc.] . . .
Art and history
      Here are entered works on the
      relation between art and history.
      Works dealing with representation of
      historical events and characters are
      entered under History in art . . .
Art in literature
Art in moving-pictures
      Here are entered works dealing with
      moving-pictures on art subjects, both
      instructional and documentary . . .
Artists . . .

MAJOR ART ORGANIZATIONS, PUBLISHERS, AND SPECIAL COLLECTIONS

At the international level, much impetus has come from various projects aided by Unesco. For example, since 1949, Unesco and its national commissions have worked with art publishers throughout the world to establish a central archives service of art reproductions. In this undertaking, Unesco has had the assistance of the International Council of Museums. Other organizations that have been active in recent years include the Artists' International Association, International Association of Art Critics, and the International Union of Architects.

Within the United States, the variety of national, regional, and state organizations is too great for more than a sampling at the national level. The American Federation of Arts (41 East 65th Street, New York, N.Y. 10021) was founded in 1909 to broaden public art appreciation, especially in those areas of the country not served by large museums, and to promote international exchanges of art. Its membership includes 500 art institutions and 3,000 individuals. The program of activities ranges from circulating exhibitions to preparation of curricula on visual education. The Federation gives editorial advice and assistance in the publication of the *American Art Directory*, *Sources of Films on Art*, and *Who's Who in American Art*.

The National Art Education Association (1201 16th Street, N.W., Washington, D.C. 20006) is an affiliate of the National Education Association, and was founded in 1947 to promote study of the problems of teaching art as well as to encourage research and experimentation. Its membership includes approximately 8,000 art teachers, supervisors, and students. Regular publications include *Art Education* and *Studies in Art Education*.

Other national organizations that should be mentioned are the American Art Association, the American Association of Museums, and the College Art Association. Of special interest to librarians is the Art Libraries

Society, with headquarters in Coventry, England, which has published *ARLIS Newsletter* since 1969, and its more recent American counterpart, Art Libraries Society/North America (c/o J. A. Hoffberg, Brand Library, Glendale, California 91201), which has published *ARLIS/NA Newsletter* since November 1972. More specialized are the American Association of Architectural Bibliographers and the Mid-America College Art Slide and Photograph Librarians.

Certain publishers have been particularly noted for their fine art books. Harry N. Abrams, of New York, has issued such series as "Pocket Library of Great Art," "Collector's Editions," "Panorama of World Art," and the "Library of Great Painters." The New York Graphic Society and Frederick A. Praeger deserve mention. The famous Swiss firm of Skira was noteworthy for "Great Centuries of Painting," and "Taste of Our Time." The British firm, Phaidon Press, has been publishing distinguished books on individual artists for over 50 years. Thames and Hudson, also of London, is noted for its "World of Art" series. Studio Vista and Penguin Press have produced high quality paperbacks. While not a specialist in art books, Prentice-Hall has produced a noteworthy series entitled "Sources and Documents in the History of Art."

Collections in the fine arts are numerous and are found in public, academic, and special libraries. Examples in public libraries are the Art and Architecture Division of the New York Public Library and Fine Arts Library of the Westminster City Libraries (London). The Avery Architectural Library, of Columbia University, the Fine Arts Library of Harvard University (which now combines holdings from the Fogg Art Museum and the Widener Library), and the Marquand Library of Princeton University (noted for its *Index of Christian Art*) are leading examples of academic libraries. Other notable art libraries in this country include the Frick Art Reference Library in New York, the Dumbarton Oaks Research Library in Washington, D.C., the Ryerson and Burnham Libraries of the Art Institute of Chicago, the Archives of American Art in Detroit, and the Henry E. Huntington Library and Art Gallery in San Marino, California. Among the notable libraries of Europe that deserve special mention are: the Victoria and Albert Museum Library, London, and the libraries of the Courtauld Institute of Art and the Warburg Institute, University of London; Rijksbureau voor Kunsthistorische Documentatie, The Hague; Bibliothèque Forney, Paris; Kunstbibliothek, Berlin; Zentralinstitut für Kunstgeschichte, Munich; Akademie der Bildenden Kunst, Vienna; Kunsthistorisches Institut, and Biblioteca Berenson, Florence; Biblioteca dell'Istituto Nazionale de Archeologia e Storia dell'Arte, Rome; and Instituto Amatller de Arte Hispanico, Barcelona. Catalogs of several of these libraries have been published by G. K. Hall and Company.

Additional information may be found in *Subject Collections*, by Lee Ash, *ASLIB Directory, Subject Collections in European Libraries*, by Lewanski, and in an excellent article by Wolfgang Freitag entitled "Art Libraries and Collections," in the *Encyclopedia of Library and Information Science* (New York: Marcel Dekker, 1968).

11 PRINCIPAL INFORMATION SOURCES IN THE VISUAL ARTS

ARTS IN GENERAL

Introductory Works and Bibliographic Guides

258.   Albrecht, Milton C., James H. Barnett, and Mason Griff, eds. **The Sociology of Art and Literature: A Reader**. New York: Praeger, 1970. 752p.

Comprehensive collection of articles and essays for use by undergraduate and graduate students as well as art critics. Extensive notes and bibliographies under major headings. More advanced and specialized coverage of American research from the 1930s to the early 1960s will be found in *Art and Archaeology*, by James S. Ackerman and Rhys Carpenter (Englewood Cliffs, N.J.: Prentice-Hall, 1963).

259.   Ayrton, Michael. **The Rudiments of Paradise: Various Essays on Various Arts**. New York: Weybright and Talley, 1971. 319p.

Essays on art appreciation by a practicing artist. Topics range from classical art to Picasso. Illustrations complement the text. Another work to consider is N. Knobler's *The Visual Dialogue: An Introduction to the Appreciation of Art* (New York: Holt, Rinehart and Winston, 1972).

260.   Carrick, Neville. **How to Find Out about the Arts: A Guide to Sources of Information**. New York: Pergamon, 1965. 164p.

Designed primarily for art students and librarians. Chapters cover such familiar topics as bibliographies, dictionaries, encyclopedias, reproductions, periodicals, etc. Arrangement follows Dewey 700-799 except for Music (780-789). Good descriptions of many reference works. Art students and general readers will find supplemental coverage in *Reading and Writing in the Arts*, by Bernard Goldman (Detroit: Wayne State University Press, 1972).

261.   Chamberlin, Mary. **Guide to Art Reference Books**. Chicago: American Library Association, 1959. 418p.

Organizes and appraises more than 2,500 titles ranging from ready reference to highly specialized works. Arrangement is basically by subject, preceded by general chapters by form (bibliographies, etc.). Annotations are descriptive and often evaluative. The last three chapters describe documents and sources; periodicals; and series of art books. Appendix describes holdings of most important special art collections and libraries in the United States and Western Europe. A book of fundamental importance.

262.   Dove, Jack. **Fine Arts**. London: Clive Bingley, 1966. 88p.

An extended bibliographic essay with chapters on general works; art history; painters and painting; sculpture; architecture; glass, ceramics and furniture; miscellanea; costume and stage design; crafts; museums and art galleries. Has a title index and a subject index. Briefer, but better in some respects, is the excellent bibliographical essay by James Humphrey entitled "Architecture and the Fine Arts" [*Library Trends* 15 (January 1967): 478-93].

263.   Faulkner, Ray Nelson, and Edwin Ziegfeld. **Art Today: An Introduction to the Visual Arts**. 5th ed. New York: Holt, Rinehart and Winston, 1969. 542p.

Covers such fields as painting, sculpture, architecture, household design, crafts, industrial design, and community planning. Has 72 color and 630 black and white illustrations.

264.   Gombrich, Ernst Hans Josef. **Meditations on a Hobby Horse, and Other Essays on the Theory of Art**. 2nd ed. New York: Phaidon, 1971. 252p.

Author has enjoyed a distinguished career at the universities of London, Oxford, and Cambridge. Critics have found these essays generally valuable and stimulating, though some have lamented his lack of sympathy for contemporary art movements. Gombrich has also written *Art, Perception, and Reality* (Baltimore: Johns Hopkins University Press, 1972), which deals primarily with the psychology of art.

265.   Holst, Niels von. **Creators, Collectors and Connoisseurs: The Anatomy of Artistic Taste from Antiquity to the Present Day**. Introduction by Herbert Read. New York: Putnam, 1967. 400p.

Based on the German edition of 1960, but with revisions and the addition of a bibliography. The book is handsomely produced, with approximately 400 illustrations (some in color). At a more popular level, planned for high school students, are *Understanding Art: People, Things and Ideas from Ancient Egypt to Chagall and Picasso*, by Luise C. Kainz and Olive L. Riley (New York: H. N. Abrams, 1966), and its sequel, *Understanding Art: Portraits and Personalities* (New York: H. N. Abrams, 1967).

266.   Krause, Joseph H. **The Nature of Art**. Englewood Cliffs, N.J.: Prentice-Hall, 1969. 324p.

Addressed to the educated layman rather than the specialist. Author adopts a comparative approach. There are chapters on the nature of art, conceptual development of art, classifications within art, line and drawing, color, texture, and composition. Many illustrations (both color and black and white). Short bibliography. Index. More informal is *The Open Eye: In Pursuit of Art*, by Katharine Kuh (New York: Harper & Row, 1971), which is a series of essays in non-technical language on a wide range of topics, originally published in *Saturday Review*.

267.   Mumford, Lewis. **Art and Technics**. New York: Columbia University Press, 1952. 162p.

Originally delivered as a series of lectures on art and the symbol; the tool and the object; from handicraft to machine art; standardization, reproduction, and choice; symbol and function in architecture; art, technics, and cultural integration. A clear, readable commentary by one of the great minds of our century.

268.   Munro, Thomas. **The Arts and Their Interrelationships**. Rev. and enl. ed. Cleveland: Press of Case Western Reserve University, 1967. 587p.

A general survey, from a philosophical point of view, rather than a book on art history or art appreciation. Great attention is paid to problems of definition and classification. Librarians will be interested in his comments on Dewey, LC, and Bliss (pp. 219-33) as well as his chapter entitled, "Four Hundred Arts and Types of Art: A Systematic Classification" (pp. 547-71). Detailed table of contents. Name and subject index. No illustrations. Another work of a philosophical nature is *Reason and Controversy in the Arts*, by Mortimer Raymond Kadish (Cleveland: Press of Case Western Reserve University, 1968). Another reflective work is Erwin Panofsky's *Meaning in the Visual Arts: Papers in and on Art History* (Garden City, N.Y.: Doubleday, 1955).

269.   Myers, Bernard Samuel. **How to Look at Art**. New York: F. Watts, 1966. 239p.

General introduction, profusely illustrated with small black and white photographs (on appropriate pages of text) and full-page color plates (with page references to text). There is also an illustrated glossary (pp. 201-232) and an index (pp. 233-39). Final volume in "Great Art and Artists of the World" series. Other titles are: *Origins of Western Art*; *Italian Art to 1850*; *Flemish and Dutch Art*; *German and Spanish Art to 1900*; *French Art from 1350 to 1850*; *British and North American Art to 1900*; *Impressionists and Post-Impressionists*; *Modern Art*; *Chinese and Japanese Art*.

270.   Myers, Bernard Samuel. **Understanding the Arts**. Rev. ed. New York: Holt, Rinehart, and Winston, 1963. 502p.

Designed for the undergraduate student in a beginning course in art appreciation, this logically organized book is illustrated with four color plates and 250 black and white photographs. Includes a brief bibliography and a good index.

271.   Osborne, Harold, ed. **The Appreciation of the Arts**. New York: Oxford University Press, 1969/70. 5 vols.

Generally well regarded by the critics, the volumes in this series are cataloged individually by LC: 1) *Architecture*, by Sinclair Gauldie (1969); 2) *Sculpture*, by Leonard Robert Rogers (1969); 3) *Drawing*, by Philip Rawson (1969); 4) *The Art of Appreciation*, by Harold Osborne (1970); 5) *Painting*, by Peter Owen (1970).

272.   Pepper, Stephen Coburn. **Principles of Art Appreciation**. New York: Harcourt, 1949. 326p.

"...An analysis of art appreciation which is based upon psychological and philosophical, as well as aesthetic, considerations ... expounds the principles of design: contrast, gradation, theme and variation, and restraint ... analyzes pattern, its elements and organization ... and treats the visual materials, color, line, mass, volume, as the artist operates with each toward artistic expression ..." (*Christian Science Monitor*, June 2, 1949, p. 2).

273.   Read, Sir Herbert Edward. **The Meaning of Art**. New and rev. ed. London: Faber and Faber, 1968. 280p.

Originally a series of articles in *The Listener*, this little book (first published in 1931) has been revised and expanded. The form is somewhat choppy, but the detailed table of contents and the index make it easy to find what Read has said on a particular subject. There are 70 black and white illustrations.

274.   Rosenberg, Jakob. **On Quality in Art: Criteria of Excellence, Past and Present**. Princeton, N.J.: Princeton University Press, 1967. 264p.

Based on the A. W. Mellon Lectures of 1964, this book attempts to clarify, for the intelligent layman, the criteria of excellence in art. The first part is devoted to critical judgments of the past. The second compares similar works of art, one by a master and one by a pupil or imitator. Comparisons are limited to drawings (which reproduce well). Highly regarded by reviewers except for the chapter on the twentieth century.

275.   Schlosser, Julius Ritter von. **La letteratura artistica: manuale delle fonti della storia dell'arte moderna**. Tr. Filippo Rossi. 3rd Italian ed. rev. by Otto Kurz. Firenze: La Nuova Italia, 1964. 792p.

An extensive bibliographical essay on the literature of art from the Middle Ages through the eighteenth century, with special emphasis on Italy. Classified arrangement supplemented by an index of artists and a general bibliographical index. An asterisk in the margin of the main work indicates that additional information will be found in the bibliographical supplement (pp. 707-735).

276.   Taylor, Joshua C. **Learning to Look: A Handbook for the Visual Arts**. Chicago: University of Chicago Press, 1957. 152p.

The material in this book was developed over a period of years for use in the art portion of the introductory humanities course at the University of Chicago. The book opens with 32 plates (two in color) and continues with chapters on art analysis; color and perspective; the visual arts (drawing and painting, graphic arts, sculpture, architecture); materials and techniques of the artist; the artist and the work of art. Emphasis is on development of critical appreciation based on first-hand experience with art. Text is supplemented by chronological table and index.

Bibliographies

277.   **Annuario bibliografico de storia dell'arte**. Modena: Societa Tipografica Modenese, 1952– . Annual.

Classified bibliography of books and periodicals acquired by the Library of the Modena Typographical Society. Abstracts. Name index.

278.   Besterman, Theodore. **Art and Architecture: A Bibliography of Bibliographies**. Totowa, N.J.: Rowman and Littlefield, 1971. 216p.

Includes archaeology. Part of "The Besterman World Bibliographies" series.

279.   **Bibliografia del libro d'arte italiano**. Roma: Carlo Bestetti–Edizioni d'arte, 1952– .

The first volume, covering 1940 to 1952 and edited by E. Aeschilimann (1952), lists about 4,000 Italian art books and gives type of illustration, size, and price. Author and subject index. Vol. 2, 1952-1962 (1964), edited by Carla Emilia Tanfani, also includes congresses, periodicals, and exhibition catalogs, and has an index of authors, artists, subjects, and localities for the two volumes.

280.   Canada. National Gallery. Library. **Catalogue of the Library of the National Gallery of Canada**. Boston: G. K. Hall, 1973. 8 vols.

Dictionary catalog. Particularly strong for all aspects of Canadian art, but also good for art history from the Renaissance to the twentieth century. Includes books, journals, exhibition catalogs, and material from pamphlet and clipping files.

281.   Harvard University. Fine Arts Library. **Catalogue of the Harvard University Fine Arts Library, the Fogg Art Museum.** Boston: G. K. Hall, 1971-72. 15 vols.
Photographic reproduction of some 360,000 cards. One of the strongest art libraries in the United States.

282.   Illinois University. Graduate School of Library Science. **A Checklist of U.S. Government Publications in the Arts.** By Donald L. Foster. Occasional Paper No. 96. Urbana: University of Illinois, June 1969.

283.   Lucas, Edna Louise. **Art Books: A Basic Bibliography on the Fine Arts.** Greenwich, Conn.: New York Graphic Society, 1968. 245p.
Based on an earlier work by Lucas entitled *The Harvard List of Books on Art.* Contains about 4,000 entries (unannotated) in nine major categories with a detailed index of authors and artists. Intended as a selection and reference tool for four-year colleges and students of art history.

284.   National Book League, London. **Art Books: An Annotated List; Based on an Exhibition at the Tate Gallery, Autumn, 1968.** London: National Book League; Tate Gallery, 1968. 136p.
Classified, annotated bibliography of 679 items, with three indexes: index to authors, editors and compilers; index to monographs; index to artists not included in monographs. Emphasis is on books in English and in print at time of publication.

285.   New York Metropolitan Museum of Art. **Library Catalog.** Boston, G. K. Hall, 1960. 25 vols. 2 suppls. to 1965. 1966.
Photographic reproduction of the dictionary card catalog. Vols. 1 through 23 cover books and periodicals; Vols. 24 and 25, sales catalogs. One of the great art libraries of this country.

286.   Rave, Paul Ortwin. **Kunstgeschichte in Festschriften.** Berlin: Mann, 1962. 314p.
Contains: list of Festschriften indexed; list, arranged by subject, of essays on art included in them; indexes of titles of Festschriften, of authors of art essays, of artists, and of places written about.

287.   **Répertoire d'art et d'archéologie: dépouillement des périodiques et des catalogues de ventes, bibliographie des ouvrages d'art français et étrangers.** Paris: Morancé, 1910– . Annual.
Classified, annotated bibliography of books, pamphlets, and periodical articles. Indexes for authors and for artists. Separate section for sales catalogs. Major international work in this field; now published with the aid of Unesco under the

auspices of the International Committee on the History of Art and the Library of Art and Archeology, University of Paris.

288. Victoria and Albert Museum, London. **National Art Library Catalogue**. Boston: G. K. Hall, 1973. 10 vols.

Over 300,000 entries, including over 50,000 exhibition catalogs.

289. **Worldwide Art Book Bibliography: A Select List of In-Print Books on the History of Art and Archaeology**. New York: Worldwide Books, 1966– .

Two issues per year. Vols. 1 and 2 entitled *Worldwide Art Book Syllabus*. Classified, annotated. Index to authors and editors. Some irregularity in publication (e.g., Vol. 4, No. 1, 1969; Vol. 4, No. 2, 1971). Vol. 5, No. 1 (issued in 1971) is entitled *LOMA 1969: Literature on Modern Art; An Annual Bibliography* and is alphabetically arranged in two parts: artists, A–Z; subjects, A–Z. Has subject and author indexes.

290. **The Worldwide Art Catalogue Bulletin**. American library ed., Vol. 1– . New York: Worldwide Books, 1963/64– . Quarterly.

The Worldwide Art Center was established in 1962 to meet the need for up-to-date information on art exhibits around the world. Supported by major national art bodies. Over 900 art museums and galleries in 30 countries send exhibition catalogs to the Center. *The Worldwide Art Catalogue Bulletin* provides the only central record of new and significant art catalogs. Descriptions and reviews by art experts. In addition, art catalogs may be purchased through the Center. Most are covered by NPAC, and LC numbers are given when available.

Indexes, Abstracts, and Current Awareness Services

291. **Art Index**. New York: H. W. Wilson, 1929– . Quarterly, with annual and two-year cumulations.

Major indexing tool in this field. Indexed museum bulletins until end of 1957. Now indexes American and some foreign periodicals in archaeology, architecture, art history, arts and crafts, fine arts, graphic arts, industrial design, interior decoration, photography and films, planning and landscape design. Method of indexing: 1) ordinary articles under author and subject or subjects; 2) book reviews under author *reviewed* and by subject; 3) exhibitions under artist; 4) illustrations listed under the article which they accompany but not individually; 5) if an illustration appears without accompanying text, it is listed under name of artist. Easiest to use of major tools. Over 70 percent of periodicals indexed are published in the United States, United Kingdom, and Canada. Considerable time lag in many cases.

292. Chicago. Art Institute. Ryerson Library. **Index to Art Periodicals**. Boston: G. K. Hall, 1962. 11 vols.

Photographic reproduction of library's card file. All entries are by subject, alphabetized within subject by periodical. Material that appears in *Art Index* is excluded.

Dictionaries and Encyclopedias

293.   Adeline, J. **The Adeline Art Dictionary, Including Terms in Architecture, Heraldry and Archaeology**. Tr. from the French with a supplement of new terms by Hugo G. Beigel. New York: Ungar, 1966. 459p.
About 4,000 terms are defined, with about 2,000 illustrations.

294.   Ehresmann, Julia M., ed. **The Pocket Dictionary of Art Terms**. Rev. ed. Greenwich, Conn.: New York Graphic Society, 1971. 1 vol. (unpaged).
Designed to be carried on museum visits, this little book opens with 12 sketches to illustrate key architectural concepts and styles, continues with brief definitions of common art terms, and concludes with a selective, classified bibliography. A quick starting point. Another popular work (which excludes technical terms relating to processes) is *A Glossary of Art, Architecture and Design Since 1945*, by John A. Walker (Hamden, Conn.: Linnet/Shoe String, 1973).

295.   **Encyclopaedia of the Arts**. Consulting ed., Herbert Read. New York: Meredith Press, 1966. 966p.
Subject coverage: architecture, sculpture, applied arts, painting, graphic arts, literature, theatre, cinema, photography, music, opera, ballet. Includes biographies, titles, styles, schools, movements, technical terms, techniques, and materials. Over 10,000 entries. More than 3,500 illustrations, with 79 color plates. Short articles. Alphabetical arrangement.

296.   **Encyclopedia of World Art**. New York: McGraw-Hill, 1959-68. 15 vols.
High on any list of vital works. Published simultaneously in Italian and English. English edition has more cross references; a more extensive article on art of the Americas; some 300 separate, short biographies to give quicker access to information about notable people mentioned in longer, monographic articles. Specialists from many parts of the world have assisted with the editorial work or have contributed signed articles, often of considerable length, with extensive bibliographies. Covers the entire field of art in all countries and periods. A major work of high quality. Plates (many in color) make up about half of each volume. Vol. 15 (index) has about 20,000 main entries and is very thorough.

297.   Haggar, Reginald George. **A Dictionary of Art Terms: Painting, Sculpture, Architecture, Engraving and Etching, Lithography and Other Art Processes, Heraldry**. New York: Hawthorn, 1962. 416p.
Approximately 2,000 brief entries and about 200 small illustrations. Cross references. Glossary of French, German, and Italian terms with English equivalents.

298.   **Harper's Encyclopedia of Art: Architecture, Sculpture, Painting, Decorative Arts**. Based on the work of Louis Hourticq . . . and tr. under the supervision of J. Leroy Davidson and Philippa Gerry, with the assistance of the staff of the Index of Twentieth Century Artists, College Art Association, New York City. New York: Harper, 1937. 2 vols.

Based on *Encyclopédie des beaux-arts . . .* by Louis Hourticq (Paris: Hachette, 1925) and later reprinted as *New Standard Encyclopedia of Art* (New York: Doubleday, 1939).

299.   Huyghe, René, gen. ed. **Larousse Encyclopedia of Modern Art: Art and Mankind from 1800 to the Present Day**. New York: Prometheus Press, 1965. 444p.

Not a true encyclopedia and of limited use for ready reference because of its arrangement. A good survey of modern art. More of a guide than a regular encyclopedia. Illustrations are in black and white.

300.   Kaltenbach, Gustave Emile. **Dictionary of Pronunciation of Artists' Names, with Their Schools and Dates, for American Readers and Students** . . . 2nd ed. Chicago: Art Institute of Chicago, 1938. 74p.

Lists about 1,500 artists.

301.   **McGraw-Hill Dictionary of Art**. Ed. by Bernard S. Myers. New York: McGraw-Hill, 1969. 5 vols.

About 125 contributors. The 2,500 illustrations are mostly black and white. Best for high school and small public libraries. Larger libraries will need *Encyclopedia of World Art*. Articles are brief, well chosen, often signed; some have bibliographies. Most of the 15,000 entries are biographies of painters, sculptors, architects, and decorative artists from all periods and countries. There are also articles on art types and art terms. Cross reference system linking art works and schools with individual artists and vice versa.

302.   Mayer, Ralph. **A Dictionary of Art Terms and Techniques**. New York: Crowell, 1969. 447p.

About 3,000 short articles, technical in nature, to help the practicing artist or serious student. Heavy emphasis on painting technology, materials, and methods.

303.   Murray, Peter, and Linda Murray. **Dictionary of Art and Artists**. New York: Praeger, 1966. 464p.

Technical terms, processes, and movements are included as well as short biographies of more than 1,000 artists. There are about 1,000 black and white illustrations and over 50 color plates. Bibliographies (classified and alphabetical) include some 3,000 items.

304.   Osborne, Harold. **The Oxford Companion to Art**. New York: Oxford University Press, 1970. 1277p.

New addition to this excellent series of guides for the general reader. Has about 3,000 entries, alphabetically arranged. Painting and sculpture are emphasized. Some attention is given to architecture and ceramics, but very little to the minor arts. Entries vary in length from a few lines to several pages and are unsigned, but the list of contributors is distinguished. Covers national and regional schools of art, art movements, art concepts, styles, techniques, iconography, names of artists, art historians, and museums. Selective bibliography of general works and specific subjects includes about 3,000 items. Illustrations are small and designed to support the text. Recommended for all types of libraries from medium-sized to large.

305.   **Phaidon Dictionary of Twentieth Century Art**. New York: Phaidon; distr. Praeger, 1973. 420, 48p.

Has 1,600 entries on painters, sculptors, and graphic artists (but not architects), and 140 entries on ideas, groups, and movements. Articles are brief (sometimes with bibliographies) and authoritative.

306.   **A Pictorial Encyclopedia of the Oriental Arts**. Ed. by Kadokawa Shoten. New York: Crown, 1969. 7 vols.

Compiled from the Oriental section of *Encyclopedia of World Art*. Devotes four volumes to Japan, two to China, one to Korea. Good quality reproductions, many in color. Brief identification, sometimes with location of original. Supplemented by lists of plates, which supply additional information on size and medium and, for early art, where excavated.

307.   **Praeger Encyclopedia of Art**. New York: Praeger, 1971. 5 vols.

About 4,000 articles, mostly signed, with over 5,000 illustrations (1,700 in color). List of 100 contributors shows international background. (Work is partly based on *Dictionnaire universel de l'art et des artistes*, Paris, Hazan, 1967. 3 vols.) About 3,000 biographies of artists. Other articles cover periods, styles, schools, movements, etc. Good bibliographies. For the general reader rather than the art specialist.

308.   Quick, John. **Artists' and Illustrators' Encyclopedia**. New York: McGraw-Hill, 1969. 273p.

Actually a dictionary of terms. Covers methods and materials used in commercial and fine art, photography, graphic arts, and printings. Bibliography.

309.   Schiller, Gertrud. **Iconography of Christian Art**. Tr. from the German by J. Seligman. Greenwich, Conn.: New York Graphic Society, 1971-72. 2 vols.

Arranged thematically rather than alphabetically, with an index at the end of Vol. 2. Thoroughly researched. Well written and well translated. Large number of excellent illustrations.

Directories and Annuals

310.   **American Art Directory**, Vol. 1– , 1898– . New York: R. R. Bowker, 1899– .

Frequency has varied. Triennial since 1952. Title has varied in the past. High on list of vital works. Prefatory matter includes information about the American Federation of Arts and state and provincial arts councils. Classified arrangement: national and regional organizations in the United States; museums, associations, and other organizations by state; children's and junior museums; Canadian art organizations by province; major museums abroad by country; art schools in the United States by state; Canadian art schools by province; art schools abroad by country; directors and supervisors of art education in school systems; art magazines; newspapers carrying art notes, and their critics; scholarships and fellowships; travelling exhibitions and booking agencies. There is a combined name and subject index at the end. The latter portion may involve searching dozens of undifferentiated page references under broad headings (e.g., PAINT-ING–AMERICAN).

311.   Cartwright, W. Aubrey. **Guide to Art Museums in the United States: East Coast–Washington to Miami; with Comprehensive Index of Artists Represented in the Permanent Collections**. New York: Duell, Sloane and Pearce, 1958– .

Designed in pocket size for convenience of museum visitors. Small black and white illustrations. Index.

312.   Christensen, Erwin Ottomar. **A Guide to Art Museums in the United States**. New York: Dodd, Mead, 1968. 303p.

Information on 88 major and regional museums in 59 cities. Part I, arranged geographically, has some detail on leading works of art in museums described, including 500 illustrations. Part II is alphabetical and gives much briefer descriptions of lesser museums. Indexes: museums alphabetically by name of museum; museums alphabetically by name of city; works of art discussed in text; museum architects, donors, etc.

313.   Faison, Samson Lane. **A Guide to the Art Museums of New England**. New York: Harcourt, Brace, 1958. 270p.

Selective guide to some 60 collections. Arranged by state and then by location within the state. After a brief general description of each museum, there are comments on a few of its works and small reproductions of works chosen.

314.   **International Poster Annual**, 1948– . New York: Hastings House. Biennial.

There are editions in English, French, and German.

315.   **Internationales Kunst-Adressbuch. International Directory of Arts**, 1952/53– . Berlin: Kaupertverlag, 1952– .

Arranged by subject groups. Vol. 1, *Public Institutions*, is divided into two chapters: "Museums and Galleries" and "Universities and Art Schools." Within these groups, addresses are alphabetical: first by country, then by city or town, then by name of institution. The section on artists is alphabetical by surnames, as is the section on collectors; the section on associations is arranged by countries and then by name of association. At the end of Vol. 1 is an alphabetical list of names of directors of museums, libraries, and art institutes, with reference to the page where the museum, etc., is listed. Vol. 2 has chapters on art and antique dealers, galleries, auctioneers, art publishers, art periodicals, antiquarian art booksellers, restorers and experts. Basic arrangement is by country, then city, then name, except for the index of experts, which is arranged first by subjects with subdivisions, and then by surnames.

316. Lewis, Samella S., and Ruth G. Waddy, eds. **Black Artists on Art**. Los
      Angeles: Contemporary Crafts, 1969– .
Distributed by Ward Ritchie Press. Vol. 1 appeared in 1969, Vol. 2 in 1971.

317. McCoy, Garnett. **Archives of American Art: A Directory of Resources**.
      New York: R. R. Bowker, 1972. 163p.
Lists 535 groups of papers held by the Archives of American Art. Basic listing is
by title of collection. Information is given about owners, donors, numbers of
items, types, dates covered, etc. Collections include personal papers of art
dealers, collectors, curators, painters, and sculptors.

318. **The Official Museum Directory: United States, Canada**. Washington,
      D.C.: American Association of Museums, 1961– .
An essential reference tool. Title and frequency of publication have varied: 1961
and 1965 editions were entitled *Museums Directory of the United States and
Canada*. Present title and biennial schedule were adopted in 1971. The 1973
edition has approximately 5,100 entries, covering museums of all types.
Prefatory material includes information about the American Association of
Museums and a display advertising section. The heart of the directory is arranged
geographically by country (United States, Canada, Puerto Rico) and then
alphabetically by state or province, subarranged alphabetically by city. Information provided includes: name, address, and date of founding; director; scope
of collections and areas of specialization; facilities; activities; hours and
admission prices. Does not mention individual paintings or other museum
objects. Supplementary access provided by these sections: institutions by name
alphabetically; directors and department heads; institutions by category;
museum associations of the United States; foreign museum associations, etc.

319. Porter, Arthur, ed. **Directory of Art and Antique Restoration: A Guide
      to Art and Antique Restorers Throughout the United States**. San
      Francisto: the Author, 1972.
Author's address: 465 California Street, San Francisco, Calif. 94104. Both firms
and individuals are listed. Arrangement is geographical (first by states and then
by cities).

320. **The Year's Art**, 1880-1947, 1968-69– . London: Hutchinson,
      1880-1947, 1969– ; distr. New York: Putnam, 1971– . Annual.
Subtitle of original: "a concise epitome of all matters relating to the arts of
painting, sculpture, engraving and architecture and to schools of design, which
have occurred during the year...." Subtitle of revised version: "Europe and the
U.S.A.: architecture–art criticism–design–museums–painting and sculpture–
people–salesrooms." Newer version gives nearly half its space to auctions and
prices.

Histories

321. **Ancient Peoples and Places**. Gen. ed., Glyn Daniels. New York: Praeger,
      1956– .

LC catalogs each title separately. Many libraries make a series added entry. For a list of titles, see *Titles in Series*, by Eleanora A. Baer (2nd ed. Scarecrow Press, 1964) and supplements.

322.   Arnason, H. Harvard. **History of Modern Art: Painting, Sculpture, Architecture**. New York: H. N. Abrams, 1968. 663p.

Chronologically arranged. Includes biographical sketches of major artists of nineteenth and twentieth centuries. Black and white illustrations are on the same page as the corresponding text. Color plates are nearby.

323.   **Art of the World: The Historical, Sociological and Religious Backgrounds**. New York: Crown, 1959– .

Highly regarded series of regional art histories. LC catalogs separately, but with a series added entry. For brief listing, see latest publisher's catalog or A. J. Walford's *Guide to Reference Material*, or supplements I and II of the second edition of *Titles in Series*, by Eleanora A. Baer.

324.   **Art Since Mid-Century: The New Internationalism**. Greenwich, Conn.: New York Graphic Society, 1972. 2 vols.

Essays on various movements cover history, relation to other movements, and leading exponents. An appendix contains personal statements of artists. Plates are keyed to the text and numbered, but not titled; they cannot be found by title in the index.

325.   **The Arts of Mankind**. Gen. eds., André Malraux and Georges Salles. New York: Golden Press, 1961– .

LC catalogs each title separately, but with a series added entry. For a list of titles, see A. J. Walford's *Guide to Reference Material* or Supplement II of the second edition of *Titles in Series*, by Eleanora A. Baer.

326.   Bazin, Germain. **A History of Art: From Prehistoric Times to the Present**. Boston: Houghton Mifflin, 1959. 574p.

An authoritative work, written by the Chief Curator of the Louvre. One British reviewer thought it less balanced than E. H. Gombrich's *The Story of Art* (12th ed. New York: Praeger, 1972), but other critics tended to regard it more highly.

327.   Bunt, Cyril George Edward. **A History of Russian Art**. New York: Studio, 1946. 272p.

Coverage of all phases of art from the pre-Christian period to time of publication. Generally authoritative and factual. The illustrations (about 200) are well selected and generally of good quality.

328.   Bussagli, Mario, and Calembus Sivara Mamurti. **5,000 Years of the Art of India**. Tr. by Anna Maria Brainerd. New York: H. N. Abrams, 1971. 335p.

Despite differences of approach by the two authors and some unevenness in the quality of the nearly 400 color illustrations, this book is generally recommended.

329.   Clapp, Jane. **Art Censorship: A Chronology of Proscribed and Pre-scripted Art**. Metuchen, N.J.: Scarecrow Press, 1972. 582p.
Covers painting, sculpture, graphic arts, decorative arts, and architecture. Excludes photography. The basic arrangement is chronological, and brief information about each incident is given. The index leads to the chronology (by date rather than page number) and includes: artists' names, titles of works of art, and various subjects (e.g., geographic locations, art forms, themes) as well as reasons for censorship (e.g., blasphemy, heresy, obscenity, etc.). The illustrations (one color, 33 black and white) are generally of unexciting quality. There is an extensive bibliography.

330.   **Columbia University Studies in Art History and Archaeology**. Gen. ed., Rudolf Wittkower. New York: Random House, 1965– .
LC catalogs each title separately, but with a series added entry. For a list of titles, see the first supplement to the second edition of *Titles in Series*, by Eleanora A. Baer.

331.   Cook, Robert Manuel. **Greek Art: Its Development, Character and Influence**. New York: Farrar, Straus and Giroux, 1973. 277p.
Author is a professor of classical archaeology at Cambridge University. Covers the eleventh to first centuries B.C. Good illustrations (96p.). Index.

332.   Gardner, Helen. **Art through the Ages**. 4th ed. New York: Harcourt, Brace, 1959. 795p.
Intended for high school and college students as well as general readers. Many illustrations. Bibliographies at the ends of chapters. Glossary. Index.

333.   Gombrich, Ernest Hans Joseph. **The Story of Art**. 12th ed. New York: Praeger, 1972. 498p.
Considered especially attractive for the beginner. British viewpoint. Criticized by some reviewers for omission of certain American and Continental European artists.

334.   Grabar, Oleg. **The Formation of Islamic Art**. New Haven: Yale University Press, 1973. 233p.
Concentrates on seventh to ninth centuries. Scholarly work, with an excellent critical bibliography. Illustrations (131) are black and white.

335.   Grousset, René. **Chinese Art and Culture**. Tr. from the French by Haakon Chevalier. New York: Orion Press, 1959. 331p.
A work by a noted scholar in the field. Now a bit out of date in some details, but still an excellent (if not easy) overview. There are 64 plates (16 in color) of high quality. Its reference value is enhanced by bibliographical footnotes, a chronology of Chinese dynasties, and a detailed index.

336.   Hare, Richard. **The Art and Artists Russia**. Greenwich, Conn.: New York Graphic Society, 1965. 294p.
Covers period from early Byzantine to twentieth century. Has 32 excellent color

plates, a bibliography, and an index. Some reviewers dispute his critical judgments on the later periods, and others point out that his scope tends to be limited to the urban art of Kiev, Novgorod, St. Petersburg, and Moscow.

337.   Hartt, Frederick. **History of Italian Renaissance Art: Painting, Sculpture, Architecture**. New York: H. N. Abrams, 1969. 636p.

First single volume in English to treat painting, sculpture, and architecture of period. Author includes at least a small reproduction of each of the more than 800 works of art he discusses. Three main sections: Late Middle Ages; Quattrocento; Cinquecento. Each is subdivided by place or form. Well written and well edited. Glossary. Chronological chart. Index to artists' works and subjects. There are 80 color prints and 731 black and white; for each is given date, medium, size, location of original.

338.   Hauser, Arnold. **The Social History of Art**. Tr. by Stanley Godman. New York: Alfred A. Knopf, 1951. 2 vols. Reprinted New York: Vintage, 1958-60. 4 vols.

A major work by a noted German scholar, reflecting more than 30 years of study. Concentrates on the manner in which social forces shaped the development of painting, architecture, sculpture, folk arts, literature, theatre, and music. Excellent subject index.

339.   Hofmann, Werner. **Turning Points in 20th Century Art: 1890-1917**. Tr. by Charles Kessler. New York: G. Braziller, 1969. 286p.

Explores what the author regards as the decline of easel painting in favor of more total expression. Not a book for beginners, but stimulating for the specialist.

340.   Janson, Horst Woldemar, and Dora Janson. **History of Art: A Survey of the Major Visual Arts from the Dawn of History to the Present Day**. Rev. and enl. New York: H. N. Abrams, 1969. 616p.

Generally regarded as a solid and comprehensive overview from a traditional Western approach. More advanced than Gombrich. Good as a text. Well illustrated, but one reviewer thought the black and white plates better than the color. Good index and bibliography.

341.   Larkin, Oliver Waterman. **Art and Life in America**. Rev. and enl. ed. New York: Holt, 1960. 559p.

Covers architecture, painting, and sculpture. More specialized is *North American Indian Arts*, by A. H. Whiteford (New York: Golden Press, 1970).

342.   **Library of Art History**. Ed. by H. W. Janson. New York: H. N. Abrams, 1971– .

LC catalogs and classifies separately, but with a series added entry. Represents the combined efforts of a distinguished editor and a major art book publisher.

343.   Louis-Frederic, pseud. **Japan: Art and Civilization**. New York: H. N. Abrams, 1971 (c.1969). 504p.

A survey of Japanese civilization and art from prehistoric times until 1868. There are 430 black and white photographs (concentrating heavily on sculpture and architecture) and 49 line drawings. Most chapters include a cultural chart at the end. Appendices include ancient calendar; tables of emperors, etc.; great schools of Japanese painting; glossary, and brief bibliography. Index. Captions describing photographs appear on pages preceding. Though photographs are clearly numbered, this paging back and forth is an inconvenience.

344.   New York Museum of Modern Art. **Masters of Modern Art**. Ed. by Alfred H. Barr, Jr. Rev. ed. New York: Doubleday, 1958. 239p.
Includes nearly 300 black and white illustrations and about 75 color plates based on the works in the Museum's permanent collection. Reviewers were generally enthusiastic about the illustrations (both selection and quality) and the accompanying commentary.

345.   **The Oxford History of English Art**. Ed. by T. S. R. Boase. New York: Oxford University Press, 1949– .
A major series, planned for 11 volumes. For a list of titles, see Walford's *Guide to Reference Material*.

346.   **Panorama of World Art**. New York: H. N. Abrams, 1968-72. 18 vols.
Another notable series by this outstanding publisher of art books. LC classifies and catalogs separately, without a series added entry. Early volumes are listed in the second supplement to *Titles in Series*, by Eleanora A. Baer.

347.   **The Pelican History of Art**. Gen. ed., Nikolaus Pevsner. Baltimore: Penguin Books, 1953– .
Planned to cover world art and architecture in 50 volumes. Highly regarded for text and illustrations. LC catalogs each title separately but with a series added entry. For a list, see A. J. Walford's *Guide to Reference Material* or Eleanora A. Baer's *Titles in Series* (2nd ed., 1964) and supplements. Considered vital by over 60 percent of the art librarians surveyed by Larsen.

348.   Pevsner, Nikolaus. **Studies in Art, Architecture, and Design**. New York: Walker, 1968. 2 vols.
A collection of 28 essays, some of which first appeared in the 1920s. Nearly 800 black and white illustrations.

349.   Robb, David Methany, and Jessie J. Garrison. **Art in the Western World**. 4th ed. New York: Harper & Row, 1963. 782p.
Long regarded as an excellent introduction to all phases of art: architecture, sculpture, painting, minor arts. Other features include a chronological and topical concordance, glossary, bibliography, chronological table, index to illustrations (over 650), general index. Considered "vital" or "recommended" by nearly a third of the art librarians surveyed by Larsen.

350.   **Sources and Documents in the History of Art**. Gen. ed., H. W. Janson. Englewood Cliffs, N.J.: Prentice-Hall, 1965– .
LC catalogs and classifies separately but with a series entry.

351. **The Taste of Our Time**. New York: Skira, 1954– .
LC catalogs each title separately. Many libraries make a series added entry. For a list, see the 1970 catalog of the World Publishing Company in the 1970 *Publishers' Trade List Annual*.

352. **Unesco World Art Series**. Greenwich, Conn.: New York Graphic Society, 1954– .
LC catalogs and classifies each title separately, but uses "United Nations Educational, Scientific and Cultural Organization" as the main entry and makes a series added entry. For a list, see Supplement I to *Titles in Series*, by Eleanora A. Baer (2nd ed. Scarecrow Press, 1964).

353. Venturi, A. **Storia dell'arte italiana**. Milan: Hoepli, 1901-1940. 11 vols. in 25 parts. Reprinted New York: Kraus, 1967.
Regarded by many critics as the most authoritative and comprehensive history of Italian art. Difficult to use because there is no combined index for all 11 volumes, although each part has its own indexes of places and artists.

354. Willett, Frank. **African Art: An Introduction**. New York: Praeger, 1971. 288p.
Hailed by reviewers as the best introduction to African art yet available, this book sets art in its wider social and historical context. There is an excellent bibliography, and the illustrations (188 black and white, 61 color) are of good quality, well chosen and titled, and carefully documented. Index.

355. Wölfflin, Heinrich. **Principles of Art History: The Problem of the Development of Style in Later Art**. Tr. by M. D. Hottinger. London: G. Bell, 1932. Reprinted New York: Peter Smith, 1950. 237p.
Long established as a classic in the field. This English translation is from the seventh German edition (1929).

356. **Yale Publications in the History of Art**. New Haven: Yale University Press, 1939– .
LC catalogs separately but with a series added entry. For a list of volumes still in print see the publisher's latest catalog.

Biographies

357. Ainesworth, Edward Maddin. **The Cowboy in Art**. New York: World, 1968. 242p.
Gives information about cowboy artists as well as paintings of cowboys. Over 200 illustrations, some in color. Text includes names, dates, and biographies.

358. Bénézit, Emmanuel. **Dictionnaire critique et documentaire des peintres, sculpteurs, dessinateurs et graveurs de tous les pays, par un groupe d'écrivains spécialistes français et étrangers**. Nouv. éd. entièrement refondue, rév. et corr. Paris: Librairie Grund, 1956-61 (c.1948-55). 8 vols.

Long a vital source of biographical information even for relatively minor figures. Rated next to *Art Index* as the second most vital source by art librarians. Includes artists from earliest times to the present. Entries vary in length, but usually include a list of chief works and the museums that owned them at the time of compilation. Reproductions of symbols and signatures are given with artists' names, and reproductions of signatures used by anonymous artists will be found at the end of each key letter of the alphabet.

359.   Bryan, Michael. **Bryan's Dictionary of Painters and Engravers**. New (4th) ed. rev. and enl. by G. C. Williamson. London: Bell, 1903-1905. Reprinted Port Washington, N.Y.: Kennikat Press, 1964. 5 vols. Largest such effort in English. About 20,000 entries. Longer articles signed by specialists. Usually lists of chief works and locations. Less current than Bénézit or Thieme and Becker. Some monograms are with articles and others are on pages 421 to 425 of Vol. 5. Still rated as vital by nearly half the art librarians in a 1971 survey.

360.   Cummings, Paul. **A Dictionary of Contemporary American Artists**. 2nd ed. New York: St. Martin's Press, 1971. 368p.
Includes 787 artists, chosen on basis of representation in museums and collections. Entries are concise and concentrate on professional activities. Each entry has a short bibliography, with citations only by surnames, leading to full citations in the bibliography at the back of the book (pp. 343-68). There are about 100 black and white illustrations of varying size and quality. (Many do, however, show the artist's most recent style.) Pronunciations of less common names are given in the "Index of Artists and Pronunciation Guide" (pp. 1-10). Interpretation of individual entries will require frequent reference to the "Key to Museums and Institutions and Their Schools" (pp. 11-34). Another useful feature is the list of addresses of "Galleries Representing the Artists in this Book" (pp. 35-42), although one could wish for more consistency in the inclusion of zip codes. More specialized is *Afro-American Artists: A Bio-Bibliographical Dictionary* (Boston: Boston Public Library, 1973).

361.   Fielding, Mantle. **Dictionary of American Painters, Sculptors and Engravers**. With an addendum containing corrections and additional material on the original entries. Comp. by James F. Carr. New York: J. F. Carr, 1965. 529p.
Covers about 8,000 artists. Rated as vital by 75 percent of the art librarians who responded in a 1971 survey.

362.   Goldstein, Franz. **Monogramm Lexikon: Internationales Verzeichnis der Monogramme Bildenden Künstler seit 1850**. Berlin: Walter de Gruyter, 1964. 931p. "About 20,000 monograms from all countries, with small but clear reproductions (p. 1-810). Supplementary lists of figures and signs, of anonymous artists, and of Cyrillic characters. Name index, p. 835-931" [A. J. Walford, *Guide to Reference Material, Vol. III: Generalities, Languages, the Arts and Literature* (2nd ed. London: Library Association, 1970), p.275]. Suggested by art museum librarians as a vital addition to the Larsen list.

363.   Havlice, Patricia Pate. **Index to Artistic Biography**. Metuchen, N.J.:
Scarecrow Press, 1973. 2 vols.
International coverage of 70,000 artists whose biographies appeared in 64
reference works published between 1902 and 1970. This source gives dates,
nationality, media, pseudonyms, variant name spellings, and coding to the 64
works indexed.

364.   **The Index of Twentieth Century Artists**, Vols. 1-4, No. 7, Oct. 1933—
April 1937. New York: College Art Association, 1933-37. 4 vols.
Reprinted New York: Arno Press, 1970. 4 vols. in 1.
Articles on 120 American artists, which appeared in the monthly issues.
Biographies included information about honors, awards, and exhibitions. The
reprint includes an index.

365.   **International Who's Who in Art and Antiques**. Totowa, N.J.: Rowman
and Littlefield, 1972. 679p.
Contains about 4,000 biographies of collectors, sculptors, painters, dealers,
educators, gallery and museum directors, etc. Covers 58 countries. Narrower in
national scope but broader in subject focus is *Creative Canada: A Biographical
Dictionary of Twentieth-Century Creative and Performing Artists* (Toronto:
University of Toronto Press, 1971—).

366.   **Khudozhnik: Narodov SSSR: Bibliograficheskii Slovar**. Moskva: Izd.
"Iskusstvo," 1970— .
A major biographical dictionary to be completed in six volumes, with entries for
20,000 painters, sculptors, architects, graphic and decorative artists, theater and
movie designers (both native and foreign) who have worked in some part of what
is now the Soviet Union from ancient times to the present.

367.   Mallett, Daniel Trowbridge. **Mallett's Index of Artists, Including
Painters, Sculptors, Illustrators, Engravers and Etchers of the Past and
Present**. New York: R. R. Bowker, 1935. Supplement, 1940. Reprinted
New York: Peter Smith, 1948. 2 vols.
Gives brief biographical information and refers to 22 general and over 1,000
specialized sources. Makes heavy use of symbols. Valuable for minor artists,
despite some inaccuracies. Regarded as vital by over half the art librarians in the
Larsen survey.

368.   New York Historical Society. **Dictionary of Artists in America,
1564-1860**. By George C. Croce and David H. Wallace. New Haven:
Yale University Press, 1957. 759p.
Biographical information concerning some 11,000 painters, draftsmen, sculptors,
engravers, lithographers, etc. Among the top ten vital titles in the Larsen survey.

369.   Thieme, Ulrich, and Felix Becker. **Allgemeines Lexikon der Bildenden
Kunstler von der Antike bis zur Gegenwart**. Leipzig: Seemann,
1907-1950. 37 vols. Reprinted by Seemann, 1965.
This is the most comprehensive and authoritative biographical directory in any

language. Lists nearly 50,000 artists (mostly painters and engravers, but sculptors and architects as well). About 400 German and foreign experts contributed articles. The longer ones are signed. Locations of art works are often given. Bibliographies are frequently included. Includes a few living persons, but these are generally reserved for Vollmer's work on twentieth century artists.

370.   Vasari, Giorgio. **Lives of the Most Eminent Painters, Sculptors and Architects**. Tr. by Gaston du C. De Vere. London: Macmillan, 1912-15. 10 vols.

First published in 1550, this is the classic source for biographies of Italian Renaissance artists. De Vere's translation is the most reliable in English. Over 500 illustrations.

371.   Vollmer, Hans. **Allgemeines Lexikon der Bildenden Kunstler des XX Jahrhunderts**. Leipzig: Seemann, 1953-62. 6 vols.

A continuation of Thieme and Becker. Includes some overlap from the nineteenth century. Gives brief biographical notes, lists of works, and bibliographical references. Approximately 6,000 entires.

372.   **Who's Who in American Art**, Vol. 1– , 1936/37– . New York: R. R. Bowker, 1935– .

Biennial, but sometimes irregular. Eleventh edition, 1973. Biographical data on 6,500 painters, sculptors, illustrators, craftsmen, engravers, museum executives and art patrons. Basic arrangement is alphabetical, supplemented by a geographical index. Separate section for Canadian biographies. Schedule of national, regional, and state open exhibitions. The 1973 edition has a Professional Classification Index.

373.   **Who's Who in Art: Biographies of Leading Men and Women in the World of Art Today–Artists, Designers, Craftsmen, Critics, Writers, Teachers, Collectors and Curators, with an Appendix of Signatures**. Havant, Hants.: Art Trade Press, 1927– .

Biennial, but sometimes irregular in the past. Usually contains about 4,000 short biographies, with British artists predominating. Appendices typically include: monograms and signatures; obituaries; abbreviations.

374.   Young, William. **A Dictionary of America's Artists, Sculptors and Engravers: From the Beginning Through the Turn of the Twentieth Century** . . . Cambridge, Mass., W. Young, 1968. 515p.

Has a large number of very brief entries. Quite useful for identification of obscure artists; less so for details on people reasonably well known. No bibliographies.

Art Reproductions

Note: Other sources are given under the heading **Painting–Reproductions**

375.   American Library Color Slide Company, Inc., New York. **The American Library Compendium and Index of World Art: Architecture, Sculpture,**

Painting and the Minor Arts as Compiled from the Archives of the American Library of Color Slides. New York: American Archives of World Art, 1961. 465p.

Arranged by period and then by country. Special section on survey sets and basic slide libraries. Slides may be obtained from the firm. Supplemented by *Teacher's Manual for the Study of Art History and Related Courses* (Rev. ed., 1968). Unfortunately, many of the slides available from this source are somewhat expensive and not of the highest quality.

376. Avid Corporation, P.O. Box 4263, Trips Lane, East Providence, R.I. 02914.

Coverage for color slides includes art and architecture, East and West, from the earliest times to the present. Slides are of high quality and are less expensive than from many alternative sources. Catalogs and other information available on request.

377. Bartran, Margaret. **A Guide to Color Reproductions**. 2nd ed. Metuchen, N.J.: Scarecrow Press, 1971. 625p.

Intended primarily as a handbook for retail print dealers but useful to art librarians as well. Covers range of art reproductions available in the United States at the beginning of 1969. Intended as a quick first step which would lead to publishers' catalogs for more detailed information. Limited to color reproductions commercially available in sheet form. The first part is alphabetical by artist (subarranged alphabetically by title); it gives information on size of reproduction, source for ordering, and price. The second part is an index of titles, which refers back to the first part. Over 12,000 reproductions are listed.

378. Clapp, Jane. **Art in Life**. Metuchen, N.J.: Scarecrow Press, 1959. 504p. Suppl., 1965. 379p.

Index (by author, title, and subject) of reproductions of paintings and graphic arts in *Life* magazine. Also includes selected photographs of architecture, sculpture, and decorative arts, plus portraits of artists and historical and literary personages.

379. Clapp, Jane. **Art Reproductions**. Metuchen, N.J.: Scarecrow Press, 1961. 350p.

List of reproductions available from 95 museums in the United States and Canada. Arrangement is by medium (e.g., painting) and then by scale. Index includes names of artists, of individuals portrayed, and a few subjects.

380. Havlice, Patricia Pate. **Art in Time**. Metuchen, N.J.: Scarecrow Press, 1970. 350p.

Indexes all the photographs and art reproductions in the art section of *Time* magazine from 1923 to 1969. Artist/title index in single alphabet, with selective (rather than comprehensive) subject entries. *Time* is not covered in *Art Index* or *Illustration Index*. Thus this work fills a need, especially for school and public libraries.

381.   International Portrait Gallery. **Basic Collection**. Detroit: Gale Research
        Co., 1968. **Supplemental Collection**, 1970.
Basic Collection has 750 black and white portraits (8½" by 11") of authors,
actors, musicians, explorers, statesmen, etc. *Supplemental Collection* has 500
portraits, including characters of fiction and mythology. Both have master
indexes by name and profession. Very expensive. No reviews concerning quality.

382.   **Multi-Media Programs for the Humanities: From Macmillan and the
        Metropolitan Museum of Art**. Riverside, N.J.: Macmillan Library
        Services, 1973– .
Each program includes: a set of slides (mostly in color); a lecture (33 1/3 rpm)
prepared by staff of The Metropolitan Museum of Art; and curriculum manuals.
Titles currently available include: *Rembrandt: Love and Compassion*; *Art of
Black Africa*; *Art of Discovery*; *Ways of Seeing Abstract Painting*; *Tutankha-
men's Treasures*; *Protest and Hope* (lecture on Picasso's "Guernica").

383.   New York Graphic Society. **Fine Art Reproductions of Old and Modern
        Masters: A Comprehensive Illustrated Catalog of Art Through the Ages**.
        8th rev. ed. Ed. by Anton Schutz. Greenwich, Conn.: New York
        Graphic Society, 1968. 420p.

384.   Pierson, William Harvey, and Martha Davidson, eds. **Arts of the United
        States: A Pictorial Survey**. New York: McGraw-Hill, 1960. 452p.
Authors surveyed American art and selected 4,000 examples to be made into
color slides for use of schools, museums, and libraries. Arranged by subject. Each
section is introduced by an essay and followed by small black and white
reproductions of the slides. Index of artists, titles, and subjects. For information
on what the New York State Library has done to make this collection available
to public library users, see "Slides of the Arts of the United States," by Jack B.
Spear, in *The Bookmark* 29 (November 1969): 77-79.

385.   Sloane, Patricia. "Color Slides for Teaching Art History," **Art Journal**
        31 (Spring 1972): 276-80.
A critical analysis of the quality of art slides available from museums and
commercial sources. The author teaches art history at the New York City
Community College of the City University of New York. At the conclusion of
the article, a letter is printed from Nancy de Laurier, University of Missouri at
Kansas City, stating that the College Art Association of America has prepared a
Slide Buyer's Guide, which evaluates both commercial and museum slides.

386.   Special Libraries Association. Picture Division. **Picture Sources**. Ed. by
        Celestine G. Frankenberg. 2nd ed. New York: Special Libraries Associa-
        tion, 1964. 216p.
Basic divisions are first by subject and then by non-commercial and commercial
sources. Of particular interest is the section on "Fine, Graphic, and Applied
Arts" (entries 201-288, pp. 52-72).

387. University Prints, Cambridge, Massachusetts. **The University Prints: Fine Art Reproductions for Students . . . Complete Catalogue**. Cambridge, Mass., University Prints, 1931– . 1972 ed., 278p.

Subtitle: "Listing by period, school and artist all 7,000 basic fine arts subjects–architecture, painting, sculpture–available both as slides and as prints. All prints a uniform 5½" x 8" in black and white . . . 275 in color. Available loose leaf or custom bound." Useful for college-level teaching. Selected and frequently revised by specialists.

388. Vance, Lucile E., and Esther M. Tracey. **Illustration Index**. 2nd ed. Metuchen, N.J.: Scarecrow Press, 1966. 527p.

Covers the period from 1950 through June 1963. Type of illustration is indicated if it is other than a photograph. Does not include furniture, nature subjects, portraits, or paintings (unless paintings portray historical events or have information of a general nature). Arranged alphabetically by subject.

Art Librarianship

389. **ARLIS Newsletter**, No. 1, October 1969– . Issued by Art Libraries Society, Coventry Collection of Art and Design, Coventry, England.

390. **ARLIS/NA Newsletter**, Vol. 1, No. 1, November 1972– .

Further information available from Judith A. Hoffenberg, Brand Library, 1601 West Mountain Street, Glendale, California 91201.

391. Broxis, Peter F. **Organising the Arts**. Hamden, Conn.: Archon Books, 1968. 132p.

A manual of practice for art librarians, covering such topics as treatment of art in general classification schemes; a faceted classification for the arts; descriptive cataloging; subject cataloging; indexing periodicals; and visual materials and art libraries. British viewpoint.

392. **Directory of Art Libraries and Art Librarians in North America**. Ed. by Martha Kehde, Art Librarian, University of Kansas. Date and publisher to be announced.

393. Freitag, Wolfgang M. **Art Libraries and Collections**. New York: Dekker, 1968.

Reprinted from Vol. 1 of *Encyclopedia of Library and Information Science* (pp. 571-622).

394. Freitag, Wolfgang M., ed. **State-of-the-Art Handbook for Art Librarianship**. Date and publisher to be announced.

Joint venture of Art Libraries Society of North America (ARLIS/NA) and Art Libraries Society of the United Kingdom (ARLIS/UK). Freitag is Librarian of Fogg Art Museum, Harvard University.

395.   Garvey, Mona. **Library Displays: Their Purpose, Construction, and Use**. New York: Wilson, 1969. 88p.

Chapters on design components, lettering, layout, cartooning. Author has background in art as well as librarianship. Especially useful for school and public libraries.

396.   Irvine, Betty Jo. "Slide Classification: A Historical Survey," **College and Research Libraries** 32 (January 1971): 23-30.

"The historical background of slide collections is treated, with bibliographic references. The major portion of the paper reports and analyzes some of the data derived from a 1968 questionnaire directed to institutions having slide collections" (Abstract).

397.   Irvine, Betty Jo. **Slide Libraries: A Guide for Academic Institutions and Museums**. Littleton, Colo.: Libraries Unlimited, 1974, 256p.

The Fine Arts Librarian, Indiana University, has prepared a manual for librarians that covers acquisitions, cataloging, facilities, equipment, organization, and administration. Includes directory of manufacturers and distributors.

398.   Larsen, John C. "The Use of Art Reference Sources in Museum Libraries," **Special Libraries** (November 1971): 481-86.

"This paper investigates the use in museum libraries of the art reference sources most commonly studied by students at ALA-accredited schools. Reference sources were rated by librarians in 45 United States art museums as vital, recommended, or peripheral. Additional titles suggested by the practising librarians are enumerated" (Abstract).

399.   **Worldwide Art and Library Newsletter**, Vol. 1, No. 1– , September 1972– .

Devoted to art librarianship. Published monthly during the academic year (nine issues). Edited (1973) by Judith C. Joy and published by Worldwide Books, Inc., 1075 Commonwealth Ave., Boston, Mass. 02215.

Handbooks

Note: This is but a small selection from the many
books available. Others will be found in
library catalogs under such headings as
"Art–Technique" and "Artists' Materials."

400.   Cooke, Hereward Lester. **Painting Techniques of the Masters**. Rev. and enl. ed. New York: Watson-Guptill, 1972. 269p.

Published in cooperation with the National Gallery of Art. Reproduces major paintings from the fifteenth to the twentieth centuries in high quality color and accompanies each by informative comments on technique, with sketches to illustrate particular points.

401.   Massey, Robert. **Formulas for Painters**. New York: Watson-Guptill, 1967. 224p.

Contains over 200 recipes for sizes, grounds, media, glazes, varnishes, fixatives, and adhesives. Cross references. Bibliography. Index.

402. Mayer, Ralph. **The Artist's Handbook of Materials and Techniques**. 3rd ed. New York: Viking Press, 1970. 750p.

This title was suggested by art librarians in the Larsen survey for addition to his basic list of vital works.

Art Sales

403. **Art at Auction: The Year at Sotheby's and Parke-Bernet**. 223rd season, 1966/67– . New York: Viking Press.

Arranged in chapters on various topics. Good table of contents. Profusely illustrated, often in color. For each item sold there is a picture, description, sale price, and date of sale. Two indexes: General Index; Index of Books, Manuscripts and Miniatures.

404. **Art Prices Current**. London: Art Trade Press, 1908– . Annual.

Arranged by medium: Pt. A, Paintings, drawings, and miniatures; Pt. B, Engravings and prints. Each part is arranged chronologically by sales, with items within that part numbered consecutively. Artist, title, size, purchaser, price, and sometimes conditions are given. Indexes of artists, engravers, and collectors.

405. Berard, Michele. **Encyclopedia of Modern Art and Auction Prices**. New York: Arco, 1972. 417p.

From impressionists to the present. Covers auctions from 1961 to 1969 and includes 282 painters whose works brought over $2,000 each.

406. Chamberlain, Betty. **The Artist's Guide to His Market**. New York: Watson-Guptill, 1970. 128p.

Written by the founder of the Art Information Center, New York. Advice on exhibiting, galleries, pricing, selling, commissions, contracts, publicity, and artists' groups. Limited to New York.

407. **International Auction Records**, 1967– . New York: Editions Publison, 1967– .

Annual. Formerly *International Yearbook of Sales*. Covers both the United States and abroad. Arranged in five parts (engravings, drawings, watercolors, paintings, sculpture), then alphabetically by artist. Gives size and price. Some illustrations. Calendar index.

408. Lancour, Harold. **American Art Auction Catalogues, 1785-1942: A Union List**. New York: New York Public Library, 1944. 377p.

A union checklist of more than 7,000 catalogs of auction sales of art objects. Locates copies in 21 libraries. Includes list of auction houses and index of owners.

409.   Lugt, Fritz. **Répertoire des catalogues de ventes publiques**. The Hague: Nijhof, 1938– . Vol. 1, to 1825 (1938); Vol. 2, 1826-1860 (1964); Vol. 3, 1861-1900 (1964); Vol. 4, 1901-1925.

Chronological list of catalogs of art sales. Information for each entry includes date and place of sale, provenance, contents, number of items and pages, auctioneers, and locations of copies in libraries. Index of names of collections sold.

Periodicals

410.   **AIA Journal**, 1900– . Monthly American Institute of Architects, 1785 Massachusetts Ave., N.W., Washington, D.C. 20036.

Indexed in: *Art Index*. A professional journal with a wide range of articles and technical information for both the practicing architect and the student.

411.   **American Artist** 1937– . Monthly (Sept.–June). Billboard Publications, Inc., 165 W. 46th St., New York, N.Y. 10036.

Indexed in: *Reader's Guide, Art Index, Abridged Reader's Guide, Public Affairs Information Service*. For the amateur or "Sunday painters." Articles on technique by well-known practitioners. Occasionally articles on famous artists from the standpoint of elementary appreciation.

412.   **Apollo: The International Magazine of Art**, 1925– . Monthly. Apollo Publications, Inc., 551 Fifth Ave., New York, N.Y. 10019.

Indexed in: *Art Index, British Humanities Index*. Articles on history of art, book reviews, news of auctions and other sales. For collectors.

413.   **Architectural Forum**, 1892– . 10 per year. Whitney Publications, Inc., 130 E. 59th St., New York, N.Y. 10022.

Indexed in: *Art Index, Applied Science and Technology Index, Reader's Guide, Current Index to Journals in Education, Public Affairs Information Service*. Concerned with total environment. Each issue has a review of notable buildings.

414.   **Architectural Record**, 1891– . Monthly. McGraw-Hill, Inc., Box 430, Hightstown, N.J. 08520.

Indexed in: *Applied Science and Technology Index, Art Index, Engineering Index, Reader's Guide, Current Index to Journals in Education*. Well illustrated. Vast amounts of technical information for architects and engineers. The emphasis on homes also makes it of more general interest.

415.   **Art Bulletin**, 1912– . Quarterly. College Art Association of America, 432 Park Ave. S., New York, N.Y. 10016.

Indexed in: *Art Index*. Long, scholarly articles on all fields of art history, and short notices. Lengthy, signed book reviews. Index to Vols. 1-21 (1917-1948) published in 1950. Major journal for art historians in the United States. Available on microform.

416.   **Art in America**, 1913– . Bi-monthly. Art in America, Inc., 150 E. 58th St., New York, N.Y. 10022.

Indexed in: *Art Index, Reader's Guide*. One of the best, perhaps the best, of the general art periodicals. Each issue has many excellent plates (both color and black and white). Coverage includes painting, sculpture, architecture, design, and photography.

417.   **Art International**, 1956– . 10 per year. James Fitzimmons, Via Maraini 17-A, Lugano, Switzerland.

Indexed in: *Art Index*. Most important periodical covering modern developments in European art. For the professional artist. Includes information on competitions, prizes, and auction sales.

418.   **Art News**, 1902– . Monthly (Sept.–May); Quarterly (June–Aug.). Newsweek, 444 Madison Ave., New York, N.Y. 10022.

Indexed in: *Art Index, Reader's Guide*. Aimed at professional artists but also of interest to collectors. Very strong on contemporary art, especially new developments in the United States. Reviews of current exhibitions.

419.   **Art Quarterly**, 1938– . Quarterly. Detroit Institute of Arts, 5200 Woodward Ave., Detroit, Mich. 48202.

Indexed in: *Art Index*. Scholarly and well illustrated. "Archives of American Art" section lists important acquisitions of American museums. Short reviews of books and museum publications.

420.   **Bollettino d'arte**, 1907– . Istituto Polygrafico dello Stato, Rome.

Indexed in: *Art Index*. Official publication of Ministry of Public Instruction. Essential tool for study of Italian art and architecture, with emphasis on classical period. Lengthy, scholarly articles and book reviews. Illustrations are well printed.

421.   **Burlington Magazine**, 1903– . Monthly. Burlington Magazine Publications, Ltd., 49 Park Lane, London, W.1, England.

Indexed in: *Art Index, British Humanities Index, Internationale Bibliographie der Zeitschriften-Literatur*. Research periodical. Covers art of all periods and countries. Both the lengthy articles and the short notices are carefully researched and written by scholars attached to universities and museums. Reviews of exhibitions. Bibliographies. Lengthy critical book reviews. The section "Publications Received" lists new books, museum publications and catalogs, and contents of periodicals. This section is particularly strong on foreign works often hard to trace.

422.   **The Connoisseur**, 1901– . Monthly. National Magazine Co., Ltd., Chestergate House, Vauxhall Bridge Road, London, S.W.1, England.

Indexed in: *Art Index, British Humanities Index*. For the art collector. Articles on painting and sculpture. Information on pottery, silverware, furniture, sales. Well printed and illustrated. Numerous color plates. Good book reviews. There is a section called "The Connoisseur in America" on American art news.

423.   **Design (U.S.)**, 1899– . Bi-monthly. Reviews Publishing Co., Inc., 1100 Waterway Blvd., Indianapolis, Ind. 46207.
Indexed in: *Reader's Guide*. Magazine of creative art for teachers, artists, and craftsmen. Book reviews. Illustrated. Also available on microform. Study and teaching of handicrafts.

424.   **Gazette des beaux arts**, 1859– . Monthly. Presses Universitaires de France, 12 rue Jean de Beauvais 12, 75 Paris (5e), France.
Indexed in: *Art Index*. Covers all aspects and periods in a scholarly manner, but with special emphasis on French art. In recent years, it has had a good many articles in English. Included with the periodical is a supplement, "La chronique des arts," which gives news of museum activities, collections, and exhibitions as well as short reviews of books.

425.   **Die Kunst und das schöne Heim**, 1885– . Monthly. Verlag Karl Thiemig KG, Pilgersheimer Str. 38, 8 Munich, 90, West Germany.
Popular articles on art and architecture, often modern, chiefly in German. Well illustrated. For collectors.

426.   **L'Oeil; revue d'art**, 1955– . Monthly. Sedo S.A., 33 Ave. de la Gare, Lausanne, Switzerland.
Indexed in: *Art Index*. Text in French. Art of many different periods. Superbly illustrated. For collectors.

427.   **Progressive Architecture**, 1920– . Monthly. Reinhold Publishing Corp., 25 Sullivan St., Westwood, N.J. 07695.
Indexed in: *Art Index, Applied Science and Technology Index. Avery Index to Architectural Periodicals, Current Index to Journals in Education*. One of the best general periodicals in the field. Emphasis on modern work. International coverage.

428.   **School Arts Magazine**, 1901– . Monthly. Davis Publications, Inc., Printers Bldg., Worcester, Mass. 01608.
Indexed in: *Education Index, Reader's Guide*. A magazine for art educators. Emphasis on arts and crafts teaching.

429.   **Studio International**, 1893– . Monthly. c/o Eastern News, 155 W. 15th St., New York, N.Y. 10011.
Indexed in: *Art Index, Internationale Bibliographie der Zeitschriften-Literatur*. Published in London, it is especially strong on modern British art. Well illustrated. For collectors. Covers book reviews, and provides information on exhibitions. Formerly titled *Studio*.

430.   **Zeitschrift für Kunstgeschichte**, 1924– . Quarterly. Deutscher Kunstverlag, Vohburger Str. 1, 8 Munich 42, West Germany.
Indexed in: *Art Index*. In a typical year, five issues appear, the last of which is a special bibliography issue devoted to art publications in the preceding year. Long scholarly articles and important book reviews.

PAINTING

Introductions

431. Barr, Alfred Hamilton. **What Is Modern Painting?** 9th ed. rev. New York: Museum of Modern Art; distr. Doubleday, 1966. 48p.

A small book that does not attempt to be art history but that does try to help the person looking at modern art for the first time. Illustrations (black and white) are numerous and closely related to the text.

432. Boas, George, and Harold Holmes Wrenn. **What Is a Picture?** New York: Schocken Books, 1966. 182p.

First published in 1964 by the University of Pittsburgh Press, this book is the result of collaboration between a philosophy professor and a practicing artist. Chapter titles: The Problem; A Picture as a Design upon a Flat Surface; Painting as Representation; Painting as Interpretation; Painting as Allegory; The Picture as an Emblem. There are 142 illustrations (black and white) representing a variety of schools from the Renaissance to the present. These are listed in the front, but there is no index of illustrations or general index.

433. Campbell, Ann. **Paintings: How to Look at Great Art**. New York: Franklin Watts, 1970. 136p.

Designed for children in grades 5 to 8, this book covers paintings from the earliest times to the beginning of the twentieth century. The color plates are excellent and are opposite the text that discusses them.

434. Gaunt, William. **A Guide to the Understanding of Painting**. New York: H. N. Abrams, 1968. 288p.

A guide by one who is both a writer and a painter.

435. Kulturmann, Udo. **The New Painting**. Tr. by Gerald Onn. New York: Praeger, 1970. 207p.

International coverage of painting since about 1950. Considered by some reviewers to be the best available guide. Arranged by subjects or formal themes. Illustrations were regarded as well chosen and reproduced, except for some of the color plates.

Dictionaries and Encyclopedias

436. Berckalaers, Ferdinand Louis. **A Dictionary of Abstract Painting, with a History of Abstract Painting by Michel Seuphor** (pseud.). New York: Tudor, 1957. 304p.

Translated from the French. Contents include history; chronology; dictionary (with short biographies of 500 abstract artists); bibliography. Many small illustrations (color).

437. Champlin, John Denison, Jr., and Charles C. Perkins. **Cyclopedia of Painters and Paintings**. Originally published 1886-87. Reissued Port Washington, N.Y.: Kennikat Press, 1969. 4 vols.

Reprinted in 1927 and again in 1969. Product of the late nineteenth century. An alphabetical arrangement of biographies of painters and descriptions of paintings. Also reproduces monograms and signatures of many painters. Relatively few plates and outline drawings. More recent sources are better for pictures. Entries have brief citations to sources, which are fully listed in Vol. 1.

438.   Daniel, Howard. **Encyclopedia of Themes and Subjects in Painting: Mythological, Biblical, Historical, Literary, Allegorical and Topical**. Introd. by John Berger. New York: H. N. Abrams, 1971. 252p.

Covers European painting from the Renaissance through the middle of the nineteenth century. Arrangement is alphabetical. About 400 subjects and about 300 illustrations (over 30 in color). List of illustrations and detailed information about originals is in the back. Lacks an overall index.

439.   **Dictionary of Modern Painting**. Gen. eds.: Carlton Lake and Robert Maillard. 3rd ed. rev. New York: Tudor, 1964. 416p.

Translated from the French, but with some additional entries. Includes art movements, artists, places, and schools of painting. Period covered: impressionists to World War II.

440.   **Encyclopedia of Painting: Painters and Painting of the World from Prehistoric Times to the Present Day**. Bernard S. Myers, ed. New York: Crown, 1955. 511p.

Covers painters, movements, styles, techniques, etc. Arrangement is alphabetical except for some Oriental painters (country and period). About 1,000 illustrations, some in color.

441.   Foskett, Daphne. **A Dictionary of British Miniature Painters**. New York: Praeger, 1972. 2 vols.

Vol. 1 gives brief information on 4,500 artists from 1520 to 1910 and includes 100 color reproductions. Vol. II consists entirely of plates (black and white), with 967 reproductions. Very expensive, but likely to remain the definitive work for many years to come. Much more comprehensive than Basil Long's *British Miniaturists, 1520-1860*, which had been the standard work on the subject since its appearance in 1929.

442.   Gaunt, William. **Everyman's Dictionary of Pictorial Art**. New York: Dutton, 1962. 2 vols.

Tries to provide brief information on painters, periods, etc., from all parts of the world from earliest times to the present. About 1,000 illustrations. Biographical sketches of 2,100 artists. Definitions of terms. Information on galleries. Some descriptions of famous paintings.

443.   Taubes, Frederic. **The Painter's Dictionary of Materials and Methods**. New York: Watson-Guptill, 1971. 253p.

Concentrates on technical advice needed when painting. Emphasizes purchase of materials now commercially available, in contrast to some older works, which contained information on preparation by hand. Numerous sketches of equipment.

Catalogs, Directories, and Annuals

444. Boston Museum of Fine Arts. **American Paintings in the Museum of Fine Arts, Boston**. Greenwich, Conn.: New York Graphic Society, 1969. 2 vols.

Scholarly, attractive catalog of over 1,000 American paintings and more than 600 illustrations, many in color. Each catalog entry gives description, measurements, provenance, a brief biography of artist, full bibliographical references, and exhibitions in which the painting has been displayed.

445. Hofstede de Groot, Cornelius. **A Catalogue Raisonné of the Works of the Most Eminent Dutch Painters of the Seventeenth Century: Based on the Work of John Smith**. Tr. and ed. by Edward G. Hawke. London: Macmillan, 1907-1927. 8 vols.

Concentrates on major painters and covers each in great detail. For each painting, the following types of information are given: condition, location, size, signature, sale date, and price. Index of collections and collectors is in Vol. 1; indexes of painters and engravers are in Vols. 2-8. No monograms or illustrations.

446. Morse, John D. **Old Masters in America**. Chicago: Rand McNally, 1955. 192p.

Lists works of 40 artists in various American galleries. A more specialized work is *Census of Pre-Nineteenth Century Italian Paintings in North American Collections*, by Burton B. Fredericksen and Federico Zeri (Cambridge: Harvard University Press, 1973).

447. Standen, Edith, and others. **Masterpieces of Painting in the Metropolitan Museum of Art**. Greenwich, Conn.: New York Graphic Society, 1970. 118p.

Excellent color reproductions of 85 European and 15 American works with comments by the Museum staff. For museum goers and others.

448. Tate Gallery, London. **The Modern British Paintings, Drawings, and Sculpture**. London: Oldbourne Press, 1964. 2 vols.

Arranged alphabetically by surnames under which artists were professionally known. Gives brief biographical sketch and then a full description of each art work in the Tate Gallery. Covers 1850 to 1963.

Histories

449. Baigell, Matthew. **A History of American Painting**. New York: Praeger, 1971. 288p.

Part of the "Praeger World of Art" series. Treatment woven around major artists. Praised by some reviewers for its good sense of proportion and its value for the beginner, it has been criticized by others for brevity and omissions. Includes notes and bibliography. Supplemental coverage may be found in *Three Hundred Years of American Painting*, by Alexander Eliot (New York: Time, Inc., 1957).

450.   Gould, B. E. **A Basic Guide to Literature on the History of Painting in the Occidental Tradition: A Thesis Submitted for the Fellowship of the Library Association**. London: Library Association, 1966; London: University Microfilms, 1969. 4 vols.

Classified arrangement with author and subject indexes. Lengthy annotations. Over 2,600 items.

451.   **The Great Centuries of Painting**. New York: Skira, 1952– .

LC catalogs each title separately. Many libraries make a series added entry. For a list, see the 1970 catalog of the World Publishing Company in the 1970 *Publishers' Trade List Annual*, or A. J. Walford's *Guide to Reference Material*.

452.   Haftman, Werner. **Painting in the Twentieth Century**. 2nd Engl. ed. New York: Praeger, 1965. 2 vols.

A history of painting in the twentieth century. Vol. I has the subtitle: "An Analysis of the Artists and Their Work"; Vol. II is subtitled: "A Pictorial Survey." Some 50 of the 1,011 illustrations are in color. The 1965 edition was substantially revised and won wide acclaim from reviewers as an excellent and comprehensive work.

453.   Marle, Raimond van. **The Development of the Italian Schools of Painting** . . . The Hague: Martinus Nijhoff, 1923-38. 19 vols. Reprinted New York: Hacker, 1971.

Scholarly approach with numerous footnotes and chapter bibliographies. Each volume has indexes of artists, iconography, and places. The final volume is a general index to the whole set.

454.   Siren, Oswald. **Chinese Painting: Leading Masters and Principles**. New York: Ronald Press, 1956-58. 7 vols.

Covers earliest times through the Ch'ing period. Over 800 plates. Lists of works by Chinese painters. Bibliographies include works in both Oriental and Western languages.

Biographies

455.   Canaday, John. **The Lives of the Painters**. New York: Norton, 1969. 4 vols.

Covers four centuries (through the nineteenth), with biographies of 450 European and American painters. Vols. 1-3 are text, and Vol. 4 is plates (both color and black and white) of artists' works.

456.   Harper, J. Russell. **Early Painters and Engravers in Canada**. Toronto: University of Toronto Press, 1970. 376p.

Restricted to artists born before 1867 or active before 1900, it includes both Canadians and foreigners working in Canada. Articles include biographies, records of exhibition, and collections where works are housed. Thorough and comprehensive.

457. **Kindlers Malerei Lexikon**. Hrsg., Germain Bazin and others. Zurich: Kindler Verlag, 1964-71. 6 vols.

Includes bibliographies, 1,000 artists' signatures, 1,200 color reproductions, and 3,000 black and white illustrations. Vols. 1-5 contain biographies of artists and reproductions of their works. Vol. 6 contains a section devoted to subjects (terms, movements, etc.) and three indexes: artists' names; places; reproductions. The quality of the reproductions is excellent.

458. Wernersbach, Geraldine. **Index to Twentieth-Century American Painters Presently Listed in National or Local Publications**. Unpublished thesis, Department of Library Science, Kent State University, 1959. 392 l.

A specialized supplement to Mallett, with references to biographical data on 8,500 painters.

Reproductions

459. Brooke, Milton, and Henry J. DuBester. **Guide to Color Prints**. Washington: Scarecrow Press, 1953. 257p.

Covers 5,000 reproductions of works by 1,000 painters. Information concerning several additional sources of reproductions may be found in "Pictures: Reproductions of Art," by Sydney Starr Keaveney, *Wilson Library Bulletin* 46 (February 1972): 494-95.

460. Monro, Isabel. **Index to Reproductions of American Paintings: A Guide to More Than 800 Books**. New York: H. W. Wilson, 1948. 731p. Supplement, 1964. 480p.

Main work lists paintings of artists in the United States in 520 books and 300 catalogs of exhibitions. Paintings are entered 1) under name of artist, followed by dates, title of picture, and abbreviated entry for book in which reproduction is found; 2) under titles; and 3) in some cases, under subjects. Locations of pictures in permanent collections are also included when available. Supplement has 400 books and catalogs from 1948 to 1961. Regarded as vital by more than half of the art librarians in the Larsen survey.

461. Monro, Isabel. **Index to Reproductions of European Paintings: A Guide to Pictures in More Than 300 Books**. New York: H. W. Wilson, 1956. 668p.

Reproductions in 328 books. Entered 1) under name of artist, followed by dates if available, by title of picture, and by abbreviated entry for book where reproduction is found; 2) under titles; 3) in some cases, under subjects. Whenever permanent locations could be obtained, this information is recorded by symbols. Regarded as vital by more than half of the art librarians in the Larsen survey.

462. United Nations Educational, Scientific and Cultural Organization. **Catalogue of Reproductions of Paintings Prior to 1860**. 9th ed. rev. New York: Unipub, Inc., 1971. 451p.

First published in 1950. Formerly entitled *Catalogue of Reproductions of*

Paintings Prior to 1860. Revised every two to three years. The title and the preface are in English, French, and Spanish. Selections are made on the basis of fidelity of color reproduction, significance of the artist, and importance of the painting. Entries are arranged alphabetically by artist (when known) and then by date. If the artist is unknown, the entries are under the country and then by date. [This is sometimes done when the artist's name is known but country identification appears more useful. For example, "Country Scene," by Cha Po-Chu, is entered under "China—Sung Dynasty (South)—1127-1267." However, this artist is noted by name in the index, with a reference to the page on which the entry appears.] Each entry is accompanied by a small black and white reproduction. Other details are similar to those given for the next title.

463. United Nations Educational, Scientific and Cultural Organization. **Catalogue of Reproductions of Paintings—1860 to 1969**. 9th ed. rev. New York: Unipub, Inc., 1969. 549p.

First published in 1949. Formerly entitled *Catalogue of Colour Reproductions of Paintings*. Revised every two to three years. Color reproductions from books and periodicals are not included unless these can be purchased separately. The basic arrangement is alphabetical by artist and then chronological by date of painting. Each entry gives the following information: 1) *(for the original painting)* name of painter; places and dates of birth and death; title of painting; date, when known; medium; size (height by width in centimeters and inches); collection of the original; 2) *(for the reproduction)* process used in printing (as described by the publisher); size; Unesco archives number; printer; publisher; price. Items are numbered consecutively, but the index of artists at the back refers to page numbers. There is also a list of publishers' names and addresses, and a page of instructions for ordering reproductions.

ARCHITECTURE

Introductions

464. Giedion, Siegfried. **Space, Time and Architecture: The Growth of a New Tradition**. 5th ed. rev. and enl. Cambridge: Harvard University Press, 1967. 897p.

Reflections, by one of the leaders of the twentieth century, on architectural history, city planning, and man's perception of space. Originally given as the Charles Eliot Norton Lectures in 1938 and 1939. Another of his works worth considering is *Architecture, You and Me: The Diary of a Development* (Cambridge: Harvard University Press, 1958). A rather different approach is found in T. F. Hamlin's *Architecture, an Art for All Men* (New York: Columbia University Press, 1947).

465. Owings, Nathaniel Alexander. **The Spaces in Between: An Architect's Journey**. Boston: Houghton Mifflin, 1973. 303p.

Combined autobiography and history of Skidmore, Owings and Merill, one of the most distinguished architectural firms in the United States. Well written.

466.   Rasmussen, Steen Eiler. **Experiencing Architecture**. 2nd ed. Cambridge: MIT Press, 1962. 245p.

Translated from the Danish by Eve Wendt. The author was both a practicing architect and a professor at the Royal Academy of Fine Arts, Copenhagen. Reviewers generally praised it as a good book for beginners.

467.   Sullivan, Louis Henry. **Kindergarten Chats and Other Writings**. New York: Wittenborn, Schultz, 1947. 252p.

Reflections by one of America's leading architects of the late nineteenth and early twentieth centuries. Originally published serially in *Interstate Architect and Builder* (1901-1902) and revised by Sullivan in 1918.

468.   Wright, Frank Lloyd. **Frank Lloyd Wright on Architecture: Selected Writings 1894-1940**. Ed. with an introduction by Frederick Gutheim. New York: Duell, Sloane and Pearce, 1941. 275p.

A good selection from the writings of one of America's foremost architects in the twentieth century.

469.   Wright, Frank Lloyd. **A Testament**. New York: Bramhall House, 1957. 256p.

Personal reflections by one of America's most creative architects, published only two years before his death at age 90.

Reference Works

470.   **American Architects Directory**. 3rd ed. Published under the sponsorship of American Institute of Architects. New York: R. R. Bowker, 1970. 1126p.

Condensed biographical sketches (of both members and non-members who responded to questionnaires) make up the main section. Supplemental information on the American Institute of Architects, a geographical index, and articles on such topics as choosing an architect are also included.

471.   American Association of Architectural Bibliographers. **Papers**, Vol. 1, 1965– . Charlottesville: University Press of Virginia, 1965– .

Annual. Bibliographies on specific topics (often historical), rather than annual coverage of current publications.

472.   Briggs, Martin Shaw. **Everyman's Concise Encyclopedia of Architecture**. With line drawings by the author and 32p. of photos. New York: Dutton, 1960.

Has about 2,000 short entries (definitions, biographies, architectural history). Illustrations are small but clear. Cross references are generally good.

473.   Columbia University. Avery Architectural Library. **Avery Index to Architectural Periodicals**. 2nd ed. Boston: G. K. Hall, 1973. 15 vols.

Contains entire original index of 1963, plus seven supplements through December 1972. Also includes decorative arts, city planning, and archaeology.

Good for information on individual architects. Most comprehensive index in architecture, with over 360,000 entries. Does not include periodicals in non-Western alphabets.

474.   Columbia University. Libraries. Avery Architectural Library. **Avery. Obituary Index of Architects and Artists**. Boston: G. K. Hall, 1963. 338p.

Reproduction of 13,000 cards. Draws on obituaries in newspapers (especially the *New York Times*) as well as periodicals in the Avery collection.

475.   Columbia University. Libraries. Avery Architectural Library. **Catalog** . . . 2nd ed. enl. Boston: G. K. Hall, 1968. 19 vols.

One of the most outstanding architectural collections in the United States. Photographic reproduction of cards in the catalog. Includes ont only the Avery collection but all Columbia University Libraries books on architecture

476.   **DAA: Dictionary of Architectural Abbreviations, Signs and Symbols**. Ed., David D. Dolon. New York: Odyssey Press, 1965. 595p.

The basic arrangement is a classified one: Abbreviations for Use in Text; Abbreviations for Associations and Societies; Abbreviations for Unions; Abbreviations for Degrees; Letter Symbols; Abbreviations for Use on Drawings; Graphic Symbols; Reinforcing Bar Designations; Color Code for Residential Wiring; Abbreviations for Use on Maps, etc. Within each, there is usually an introduction and then a two-fold division: alphabetically by abbreviation, and alphabetically by name. There is no general index, but scrutiny of the table of contents and introductory material should readily lead to the information needed.

477.   **Dizionario enciclopedico do architettura e urbanistica**. Diretto da Paolo Portoghesi. Roma: Istituto Editoriale Romano, 1968-71(?). 6 vols.(?)

A major encyclopedic dictionary of architecture and city planning. International in coverage, but with Italian emphasis and viewpoint. Alphabetical arrangement.

478.   Fleming, John, Hugh Honour, and Nikolaus Pevsner. **The Penguin Dictionary of Architecture**. Drawings by David Etherton. Baltimore: Penguin Books, 1966. 247p.

In addition to definitions of terms, it includes brief biographical notes on leading architects.

479.   Hatje, Gerd, ed. **Encyclopaedia of Modern Architecture**. London: Thames and Hudson, 1963. 336p.

Translated from German. Articles, except for very brief ones, are signed and many include bibliographies. Covers architects, schools, styles, associations, countries, construction terms, and materials that, since the mid-nineteenth century, have contributed to modern architecture.

480.   Saylor, Henry. **Dictionary of Architecture**. New York: Wiley, 1952. 221p.

A dictionary of about 4,000 technical terms which indicates pronunciation and gives brief definitions. American viewpoint. A more recent work is *Dictionary of Architecture and Construction*, edited by Cyril M. Harris (New York: McGraw-Hill, 1974).

481.   Smith, Denison Langley. **How to Find Out in Architecture and Building: A Guide to Sources of Information**. New York: Pergamon Press, 1967. 232p.

A guide to the literature of the field, prepared by a British librarian. Supplementary approaches are provided in *Guide to Architectural Information* (1971), by Margaret Phillips (Design Data Center, P.O. Box 566, Lansdale, Pa. 19446).

482.   Sturgis, Russell. **A Dictionary of Architecture and Building: Biographical, Historical and Descriptive**. New York: Macmillan, 1901. 3 vols.

Actually a short encyclopedia, which includes many illustrations of buildings and their components.

483.   Ware, Dora. **A Short Dictionary of Architecture**. 3rd ed. London: Allen and Unwin, 1953. 135p.

A small, useful dictionary of terms commonly used in classical and modern architecture, well illustrated with line drawings.

Histories

484.   Adams, Henry. **Mont-Saint-Michel and Chartres**. Boston and New York: Houghton, 1933. 397p.

A classic, both as history and literature. It is better reading than *History of Modern Architecture*, by Leonardo Benevolo (Cambridge: MIT Press, 1971), but less detailed. The Benevolo work, a translation of the 1966 Italian edition, covers architecture and city planning from 1760 to the present.

485.   Fletcher, Sir Banister Flight. **A History of Architecture on the Comparative Method**. 17th ed. New York: Scribner's, 1967. 1366p.

The seventeenth edition (1967), by the Royal Institute of British Architects and the University of London, has major changes in text from earlier ones. Pt. 1, Ancient Architecture and Western Succession; Pt. 2, Architecture of the East. Each style is considered under five sections: influences; characteristics; examples; comparative analysis of structural patterns; reference books.

486.   Hamlin, Talbot Faulkner. **Architecture through the Ages**. Rev. ed. New York: Putnam, 1953. 684p.

An excellent survey history from a social point of view. Another work of importance by the same author is *Forms and Functions of Twentieth-Century Architecture* (New York: Columbia University Press, 1952).

487.   Pevsner, Nikolaus. **An Outline of European Architecture**. Baltimore: Penguin, 1960. 740p.

A valuable work, usefully complemented by Ian McCallum's *Architecture USA* (New York: Reinhold, 1959).

488.   Simpson, Frederick Moore. **History of Architectural Development**. New ed. New York: Longmans, Green, 1954– .
First published in three volumes (1905-1911); the new edition was planned for completion in five. The first four (covering ancient times through the Renaissance) have appeared, and Vol. 5 will cover 1837 to the present.

SCULPTURE

489.   Bazin, Germain. **The History of World Sculpture**. Greenwich, Conn.: New York Graphic Society, 1969. 459p.
The text (87 pages) is regarded by most reviewers as sound, but the quality of the 1,024 colored illustrations is considered uneven. Many are excellent, but some colors are not true and some illustrations have been too harshly cropped. The range of coverage makes it very useful despite these defects.

490.   Chase, George Henry, and Chandler Rathfon Post. **A History of Sculpture**. New York: Harper, 1925. 582p.
Long regarded as the standard work. Chapter bibliographies. Indexes of sculptors, monuments and places.

491.   Clapp, Jane. **Sculpture Index**. Metuchen, N.J.: Scarecrow Press, 1970-71. 2 vols.
Vol. 1, *Sculpture of Europe and the Contemporary Middle East*; Vol. 2, *Sculpture of the Americas, the Orient, Africa, Pacific Area and the Classical World*. Indexes pictures of works of sculpture in more than 900 publications. Listings are under name of artist, title and subject, with dimensions (original and present). Limitations and inclusions are not clearly defined, but the set is essential for most art collections despite these defects.

492.   Craven, Wayne. **Sculpture in America from the Colonial Period to the Present**. New York: Crowell, 1968. 722p.
Favorably received by most critics as a solid contribution to the field, it treats both the social background and the works of individual sculptors. Commended for its documentation, bibliography, and index. Fullest account since *The History of American Sculpture*, by Lorado Taft (1903).

493.   Gunnis, Rupert. **Dictionary of British Sculptors, 1660-1851**. New rev. ed. London: Murrays Book Sales, 1968. 515p.
Scholarly, thorough, and more complete than any other source. Over 1,700 biographies. Bibliographical citations of sources. Indexes of names and places.

494.   Lami, Stanislas. **Dictionnaire des sculpteurs de l'école française**. Paris: Champion, 1898-1921. 8 vols.
Volumes cover historical periods. Within each period, the material is arranged

alphabetically by artist. Information given includes a short biography, list of works, and bibliography. Includes foreigners who worked in France until they died. Does not include anyone still alive in 1914.

495.   **Masterpieces of European Sculpture**. 167 photogravure plates, 10 color plates from photos. By Martin Hurlimann and others. With a prefatory note by Eric Newton. New York: H. N. Abrams, 1959. 54p.

The period covered is immense—from the sixth century B.C. to the middle of the twentieth century A.D. Reviewers varied in their assessments, but several praised the photographs.

496.   Meauze, Pierre. **African Art: Sculpture**. Cleveland: World Publishing Co., 1968. 219p.

Concentrates on black African tribal art south of the Sahara. A good introduction for the beginner, but not adequate for the scholar. Both the color plates and the black and white photographs are beautifully done.

497.   **New Dictionary of Modern Sculpture**. Gen. ed., Robert Maillard. Tr. from the French by Bettina Wadia. New York: Tudor, 1971. 328p.

The new edition covers nearly 200 more artists (for a total of almost 600) and takes greater account of new uses of materials (e.g., metal and resins). Articles, signed with the initials of contributors, give brief biographical information about the sculptor and concentrate on professional accomplishments (leading works, exhibitions, etc.). Illustrations (black and white) are both numerous and good.

498.   Newton, Eric. **European Painting and Sculpture**. 4th ed. London: Cassell, 1961 (also Penguin paperbound). 245p.

Author was Slade Professor of Fine Arts, Oxford University. Purpose of book is "to induce my readers to tune in to painting and sculpture in whatever form they may manifest themselves, at whatever period or in whatever country" (Foreword to first edition). There are 32 black and white reproductions in the middle of the book. In the copy examined, these appeared dark and were somewhat lacking in clarity of detail. There are two appendices: a diagram of schools and influences, and a classified list of artists. There is a brief name index.

499.   Pope-Hennessy, John. **An Introduction to Italian Sculpture**. 2nd ed. New York: Phaidon; distr. Praeger, 1971. 3 vols.

Contents: Vol. I, *Italian Gothic Sculpture*; Vol. II, *Italian Renaissance Sculpture*; Vol. III, *Italian High Renaissance and Baroque Sculpture*. The typical pattern for each volume includes introductory chapters on leading sculptors and trends; plates; notes on sculptors and plates; index of places; index of sculptors. The plates conveniently related to the text, even when not directly beside it, are handsome black and white photographs remarkable for their clarity and detail.

500.   Rich, Jack C. **The Material and Methods of Sculpture**. New York: Oxford University Press, 1947. 416p.

Covers techniques for a wide range of media. Contains a bibliography, glossary, and tables. Excellent detailed index. Another work to be considered is

Sculpture: Techniques in Clay, Wax, Slate . . ., by Frank Eliscu (Philadelphia: Chilton, 1959).

501. Schaefer-Simmern, Henry. **Sculpture in Europe Today**. Berkeley: University of California Press, 1955. 33p. 128 plates.
Contains 128 full-page plates, illustrating the work of 60 leading sculptors of the mid-twentieth century. Brief but good introduction on trends.

502. Zorach, William. **Zorach Explains Sculpture: What It Means and How It Is Made**. New York: Tudor, 1961. 308p.
First published in 1947 by the American Artists Group, New York. The chapters on technique are generally regarded as clear and helpful for the beginner.

MINOR ARTS

503. Aronson, Joseph. **The Encyclopedia of Furniture**. 3rd ed. New York: Crown, 1965. 484p.
First published in 1938. Latest edition includes 1,400 photographs and many line drawings.

504. Bishop, Robert Charles. **Centuries and Styles of the American Chair, 1640-1970**. New York: Dutton, 1972. 516p.
Most comprehensive book to date. Nearly 1,000 black and white photographs, arranged by period and style. Detailed index: furniture makers, chair types, chair parts.

505. Boger, Louise Ade. **The Complete Guide to Furniture Styles**. Enl. ed. New York: Scribner's, 1969. 500p.
A history of furniture by a noted writer in the field of antiques. She has also written an illustrated history entitled *Furniture Past and Present* (Garden City, N.Y.: Doubleday, 1966).

506. Boger, Louise Ade. **The Dictionary of World Pottery and Porcelain**. New York: Scribner's, 1971. 533p.
Persons, places, manufacturers, trends, etc., are subjects of short articles in one alphabetical sequence, illustrated with numerous line drawings and generously provided with cross references. There are 57 beautiful illustrations in color and 562 small black and white photographs, with extensive notes. Coverage ranges from the primitive world to our own time. Short bibliography.

507. Boger, Louise Ade, and H. Batterson Boger. **The Dictionary of Antiques and the Decorative Arts: A Book of Reference for Glass, Furniture, Ceramics, Silver, Periods, Styles, Technical Terms, etc.** New York: Scribner's, 1967. 662p.
Illustrated with color plates, line drawings, and black and white photographs. Dictionary section has numerous cross references and is supplemented by a classified list of subjects and terms. Short bibliography. Supplement (pp. 567-662) contains nearly 700 entries.

508. Boston. Museum of Fine Arts. **American Furniture in the Museum of Fine Arts, Boston.** Comp. by Richard H. Randall, Jr. Boston: Museum of Fine Arts: distr. New York: October House, 1965. 276p.

A classified arrangement by types of furniture, with 218 black and white photographs. General index and index of former owners. Each item is rather fully described as to general appearance, structure, size, history, etc.

509. Bradley, John William. **A Dictionary of Miniaturists, Illuminators, Calligraphers, and Copyists, with References to Their Works, and Notices of Their Patrons, from the Establishment of Christianity to the Eighteenth Century.** London: Quaritch, 1887-99. 3 vols. Reprinted New York: Burt Franklin, 1958.

510. Chu, Arthur, and Grace Chu. **Oriental Antiques and Collectibles: A Guide.** New York: Crown, 1973. 248p.

Chinese and Japanese art objects (bronzes, jades, porcelains, cloisonné, textiles, and glass) are covered, with emphasis on the last hundred years. Illustrations (some in color). Bibliography. Index.

511. Comstock, Helen. **American Furniture: Seventeenth, Eighteenth and Nineteenth Century Styles.** New York: Viking Press, 1966 (c.1962). 336p.

Chapters on major periods: 1) Jacobean—William and Mary: 1640-1720; 2) Queen Anne: 1720-1755; 3) Chippendale: 1755-1790; 4) Classical Period: 1790-1830; 5) Early Victorian: 1830-1870. There are 665 black and white photographs (with excellent clarity of detail) and eight color plates. Each chapter has a summary chart at the end. Additional sources of information are given in the notes and selected bibliography. There is a name and subject index that covers both text and illustrations.

512. Comstock, Helen, ed. **The Concise Encyclopedia of American Antiques.** New York: Hawthorn Books, 1958. 2 vols.

Pages are numbered consecutively through the two volumes. The essay-type articles cover broad topics. Some have glossaries and bibliographies; all are illustrated with good, clear, black and white photographs. Complete table of contents and index are repeated in both volumes.

513. Coysh, Arthur Wilfred. **The Antique Buyer's Dictionary of Names.** New York: Praeger, 1970. 278p.

Divided into 17 categories. Gives information on 1,700 European and American artists, craftsmen, designers and firms. Often includes museum locations. Each section has a bibliography.

514. Davenport, Millia. **The Book of Costume.** New York: Crown, 1964. 2 vols.

Historical coverage from the early days to the end of the U.S. Civil War. About 3,000 illustrations (some in color). Usually gives locations of originals.

515.   Fales, Dean A., Jr. **American Painted Furniture, 1660-1880**. New York: Dutton, 1972. 299p.

Chapters deal with various historical styles: 1) Early Colonial; 2) Late Colonial; 3) Federal; 4) American Empire; 5) Nineteenth Century; 6) Cultural Patterns; 7) Victorian. There are 511 photographs (many in color). Additional sources of information are given in "Notes" and "Bibliography." There is a brief name and subject index and an index of owners.

516.   Hiler, Hilaire, and Meyer Hiler. **Bibliography of Costume: A Dictionary Catalog of about Eight Thousand Books and Periodicals** ... Ed. by Helen Grant Cushing, assisted by Adah V. Morris. New York: H. W. Wilson, 1939. Reprinted New York: Benjamin Blom, 1967. 911p.

517.   Hollister, Paul, Jr. **The Encyclopedia of Glass Paper Weights**. New York: Crown, 1969. 312p.

Covers entire history from ancient Egypt to the present. Many illustrations. Glossary of terms. Bibliography. List of museums with paperweight collections.

518.   Honey, William Boyer. **European Ceramic Art from the End of the Middle Ages to about 1815**. London: Faber and Faber, 1949-53. 2 vols.

Contents: Vol. I, *A Dictionary of Factories, Artists, Technical Terms, etc.*; Vol. II, *Illustrated Historical Survey*. Vol. I is copiously illustrated with line drawings and has a special "Index to Marks" (pp. 683-788). Vol. II has 24 plates in color and 192 plates in black and white. (Many of the latter have several small photographs on one page.) There are lists of plates and an index of plates. Compiler was keeper of the Department of Ceramics, Victoria and Albert Museum, London.

519.   Hornung, Clarence P. **Treasury of American Design** New York: H. N. Abrams, 1972. 2 vols.

520.   Monro, Isabel Stevenson, and Dorothy E. Cook. **Costume Index: A Subject Index to Plates and to Illustrated Texts**. New York: H. W. Wilson, 1937. 338p. **Supplement**. Ed. by I. S. Monro and K. M. Monro. New York: H. W. Wilson, 1957. 210p.

Excellent, detailed indexing of more than 900 works. Accessible by places, types of persons, and kinds of costumes.

521.   Papert, Emma. **Illustrated Guide to American Glass**. New York: Hawthorn, 1972. 289p.

522.   Porter, Arthur, ed. **Directory of Art and Antique Restoration: A Guide to Art and Antique Restorers Throughout the United States**. San Francisco: the Author, 1971. 240p.

523.   **The Practical Encyclopedia of Crafts**. Comp. by Maria Di Valentin and others. New York: Sterling, 1970. 544p.

Covers a wide range of crafts (clay, fabrics, metal, glass, etc.). Almost 1,200 illustrations (about 40 in color). Good index.

524.   Safford, Carleton L., and Robert Bishop. **America's Quilts and Coverlets**. New York: Dutton, 1972. 313p.

525.   Savage, George. **Dictionary of Antiques**. New York: Praeger, 1970. 534p.
Prepared to help collectors and dealers to recognize and date the specimens they examine. Short articles on persons, objects, and trends are in one alphabet, illustrated in many cases with black and white photographs and provided with cross references. There is an appendix of marks and a select bibliography. The 45 color plates are of uneven quality. Some are too yellowish, while others verge toward blue.

526.   Turner, Noel D. **American Silver Flatware, 1837-1910**. New York: Barnes, 1972. 473p.

527.   Wanscher, Ole. **The Art of Furniture: 5,000 Years of Furniture and Interiors**. Tr. from the Danish by David Hohnen. New York: Reinhold, 1967. 419p.
Each chapter consists of a brief introduction to the period, followed by a copious array of illustrations (black and white photographs and some line drawings). There is a short bibliography and an index of names and places.

PERFORMING
ARTS

12   TRENDS IN THE PERFORMING ARTS

The performing arts (except for the film) are almost as old as mankind itself. Throughout much of human history, religious and symbolic meanings have been more important than entertainment. In addition, music, theater, and the dance have frequently been so intertwined that separation is difficult. This chapter will deal briefly with historical trends in music, the dance, theater, and the film.

MUSIC

Historians differ as to whether song or use of rhythmic instruments constituted the earliest form of music. In most primitive tribes, music was associated with daily life—birth, marriage, harvest, success in the hunt—and was a communal activity.

Oriental

Ancient Oriental music differed from primitive music in that it used expert performers and evolved a theoretical structure. This music has not survived, except for a few Hindu chants. India and Pakistan exhibit some of the richest and most complex forms, with octaves of five, six, or seven steps, grace notes, and subtle rhythms. In China, the music is somewhat less varied, although large orchestras existed as early as the T'ang dynasty (618-906 A.D.). Music of Bali and Java is also written for large orchestras, with extensive use of gongs and chimes. Islamic music, which is closer to that of India, somewhat resembles Western chamber music. Individual composers are not accorded the same amount of recognition as in the West.

Western

The history of Western music may be divided into six major periods: monophonic (early antiquity to 1300 A.D.); polyphonic (800-1600); baroque (1600-1750); classical (1750-1820); romantic (1820-1900); and the twentieth century.

Monophonic

Music in the monophonic period was characterized by the use of a single melodic line without accompaniment. Virtually no music has been preserved from antiquity, but we are able to gather information from ancient writings about music. The Hebrews used music in their worship, commonly in the forms of unison singing, chanting, and antiphonal singing (one choir or group of singers answered by another). The shofar (or ram's horn, a member of the trumpet family) and cymbals were instruments commonly used. The harp was used in ancient Egypt.

The Greeks made several contributions. With their usual philosophic genius, they developed musical theories that greatly influenced Christian thought in the Middle Ages. They also developed an instrumental notation that used the Phoenician letters and a vocal notation that used the Ionian letters. Among the instruments used by the Greeks were the panpipes, the cithara (a plucked, stringed instrument) and the aulos (a double-reed wind instrument.)

Monophonic music continued to dominate during much of the Christian era, although polyphonic music (two or more parts) began to be heard around 800 A.D. Most of the music was religious: plainsong, plain chant, and Gregorian chant. It was nonmetric and unaccompanied, using a free prose rhythm and having a limited range. There was very little secular music before the tenth century, when musical entertainers, known as jongleurs, began to appear in France. Later, the troubadours appeared in Southern France and the trouvères in the North. The Minnesingers appeared in Germany in the twelfth and thirteenth centuries and the Meistersingers in the fourteenth, fifteenth, and sixteenth centuries.

Polyphonic

Music in the polyphonic period underwent a number of changes. In the ninth century, the practice of singing plainsong melody simultaneously in two parts (parallel, a fourth or fifth apart) came into prominence. This form was known as organum. Melodic and rhythmic independence developed later.

In the twelfth and thirteenth centuries, Paris became the cultural center and voice polyphony became dominant. The two-part arrangements continued and four-part singing came into existence. The most important form was the Paris motet, in which the lowest part (tenor) was plainsong with a slow tempo while the two upper parts had different rhythms and a faster tempo. The upper voices also used different texts.

The term *ars nova* is used for the music of the fourteenth century. By this time, secular music predominated. There were new polyphonic forms, with little parallelism, and new rhythmic freedom. Dissonance was treated boldly. In the fifteenth century, the locus shifted from France and Italy to the Netherlands. The Flemish school was particularly important in the transition from the Middle Ages to the Renaissance. The bass part was added to produce four-voice polyphony and greater equality of parts.

The sixteenth century has been called the "golden age of polyphony." Under the influence of Renaissance humanism, secular music increased in importance, encouraged by the nobility. The madrigal was the chief form. The religious music that was still composed within the Catholic Church was characterized by tranquillity of mood. The Mass and the motet were the chief forms, intended to be sung by the choir alone, without instrumental accompaniment. An important new force was the Protestant Reformation (with Martin Luther its leading musical figure); its emphasis on congregational singing led to the rise of the chorale.

The chief developments before 1600 were in the field of vocal music, but the Renaissance brought an awakening of interest in instrumental music. Most of the musical instruments of the period have since fallen into disuse, with the exception of the organ and the oboe.

Baroque

Baroque music was characterized by large-scale productions, spectacular effects, contrasts, and overall grandeur. Secular music began to take precedence over religious, while the influence of the nobility continued to increase. The court of Louis XIV of France (1643-1715) was an especially brilliant musical center. Instrumental music began to surpass vocal in importance, and national styles began to emerge. The development of operas, oratorios, and cantatas emphasized the dramatic element. New forms were the dance suite, solo sonata, trio sonata, concerto, and fugue.

Among the important baroque composers were: Claudio Monteverdi (madrigals and operas); Alessandro Scarlatti (opera); Domenico Scarlatti (keyboard pieces); Arcangelo Corelli and Antonio Vivaldi (chamber and concert music for strings); Henry Purcell (dramatic and instrumental music); Johann Herman Schein and Samuel Scheidt (keyboard music); Heinrich Schütz (choral music—cantatas, oratorios, Passion music); Johann Jakob Froberger (keyboard music); Michael Pretorius (choral music); Dietrich Buxtehude and Johann Pachelbel (organ music); Johann Sebastian Bach (choral, instrumental, and keyboard music); and George Frederick Handel (operas and oratorios). In this period the modern form of musical notation replaced earlier forms developed in the Middle Ages.

Classical

Classical music was noted for objectivity, restraint, clarity of form, and adherence to certain structural principles. Vienna was the leading musical center in this period. The predominant philosophy was rationalism, as exemplified in the work of Kant. The classical spirit was most evident in instrumental music, where emphasis was placed on the clarification of formal structure. The modern sonata emerged in this period, as did a new style of melody—simpler and clearer than the baroque. Counterpoint became less important. Harmonies were simpler. The basis for modern orchestration was established—strings, brass, woodwinds, percussion—and the piano made its appearance. Music publishing was greatly expanded. Christoph Willibald Gluck (operas) and Franz Joseph Haydn (symphonies, piano music, chamber music, oratorios) were two of the great classical composers. Wolfgang Amadeus Mozart was distinguished by the wide range of his compositions; he excelled in all forms of the period—concerto, opera, chamber music, sonata, symphony, and oratorio. Ludwig van Beethoven is often regarded as a transitional figure between classicism and romanticism; his works include symphonies, piano music, chamber music, Masses, oratorios, and one opera.

Romantic

The general characteristics of romanticism (individualism, emotionalism, subjectivity, nationalism, interest in nature, in the medieval, and in the supernatural) also are evident in music. The piano was the most important instrument of the period. Works written for the piano became more and more free in form as the romantic period developed and as the piano itself improved. Short forms—nocturnes, arabesques, fantasies—predominated, and they were given descriptive titles. Styles were diverse and inventive, and melodies were often warm and personalized. Orchestras of the period were larger than classical orchestras, and extensive use was made of brasses, woodwinds, and percussion instruments. Like the music written for the piano, orchestral music became freer in form, with the development of symphonic poems, suites, etc.

The romantic period was the golden age of opera. Prominent Italian opera composers were Gioacchino Rossini, Vincenzo Bellini, Gaetano Donizetti, Giuseppe Verdi, and Giacomo Puccini. Operatic composers in France included Georges Bizet, Giacomo Meyerbeer, and Charles Gounod. Germany contributed Richard Wagner, whose "music drama" provided a new direction for the form.

Far from being a monolithic movement, romanticism in music contained conservative as well as radical elements. An example of the former approach is found in the works of Johannes Brahms (symphonies, piano music, chamber music, songs, and choral works), while the radical trend is exemplified in the programmatic titles of Franz Liszt's orchestral and piano works.

Among the major romantic composers are Felix Mendelssohn (oratorios, songs, and piano compositions); Franz Schubert (songs, symphonies, and piano works); Frederic Chopin (piano works); Robert Schumann (piano pieces and symphonies); Anton Bruckner (symphonies); Hector Berlioz (symphonies); Richard Strauss (symphonies and operas); Nicolai Rimsky-Korsakov (symphonies); and Peter Ilich Tchaikovsky (symphonies).

Twentieth Century

The twentieth century has been a revolutionary time in the history of music, with an increase in both the amount and the variety of music composed and performed. Changes in communications technology (the phonograph, radio, and TV) have brought music to millions who could not or would not attend a performance in a concert hall or an opera house. Because individualism has been a prominent feature, accurate discernment of trends is somewhat difficult. One trend is neo-romanticism, a continuation of the German romantic traditions, with emphasis on heavy emotionalism and the use of large orchestras. Another is impressionism, led by Claude Debussy. This reaction against romanticism, characterized by delicacy, vagueness, and refinement, is linked to a similar movement in painting. Expressionism, another term borrowed from painting, refers to music that is an expression of the inner self, especially the subconscious; it emphasizes the dissonant and the atonal. Neo-classicism represents a return to the ideals of the late eighteenth century, but in the context of modern techniques. Jazz, which originated with the Negro in the United States, began to emerge around 1910 out of ragtime and blues. Jazz is noted for its sustained melody with a throbbing accompaniment, complex rhythm patterns, and prominence of percussion and woodwinds (especially the saxophone).

Among the noted composers of the twentieth century are: Maurice Ravel; Frederick Delius; Ottorino Respighi; Alexander Scriabin; Arthur Honegger; Darius Milhaud; François Poulenc; Arnold Schönberg; Igor Stravinsky; Sergei Prokofiev; Béla Bartók; Jean Sibelius; Ralph Vaughan Williams; Ernest Bloch; Charles Ives; Virgil Thomson; George Gershwin; Aaron Copland; Roger Sessions; John Cage; Dmitri Shostakovich; Karlheinz Stockhausen; Samuel Barber; and Gian Carlo Menotti.

DANCE

Like music, with which it is nearly always linked, the dance was a means by which primitive man not only expressed his feelings but also sought to communicate with the gods and thus to control events. Elements of this link with religion remain today in the dances of the North American Indians and in traditional dances of India, China, and Japan. More settled agricultural societies considered dancing a form of pleasure; it was usually a communal activity, as exemplified in folk dances. Modern ballroom dancing arose in the fifteenth and sixteenth centuries among the nobility. Theater dancing was known in ancient Egypt and in Greece, but modern ballet is derived from the court dances of the Renaissance. The paragraphs that follow will concentrate on theater dance and ballet.

Eastern Dance

In ancient Egypt, it was customary for kings and nobles to have slaves dance at their banquets. In Greece, a trained chorus of dancers would be part of many theater performances. In the Orient, temple dancers passed instructions from generation to generation. A classic work on this subject from India was the *Natya Shastra*, written in the fifth century A.D., which included descriptions of the gestures to accompany the chanting of hymns from the *Rig Veda*. Indian influence spread to Japan, where the Suragaku, performed at Shinto and Buddhist festivals, gave rise to the Noh drama in the fourteenth century. Kabuki, a popular dance drama, evolved from Noh in the seventeenth century.

Western Dance

In the West, indoor theatrical entertainments known as "masques" were common by the seventeenth century. These would include dramatic scenes, accompanied by songs and dances. In Stuart England, Inigo Jones designed many of these and Ben Jonson supplied some of the lyrics. In France, Catherine de Medicis gave encouragement and commissioned the first real ballet (*Ballet comique de la reine*) in 1581. In 1661, Louis XIV founded the Académie Royale de Danse. In the eighteenth century, Jean Georges Noverre succeeded in making ballet an art form in its own right.

The nineteenth century witnessed a flowering of classical ballet, especially in state-subsidized theaters such as l'Opéra, in Paris, La Scala, in Milan, and the Imperial Mariinsky Theater, in St. Petersburg. Notable ballerinas of the period, Maria Taglioni and Carlotta Grisi, performed in such productions as *La Sylphide* (1832) and *Giselle* (1841). A high point was reached in 1890 with the production in St. Petersburg of *The Sleeping Beauty*, with choreography by Marius Petipa and a musical score by Tchaikovsky.

Early in the twentieth century, Sergei Diaghilev began to revolutionize and revitalize ballet. A notable event was the performance of the Ballets Russes in Paris in 1909. Famous dancers from his company included Anna Pavlova, Vaslav Nijinsky, and Léonide Massine. Choreographers included Michel Fokine, Léonide Massine, and George Balanchine. The influence of Russian ballet has been strong in Western Europe and the United States. George Balanchine's productions at the New York City Ballet included *Serenade*, with music by Tchaikovsky, *Concerto Barocco*, with music by Bach, and *Agon*, with a score by Stravinsky. The best-known contemporary Soviet companies are the Bolshoi Ballet, of Moscow, and the Kirov Ballet, of Leningrad (successor to the Imperial Mariinsky Ballet). In Great Britain, the Royal Ballet (formerly Sadler's Wells Ballet), under the direction of Ninette de Valois, has been noted for the technical excellence of its productions, many with choreography by Frederick Ashton and featuring Margot Fonteyn. The Royal Danish Ballet has also been noteworthy since World War II, and the National Ballet of Canada, under the direction of Celia Franca, has risen to prominence. In the United States, some productions have been inspired by American folklore, such as Agnes de Mille's *Fall River Legend*, based on the Lizzie Borden story, and her *Rodeo*. A number of American companies have produced works by the English-born choreographer Antony Tudor, notably *Pillar of Fire* and *Lilac Garden*. Jerome Robbins combined ballet and jazz dancing in *Fancy Free*. The American Ballet Theatre, founded in 1940, and the New York City Ballet, founded in 1948, have been the leading companies in the United States, although some regional ballet companies (such as the Washington Ballet, of Seattle) began to achieve prominence in the 1960s.

Dance Notation

As the movements of the dance became more complex, systems of notation became increasingly necessary. There are two major systems in use today. The Benesh method, widely used in England, takes its name from Rudolf and Joan Benesh, whose book *Introduction to Benesh Dance Notation* (New York: Pitman, 1956) is the standard work on the subject. More widely used, especially in the United States, is the system devised by Rudolf von Laban and known as "Labanotation." Two of Laban's works are *Principles of Dance and*

Movement Notation (New York: Dance Horizons, Inc., n.d.) and *Choreutics* (London: Macdonald & Evans, 1966). The system is also described by Ann Hutchinson in *Labanotation* (New York: New Directions, 1954).

THEATER

Origins

The origins of the theater are lost in the mists of antiquity. A religious origin appears probable. There is evidence of a kind of passion play in Egypt as early as the nineteenth century B.C. In 534 B.C. the ruler of Athens decreed that performance of tragedies should be a part of the Great Dionysia, an annual celebration in honor of the god of wine. Indian tradition holds that Brahma himself founded the theater. Religious plays were produced in China as early as the first millenium B.C. In Japan, the Noh theater can be traced to priestly dances used in Shinto worship.

In time, the influence of the court became more important than that of the temple. In the great period of the Hindu theater (320-800 A.D.), plays were written and performed in Sanskrit rather than in the language of the common people. A similar development occurred in 13th century China. In Japan, full understanding of the Noh drama was possible only for an educated elite. The Kabuki drama, which appealed to the masses, did not become widespread until the seventeenth century. It was soon rivalled in popularity by the Bunraku, or puppet theater.

The great period of Greek theater corresponded with the rise of Athens to a position of imperial leadership. Major tragic dramatists included Aeschylus (524?–456 B.C.), Sophocles (496-406 B.C.), and Euripedes (484?–406 B.C.). Among the writers of comedy, Aristophanes (c.450–c.385 B.C.) is best remembered for his social and political satire. Performances were given in the Dionysian theater, on a hillside where a natural amphitheater seating 14,000 was formed by the contours of the land.

The theater played a less important role in Roman civic life than in Greek. Some tragedies by Seneca (4 B.C.–65 A.D.) and a few comedies by Plautus (c.254–c.184 B.C.) and Terence (c.195–159 B.C.) have survived. Roman theaters were built on flat ground but imitated the natural amphitheaters of the Greeks. With the fall of Rome in 476 A.D., the theater vanished from the West until the tenth century.

Western Theater

When theatrical activity revived in France and, later, in the rest of Europe, it took the form of religious dramas, usually featuring the women at the empty tomb, or scenes from the life of Christ. Later, three distinct types evolved: mystery plays, which dealt with episodes from the Old or New Testament; miracle plays, or scenes from the lives of the saints; and morality plays, in which the characters represented abstract virtues and vices. On the Continent, different scenes would be performed on fixed stages at various locations. In England, a stage would be constructed on a wagon and moved from place to place. Festivals that involved whole communities were common until the sixteenth century.

As religious drama declined in importance, two newer forms arose. The first, addressed to mass audiences, was known in Italy as *commedia dell'arte*. The second, intended for the elite, was known as *commedia erudita*. Greek and Latin plays (and Italian imitations) were performed in such places as the Teatro Olimpico, in Vicenza, designed by Andrea Palladio and opened in 1585.

During the seventeenth and eighteenth centuries many court theaters were built. The popular tradition was particularly strong in England, where English actors established a native repertory, permanent playhouses, and the first commercial theater in Europe. Players were granted permission to perform daily in London in 1572. In 1576, James Burbage built the first permanent playhouse, called the Theatre. Seven open-air playhouses, usually seating about 2,500, were built in the next 40 years, the most notable being the Globe (erected in 1599) where the Lord Chamberlain's Men (including William Shakespeare) performed. Court influence became stronger under James I, and Inigo Jones (1513-1652) designed several theaters. In France, the court was even more dominant. Cardinal Richelieu was most displeased with Pierre Corneille's *Le Cid* (1636) and influenced the French Academy to set neo-classical standards for the drama. In 1658, Molière's company received permission to perform in Paris. Giacomo Torelli (1608-1678) devised new machinery for moving heavy scenery.

Although French influence was predominant for the next 150 years, important changes did take place in the eighteenth and nineteenth centuries. Theaters were no longer controlled by actors but by full-time managers; in addition, theaters grew in size. Among the more famous ones were the Opernhaus in Bayreuth (1748), designed by Giuseppe Galli-Bibiens; the Residenztheater in Munich (1752), by François Cuvilliés; the Theatre Royal, Drury Lane, London (1674), by Christopher Wren; and the Grand Theatre de Bordeaux (1780), by Victor Louis.

German playwrights, led by Lessing, Goethe, and Schiller, rebelled against French neo-classicism in favor of a native drama. In the English theater, historical accuracy in costuming was stressed by Charles Kean (1811-1868). Toward the end of the nineteenth century the "free theater" movement arose as a vehicle for social criticism. Examples were the Théâtre Libre, Paris (1887); the Freie Bühne, Berlin (1889); the Independent Theater, London (1891); and the Moscow Art Theater (1898). These served as congenial settings for the plays of Henrik Ibsen (1828-1906) and Anton Chekhov (1860-1904).

The first true theater in the United States was the Chestnut Street Theatre in Philadelphia (1793), quickly followed by the Newport (R.I.) Theatre (1793), the Federal Street Theatre in Boston (1794), and the Park Street Theatre in New York (1795). In the nineteenth century, the number of seats was greatly enlarged, reaching 4,600 in the New York Academy of Music (1854). The comfort of theatergoers was enhanced with the introduction of padded seats, and the advent of electric lights around 1880 made greater realism and fantasy possible on stage.

Twentieth Century

The twentieth century has been a time of mixed fortunes for commercial theaters (which still survive in London and New York) but a time of greater stability for national or civic theaters. Playwrights like George Bernard Shaw (1856-1950) and Eugene O'Neill (1888-1953) received stimulus from both the "free theater" and "little theater" movements. The rise of festivals in many countries has encouraged both actors and writers. Notable among these are the Shakespeare Festival in Stratford, Ontario, Canada, and the festival of the Théâtre des Nations, Paris. Among the notable new buildings of recent years are the Vivian Beaumont Theater in the Lincoln Center for the Performing Arts (New York City), the Experimental Theatre in the National Center for the Arts (Ottawa, Canada), the John F. Kennedy Center for the Performing Arts (Washington, D.C.) and the Tyrone Guthrie Theatre (Minneapolis, Minnesota). Playwriting in the twentieth century has reflected literary trends. Naturalism is exemplified in the works of August Strindberg, Gerhart Hauptmann, John Galsworthy, John Millington Synge, Sean O'Casey, Eugene O'Neill, Maxwell Anderson, Elmer Rice, Clifford Odets, and Lillian Hellman. Symbolism began to appear in the later writings of Henrik Ibsen and Gerhart Hauptmann, gaining momentum in the plays of Jean Giraudoux and Bertolt Brecht. A blend of realism and symbolism is evident in the plays of Thornton Wilder, Tennessee Williams, Arthur Miller, Edward Albee, and Harold Pinter. The problem of how to know the truth is uppermost in several works by Luigi Pirandello. A major Spanish playwright was Federico Garcia Lorca. The social satire of George Bernard Shaw occupies a unique place, and the "theater of the absurd" is represented by Eugène Ionesco, Arthur Adamov, Samuel Beckett, and Jean Genet.

FILM

Motion pictures were a late nineteenth century invention, and the art of the film belongs to the twentieth century. A famous early silent film was *The Great Train Robbery* (1903). By 1915, significant artistic progress had been made by D. W. Griffith in *The Birth of a Nation*. The first technicolor film, *The Toll of the Sea*, appeared on Broadway in 1922, while the first sound film—*Don Juan*, with John Barrymore—appeared in 1926. During these years Charles Chaplin made major contributions in a series of films featuring "Charlie." A succession of comic artists includes Buster Keaton, W. C. Fields, the Marx Brothers, Bing Crosby, and Bob Hope. A landmark among Soviet films was S. M. Eisenstein's *Armored Cruiser Potemkin* (1925).

The production of sound and color films proceeded rapidly in the 1930s. After World War II, the development of television brought about a decline in the patronage of movie houses. Nevertheless, many films of distinction were produced. In Italy, Roberto Rossellini led the way with *Open City* (1945) and *The Bicycle Thief* (1948). Federico Fellini's *La Strada* (1954) and *La Dolce Vita* (1960) were noteworthy. In France, major film makers included Jean-Luc Godard, François Truffaut, and Marcel Camus. In Sweden, the work of Ingmar

Bergman, Lars Magnus Lindgren, Vilgot Sjoman, and Bo Widerberg was noteworthy. Luis Buñuel made films in France, Spain, and Mexico. Sergei Bondarchuk (U.S.S.R.) and Roman Polanski (Poland) produced films widely admired in the West. Major British film directors included Tony Richardson, David Lean, Joseph Losey, Richard Lester, John Schlesinger, Byran Forbes, Carol Reed, and Jack Clayton. American directors who continued to produce included John Fors, George Cukor, Alfred Hitchcock, and Otto Preminger. New directors included Elia Kazan, Joseph Mankiewicz, George Stevens, Stanley Donen, John Dassin, Delbert Mann, Fred Zinnemann, Stanley Kubrick, Robert Wise, Arthur Penn, and Mike Nichols.

13 ACCESSING INFORMATION IN THE PERFORMING ARTS

MAJOR DIVISIONS OF THE FIELD

The term "performing arts" has not become fully standardized in its usage. Generally, however, three elements are considered necessary: the performer, the piece performed, and the audience. As used in this book, the term will include music, the dance, the theater, and film.

Music is commonly defined as the art of organizing sounds. Its principal elements are melody (single sounds in succession), harmony (sounds in combination), and rhythm (sounds in a temporal relationship). The two major divisions are vocal music and instrumental music. Vocal music includes songs, operas, oratorios, etc., while instrumental music includes solos, chamber music, and orchestral music. Musical instruments may be classified as stringed (violin, harp, guitar, etc.), woodwind (flute, bassoon, oboe, English horn), brass (trumpet, cornet, bugle, trombone), percussion (drums, chimes, bells, gongs, etc.), keyboard (piano, organ), and other (accordion, concertina, harmonica, bagpipes, etc.). The modern system of musical notation began to be used around 1700.

The librarian responsible for a music collection will need to keep in mind three major elements: 1) the music itself, which will follow somewhat the divisions outlined above; 2) the literature about music, which will divide itself rather more along the conventional lines for all disciplines, but with some special characteristics; 3) the vast array of recordings on discs, tapes, cassettes, etc., which are a part of any modern music library and which pose problems all their own in terms of organization, retrieval, and use.

The dance may be defined as movement of the body to a certain rhythm. There are three major divisions of the field: folk dancing, ballroom dancing, and theater dancing. Folk dancing, which originated in open-air activities, is characterized by great vigor and exuberance of movement. Ballroom dancing had its origin in the European courts of the Renaissance and is an indoor, participant activity. Theater dancing is a spectator activity that may be traced to religious dances in the ancient world and to performances known as "masques" in the courts of Renaissance Europe. Its most characteristic modern form is the ballet. The dance is usually (though not necessarily) accompanied by music.

Theater is the art of presenting a performance to an audience. In modern usage the term is normally restricted to live performances of plays. A distinction is sometimes drawn between theater and drama; theater is restricted in meaning to those matters having to do with public performance, while drama includes the literary basis for performance (i.e., the texts of plays). Frequently, the texts of plays are classed with literature. Libraries with subject departments often put plays in a literature department and other works about the theater in a performing arts department. Topics closely related to theatrical performance are acting, costume, makeup, directing, and the architecture of theaters.

Films may conveniently be divided into feature-length (an hour or more) and shorts. Many feature-length films are fictional, often based on books of some popularity. Others, known as documentaries, are prepared for informational purposes. A blending of these forms may result in stories that are essentially colorful travelogues. Two other forms are animated cartoons and puppet features. Short subjects are often filmed by independent producers and sold to distributors of feature-length films to complete an entertainment package. However, they are also widely used by schools, universities, churches, clubs, businesses, etc., for informational and educational purposes. Indeed, films of this latter kind will probably constitute the bulk of those included in most library film collections.

MAJOR CLASSIFICATION SCHEMES

Despite some special efforts in the field of music, Dewey and LC are the most widely used systems of classification for the performing arts. Two music classification efforts deserve particular mention. The first is the faceted classification system devised by E. J. Coates and others for the *British Catalogue of Music*, and the second is the one used for *RILM Abstracts of Music Literature*.

The *British Catalogue of Music* assigns the letters A and B to literature about music and the letters C through Z (except for I and O) to music scores and parts. Classes A and B may be subdivided by combining with C through Z (e.g., AC = works about opera). Five main facets (or aspects) of music are also identified: 1) medium (e.g., ensemble, viola, woodwind); 2) form (e.g., fugue, sonata, opera); 3) elements (e.g., tonality, rhythm, intervals); 4) character (e.g., religious, film, incidental); 5) musical activities (e.g., extemporization, composition, conducting). There are nine form subdivisions, which appear in round brackets (e.g., A (C) = music encyclopedias). Oblique strokes are also used for certain subdivisions.

The main divisions of *RILM Abstracts of Music Literature* are: reference and research materials; historical musicology; ethnomusicology; instruments and voice; performance practice and notation; theory and analysis; pedagogy; music and other arts; music and related disciplines; music and liturgy.

Dewey places music in "The Arts" between "Photography" and "Recreational and Performing Arts." The main outlines are as follows:

780	Music
781	General principles
782	Dramatic music
783	Sacred music
784	Voice and vocal music
785	Instrumental ensembles & their music
786	Keyboard instruments & their music
787	String instruments & their music
788	Wind instruments & their music
789	Percussion, mechanical, electrical

One major defect of Dewey is the failure to make a clear separation of works *of* music and works *about* music. Recent editions recommend use of the letter "M" and offer certain other alternatives.

By contrast, the Library of Congress is very explicit about Class M, which has three main divisions: M—Music; ML—Literature of Music; MT—Musical Instruction and Study. The main subdivisions of M are as follows:

1	Miscellaneous collections
2	Monuments, sources, reprints, etc.
3-4	Complete and collected works of individual masters
5-1450	Instrumental music
5	Miscellaneous collections
6-176	One instrument
177-993	Several (solo) instruments . . .
1000-1360	Orchestral, band, etc., music . . .
1375-1420	Juvenile
1450-1459	Dance music. General
1490	Music before 1700
1495-2199	Vocal music
1495	Miscellaneous collections
1497-1998	Secular vocal music . . .
1999-2199	Sacred vocal music . . .

Some of the main subdivisions of ML are:

1-5	Periodicals
15-21	Almanacs, directories, etc.
25-28	Societies and organizations . . .
40-44	Programs . . .
100-110	Dictionaries, lexica, encyclopedias
111-158	Bibliography
159-3790	History and criticism
159-161	General
162-197	Periods
200-360	Countries
385-429	Biography
430-455	Composition
457	Conducting and interpretation
460-1090	Instruments and instrumental music . . .
1400-3275	Vocal music . . .
3800-3920	Philosophy and physics . . .
3925	Fiction
3930	Juvenile literature of music

A few key subdivisions from MT are:

1	Theory of musical instruction and study in general
2-5	History and criticism
6-950	Instruction and study
6	General
7-38	Rudiments, notations, etc.
40-74	Composition
78-85	Interpretation, conducting, etc. . . .
165	Tuning
170-810	Instrumental technics . . .
820-949	Singing and voice culture . . .
950	Choreographical instruction

Dewey places the dance (except for ballet) in 793—"Indoor Games and Amusements." Ballet is placed in 792—"Theater (Stage Presentations)." Highlights of the more general section on the dance are as follows:

793.3	Dancing
793.31	Folk and national dances
793.319	Historical and geographical treatment . . .
793.32	Theatrical dancing (except ballet) . . .
793.33	Ballroom dancing (Round dances)
793.34	Square dancing
793.35	Dances with accessory features
793.38	Balls

The divisions for ballet are:

792.8	Ballet
792.809	Historical and geographical treatment
792.82	Ballet dancing (including choreography)
792.84	Specific ballets
	Description, critical appraisal, production scripts (stage guides)
	Including stories, plots, analyses, librettos, stage guides.

LC places the dance in Class G—"Geography, Anthropology, Folklore, Manners and Customs, Recreation." Specifically, all forms of the dance, including ballet, are placed in GV—"Recreation." Highlights of the schedule are as follows:

1580	Periodicals . . .
1585	Dictionaries
1590-1599	General works . . .
1601-1728	History
	By period . . .
	By country . . .
1740-1741	Ethics
1743	National dances. Folk dances and dancing . . .
1746-1771	Social dancing. Ballroom dancing . . .
1779	Dancing in motion pictures, television, etc. . . .
1781-1795	Theatrical dancing (including biography) . . .
1787-1790	Ballet
1787	General works
	Biography—See GV 1785
1788	Technique. Instruction
1790	Ballets
1796	Special dances, A–Z
1797	Drills, parades, etc.
1798	Gymnastic dancing. Rhythmic exercises.
1799	Children's dances. Dances for schools.

Dewey places theater in 792—"Theater (Stage Presentations)" with the following breakdown:

792	Theater (Stage Presentations)
	Class texts of plays in 800
	For miniature, toy, shadow theaters, see 791.5
792.01	Philosophy and esthetics . . .
792.02	Handbooks, techniques, apparatus, equipment, materials, miscellany
792.022	Types of stage presentations . . .
792.023	Supervision
792.023 2	Production
792.023 3	Direction . . .
792.026	Costuming
792.027	Make-up
792.028	Acting . . .
792.1	Tragedy and serious drama
792.2	Comedy and melodrama . . .
792.8	Ballet
792.9	Specific productions (except ballet) . . .

LC places theater within the context of Class P—"Literature." The key elements in the PN (Drama) schedules are:

1600-1609	Periodicals . . .
1625	Dictionaries . . .
1654-1657	General works on the drama and the stage
1660-1691	Technique of dramatic composition . . .
1701	Study and teaching
1707	Criticism . . .
1720-1861	History (Subdivided by period) . . .
1870-1998	Special types (historical plays, tragedies, etc.) . . .
2000-(3300)	Dramatic representation. The theater . . .
2012	Yearbooks . . .
2035	Dictionaries . . .
2053	Management . . . See PN2085-2091
2055	Acting as a profession . . .
2085-2091	The stage and accessories . . .
2100-2193	History . . .
2205-2217	Biography . . .
2220-3030	Special countries
2220-2298	United States . . .
3151-3171	Amateur theatricals
3175-3191	College theatricals
3195	Negro minstrels
3203-3299	Spectacles, tableaux, pageants
(33))	Lyceum courses, etc. See LC 6551-6560.

The actual texts of plays are placed with the literature of each country.

Dewey places the film in 791—"Public Performances"—and devotes 791.4 to "Motion Pictures, Radio, Television." The specific breakdown is as follows:

791.43	Motion pictures
791.433	Types of presentation
791.435 ●	Kinds of motion pictures
791.435 2	Dramatic films (class texts of plays in 800)
791.435 3	Educational and documentary films

791.437	Specific films
	Description, critical appraisal, production scripts.
791.438	Bibliographies and catalogs of films
	(Use of this number is optional; prefer 010

LC places the film in PN (Drama), immediately after "Ballet" and before "Dramatic Representation. The Theater." The breakdown is as follows:

1993–1999	Motion Pictures
1993	Periodicals and societies
1994	General works
	.A1–5, By country
1995	General special (e.g., acting, criticism, aesthetics)
1996	Authorship, Scenario writing, etc.
1997	Plays, Scenarios, etc.
1998	Miscellaneous: Directories, Catalogs, etc.
1999	Special corporations

SUBJECT HEADINGS FREQUENTLY USED

Apart from the New York Public Library, which has published *Music Subject Headings* (2nd ed. enl. Boston: G. K. Hall, 1966), most libraries use the Library of Congress subject headings. A general, comprehensive heading was added by LC in 1972, with the following divisions:

Performing Arts
 xx Amusements
 −Law and legislation (Direct)
  xx Law and art
 −Reviews
Performing arts and children
 x Children and the performing arts
Performing arts and youth
 x Youth and the performing arts.

Most information about the performing arts will be found under the specific headings and subdivisions of the individual fields.

A sampling of the headings and structure of divisions and cross references for "Music" is given as follows:

Music (Indirect)
 sa Advent music
 Arrangement (Music) . . .
 Chamber music . . .
 Choral music . . .
 Electronic music . . .
 Folk dance music
 Folk music . . .
 Impressionism (Music) . . .
 Opera . . .
 Symphony orchestras
 Television music . . .

also subdivision Songs and music *under specific subjects, classes of persons, names of individuals, institutions, societies, etc.; also headings beginning with the words* Music or Musical . . .
−Acoustics and physics . . .
−Aesthetics
 See Music−Philosophy and aesthetics
−Analysis, appreciation
−Bibliography
 sa International inventory of musical sources
 Music libraries
 −Catalogs . . .

—Bio-bibliography . . .
—Biography
   See Composers
      Conductors (Music) . . .
—Classification
   See Classification—Music . . .
—Dynamics, phrasing
   See Music—Interpretation (Phrasing,
      dynamics, etc.) . . .
—History and criticism . . .
  —Methods . . .
  —Outlines, syllabi, etc. . . .
  —Ancient
    sa Bible—Music
      Music—Jews
      Music, Greek and Roman . . .
    xx Bible—Music
  —Medieval
    sa Chants (Plain, Gregorian, etc.)
      —History and criticism
      Madrigal
      Motet . . .
  —16th century . . .
  —20th century . . .
—Performance
   sa Concerts
      Conducting . . .
      Piano—Performance . . .
   xx Concerts
      Conducting
      Embellishment (Music)
      Embellishment (Vocal music). . .
—Therapeutic use
   See Music therapy

—Yearbooks
   See Music—Almanacs, yearbooks, etc.
—Africa [Brazil, Germany, etc.] . . .
—Russia
  -1917-
Music, Baroque . . .
Music, Byzantine . . .
Music, Incidental . . .
Music, Oriental . . .
  sa Microtones
  x Oriental music
  xx Microtones
    Microtonic music
Music, African [Brazilian, German, etc.] . . .
Music and literature . . .
Music and television
   See Television and music . . .
Music in art
  Here are entered works dealing with
   the representation of musical
   subjects in art.
Music in churches . . .
  sa Church music
    Music in synagogues . . .
Musical form
  sa Anthem
    Ballad opera . . .
Musical instruments (Mechanical) . . .
Musical instruments, Electronic . . .
Musical notation . . .
Musicians . . .
Musicians, Women . . .
Musicians, Austrian [English, German,
   etc.] . . .

The headings for the dance, which have not been developed as fully as those for music, can be treated more briefly:

Dancing (Indirect)
  sa Ballet
    Ballroom dancing
    Balls (Parties)
    Choreography
    Clog-dancing
    Dance etiquette
    Dance music . . .
    Folk dancing . . .
    Rock and roll dancing
    Round dancing
    Square dancing . . .

—Libraries and museums
   see Music libraries
     Music museums . . .
—Philosophy
   x Dancing—Aesthetics
   xx Aesthetics . . .
—Production and direction
   see Dance production
  —Stage—setting and scenery . . .
Dancing (in religion, folklore, etc.) . . .
Dancing in moving-pictures, television,
   etc. . . .

Although the LC headings for the theater are more fully developed than those for the dance, they are much less complex than the ones for music:

Theater (Direct)
  Here are entered works which deal with
    the drama as acted upon the stage,
    and works treating of the historical,
    legal, moral, and religious aspects of
    the theater. Works treating of
    the drama from a literary point of
    view only are entered under Drama,
    English drama, French drama, etc.
  Works dealing with the architecture,
    construction, decoration, etc., of
    theaters are entered under the heading
    Theaters.
  sa   Acting
       Actors . . .
       Drama
       Dramatic criticism . . .
       Moralities . . .
       Mysteries and miracle-plays
       Opera . . .
       Theaters . . .
  —Censorship
  x Censorship of the stage . . .
  —Laws and regulations
  sa Actors—Legal status, laws, etc.
       Copyright—Drama

  —Little theater movement . . .
  —Production and direction . . .
  —Research . . .
  —Greece . . .
  —New York (City)
    sa Off-Broadway theater . . .
Theater, Municipal . . .
Theater as a profession
  sa Acting as a profession
  x Theater—Vocational guidance . . .
Theater programs
  sa Playbills
  xx Playbills . . .
Theaters
  Here are entered works dealing only with
    the physical aspects of theaters,
    their architecture, construction,
    decoration, sanitation, etc. Works
    treating of the historical, legal,
    moral and religious aspects of the
    theater are entered under the heading
    Theater.
  The theaters of a particular city are
    entered under the name of the city,
    with subdivision Theaters, e.g.,
    Paris—Theaters.

The Library of Congress does not use the word "Film" (except in very minor ways) in its system of subject headings. The terms "Photography" and "Moving-pictures" are used instead. The latter is more productive for most searches of the sort envisioned in this book:

Moving-pictures (Direct) . . .
  sa Art in moving-pictures
       Ballet in moving-pictures, television,
         etc. . . .
       Comedy films . . .
  x Motion pictures . . .
  —Academy awards
    see Academy awards (Moving-pictures)
  —Aesthetics
    xx Aesthetics . . .
  —Audiences
    see Moving-picture audiences . . .
  —Biography
    xx Actors
         Actresses
  —Cataloging
    see Cataloging of moving pictures
  —Catalogs
    sa *subdivision* Film catalogs *under*
         specific subjects, e.g.
         Geology—Film catalogs
  —Direction
    see Moving-pictures—Production and
         direction . . .
  —Setting and scenery . . .

**Moving-pictures, American, [French, etc.]
    (Direct) . . .**
Moving-pictures, Talking
  sa Sound—Recording and reproducing. .
Moving-pictures and television . . .
Moving-pictures as a profession
  sa Acting as a profession . . .
Moving-pictures in education
  sa Libraries and moving-pictures
       Moving-pictures—Evaluation . . .
       Moving-pictures in teacher
         training
  xx Education
       Teaching—Aids and devices
       Visual education . . .
Moving-pictures on television
  see Television broadcasting
       of films.

MAJOR ORGANIZATIONS, PUBLISHERS,
INFORMATION CENTERS, AND SPECIAL COLLECTIONS

The number of national and international organizations in the field of music is so great that attention can be given here only to a small number of those most significant to the librarian. The International Association of Music Libraries has branches in most of the developed countries (U.S. branch: 80 Codornices Road, Berkeley, Calif. 94708). It is currently sponsoring the *International Inventory of Musical Sources/Répertoire international des sources musicales* (RISM). Since 1954, it has published *Fontes Artis Musicae*. The International Music Council (1 rue Miollis, Paris 15e, France), one of the first non-governmental organizations established under Unesco sponsorship, studies the development of music throughout the world and produces numerous books and recordings. The International Musicological Society (Neuweilstr. 15, CH 4000 Basel 15, Switzerland), founded in 1927 to promote research, has published *Acta Musicologica* since 1928. The Music Library Association (343 S. Main St., Room 105, Ann Arbor, Mich. 48108) supports a wide range of activities, including publication of *Music Cataloging Bulletin* (1970–) and *Notes* (1943–). The Association for Recorded Sound Collections (c/o Rogers & Hammerstein Archives, 111 Amsterdam Ave., New York, N.Y. 10023), founded in 1966, includes in its membership people in the broadcasting and recording industries as well as librarians. Its principal publications are *ARSC Journal* (3 per year) and *ARSC Bulletin* (irregular). The Music Educators' National Conference (1201 16th St., N.W., Washington, D.C. 20036) was founded in 1907 and now has over 60,000 members. It supports a wide range of publications, including *Music Educators' Journal* (monthly) and *Journal of Research in Music Education* (quarterly). The American Musicological Society (University of Pennsylvania, 201 S. 34th St., Philadelphia, Pa. 19104) promotes research in various fields of music. Its publications include the *Journal of the American Musicological Society* (3 per year) and lists of master's theses and doctoral dissertations. The American Guild of Organists (630 Fifth Ave., New York, N.Y. 10020), one of the oldest and largest of the specialized groups, publishes *Music/AGO–RCCO* (monthly).

By contrast with music, the number of organizations devoted to the dance is comparatively small; those that do exist seem to be largely concentrated in two areas—ballet and the teaching of dancing. The North American Ballet Association (2801 Connecticut Ave., N.W., Washington, D.C. 20008) consists of professional ballet companies, whereas the Ballet Theatre Foundation (888 Seventh Ave., New York, N.Y. 10019) appeals to a broad public for support.

The National Association for Regional Ballet (1564 Broadway, New York, N.Y. 10036) promotes festivals and other educational activities in the United States and Canada. The Imperial Society of Teachers of Dancing (70 Gloucester Place, London W.1, Englnad) has a branch in the United States (Box 90, Vernon, N.J. 07462) and publishes *Imperial Dance Journal* (quarterly). The National Council of Dance Teacher Organizations (325 W. 45th St., New York, N.Y. 10036) coordinates activity on a national basis, cooperates with international organizations, and publishes a *Bulletin* (5/6 per year). The Dance Educators of America (21 Club Road, Sea Cliff, Long Island, N.Y. 11579) and the Dance Masters of America (146 E. Water St., Elmira, N.Y. 14901) both consist of dance teachers; both have regional groups to supplement national activities.

The International Federation for Theatre Research (14, Woronzow Rd., London, N.W.8, England) disseminates scholarly information through *Theatre Research* (semi-annual). The International Theatre Institute, established in 1948 by Unesco, has a branch in the United States (245 W. 52nd St., New York, N.Y. 10010); it publishes *Theatre Notes* (10 per year) and *International Theatre Information* (quarterly). The American branch, known as the American National Theatre and Academy, has a variety of programs of its own, including publication of *ANTA Bulletin* (quarterly), *World Premieres*, and *World Theatres*. The American Theatre Association (1317 F St., N.W., Washington, D.C. 20004) is concerned with all phases of the educational theater; its divisions include American Community Theatre Association; Army Theatre Arts Association; National Association of Schools of Theatre; Children's Theatre Association; Secondary School Theatre Association; University and College Theatre Association; and University Resident Theatre Association. Publications include: *Theatre News* (monthly); *Educational Theatre Journal* (quarterly); *Children's Theatre Review* (quarterly); *Onstage* (quarterly); and *Secondary School Theatre* (quarterly). The Theatre Library Association (111 Amsterdam Ave., Room 513, New York, N.Y. 10023) includes actors, booksellers, writers and researchers in its membership, and issues an irregular publication entitled *Broadside*.

The University Film Association (Department of Communication Arts, University of Windsor, Windsor 11, Ontario, Canada) publishes *UFA Digest* (5/6 per year) and *Journal* (quarterly). The American Federation of Film Societies (144 Bleecker St., New York, N.Y. 10012) includes teachers, librarians and students and publishes *Film Society Bulletin* (monthly) and *Film Critic* (monthly). The American Film Institute (John F. Kennedy Center for the Performing Arts, Washington, D.C. 20566) supports a wide range of archival, research, and production activities. Publications include *Filmfacts* (bi-weekly) and *AFI Report* (6 per year). The Federation of Motion Picture Councils (110 Rose Lane, Springfield, Pa. 19064) includes 33 state and local groups that review or endorse films; it publishes *News Reel* (monthly) as well as *Motion Picture Ratings Preview Reports*. The International Federation of Film Archives (74 Galerie Ravenstein, Brussels 1, Belgium) publishes books (in English, French, and German) on the preservation of film. The Educational Film Library Association (17 W. 60th St., New York, N.Y. 10023) evaluates books and films through *EFLA Evaluations* (on 3" by 5" cards) and *Sightlines* (bi-monthly). The Film Library Information Council (Box 348, Radio City Station, New York, N.Y. 10019) gathers and disseminates information about actual library performance of films and other nonprint media. It publishes *Film Library Quarterly*.

Music publishing often occurs outside the normal trade channels. One of the best-known firms is Breitkopf and Härtel (Postbox 74, Walkmuhl-strasse 52, Wiesbaden, West Germany), which has published serious and classical music since about 1750. C. F. Peters (U.S. office: 373 Park Ave. South, New York, N.Y.) was founded in Leipzig in 1800. The famous British firm of

Novello & Co. Ltd. (Borough Green, Sevenoaks, Kent, England) was founded in 1811. A major American firm is G. Schirmer (609 Fifth Ave., New York, N.Y. 10017), founded in 1861. In 1883, the Theodore Presser Co. (Presser Place, Bryn Mawr, Pa.) was founded. Brief information about other music publishers will be found in the "Overseas Section" of the latest edition of *Who's Who in Music and Musicians' International Directory* (6th ed. New York: Hafner, 1972). Further information about publishers of serious and educational music may be obtained from the Music Publishers' Association of the United States (609 Fifth Ave., New York, N.Y. 10017), while information about publishers of popular music is available from National Music Publishers' Association (110 E. 59th St., New York, N.Y. 10022).

The American Music Center (2109 Broadway, Suite 1579, New York, N.Y. 10023) was appointed official U.S. Information Center on Music in 1962 by the National Music Council. The Institute of Ethnomusicology (University of California at Los Angeles, 405 Hilgard Ave., Los Angeles, Calif. 90024) is interested in musical cultures throughout the world, while the American Institute of Musicology (P.O. Box 30665, Dallas, Tex. 75230) concentrates on medieval and Renaissance music and the American Composers' Alliance (Library and Information Center, 170 W. 74th St., New York, N.Y. 10023) specializes in manuscripts and published music of contemporary American composers.

The Committee on Research in Dance (c/o Dr. Patricia Rowe, Department of Dance Education, New York University, Washington Square, New York, N.Y. 10003) serves as a clearinghouse for research information about the dance. The National Council of Dance Teacher Organizations (325 W. 45th St., New York, N.Y. 10036) prepares syllabi, examinations, and material for the public schools.

The International Theatre Studies Center (University of Kansas, Lawrence, Kansas 66044) publishes the results of its research in various professional journals and issues the following semi-annual publications: *Theatre Documentation*; *Afro-Asian Theatre Bulletin*; and *Latin-American Theatre Review*. The Wisconsin Center for Theatre Research (University of Wisconsin, 1166 Van Hise Hall, 1220 Linden Drive, Madison, Wisc. 53706) concentrates on the performing arts in America. The Institute of Outdoor Drama (University of North Carolina, Chapel Hill, N.C. 27514) provides advisory and consultation services, research and bibliographical work.

The most outstanding music collection in the United States is in the Library of Congress, which benefits from copyright deposit. The Music Division, established in 1897, has issued numerous catalogs, several of which are listed elsewhere in this book. Another notable collection is found in the Music Division of the Research Library of the Performing Arts in Lincoln Center (part of the New York Public Library). Music from the twelfth to the eighteenth centuries is a specialty of the Isham Memorial Library of Harvard University, while primary sources in early opera scores and librettos are a special strength of the University of California Music Library in Berkeley. In Europe, the Austrian National Library in Vienna, the Royal Library of Belgium in Brussels, the University Library in Prague, the Bibliothèque Nationale in Paris, the Deutsche Staatsbibliothek in Berlin, the British Museum in London, the Biblioteca Nazionale Centrale in Florence, and the Vatican Library in Rome have outstanding collections.

The Dance Collection in the Research Library of the Performing Arts

(New York Public Library) includes photographs, scores, programs, prints, posters, and playbills as well as instruction manuals and other literature on the dance. The Archives of Dance, Music and Theatre (University of Florida Libraries) contains about 20,000 similar memorabilia relating to the performing arts in the twentieth century.

The Theater Arts Library (University of California at Los Angeles) has screenplays and pictures in addition to the general collection of English and foreign language books on the film. The Harvard Theatre Collection (Houghton Library) has rare letters, account books, diaries, drawings, promptbooks, and playbills from the United States, Britain, and Europe. Similar materials relating to British and American theater from 1875 to 1935 (especially the Chicago Little Theatre Movement 1912-1917) are found in the Department of Rare Books and Special Collections, University of Michigan. The Theatre Collection in the Research Library of the Performing Arts (New York Public Library) is one of the most notable anywhere. Bibliographic access is provided through its published catalog. The Free Library of Philadelphia has over 1,200,000 items relating to the theater, early circuses, and minstrel and vaudeville shows.

The Library of Congress has several notable film collections, including those received on copyright deposit. The Dell Publishing Company has about 3,500,000 pictures dealing with movie and TV personalities.

These represent but a small sampling of the collections in the United States and Europe that contain specialized information about the performing arts. The previously mentioned works by Ash, Lewanski, and ASLIB should be consulted for more details.

14 PRINCIPAL INFORMATION SOURCES IN THE PERFORMING ARTS

Dance (cont.)
  Directories and Annuals
  Histories
  Biographies
  Ballet Digests
  Periodicals
Theater
  Introductory Works and Bibliographic Guides
  Bibliographies
  Indexes, Abstracts, and Current Awareness Services
  Dictionaries and Encyclopedias
    Dictionaries
    Encyclopedias
  Directories and Annuals
  Histories
    General
    Particular Topics and Countries
  Biographies
  Anthologies and Digests of Plays
  Reviews
  Production and Direction
  Periodicals
Film
  Introductory Works and Bibliographic Guides
  Bibliographies
  Indexes, Abstracts, and Current Awareness Services
  Dictionaries and Encyclopedias
  Directories and Annuals
  Histories
  Biographies
  Reviews
  Periodicals

GENERAL AND MISCELLANEOUS

528. Association for Recorded Sound Collections. **A Preliminary Directory of Sound Recordings Collections in the United States and Canada**. Prep. by a Program Committee. New York: New York Public Library, 1967. 157p.

529. **Guide to the Performing Arts**. Metuchen, N.J.: Scarecrow Press, 1960– . Annual. Years covered, 1957– .
This guide began as a supplement to *Guide to the Musical Arts* (1935-56), which it has superseded. Indexes articles in over 50 periodicals, mainly in English. From 1957 to 1965 a separate section on "Television Arts" was incorporated in the main work, starting with coverage for 1956. S. Yancey Belknap compiled the volumes for the years 1957 to 1967. Volume for 1968 (published in 1972) was compiled by Louis Rachow and Katherine Hartley. Now includes *Guide to Dance Periodicals*.

530. **The National Directory for the Performing Arts and Civic Centers**. Dallas, Handel & Co., 1973– . Annual.

Arranged by state and then by city. Includes permanent performing arts organizations, civic centers, and performing arts facilities in the United States.

531.   Philpott, Alexis Robert. **Dictionary of Puppetry**. Boston: Plays, Inc., 1967. 128p.

Covers all forms of puppetry, past and present. Technical terms, literature, individuals, history, associations. Many cross references. Compiled in England, it has a British emphasis, though coverage is international. Designed to aid the reader who knows little about the subject. The American edition lacks the bibliography. Libraries should also consider Philpott's *Modern Puppetry* (Boston: Plays, Inc., 1967).

532.   Roach, Helen Pauline. **Spoken Records**. 3rd ed. Metuchen, N.J.: Scarecrow Press, 1970. 288p.

Covers speeches, documentaries, authors' readings, other readings from English and American literature, plays, and children's records. Evaluative comments by compiler. An appendix contains articles by other people on a variety of related topics. Index.

533.   Schoolcraft, Ralph Newman, ed. **Performing Arts Books in Print: An Annotated Bibliography**. New York: Drama Book Specialists, 1973. 761p.

A classified, annotated bibliography with four main divisions: Books on Theatre and Drama; Books on Motion Pictures, Television, and Radio; Books on the Mass Media; and the Popular Arts. Detailed table of contents indicates subdivisions, while scope and limitations are carefully explained in the introduction. Supplemented by Author and Editor Index; Title Index; List of Publishers. Revision and updating of *Theatre Books in Print* (2nd ed., 1966). Supplemented and updated by a quarterly publication entitled *Annotated Bibliography of New Publications in the Performing Arts*.

534.   Sharp, Harold S., and Marjorie Z. Sharp, comps. **Index to Characters in the Performing Arts**. Metuchen, N.J.: Scarecrow Press, 1966-73. 6 vols.

Part I, Non-Musical Plays: An Alphabetical Listing of 30,000 Characters (1966, 2 vols.); Part II, Operas and Musical Productions (1969, 2 vols.); Part III, Ballets (1972); Part IV, Radio and Television (1973). The basic pattern consists of two sections for each part: 1) alphabetical listing of characters, with cross references linking the characters in each production; 2) alphabetical list of citation symbols, with full title, type of production, number of acts, author or composer, name of theater, and place and date of first performance.

535.   Stevenson, Gordon, issue ed. "Trends in Archival and Reference Collections in Recorded Sound," **Library Trends** 21 (July 1972): 3-155.

A comprehensive state-of-the-art survey. The articles on such topics as sound archives, oral history, and discography are rich in bibliographical citations.

536. Sutton, Roberta Briggs. **Speech Index: An Index to 259 Collections of World Famous Orations and Speeches for Various Occasions.** 4th ed. Metuchen, N.J.: Scarecrow Press, 1966. 947p. **Speech Index,** 1966-1970, 1972. 275p.
Includes material from the three preceding volumes plus new items. Covers 1935 to 1970. Dictionary-type arrangement with entries for each oration under author, subject, and type of speech.

537. **Who's Who in Show Business: The International Directory of the Entertainment World.** New York: Who's Who in Show Business, 1950– . Biennial.
International coverage of personalities in the performing and creative arts. For many artists, it gives portraits, credits, and an address where the artist or his representative can be reached. Classified arrangement by entertainment categories, with a name index. Detailed table of contents.

538. Woodson, Carter G. **Negro Orators and Their Orations.** Washington, D.C.: Associated Publishers, 1925. 711p.
Compiled by the editor of *The Journal of Negro History*, it attempted to include all extant orations of consequence delivered up to that time by American Negroes. A short sketch of the orator and a description of the circumstances of the speech appear with each oration. Arrangement is chronological, with a brief name and subject index.

MUSIC

Introductory Works and Bibliographic Guides

539. Backus, John. **The Acoustical Foundations of Music.** New York: McGraw-Hill, 1957. 312p.
Generally regarded as a sound, reasonably comprehensive, modern work for the layman with some musical and scientific background. Another recommended work is *Musical Acoustics*, by Charles Aaron Culver (4th ed. New York: McGraw-Hill, 1956).

540. Bernstein, Leonard. **Young People's Concerts.** Drawings by Isadore Seltzer. Rev. and enl. ed. New York: Simon and Schuster, 1970. 233p.
Based on Bernstein's television series. Discusses various aspects of music such as: What is melody? What does music mean? What is classical music? Gives examples that can be played on the piano. Planned for ages 12 to 18, this book has much to offer the adult listener as well.

541. Bryant, Eric Thomas. **Music.** New York: Philosophical Library, 1965. 84p.
About 250 books are covered in this evaluative bibliography. It follows the pattern that is standard for such guides, with seven chapters: 1) Dictionaries, Encyclopedias and Bibliographies; 2) Histories of Music; 3) Voices and

Instruments; 4) The Repertoire: Aids to Selection; 5) Some Technicalities; 6) Musical Appreciation; 7) Gramophone Records. Author and title index, general index. The author is a British librarian.

542.   Copland, Aaron. **What to Listen for in Music**. Rev. ed. New York: McGraw-Hill, 1957. 307p.
A book on music appreciation for the layman by one of America's foremost composers. Other useful works are *The Art of Listening: Developing Musical Perception*, by Howard Brofsky and Jean Shapiro Bamberger (2nd ed. New York: Harper & Row, 1972), and *Understanding and Enjoying Music*, by John D. White (New York: Dodd, Mead, 1968).

543.   Duckles, Vincent. **Music Reference and Research Materials**. 2nd ed. New York: Free Press, 1967. 385p.
An excellent guide for teachers and students of musicology and for reference librarians. Contains annotated entries and bibliographical information. Arranged by form: dictionaries, encyclopedias, catalogs, histories, etc. Reviews are cited for items. Includes an author index.

544.   Ferguson, Donald Nivison. **The Why of Music: Dialogues in an Unexplored Region of Appreciation**. Minneapolis: University of Minnesota Press, 1969. 309p.
Cast in the form of a dialogue, this book probes the meaning of music in a pleasantly discursive way. It is a sequel to Ferguson's earlier book, *Music as Metaphor* (Minneapolis: University of Minnesota Press, 1960).

545.   Haggin, Bernard H. **The New Listener's Companion and Record Guide**. 3rd ed. New York: Horizon Press, 1971. 365p.
The first part, devoted to music appreciation, covers such topics as form, major periods, and works of selected individual composers. The second part is an annotated discography. Index of musical procedures, forms and terms; general index; index of performers. Another work of music appreciation (with records to accompany the book) is *Music: A Design for Listening*, by Homer Ulrich (3rd ed. New York: Harcourt Brace Jovanovich, 1970).

546.   Hansen, Peter S. **An Introduction to Twentieth Century Music**. 2nd ed. Boston: Allyn and Bacon, 1967. 420p.
Generally regarded as one of the better books on the subject, despite some lack of sympathy with avant-garde movements. This slight deficiency may be partly remedied by turning to *Electronic Music: A Listener's Guide*, by Elliott Schwartz (New York: Praeger, 1973).

547.   Hoffer, Charles R. **The Understanding of Music**. 2nd ed. Belmont, Calif., Wadsworth, 1971. 484p.
A record album is available to accompany this book. The first four chapters form an introductory unit on aesthetics, listening techniques, basic music materials, and the nature of musical performance. The next ten chapters are a chronological survey from Gregorian chant to the twentieth century. There are

special chapters on Beethoven, chamber music, and opera, as well as more general period chapters. The last three chapters deal with modern music: folk music, jazz, commercial music, and musical comedy as well as leading modern composers of serious music.

548.   Hood, Mantle. **The Ethnomusicologist**. New York: McGraw-Hill, 1971. 386p.

A well-written book, designed for a professional audience, which considers such practical matters as field equipment, research techniques, and problems of recording non-Western music in the Western notation. Three seven-inch LP records are included in a pocket in the back.

549.   Ratner, Leonard. **Music: The Listener's Art**. 2nd ed. New York: McGraw-Hill, 1966. 463p.

Written by a professor at Stanford University, this book is generally regarded as fairly free of technical jargon and valuable for student and layman alike. One reviewer noted that it has been used in elementary and secondary schools as well as colleges and universities. There is an appendix dealing with musical notation.

550.   Sachs, Curt. **Our Musical Heritage**. 2nd ed. Englewood Cliffs, N.J.: Prentice-Hall, 1955. 351p.

A useful introduction by one of the most distinguished musicologists of the twentieth century. Can be used as a text for the student (with its bibliographies) or for the interested layman who will persevere in the more difficult portions.

551.   Sessions, Roger. **Questions about Music**. Cambridge: Harvard University Press, 1970. 166p.

Based on the Charles Eliot Norton lectures for 1968/69, this book will interest the composer as well as the layman in its exploration of such topics as listening to music with knowledge and understanding, thinking and communicating about music, performance, and criteria for evaluation.

552.   Watanabe, Ruth. **Introduction to Music Research**. Englewood Cliffs, N.J.: Prentice-Hall, 1967. 237p.

Prepared by a librarian at the Eastman School of Music, this book offers valuable assistance to the graduate student. It discusses use of libraries, preparation of a research paper, and music reference books and periodicals. Chapter bibliographies. Index of proper names; index of works and periodicals; index of subjects.

Bibliographies of Music Literature

553.   Adkins, Cecil, ed. **Doctoral Dissertations in Musicology**. 5th ed. Philadelphia: American Musicological Society, 1971. 203p.

General arrangement is by period, subdivided by broad subjects. Author and subject indexes. Coverage begins with 1905. German dissertations are covered in Richard Schaal's *Verzeichnis deutschsprachiger Musikwissenschaftlicher Dissertationen, 1861-1960* (Kassel: Bärenreiter, 1963).

554. Basart, Ann Phillips. **Serial Music: A Classified Bibliography of Writings on Twelve-Tone and Electronic Music**. Berkeley: University of California Press, 1961. 151p.

Contains 823 items. Author and subject indexes.

555. Blum, Fred. **Music Monographs in Series**. New York: Scarecrow Press, 1964. 197p.

A bibliography of numbered monograph series in the field of music current since 1945. Lists more than 250 series from 30 countries, arranged alphabetically by title of series or issuing organization. Entries for each volume give author, title, and date. Includes list of publishers and their agents, and an alphabetical list of series and issuing organizations. Index of names.

556. Chase, Gilbert. **A Guide to the Music of Latin America**. 2nd ed. Washington: Pan American Union, 1962. 411p.

An annotated bibliography, with introductory comments for each country. Subheadings for each country vary somewhat but usually include introduction; general and miscellaneous; biography and criticism; national anthem; folk and primitive music.

557. Darrell, Robert Donaldson, comp. **Schirmer's Guide to Books on Music and Musicians: A Practical Bibliography**. New York: Schirmer, 1951. 402p.

Classified list of books in print (at that time) in English. Highly selective supplement of non-English books.

558. De Lerma, Dominique-René. **The Black-American Musical Heritage: A Preliminary Bibliography**. Ann Arbor, Mich., Music Library Association, 1969. 45 l.

Covers both literature *about* music and music itself.

559. Kennington, Donald. **The Literature of Jazz: A Critical Guide**. Chicago: American Library Association, 1971. 304p.

First published in 1970 by the Library Association of Great Britain. Chapters on: general background; histories; biographies; analysis; theory and criticism; periodical literature; organizations. Appendix: jazz on film. Good coverage of books in English, but much poorer coverage of foreign languages.

560. Mecklenburg, Carl Gregor. **International Jazz Bibliography: Jazz Books from 1919 to 1968**. Strasbourg: P. H. Heitz, 1969. 198p.

Bibliography of literature about jazz. Includes 250 monographic discographies and 300 discographies published as appendices in books. Omits periodical articles.

561. New York Public Library. **Dictionary Catalog of the Music Collection**. Boston: G. K. Hall, 1965. 33 vols. Supp. I, 1966. 811p. Supp. II, 1973. 10 vols.

Main set and supplements together contain over 700,000 entries. Special strengths include folk songs, full scores of operas, American music, vocal music, programs, record catalogs, and manuscripts.

562. **Répertoire international des sources musicales. International Inventory of Musical Sources.** Munich: Henle, 1960– .
A joint effort by the International Musicological Society and the International Association of Music Libraries, attempting to list all bibliographies of music, writings about music, and textbooks on music published by 1800. Gives locations. Over 1,000 libraries in 30 countries took part. Published as individual titles and cataloged by LC as such. Most libraries class together and connect by series entry in card catalog. Commonly referred to as RISM.

563. U.S. Library of Congress. Music Division. **Catalogue of Early Books on Music (before 1800).** Washington, D.C.: 1913. 312p. Supp. 1913-42, 1944. 143p.

564. Weichlein, William J. **A Checklist of American Music Periodicals 1850-1900.** Detroit: Information Coordinators, 1970. 103p. (Detroit Studies in Music Bibliography, 16).
Excludes periodicals that published *only* music; lists 309 titles, arranged alphabetically, plus a chronological register. Full bibliographic information is given, and at least one library location. Sometimes "not in ULS." Good for interlibrary loan as well as reference. LC catalogs and classifies Detroit Studies in Music Bibliography as separates.

Bibliographies of Music

General

565. Aronowsky, Salomon. **Performing Times of Orchestral Works.** London: Benn, 1959. 802p.
Includes some 15,000 pieces, with entries under composers. Information given includes name of work, English translation, and opus number (if any); instruments taking part; movements and time for each; and total performing time.

566. **British Catalogue of Music.** London: Council of the National Bibliography, 1957– . Quarterly, with annual cumulations.
Record of music and books about music published in the United Kingdom. Classified arrangement with alphabetical index under composers and titles.

567. **British Union Catalogue of Early Music Printed before the Year 1801: A Record of the Holdings of Over One Hundred Libraries throughout the British Isles.** Ed. by Edith B. Schnapper. London: Butterworth, 1957. 2 vols.
This scholarly effort lists works generally by composer or anonymous title. Periodicals are grouped under "Periodical publications." Extensive index of first words and song titles.

568.   Brown, Howard Mayer. **Instrumental Music Printed before 1600: A Bibliography**. Cambridge: Harvard University Press, 1965. 559p.

Chronological arrangement of works published from the 1480s to 1599. Has five indexes: 1) List of Libraries and Their Holdings; 2) Volumes Described, Arranged by Types of Notation; 3) Volumes Described, Arranged by Performing Medium; 4) Names; 5) First Lines and Titles. Excellent, scholarly work.

569.   Fuld, James M. **The Book of World-Famous Music, Classical, Popular and Folk**. New rev. ed. New York: Crown, 1971. 688p.

Alphabetical by English form of titles. Gives opening bars, biographical notes, and references. Index of personal names.

570.   Henry E. Huntington Library and Art Gallery, San Marino, California. **Catalogue of Music in the Huntington Library Printed before 1801**. San Marino, 1949. 773p.

Includes music published in periodicals, omitting manuscripts, song texts, and opera librettos. Entry is under composer (title for anonymous works). There is an index of composers and editors.

571.   Heyer, Anna Harriet. **Historical Sets, Collected Editions, and Monuments of Music: A Guide to Their Contents**. 2nd ed. Chicago: American Library Association, 1969. 573p.

First published in 1957, this work covers about 900 major anthologies of music, attempting comprehensive coverage of nineteenth and twentieth century sets. The main part is alphabetical by composer and gives major editions, indicating contents and providing complete bibliographical information. Index includes entries for composers, titles, and form or medium. Similar coverage is given in *A Handbook of Music and Music Literature in Sets and Series*, by Sydney Robinson Charles (New York: Free Press, 1972).

572.   Hixon, Donald L. **Music in Early America: A Bibliography of Music in Evans**. Metuchen, N.J.: Scarecrow Press, 1970. 607p.

Hixon is a reference librarian at the University of California, Irvine. Useful for seventeenth and eighteenth century music. The first part is arranged by composer, editor or compiler; title entries are used only if the composer, editor, or compiler is unknown. Second part lists works *not* in microprint edition. Third part gives biographical sketches of lesser-known composers and compilers. There are also three indexes.

573.   Pierpont Morgan Library, New York. **The Mary Flagler Cary Music Collection: Printed Books and Music Manuscripts, Autograph Letters, Documents, Portraits**. New York: Pierpont Morgan Library, 1970. 108p.

Has 49 pages of illustrations and 108 pages of text. Collection includes over 150 autographed musical manuscripts and over 3,000 letters and documents. Valuable source for music research.

574.   Reddick, William. **The Standard Musical Repertoire, with Accurate Timings**. Garden City, N.Y.: Doubleday, 1947. 192p.

Classified arrangement. Includes overtures, orchestral works, songs, and choral numbers. Especially useful for radio program directors.

575.   Sonneck, Oscar. **A Bibliography of Early Secular American Music (18th Century)**. Rev. and enl. by William Treat Upton. Washington, D.C.: Library of Congress, 1945. Reprinted New York: Da Capo, 1964. 616p.

Lists works by title with complete bibliographical information including first lines. Also contains a list of articles and essays relating to music, and a list of composers and their works. Shows locations.

576.   Taylor, Jed H. **Vocal and Instrumental Music in Print**. New York: Scarecrow Press, 1965. 166p.

A "selective" bibliography.

577.   U.S. Information Agency. **Catalog of Published Concert Music by American Composers**. Washington, D.C.: U.S. Information Agency, 1964. 175p. Supplements, 1– , 1965– .

578.   U.S. Library of Congress. Card Division. **Library of Congress Catalog: Music and Phonorecords**, 1953– .

Issued twice a year with five-year cumulations. Earlier listings are in the main LC *Author Catalog*. "Contains entries for music scores in the broadest sense, i.e. music intended for performance, regardless of its classification. It also includes phonorecords, e.g. sound recordings, musical or non-musical, reproduced on all kinds of material, including cylinders, discs, tape and wire" (Introduction).

579.   Wolfe, Richard J. **Secular Music in America, 1801-1825: A Bibliography**. New York: New York Public Library, 1964. 3 vols.

Lists approximately 10,000 titles and editions published in America–not confined to American composers. Includes sacred music when printed in secular collections or in series and religious pieces written by American composers and published in sheet form. Arranged alphabetically by composer or anonymous title with detailed bibliographical information. Short biographical sketches of lesser-known composers. Indexes of titles, first lines, publishers, etc., and a general index. A scholarly work useful to research workers and students of American history, as well as to music scholars. Locates copies.

Vocal Music

580.   British Broadcasting Corporation. Central Music Library. **Song Catalogue**. London: B.B.C., 1966. 4 vols.

Contents: Vols. 1-2, Composers A–Z; Vols. 3-4, Titles A–Z. Basically devoted to solo songs with keyboard accompaniment, but also includes unaccompanied songs and duets; duets with piano; recitations with piano; songs with instrumental obligati; popular song annuals; and folk, national, and patriotic songs.

581.   Coffin, Berton. **The Singer's Repertoire** 2nd ed. Metuchen, N.J.:
       Scarecrow, 1960-62. 5 vols.
Contents: Vol. 1, coloratura soprano, lyric soprano and dramatic; Vol. 2,
mezzo-soprano and contralto; Vol. 3, lyric and dramatic tenor; Vol. 4, bariton
and bass; Vol. 5, program notes. A list of approximately 8,000 songs, arranged
by vocal classification, and further subdivided by nationality, mode, etc.

582.   Shoep, Arthur, and Daniel Harris. **Word-by-Word Translations of Songs
       and Arias**. Metuchen, N.J.: Scarecrow Press, 1966-72. 2 vols.
Part I, French and German (1966); Part II, Italian (1972).

583.   Stecheson, Anthony, and Anne Stecheson, comps. **The Stecheson
       Classified Song Directory**. Hollywood: Music Industry Press, 1961.
       503p.
Arranged under some 400 catchwords and composers; gives titles, publishers,
and sometimes dates for about 100,000 popular songs. Includes list of publishers
with addresses. No title index.

584.   U.S. Library of Congress. Music Division. **Catalogue of Opera Librettos
       Printed before 1800** . New York: Franklin, 1967. 4 vols. in 3.
Paged continuously. Reprint of 1914 edition. About 6,000 entries, arranged
alphabetically under title, are accompanied by historical, descriptive, and
bibliographical notes. Contents: Vols. I and II, Title Catalog; Vol. III, Author
Index; Vol. IV, Composer List and Aria Index.

585.   U.S. Library of Congress. Music Division. **Dramatic Music: A Catalogue
       of Full Scores**. Washington, D.C.: Government Printing Office, 1908.
       170p.
Arrangement is alphabetical by composer.

Specific Instruments and Combinations

586.   American Society of Composers, Authors and Publishers. **ASCAP
       Symphonic Catalog**. 2nd ed., incl. 1966 supp. New York: American
       Society of Composers, Authors and Publishers, 369, 376p.
Symphonic literature controlled by ASCAP is listed alphabetically by composers
and arrangers. Information is given about instrumentation, duration, and
publisher. For symphonies controlled by a rival organization, see entry 589.

587.   British Broadcasting Corporation. Central Music Library. **Chamber
       Music Catalogue: Chamber Music, Violin and Keyboard, Cello and
       Keyboard, Various**. London: B.B.C., 1965. Various paging.
The first volume of a series of catalogs listing both printed and manuscript
material from the BBC's vast collection. Various paging. Four parts, as indicated
in the subtitle. Arranged by composers in four columns: selection; arranger;
publishers and date; location. Short bibliography.

588. British Broadcasting Corporation. Central Music Library. **Piano and Organ Catalog**. London: B.B.C., 1965. 2 vols.
Contents: Vols. 1 and 2, Composers, A–Z. Has sections for piano solos, duets, trios, works for two or more pianos, selected works for left hand and right hand only, organ solos, and selected organ works other than solos.

589. Broadcast Music, Inc. **BMI Symphonic Catalog**. New York: Broadcast Music, Inc., 1963. 132p.
Lists, alphabetically by composer, works controlled by BMI. Information is given on instrumentation, duration, and publisher. For works controlled by rival organization, see entry 586.

590. Daniels, David. **Orchestral Music: A Source Book**. Metuchen, N.J.: Scarecrow Press, 1972. 319p.
Designed to aid in planning programs and organizing rehearsals. Covers standard repertoire (over 2,500 works) for American orchestras, providing instrumentation, duration, and publisher. A valuable older work is *Catalogue of Music for the Small Orchestra*, by Cecilia D. Saltonstall and H. C. Smith (Washington, D.C.: Music Library Association, 1947).

591. Farish, Margaret K. **String Music in Print**. 2nd ed. New York: R. R. Bowker, 1973. 464p.
Tries to cover all music for stringed instruments published in the United States.

592. Friskin, James, and Irwin Freundlich. **Music for the Piano: A Handbook of Concert and Teaching Material from 1850 to 1952**. New York: Rinehart, 1954. 432p.
Classified, selective bibliography. Comments deal mainly with technical requirements and interpretation. Updated and to some extent superseded by Maurice Hinson's *Guide to the Pianist's Repertoire*, edited by Freundlich (Bloomington, Indiana University Press, 1973. 831p.).

Individual Composers

593. Deutsch, Otto Erich, and D. R. Wakeling. **Schubert: Thematic Catalogue of All His Works, in Chronological Order**. London: Dent, 1951. 566p.
Separate sections for undated works and addenda. For each piece, the following information is given: title; date; examples; notes on manuscript and form; location of autograph; first edition; and (usually) details about first performance.

594. Zimmerman, Franklin. **Henry Purcell, 1659-95: An Analytical Catalogue of His Music**. New York: St. Martin's, 1963.
A thematic catalog with music examples. Main part divided as follows: Sacred Vocal Works; Secular Vocal Works; Dramatic Music; Instrumental Music. Numerous appendices and the following indexes: First Lines, Titles and Sub-Titles; Instrumental Forms and Titles; Authors, Translators, Paraphrasers, and Sources of Text; General Index.

Indexes, Abstracts, and Current Awareness Services

595.　Blom, Eric. **A General Index to Modern Musical Literature in the English Language, Including Periodicals, for the Years of 1915-26.** Philadelphia: Curwen, 1927. 159p.

Author entries for whole books and subject entries for parts of books are in one alphabet.

596.　Bryden, John Rennie, and David G. Hughes, comps. **An Index to Gregorian Chant.** Cambridge: Harvard University Press, 1969. 2 vols.

Vol. 1, Alphabetical index; Vol. 2, Thematic index. Chants are drawn from 19 sources chosen for general availability. Vol. 1 lists textual incipits alphabetically and cross-indexes verses and variants. Vol. 2 has a special arrangement explained in the introduction. Useful for specialized collections in music or liturgy.

597.　Chipman, John H., comp. **Index to Top-Hit Tunes, 1900-1950.** Boston: Humphries, 1962. 249p.

Contains 3,000 titles of American popular songs that have sold at least 100,000 copies of sheet music or 100,000 records. Listed by title, alphabetically and chronologically. Gives composer, publisher, date. Indicates if featured in film or musical.

598.　Cushing, Helen Grant, comp. **Children's Song Index.** New York: H. W. Wilson, 1936. 798p.

Covers more than 22,000 songs in 189 collections. Main entry, with full information, is under title, with cross references from alternate titles, different titles in different collections, translated titles, and original titles in certain languages (e.g., Russian), and from first lines (and sometimes first lines of chorus) and added entries under composer, author, and subject.

599.　de Charms, Désirée, and Paul F. Breed. **Songs in Collections: An Index.** Detroit: Information Service, Inc., 1966. 588p.

Indexes over 9,000 songs in over 400 collections. Separate sections for composed songs, anonymous and folk songs, carols and sea chanties. An index to all titles and first lines—and an author index. A useful supplement to Sears' *Song Index*.

600.　Gerboth, Walter. **An Index to Musical Festschriften and Similar Publications.** New York: Norton, 1969. 136p.

"Lists about 3,000 articles from nearly 600 volumes under broad areas and eras, with an appended author and subject index" (Frances Neel Cheney, *Wilson Library Bulletin*, May 1970, p. 973). Includes biocritical and bibliographical sources on music and musicians from a wide range of books and journals, chiefly foreign, often hard to locate.

601.　Goodkind, Herbert. **Cumulative Index 1915 through 1959 to "The Musical Quarterly."** New York: Goodkind Indexes, 1960. 204p. Supp. 1960-64.

Another focus is provided by Hazel Gertrude Kinscella's *Americana Index to "The Musical Quarterly," 1915-1957...* (Washington, D.C.: Music Educators' National Conference, 1959).

602. International Repertory of Music Literature (Organization). **RILM: Abstracts of Music Literature**. Flushing, N.Y.: International RILM Center, Queen's College, 1967– . Quarterly.

RILM (Répertoire International de la Littérature Musicale) was set up by the International Musicological Society and the International Association of Music Libraries. Classified arrangement, with nine main divisions: Reference and Research Materials; Collected Writings; Historical Musicology; Ethnomusicology; Instruments and Voice; Performance Practice and Notation; Theory and Analysis; Pedagogy; Music and Other Disciplines. Each issue has author and subject indexes. Includes dissertations.

603. Krohn, Ernest Christopher. **The History of Music: An Index to the Literature Available in a Selected Group of Publications**. St. Louis: Baton Music Co., 1958. 463p.

An index to material on the history of music appearing in some 40 periodicals, mainly German and English. Arrangement is by broad period divisions, further subdivided by such headings as "General Studies," "Composers," and the various musical forms. Includes book reviews. Indexes by authors and composers.

604. Leigh, Robert, comp. **Index to Song Books: A Title Index to Over 11,000 Copies of 6,800 Songs in 111 Books Published between 1933 and 1962**. Stockton, Calif.: the Compiler, 1964. 237p.

Coverage includes American and foreign folk songs, popular songs, children's songs, carols, hymns, operatic arias, etc. Includes only sources that have both words and music. Cross references for alternate titles and famous lines. No entries for authors or composers. Serves as a partial continuation of Sears' *Song Index*.

605. **The Music Index: The Key to Current Music Periodical Literature**. Detroit, Information Service, 1949– . Monthly, with annual cumulations.

Indexes, by author and subject, about 180 periodicals representing various aspects of the music field, ranging from musicology to the retailing of music. Gives complete indexing for musical periodicals, and indexes articles pertinent to music in some more general ones. All first performances and obituaries are indexes. Music reviews under: composer, title, and medium. Good evaluative criticism of published music can also be located through *Music and Letters: Index to Vols. I-XL, 1920-1959* (New York: Oxford University Press, 1962). Information on illustrations may be found in *Guide to the Musical Arts: An Analytical Index of Articles and Illustrations 1953-56* (New York: Scarecrow Press, 1957), which otherwise largely duplicates *The Music Index*.

606. Sears, Minnie. **Song Index ... to More Than 12,000 Songs in 177 Song Collections ...** New York: H. W. Wilson, 1926. 650p. Supp., 1934. **Another 7,000 Songs in 104 Collections**. 367p.

An important index, once widely used in public, college, and school libraries as well as music libraries. Contains titles, first lines, authors' names and composers' names in one alphabet.

Dictionaries and Encyclopedias

Dictionaries of Terms

607. Ammer, Christine. **Harper's Dictionary of Music**. New York: Harper & Row, 1972. 414p.

Includes musical terms, entries in music history, and biographies of composers (concentrating on their works). Charts present lists of composers associated with particular styles, periods, or forms. Illustrated with short specimens of music and line drawings of musical instruments.

608. Apel, Willi, and Ralph T. Daniel. **Harvard Brief Dictionary of Music**. Cambridge: Harvard University Press, 1960. 341p.

Brief articles for the non-specialist who does not need the lengthier explanations in the *Harvard Dictionary of Music*. Includes opera plots, songs and compositions, but *no* composers.

609. Apel, Willi. **Harvard Dictionary of Music**. 2nd ed., rev. and enl. Cambridge, Harvard University Press, 1969. 935p.

Probably the best work of its kind available, despite reservations about the cutting necessary to keep it in one volume and make room for new topics like Africa and iconography. Omits biographies. Some entries (e.g., periodicals) were not thoroughly updated. A necessity for every library. One reviewer estimates that it will answer 80 percent of reference questions in music. Larger libraries will want to retain the 1944 edition because of the number of monographic articles that have been drastically shortened.

610. Baker, Theodore A. **Dictionary of Musical Terms, Containing Upwards of 9000 English, French, German, Italian, Latin and Greek Words and Phrases . . . with a Supplement Containing an English-Italian Vocabulary for Composers**. New York: Schirmer, 1923. 257p.

Words and phrases are carefully defined, and rules are given for pronunciation of Italian, German, and French. Has gone through many reprintings and some revisions. First published in 1895. The 1923 version describes itself as "Twenty-first edition, thoroughly revised and augmented by an appendix of 700 additional wrods and phrases."

611. Blom, Eric, comp. **Everyman's Dictionary of Music**. 5th ed. Rev. by Jack Westrup. New York: St. Martin's Press, 1972. 793p.

Concise treatment of terms and biographical information. Over 10,000 entries, with numerous cross references.

612. Carter, Henry Holland. **A Dictionary of Middle English Musical Terms**. Ed. by George B. Gerhard and others. Bloomington: Indiana University Press, 1961. 655p.

Indiana University Humanities Series, No. 45. A standard work for the period 1100 to 1500.

613.   Coover, James B. **Music Lexicography: Including a Study of Lacunae in Music Lexicography and a Bibliography of Music Dictionaries**. 3rd ed. Carlisle, Pa.: Carlisle Books, 1971. 175p.

Began in 1952 as a bibliography of music dictionaries. Later editions have been expanded to include a substantial essay portion as well as greater bibliographical coverage. Considered by one reviewer to be the most comprehensive and authoritative bibliography in the field.

614.   Marcuse, Sibyl. **Musical Instruments: A Comprehensive Dictionary**. Garden City, N.Y.: Doubleday, 1964. 608p.

A standard work. Bibliography of sources consulted is on pages 603 to 608.

615.   Riemann, Hugo. **Musik-Lexikon**. 12th ed. Ed. by Wilibald Gurlitt. New York: Schott Music Corp., 1959-67. 3 vols.

Originally a student's pocket dictionary in 1881. Vols. 1 and 2 are geographical. Vol. 3 deals with musical terms.

616.   Wright, Rowland. **Dictionnaire des instruments de musique: étude de lexicologie**. London: Battley Brothers, 1941. 192p.

"Wright traces the names for musical instruments employed in French literature from the earliest times to the end of the nineteenth century. Although published more than twenty-five years ago, it remains one of the few music dictionaries based on a careful study of word origins" [Vincent Duckles, "Music Literature, Music, and Sound Recordings," *Library Trends* 15 (January 1967): 499].

Sources of Longer Descriptive Articles

General

617.   Cooper, Martin, ed. **The Concise Encyclopedia of Music and Musicians**. Contribs.: Sir John Barbiroll and others. New York: Hawthorn Books, 1958. 516p.

Half of the 18 contributors were musicians and the others were critics. Short articles on technical terms, foreign words, musical instruments, and lives of both well-known and obscure figures. Handsomely printed with excellent illustrations. British slant. Lacks adequate cross references. Articles unsigned.

618.   Cross, Milton John, and David Ewen. **The Milton Cross New Encyclopedia of the Great Composers and Their Music**. Garden City, N.Y.: Doubleday, 1969. 2 vols.

Conservative. Designed for home use. Revision of 1953 and 1962 editions. Very little on pre-Bach and very little on contemporary composers or recent music. Intended for casual music lover, but there are useful bibliographies. Other encyclopedias are better for libraries.

619. **Enciclopedia della musica**. Ed. by Claudio Sartori. Milan: Ricordi, 1963-64. 4 vols.

Has over 15,000 signed articles by more than 200 contributors, both Italian and foreign. Over 300 black and white photographs and 48 color plates.

620. **Encyclopédie de la musique**. Ed. by François Michel. Paris: Fasquelle, 1958-63. 3 vols.

The work opens with essays and a chronological table. Encyclopedia portion begins on page 239 of the first volume. Many short biographies and definitions of terms; longer articles on major topics are signed.

621. Grove, Sir George, ed. **Grove's Dictionary of Music and Musicians**. 5th ed. Ed. Eric Blom. London: Macmillan; New York: St. Martin's, 1954. 9 vols. Supp. 1961.

The standard encyclopedia in English, covering the whole field from 1450 with special emphasis on English subjects. Includes musical history, theory, and practice; terms; biographies; songs and operas, etc. Does *not* give opera plots. Signed articles by specialists. Bibliographies in this edition have been improved by inclusion of periodical articles.

622. **Larousse Encyclopedia of Music**. Intro. by Anthony Hopkins. Ed., Geoffrey Hindley, with special contributions by Benny Green. New York: World Publishing Co., 1971. 576p.

"Based on *La Musique, les hommes, les instruments, les oeuvres*, edited by Norbert Dufourcq." Classified arrangement by historical periods, with many biographies. Detailed table of contents. Profusely illustrated with black and white photographs (mainly portraits) and 60 color plates. Index includes names, titles, subjects, and illustrations.

623. Lloyd, Norman. **The Golden Encyclopedia of Music**. New York: Golden Press, 1968. 720p.

An informal work for high school readers or adult laymen. Excellent illustrations, especially of musical instruments. Good index. Weak in biographies. No bibliographies, cross references, or geographical articles.

624. **Die Musik in Geschichte und Gegenwart**. Kassel: Bärenreiter, 1949-68. 14 vols.

A scholarly, comprehensive work, international in scope, with long, signed articles by specialists, including extensive bibliographical notes. Profusely illustrated. An indispensable reference book in this field. An index is now in preparation.

625. Scholes, Percy Alfred. **The Oxford Companion to Music**. 10th ed. rev. and reset. Ed. by John Owen Ward. New York: Oxford University Press, 1970. 1189p.

The present editor was a colleague of Scholes, who died in 1958. New edition, pruned and updated (90 new articles), represents an improvement over the ninth edition (1955). Alphabetical by topic. No index or bibliographies. Authoritative, accurate, and well written.

626.   Thompson, Oscar. **International Cyclopedia of Music and Musicians**.
       9th ed. Ed. by Robert Sabin. New York: Dodd, Mead, 1964. 2476p.
Alphabetical. Most articles are short, but there are some lengthy, signed
monographs in the same alphabet on important composers and special subjects
like history of music, music criticism, folk music, opera, etc. Each biographical
article is followed by a calendar of the composer's life and a classified list of his
works. Strong in biographies. Many contemporary names. Appendixes on opera
plots and bibliography *omitted* from latest edition.

Specialized

627.   Ayre, Leslie. **The Gilbert and Sullivan Companion**. Foreword by
       Martyn Green. Illustrations from the Raymond Mander and Joe
       Mitchenson Theatre Collection. New York: Dodd, Mead, 1972. 485p.
Favorably received on both sides of the Atlantic, the book describes the famous
partnership and then moves on to a series of alphabetical entries on artists, plot
summaries, title and full text for each song, and explanations of obscure
references. Song texts are found under names of operettas. Does not provide
complete libretti.

628.   Berkowitz, Freda Pastor. **Popular Titles and Subtitles of Musical
       Compositions**. New York: Scarecrow Press, 1962. 182p.
A listing of some 500 titles associated with works of serious music from 1600 to
the present, with notes as to origin of name. Arranged alphabetically in English
except where foreign title is well known. Includes bibliography and list of
composers.

629.   Bowers, Q. David. **Encyclopedia of Automatic Musical Instruments**.
       Vestal, N.Y.: Vestal Press, 1972.
Covers such instruments as cylinder and disc music boxes, player and
coin-operated pianos, orchestrions, calliopes, etc. Many illustrations. Glossary.

630.   Cobbett, Walter Willson. **Cyclopedic Survey of Chamber Music**.
       London: Oxford University Press, 1929-30. 2 vols. 2nd ed., 1963.
       3 vols.
Vols. 1 and 2 are a reissue of the 1929/30 edition, with a few minor changes in
text and insertion of symbols in the margin to indicate further references in
Vol. 3. Signed articles on subjects concerned with chamber music: topics,
persons, instruments, organizations, etc. Includes biographies and lists of
composers' works. Vol. 3 contains a selective survey since 1929, a bibliography,
and additions and corrections to the 1929/30 volumes. Index of composers.

631.   Ewen, David. **New Complete Book of the American Musical Theater**.
       New York: Holt, Rinehart, and Winston, 1970. 800p.
A guide to publications of the American musical theater, with plot, production
history, stars, songs, composers, librettists and lyricists, illustrated with
photographs. Text is arranged alphabetically by composer. Lists of shows and
songs. Full index. Ewen's *The Book of European Light Opera* (New York: Holt,
1962) is a popularized treatment of a related field.

632.   Ewen, David. **The New Encyclopedia of the Opera**. New York: Hill and
         Wang, 1971. 759p.
Earlier editions were entitled *Encyclopedia of the Opera*. The author indicates
that only about 25 percent is from earlier editions. Includes 1,500 new entries
and 100,000 words of new text. Arrangement puts stories, characters,
biographies, opera houses, etc., in one alphabetical sequence.

633.   Feather, Leonard G. **The Encyclopedia of Jazz**. Rev. ed. New York:
         Horizon, 1960. 527p.
Contains biographical sketches of more than 2,000 jazzmen, with a guide to
their recordings; history of jazz on records; recommended jazz records;
bibliography and discography. A companion volume is *The Encyclopedia of Jazz
in the Sixties* (New York: Horizon, 1966).

634.   Gentry, Linnell. **A History and Encyclopedia of Country, Western, and
         Gospel Music**. Nashville, Tenn.: McQuiddy Press, 1961. 380p.
Begins with an anthology of periodical articles since 1904. Continues with a
listing of shows since 1924. Concludes with a biographical section. Very
important work in this field.

635.   Henley, William. **Universal Dictionary of Violin and Bow Makers**.
         Brighton, England: Amati Pub., Ltd., 1959-60. 5 vols.
Continued as *Dictionary of Contemporary Violin and Bow Makers*, by Cyril
Woodcock (Brighton: Amati, 1965).

636.   Lewine, Richard. **Encyclopedia of Theatre Music**. New York: Random
         House, 1961. 248p.
Covers more than 4,000 songs from Broadway and Hollywood. Contents:
Theatre songs, 1900-1924; Theatre songs, 1925-1960; Motion picture songs;
Show chronology, 1925-60; Complete vocal scores published. Index. The lists of
songs are arranged alphabetically by title, giving composer, lyricist, show, and
year. The show chronology gives dates of Broadway openings and songs from
each show.

637.   Moore, Frank Ledlie. **Crowell's Handbook of Gilbert and Sullivan**. New
         York: Crowell, 1962. 264p.
The 14 comic operas are arranged chronologically, with casts, settings, songs,
choruses, and plot synopses. Appendices: biographies of Gilbert, Sullivan, and
D'Oyly Carte; chronology of the lives of Gilbert and Sullivan; roles in the operas;
first and famous lines; themes and texts of famous musical numbers.
Bibliography. No index.

638.   Moore, Frank Ledlie. **Crowell's Handbook of World Opera**. New York:
         Crowell, 1961. 683p.
Brief information on individual operas, operatic characters, famous numbers,
and performers. Chronology of major operas. Glossary. Indexes of singers by
voice ranges.

639.   Roxon, Lillian. **Rock Encyclopedia**. New York: Grosset and Dunlap, 1969. 611p.

Highly personal evaluation of individuals and groups. Rock terms are defined, sometimes at length. Some may be hard to find in other places. Many listings of albums and singles by performers, including *Billboard*'s weekly No. 1 hits listed chronologically through 1968. Supplementary coverage is provided in Irwin Stambler's *Encyclopedia of Popular Music and Rock* (Rev. ed. New York: St. Martin's, 1973).

640.   Stambler, Irwin, and Grelun Landon. **Encyclopedia of Folk, Country and Western Music**. New York: St. Martin's, 1969. 396p.

Most of the 500 alphabetically arranged entries are devoted to biographies, but there are also definitions of terms, descriptions of instruments, special events, etc. Appended are a list of awards, a discography of the most popular long-play albums, and a bibliography. Some photographs. Adequate cross references.

Specific Musical Compositions—Thematic Dictionaries

641.   Barlow, Harold A., and Sam Morgenstern. **Dictionary of Musical Themes**. 13th printing. New York: Crown, 1968. 656p.

The "Bartlett" for musical themes. Contains some 10,000 themes of instrumental music arranged by composers, with a notation index arranged alphabetically by the first notes of the themes. Index of titles.

642.   Barlow, Harold A., and Sam Morgenstern. **A Dictionary of Opera and Song Themes, Including Cantatas, Oratorios, Lieder, and Art Songs**. New York: Crown, 1966 (c.1950). 547p.

Originally published under the title *A Dictionary of Vocal Themes* (1950). Companion volume to *Dictionary of Musical Themes*. Contains themes from operas, oratorios, cantatas, art songs, and miscellaneous vocal works. Includes index to songs and first lines.

643.   Brook, Barry S. **Thematic Catalogues in Music: An Annotated Bibliography**. Hillsdale, N.Y.: Pendragon Press, 1972. 347p.

Most comprehensive treatment of subject to date. Published under sponsorship of Music Library Association and RILM/Abstracts of Music Literature. Supersedes *Music Library Association's Checklist of Thematic Catalogues* (1954) and *Queens College Supplement* (1966).

644.   Burrows, Raymond Murdock, and Bessie Carroll Redmond. **Concerto Themes**. New York: Simon and Schuster, 1951. 296p.

Alphabetical by composer with index of concerto titles, keys, and solo instruments. No thematic index. More concertos than in Barlow's *Dictionary of Musical Themes*.

645.   Burrows, Raymond Murdock, and Bessie Carroll Redmond. **Symphony Themes**. New York: Simon and Schuster, 1942. 295p.

Major themes of 100 great symphonies, with list of recommended recordings and chart of performance times. Lists of instruments. Bibliography. Index by keys and by titles of symphonies.

Specific Musical Compositions—Plots

646. Fellner, Rudolf. **Opera Themes and Plots**. New York: Simon and Schuster, 1958. 354p.

647. Kobbé, Gustave. **Complete Opera Book**. Ed. and rev. by the Earl of Harewood. New York: Putnam, 1972.
Discusses development of the opera and includes the stories of more than 200 operas. Brief notes on composers and musical motifs. Includes older works still being produced and modern works not yet popular but thought likely to become so. Most complete general guide available.

648. McSpadden, Joseph. **Operas and Musical Comedies**. Enl. ed. New York: Crowell, 1954. 637p.

649. O'Connell, Charles. **The Victor Book of Overtures, Tone Poems and Other Orchestral Works**. New York: Simon and Schuster, 1950. 614p.

650. Upton, George Putnam. **The Standard Cantatas: Their Stories, Their Music, and Their Composers; A Handbook**. Chicago: A. C. McClurg, 1888. 367p.

651. Upton, George Putnam. **The Standard Oratorios: Their Stories, Their Music, and Their Composers; A Handbook**. Chicago: A. C. McClurg, 1886. 335p.

Specific Musical Compositions—Program Notes

652. Baldwin, Lillian Luverne. **A Listener's Anthology of Music**. Cleveland: Kulas, 1948. 2 vols.

653. Ewen, David. **The Complete Book of Twentieth Century Music**. 2nd ed. New York: Prentice-Hall, 1959. 527p.

654. O'Connell, Charles. **The Victor Book of Symphonies**. New York: Simon and Schuster, 1948. 556p.

655. Tovey, Donald F. **Essays in Musical Analysis**. London: Oxford, 1935-39. 6 vols.
Contents: Vol. I, *Symphonies*; Vol. II, *Symphonies, Variations and Orchestral Polyphony*; Vol. III, *Concertos*; Vol. IV, *Illustrative Music*; Vol. V, *Vocal Music*; Vol. VI, *Miscellaneous Notes, Glossary, and Index*.

656. Veinus, Abraham. **Victor Book of Concertos**. New York: Simon and Schuster, 1948. 450p.

657. Voorhees, Anna Tipton. **Index to Symphonic Program Notes in Books**. Kent, Ohio: Kent State University, School of Library Science, 1970. 136p.

Directories and Annuals

658. **Directory of Music Faculties in Colleges and Universities, U.S. and Canada**. Binghamton, N.Y.: College Music Society, 1967/68– .
Title varies: from 1967/68 to 1970/72, it was *Directory of Music Faculties in American Colleges and Universities*. Consists of three parts: 1) Directory of Departments of Music; 2) Directory of Areas of Interest; 3) National Alphabetical Listing. Computer produced. Data bank can be used for searches, address labels, etc.

659. **Hinrichsen's Musical Yearbook**. London: Hinrichsen, 1944– .
Irregular; 11 volumes published to 1961, none since. Volume 11 (published in 1961) contains a cumulative index to Vols. 1-11.

660. International Association of Music Libraries. Commission of Research Libraries. **Directory of Music Research Libraries**. Iowa City: International Association of Music Libraries, 1967– .
Part I, which covers music research libraries in the United States and Canada, was issued in 1967. Part II, issued in 1970. covers 13 European countries (784 libraries). Part III (not yet published) will cover other parts of the world. For each library is given address, type and size of collection, lending code service. Indexes are arranged by country, then alphabetically. Indexes include entries by present and former names of libraries, parent institutions, donors, etc. This is intended to be used with Répertoire International des Sources Musicales (RISM)/International Inventory of Musical Sources.

661. Long, Maureen W., comp. **Music in British Libraries: A Directory of Resources**. London: Library Association, 1971. 183p.

662. **The Music Magazine/Musical Courier: The Annual Directory of the Concert World**. Evanston, Ill.: Summy-Birchard, 1962– .
Preceded by *Musical Courier: Directory Issue of the Musical Arts and Artists*, 1957-61. Title varied. Information on music organizations (American and foreign), artist and concert managers, orchestras, opera producers, festivals, foundations, schools of music, music publishers, music periodicals, recording firms, music dealers, etc.

663. **The Music Yearbook: A Survey and Directory with Statistics and Reference Articles for 1972/73–** . Ed. by Arthur Jacobs. New York: St. Martin's Press, 1972– .
First number of a planned British annual. Survey articles and statistics for 1971.

664. **The Musician's Guide**. Detroit: Music Information Service, 1954– .
American coverage.

Histories

General

665. Eisler, Paul E., comp. and ed. **World Chronology of Music History**.
      Vol. 1, 4000 B.C.–1594 A.D. New York: Oceana, 1972.
First of a set which will run to eight or ten volumes, including index. Reviewer
in *Library Journal* (Nov. 1, 1972, p. 3571) felt it was less helpful for most
purposes than conventional histories, and recommended it only for large
specialized music collections.

666. Grout, Donald Jay. **A History of Western Music**. Rev. ed. New York:
      Norton, 1973. 818p.
A survey intended as a text for music students, or for general readers. Contains
glossary, bibliography, and music chronology. Numerous illustrations. Has title,
subject, and name index.

667. Lang, Paul Henry. **Music in Western Civilization**. New York: Norton,
      1941. 1107p.
Sets music in its social, political, and cultural context. A major work, translated
into several foreign languages. Multilingual, alphabetical bibliography is on pages
1045 to 1065.

Specific Periods

668. **New Oxford History of Music**. New York: Oxford University Press,
      1954– .
Vol. 1, *Ancient and Oriental Music*, edited by Egon Wellesz (1957); Vol. 2, *Early
Medieval Music up to 1300*, edited by Dom Anselm Hughes (1954); Vol. 3, *Ars
Nova and Renaissance, 1300-1540*, edited by Dom Anselm Hughes and Gerald
Abraham (1960); Vol. 4, *The Age of Humanism, 1540-1630*, edited by
G. Abraham (1967). The following volumes are planned: Vol. 5, *Opera and
Church Music, 1630-1750*, edited by J. A. Westrup; Vol. 6, *The Growth of
Instrumental Music, 1630-1750*, edited by J. A. Westrup; Vol. 7, *The Symphonic
Outlook, 1745-1790*, edited by E. Wellesz; Vol. 8, *The Age of Beethoven,
1790-1830*, edited by G. Abraham; Vol. 9, *Romanticism, 1830-1890*, edited by
G. Abraham; Vol. 10, *Modern Music, 1890-1960*, edited by E. Blom; Vol. 11,
Chronological Tables and Index.

669. **The Norton History of Music Series**. New York: Norton, 1940– .
Written by distinguished music historians, the individual volumes in this series
deal with specific periods. Taken as a group, they constitute a history of music
from the earliest times to the present: Curt Sachs, *The Rise of Music in the
Ancient World: East and West* (1943); Gustave Reese, *Music in the Middle Ages*
(1940); Gustave Reese, *Music in the Renaissance* (rev. ed., 1959); Manfred F.
Bukofzer, *Music in the Baroque Era: From Monteverdi to Bach* (1947); Alfred
Einstein, *Music in the Romantic Era* (1947); Adolfo Salazar, *Music in Our Time:
Trends in Music Since the Romantic Era* (1946); William W. Austin, *Music in the
Twentieth Century: From Debussy through Stravinsky* (1966).

670.   **Prentice-Hall History of Music Series**. Englewood Cliffs, N.J.: Prentice-Hall, 1965– .

LC catalogs and classifies these volumes separately. For a list, consult Eleanor A. Baer's *Titles in Series* and supplements.

671.   Slonimsky, Nicholas. **Music Since 1900**. 3rd ed. New York: Coleman-Ross, 1949. 759p.

Contents: Tabular views of stylistic trends in music, 1900-1948; Descriptive chronology, 1900-1948; Letters and documents.

Special Topics and Countries

672.   Bessaraboff, Nicholas. **Ancient European Musical Instruments . . .** Cambridge: Published for the Museum of Fine Arts, Boston, by Harvard University Press, 1941. 503p.

An authoritative historical study with excellent illustrations. Includes a useful bibliography of books about musical instruments and catalogs of collections.

673.   Grout, Donald Jay. **A Short History of Opera**. 2nd ed. New York: Columbia University Press, 1965. 852p.

Divided into five parts, each covering a century from the sixteenth to the twentieth (to 1960). Long bibliography (pp. 585-786) arranged by chapters. Appendices: modern versions or excerpts from operas before 1800; sources of examples and translations. Major work, first published in 1947. Both editions very favorably received by critics.

674.   Howard, John Tasker. **Our American Music: A Comprehensive History from 1620 to the Present**. 4th ed. New York: Crowell, 1965. 944p.

Very detailed history with extensive bibliography (pp. 769-845). Major composers receive detailed treatment. Numerous illustrations. Index (pp. 847-944) includes titles of compositions if at all distinctive.

675.   Humphries, Charles, and William C. Smith. **Music Publishing in the British Isles from the Earliest Times to the Middle of the 19th Century**. London: Cassell, 1954. 355p.

Standard work, essential for dating. Includes a dictionary section, a general bibliography, an index of firms outside London, and a list of instrument makers and repairers.

676.   King, Alexander Hyatt. **Some British Collectors of Music c.1600-1960**. Cambridge: Cambridge University Press, 1963. 178p.

Describes about 200 collections of music and music literature. Classified lists (pp. 130-48) of collections sold at auction (1711-1960) and collections kept intact or dispersed (1627-1961).

677.   Kinsky, Georg. **A History of Music in Pictures**. New York: Dover, 1951 (reprint). 363p.

A collection of approximately 1,500 illustrations—portraits, instruments, facsimiles, etc.—forming a pictorial history of music from the earliest times to the present. Pictures are the most important element; text is brief: 1) explanatory note for each picture; 2) indexes and tables of contents; 3) introduction and foreword. Three editions (German, French, English) were published in 1930. Detailed coverage may be found in *Musikgeschichte in Bildern*, edited by H. Bessler and M. Schneider (Leipzig: VEB Deutscher Verlag für Musik, 1961–).

678.   Loewenberg, Alfred. **Annals of Opera, 1597-1940**. 2nd ed., rev. plus corr. by Frank Walker. Genève: Societas Bibliographica, 1955. 2 vols.

Vol. 1, Text; Vol. 2, Indexes. Lists nearly 4,000 operas, arranged chronologically by date of first performance, followed by name of composer and title of opera (given in original language), name of town where first performed, sometimes name of theater, and history of performances. References to translations, revivals, etc. Indexes: 1) Operas; 2) Composers, with dates of birth and death, giving names of operas by each, with dates; 3) Librettists; 4) General index.

679.   Mattfeld, Julius. **Variety Music Cavalcade, 1620-1969: A Chronology of Vocal and Instrumental Music Popular in the U.S.** 3rd ed. Englewood Cliffs, N.J.: Prentice-Hall, 1971. 766p.

Lists popular music chronologically, with brief account of various events occurring each year. Also includes hymns, secular and sacred songs, choral compositions, and instrumental and orchestral works. Only the musical items are indexed.

680.   Rublowsky, John. **Black Music in America**. New York: Basic Books, 1971. 150p.

Written in a popular style, this book sketches the history of black music from its origins in Africa to the present. Many illustrations from old prints and contemporary photographs. Illustrations are not included in the brief index.

681.   Sachs, Curt. **The History of Musical Instruments**. New York: Norton, 1940. 515p.

Scholarly history divided into four parts: The Primitive and Prehistoric Epoch; Antiquity; The Middle Ages; The Modern Occident. Glossary is on pages 454 to 467; bibliography, on pages 469 to 487; index, on pages 489 to 505.

682.   Seltsam, William H. **Metropolitan Opera Annals: A Chronicle of Artists and Performances**. New York: H. W. Wilson, 1947. 751p. Supplement, 1947-57. Wilson, 1957.

A chronological record of the casts of the operas performed from the first season in 1883/84. Also gives excerpts from press reviews for each season, especially those covering important débuts and first performances. Profusely illustrated with photographs of leading singers in typical roles. Index traces all references to artists, performances, reviews, portraits.

683.   Shapiro, Nat. **Popular Music: An Annotated Index of American Popular Songs**. New York: Adrian Press, 1964– .

Contents: Vol. 1, 1950-59; Vol. 2, 1940-49; Vol. 3, 1960-64; Vol. 4, 1930-39. A selective list of popular songs. Arranged by year, then alphabetically by title. Gives author, composer, publisher, and first or best-selling record, indicating performer and record company.

684.   Slonimsky, Nicholas. **Music of Latin America**. New York: Crowell, 1945. 374p.
Includes "Dictionary of Latin American musicians, songs and dances, and musical instruments" (pp. 295-325).

685.   Spaeth, Sigmund. **History of Popular Music in America**. New York: Random House, 1948. 729p.

686.   Yerbury, Grace D. **Song in America: From Early Times to about 1850**. Metuchen, N.J.: Scarecrow Press, 1971. 305p.

Collections of Original Literary Sources

687.   Strunk, William Oliver, ed. **Source Readings in Music History**. New York: Norton, 1965. 5 vols.
Writings of composers and theorists from ancient times, translated into English where necessary. Most are abstracts.

Historical Anthologies of Music

688.   Davison, Archibald Thompson. **Historical Anthology of Music**. Cambridge: Harvard University Press, 1946-50. 2 vols.

689.   Lang, Paul Henry, ed. **The Symphony 1800-1900: A Norton Music Anthology**. New York: Norton, 1969. 873p.
Selections from Beethoven, Berlioz, Brahms, Bruckner, Dvorak, Mendelssohn, Schumann, Tchaikovsky. Clearly reproduced. Edited by a professor of musicology at Columbia University. Recommended for circulation as well as reference.

690.   Marrocco, William Thomas, ed. **Music in America: An Anthology from the Landing of the Pilgrims to the Close of the Civil War, 1620-1865**. Comp. and ed., with historical and analytical notes, by William Thomas Marrocco and Harold Gleason. New York: Norton, 1964. 371p.

691.   Parrish, Carl. **Masterpieces of Music before 1750**. New York: Norton, 1951. 235p.

692.   Parrish, Carl. **A Treasury of Early Music**. New York: Norton, 1958. 331p.

Biographies

693.   American Society of Composers, Authors and Publishers. **The ASCAP Biographical Dictionary of Composers, Authors and Publishers**. 3rd ed. New York: ASCAP, 1966. 845p.

Includes sketches of lyric-writers and composers, the majority of whom are writers of popular music. It also lists publishers that publish the works of ASCAP members.

694.   Baker, Theodore. **Baker's Biographical Dictionary of Musicians**. 5th ed. Completely rev. by Nicolas Slonimsky. New York: Schirmer, 1965 (c.1958). 1855, 143p.

A useful and reliable dictionary, giving compact biographies (varying from a few lines to several pages) of musicians of all periods and countries, with bibliographies of the musicians' own works and books about them. Pronunciation of foreign names is indicated. The so-called "6th edition" of 1965 is actually the 5th edition with a 1965 supplement.

695.   Bull, Storm. **Index to Biographies of Contemporary Composers**. New York: Scarecrow, 1964. 405p.

Indexes 69 sources containing biographical information on composers who are now living, who were born in 1900 or later, or who, if deceased, died after 1949.

696.   Eitner, Robert. **Biographisch-bibliographisches Quellen-Lexikon der Musiker und Musikgelehrten der christlichen Zeitrechnung bis zur Mitte des 19. Jahrhunderts**. Leipzig: Breitkopf und Härtel, 1900-1904. 10 vols. (Reprinted New York: Musurgia, 1947; Graz: Akademische Druck und Verlagsanstalt, 1959). Vol. 11, Nachträge und Miscellanea. Graz, 1960.

Major location tool for music sources from the beginning of the Christian era to the middle of the nineteenth century.

697.   Ewen, David. **Composers of Tomorrow's Music: A Non-Technical Introduction to the Musical Avant-Garde Movement**. New York: Dodd, Mead, 1971. 176p.

Contents: Charles Ives; Arnold Schoenberg; Anton Webern; Pierre Boulez; Edgar Varèse; Karlheinz Stockhausen; Yannis Xenakis; Milton Babbitt; John Cage; and Henry Partch.

698.   Ewen, David, ed. **Composers since 1900: A Biographical and Critical Guide**. New York: H. W. Wilson, 1969. 639p.

Covers 70 North and South Americans, 147 Europeans and three Australians. Informal biographical and critical sketches, photographs, lists of major works and references to books and articles about the composers. Ewen interviewed more than half of those selected for inclusion. Replaces three of Ewen's earlier books: *Composers of Today*; *American Composers Today*; *European Composers Today*.

699.   Ewen, David. **Great Men of American Popular Song**. Rev. and enl. ed.
        Englewood Cliffs, N.J.: Prentice-Hall, 1972. 404p.
For the general reader. Covers life and works of about 30 men from the
American Revolution to the present. Index. Other popular works by Ewen
include *Men of Popular Music* (New York: Prentice-Hall, 1952), *New Book of
Modern Composers* (3rd ed. New York: Knopf, 1961), and *Popular American
Composers from Revolutionary Times to the Present* (New York: H. W. Wilson,
1962. Supp. 1972).

700.   Ewen, David, comp. **Living Musicians**. New York: H. W. Wilson, 1940.
        390p. Supplement, 1957. 178p.
Biographies of 500 living musicians in the main work and 150 in the supplement.
Includes singers, conductors, instrumentalists. Mainly those of interest to the
American public. Includes articles on msuical groups such as quartets, chamber
music ensembles, etc.

701.   Kaiser, Joachim. **Great Pianists of Our Time**. New York: Herder and
        Herder, 1971. 230p.
Translated from German. Based on a series of radio talks, it covers major figures
and many minor ones. A serious study that will be of special interest to students
of the piano.

702.   Kutsch, K. J., and Leo Riemans. **A Concise Biographical Dictionary of
        Singers: From the Beginning of Recorded Sound to the Present . . .**
        New York: Chilton, 1969. 950p.
A collection of brief biographies of singers of opera and classical music who
made phonograph recordings. Lists many singers not found in other standard
sources. At least one recording label is given for each singer.

703.   Lawless, Ray McKinley. **Folksingers and Folksongs in America: A
        Handbook of Biography, Bibliography, and Discography**. Rev. ed. New
        York: Duell, 1965. 750p.
Biographical sketches of singers. Annotated bibliography of collections of folk
songs. Checklists of titles and discography, chapters on instruments, societies,
festivals. Indexes of names, titles, subjects.

704.   Pulver, Jeffrey. **Biographical Dictionary of Old English Music**. New
        York: Dutton, 1927. 537p.
Covers English musicians from about 1200 to the death of Purcell in 1695. Cites
manuscripts, contemporary publications, and some modern ones.

705.   Reis, Claire. **Composers in America: Biographical Sketches of Contem-
        porary Composers with a Record of Their Works**. Rev. and enl. ed. New
        York: Macmillan, 1947. 399p.
Biographies of 332 serious composers from 1915 to 1947, with a classified
listing of their works. There is a supplementary list of 125 without biographical
information.

706.   Vodarsky-Shiraeff, Alexandria. **Russian Composers and Musicians: A Biographical Dictionary** New York: H. W. Wilson, 1940. 158p.
Includes composers, performers, teachers, and critics. Classified lists of major works. Variant spellings of Russian names are cross-referenced.

707.   **Who's Who in Music and Musicians' International Directory.** 6th ed. New York: Hafner, 1972. 498p.
Short biographical sketches of a large number of musicians, mainly British. Includes lists of journals, publishers, festivals, organizations, etc. Some introductory material on a number of British musical organizations precedes the main section.

Music Education

708.   Boyden, David Dodge. **An Introduction to Music.** Foreword by Percy A. Scholes. 2nd ed. New York: Knopf, 1970. 554p.
Written by a former chairman of the Department of Music, University of California at Berkeley, this college textbook is designed to offer the teacher of a beginning course a variety of alternatives. Topics covered include: elements, structure, aesthetics, performance, history, repertory, and suggestions for study and listening.

709.   De Lerma, Dominique-René, ed. **Black Music in Our Culture: Curricular Ideas on the Subjects, Materials and Problems.** Kent, Ohio: Kent State University Press, 1970. 263p.

710.   Dykema, Peter W., and Hannah Cundiff. **School Music Handbook: A Guide for Music Educators.** Rev. ed. Boston: Birchard, 1955; Ann Arbor, Mich.: University Microfilms, 1968. 669p.

711.   Glidden, Robert Burr. **The Development of Content and Materials for a Music Literature Course in the Senior High School.** Iowa City: University of Iowa, 1966. 2 vols.
Prepared as a doctoral thesis. Vol. 1 consists of the text, and Vol. 2 deals with audiovisual source materials, including 33 portfolios.

712.   Juilliard School of Music, New York. **Juilliard Report on Teaching the Literature and Materials of Music.** New York: Norton, 1953. 223p.

713.   Kagen, Sergius. **Music for the Voice: A Descriptive List of Concert and Teaching Material.** Rev. ed. Bloomington: Indiana University Press, 1968. 780p.
Originally published in 1949, and revised by the author before his death in 1964. Does not try to include every song, but does represent as many composers as space permits. Information for each title includes: range of song, type of voice, descriptive remarks. References to preferred editions. No title index. Necessary for any music collection.

714. Mursell, James. **Music Education, Principles and Programs**. Morristown, N.J.: Silver, Burdette, 1956. 386p.

715. Music Educators' National Conference. **Doctoral Dissertations in Music and Music Education, 1957-63**. Washington, D.C.: Music Educators' National Conference, 1964. 119p. Supp. 1963-67. 1968. 224p.

716. Music Educators' National Conference. **Selective Music Lists, 1968**. Washington, D.C.: Music Educators' National Conference, 1968. 82p.
Contents: Vocal Solos; Small Vocal Ensembles; Large Choral Groups; Junior High Chorus.

717. Music Educators' National Conference. **Selective Music Lists: Band, Orchestra, String Orchestra** .... Washington, D.C.: Music Educators' National Conference, 1971. 58p.

718. Music Educators' National Conference. **Selective Music Lists: Instrumental Solos, Instrumental Ensembles** . . Washington, D.C.: Music Educators' National Conference, 1972. 167p.

719. Music Educators' National Conference. Commission on Teacher Education. **Teacher Education in Music: Final Report**. Washington, D.C.: Music Educators' National Conference, 1972. 58p.

720. Music Educators' National Conference. Committee on Bibliography of Research Projects Theses. **Bibliography of Research Studies in Music Education, 1932-48**. Chicago: Music Educators' National Conference, 1949. 119p. Supp., 1949-56. 1957.
Main work has about 1,600 titles; the supplement, 350.

721. Music Educators' National Conference. Committee on Music Buildings, Rooms, and Equipment. **Music Buildings, Rooms, and Equipment** ... Ed. by Charles L. Gary. 5th ed. Washington, D.C.: Music Educators' National Conference, 1966. 119p.

722. Music Educators' National Conference. Committee on Music in General Education. **Music in General Education**. Ed. by Karl D. Ernst and Charles L Gary. Washington, D.C.: Music Educators' National Conference, 1965. 223p.

723. Music Educators' National Conference. Music Education Curriculum Committee. **Music Education Source Book** ... Ed. by Hazel N. Morgan. Chicago: Music Educators' National Conference, 1951. 268p.
First published in 1947. the 1951 edition has an appendix of revisions and additions.

724. Music Educators' National Conference. Music in American Education Committee. **Music in American Education: Music Education Source**

Book Number Two. Chicago: Music Educators' National Conference, 1955. 365p.

725. United Nations Educational, Scientific and Cultural Organization. **International Directory of Music Education Institutions** ... Paris: Unesco, 1968. 115p.

A directory of music education programs in 71 countries, prepared by the International Society for Music Education.

Music Librarianship

General

726. **Anglo-American Cataloging Rules: North American Text**. Prep. by the American Library Association, the Library of Congress, the Library Association, and the Canadian Library Association. Chicago: A.L.A., 1967. 400p.

See Chapter 13, Music (pp. 294-320), and Chapter 14, Phonorecords (pp. 321-28).

727. Brown, Howard Mayer, and Joan Lascelle. **Musical Iconography: A Manual for Cataloging Musical Subjects in Western Art before 1800**. Cambridge: Harvard University Press, 1972. 220p.

728. Bryant, Eric Thomas. **Music Librarianship: A Practical Guide**. New York: Hafner, 1959. 503p.

729. International Association of Music Libraries. International Cataloging Code Commission. **Code internationale de catalogage de la musique**. Frankfurt and New York: C. F. Peters, 1957– .

Contents: Vol. 1, *The Author Catalog of Published Music*; Vol. 2, *Limited Code*; Vol. 3, *Code for Full Cataloging*; Vol. 4, *Code for Cataloging Manuscripts*; Vol. 5, *Code for Catalogoing Sound Recordings*.

730. International Association of Music Libraries. **Music, Libraries and Instruments**. London: Hinrichsen, 1961. 300p.

Consists of papers read at the Joint Congress (Cambridge, 1959) of the International Association of Music Libraries and the Galpin Society.

731. Joint Committee on Music Cataloging. **Code for Cataloging Music and Phonorecords**. Prep. by a Joint Committee of the Music Library Association and the American Library Association, Division of Cataloging and Classification. Chicago: American Library Association, 1958. 88p.

732. Long, Maureen W. **Musicians and Libraries in the United Kingdom**. London: Library Association, 1972. 152p.

733. McColvin, Lionel Roy. **Music Libraries.** London: A. Deutsch, 1965. 2 vols.

Completely rewritten, revised and extended by Jack Dove.

734. Music Library Association. **Manual of Music Librarianship.** Ann Arbor, Mich.: Music Library Association, 1966. 140p.

735. New York Public Library. Reference Department. **Music Subject Headings.** 2nd ed. Boston: G. K. Hall, 1966. 610p.

736. U.S. Library of Congress. Subject Cataloging Division. **Classification. Class M.** 2nd ed. With supplementary pages. Washington, D.C.: Library of Congress, 1963.

"Additions and changes" are contained in a 101-page supplement at the end.

737. U.S. Library of Congress. Subject Cataloging Division. **Music Subject Headings Used on Printed Catalog Cards of the Library of Congress.** Washington, D.C.: Library of Congress, 1952. 133p.

Organizing a Record Collection

738. International Association of Music Libraries. United Kingdom Branch. **Phonograph Record Libraries: Their Organization and Practice.** 2nd ed. Henry F. J. Currall, ed., with a Preface by A. Hyatt King. Hamden, Conn.: Archon Books, 1970. 303p.

The British edition (London: Lockwood, 1970) has the title *Gramophone Record Libraries.*

739. Langridge, Derek Wilton. **Your Jazz Collection.** Hamden, Conn.: Archon Books, 1970. 162p.

A recommended work dealing with collecting and classifying jazz records.

740. Marco, Guy A., and Walter M. Roziewski. "Shelving Plans for Long-Playing Records," **Library Journal** 84 (May 15, 1959): 1568-69.

741. Pearson, Mary D. **Recordings in the Public Library.** Chicago: American Library Association, 1963. 153p.

742. Pickett, Andrew G., and Meyer M. Lemcoe. **Preservation and Storage of Sound Recordings: A Study Supported by a Grant from the Rockefeller Foundation.** Washington, D.C.: Library of Congress, 1959. 74p.

The major work in this field. Still useful, despite technological changes.

743. Rosenberg, Kenyon C. "The State of Record Cataloging," **Library Journal/School Library Journal Previews: News and Reviews of Non-Print Media** 1 (April 1973): 11.

744.   Saheb-Ettaba, Caroline (Squire), and Roger B. McFarland. **ANSCR: The Alpha-Numeric System for Classification of Recordings**. Williamsport, Pa.: Bro-Dart Pub. Co., 1969. 212p.

745.   Scholz, Dell. **A Manual for the Cataloging of Recordings in Public Libraries**. Rev. ed. Baton Rouge: Louisiana State Library, 1964. 45 l.

746.   U.S. Library of Congress. Descriptive Cataloging Division. **Rules for Descriptive Cataloging ... Phonorecords**. 2nd prelim. ed. Washington, D.C.: Library of Congress, 1964. 11p.

Recordings (Discs and Tapes)

Bibliographies and Guides

747.   Bescoby-Chambers, John. **The Archives of Sound: Including a Selective Catalogue of Historical Violin, Piano, Spoken, Documentary Orchestral and Composer's Own Recordings**. Lingfield, Surrey: Oakwood Press, 1966. 153p.

748.   **The Classical Record Catalogue and Recommended Recordings**. Kenton, Middlesex: The Gramophone, 1953– . Quarterly.

749.   Clough, Francis F., and G. J. Cuming, comps. **The World's Encyclopedia of Recorded Music**. London: Sidgwick and Jackson, 1952. 890p. (includes a supp.). 2nd supp., 1951-52. 1953. 262p. 3rd supp., 1953-55. 1957. 564p.

A comprehensive list of recorded music to date of publication. Information detailed. Arrangement convenient. Indispensable for works up to the date covered in the last supplements.

750.   **Consumers Union Reviews Classical Recordings**. By CU's Musical Consultant and the Editors of Consumer Reports. Indianapolis: Bobbs-Merrill, 1973. 376p.

Collection of record reviews from the past 10 years of *Consumer Reports*. Reviews are unsigned. Basic arrangement is by composers, with cross references from performers, conductors, and orchestras. Contains 358 reviews plus a basic discography of 500 selections.

751.   Haggin, Bernard H. **The New Listener's Companion and Record Guide**. 3rd ed. New York: Horizon Press, 1971. 365p.

An evaluative guide by an outstanding music critic. For more complete description, see No. 545.

752.   **The Harrison Catalog of Stereophonic Tapes**. New York: M. and N. Harrison, 1955– . Bimonthly.

753. Hurst, Peter Geoffrey. **The Golden Age Recorded**. New and rev. ed. Lingfield, Surrey: Oakwood Press, 1963. 187p.

Intended to help the collector build a private collection. General discussion of record collecting, biographical information about artists, and a list of recordings that have ranked very high in critical esteem.

754. **Imported Records and Tapes**. New York: Peters International, Inc., 1971(?)– .

This firm imports records from 14 countries on nearly a hundred labels. The 1971 issue was reported to contain 4,000 records not listed in Schwann or its supplements.

755. **Katalog der schallplatten Klassischer Musik**. Bielefeld: Bielefelder Verlagsanstalt KG, 1953– .

Issued twice a year. Lists a smaller number of records than Schwann, but many classical records not listed by Schwann. Main entries under composers. Complete analytics. Selective cross references. New releases indicated by dots preceding entries. Artist listings.

756. **Kemp's Music and Recording Industry International Year Book**. New York: British Book Center, 1965– .

757. Myers, Kurtz, and Richard S. Hill. **Record Ratings: The Music Library Association's Index of Record Reviews**. New York: Crown, 1956. 440p.

Cumulation of "Index of Record Reviews" originally appearing in quarterly issues of *Notes*. Lists each release with complete information, and gives references to reviews in 28 reviewing media. In two parts: 1) Composer and subject; 2) Composite releases. Includes performer index.

758. **Phonolog: The All-in-One Record Reporter**. Los Angeles: Trade Services, 1948– .

Looseleaf system updated three times per week. Covers more than 500 labels: classical, popular, LPs, 45s, cassettes, cartridges. Weekly report on new releases for the week. Separate sections for classical and popular, with subdivisions for special categories. Main entries by title. Classical composers section (cross-reference list). Most recent recordings are indicated by symbols. Analytical entries for collections. Expensive–but useful for large collections, especially of popular music.

759. **Polart Index to Record Reviews**. Detroit: Polart, 1960– . Annual.

Indexes reviews published in 14 periodicals. Arranged by composer, collections, miscellaneous, and several broad subjects.

760. **Record and Tape Reviews Index**, 1971– . Comp. by Antoinette O. Maleady. Metuchen, N.J.: Scarecrow Press, 1972– .

761.   **Recorded Sound**. London: British Institute of Recorded Sound, 1961– .
Publishes research in discography and reviews of new books.

762.   Russcol, Herbert. **Guide to Low-Priced Classical Records**. New York: Hart, 1969. 831p.
Restricted to discs costing $2.00 to $3.00 at time of compilation—about 3,000 items. Sections on major composers have brief biographical sketches and guides to essential works. Valuable to libraries with limited budgets.

763.   **Schwann Record and Tape Guide**. Boston: W. Schwann, 1949– . Monthly.
A listing of currently available eight-track cartridges, cassettes, and stereo discs, revised each month. Arranged by composer. Includes price list. Sections on: electronic music; new listings for month; new books on music; classical collections; spoken and miscellaneous records; musical shows, operettas, films, TV; current popular; jazz; ballets; operas. Although not attempting to be an encyclopedia, the Schwann Catalog does include dates of composers, of compositions if available, opus numbers, languages used in vocal music. Special care is taken to list contemporary American composers as completely as possible. This basic work is now supplemented by *Schwann Children's Record and Tape Guide* and *Schwann Supplementary Record and Tape Guide*. The latter covers monaural records, popular releases more than two years old, classical music on lesser-known and foreign labels, the spoken word, religious music, and international folk and popular music.

Some Examples of Specialized Discographies

764.   Burks, John. "Songs and Sounds óf the Sixties," **American Libraries**, 3 (February 1972): 122-33.
Discusses the rock music of the 1960s, covering both records and, more briefly, publications.

765.   Coover, James B., and Richard Colvig. **Medieval and Renaissance Music on Long-Playing Records**. Detroit: Information Service, Inc., 1964. 122p. Supp., 1962-71. Detroit: Information Coordinators, Inc., 1973. 258p.

766.   Dearborn, Michigan. Public Library. Audio-Visual Department. **A Selected List of Recorded Musical Scores from Radio, Television and Motion Pictures**. Comp. by James L. Limbacher. 4th ed. Dearborn, Mich.: Dearborn Public Library, 1967. 48 l.

767.   Dearborn, Michigan. Public Library. Audio-Visual Department. **Theatrical Events—1900-1962: A Selected List of Musical and Dramatic Performances on Long-Playing Records**. Comp. by James L. Limbacher. Dearborn, Mich.: Dearborn Public Library, 1962. 9 l.

768. Douglas, John R. "Classic Recordings for a Song: A Discography of Historic Reissues," **Library Journal** 96 (Feb. 15, 1971): 597-607.

769. International Folk Music Council. **International Catalogue of Recorded Folk Music**. London: Oxford University Press, 1954. 201p.
With text in English and French, this catalog is in two parts: 1) commercial records; 2) recordings held by institutions. Locates collections of authentic folk music in different countries.

770. Koenigsberg, Allen. **Edison Cylinder Records, 1889-1912: With an Illustrated History of the Phonograph**. New York: Stellar Productions, 1969.
Brief historical sketch, then a listing by recording artists' names. Reproductions of early catalogs, insert slips, and containers. Supplements *Vertical-Cut Cylinders and Discs* by Victor Girard and Richard M. Barnes. Both are useful for dating and other documentation.

771. Merriam, Alan P. **African Music on LP: An Annotated Discography**. Evanston, Ill.: Northwestern University Press, 1970. 200p.

772. **Russian Music on Records**. New York: Four Continents Book Corp., 1968– .
Two catalogs (both of which are published in Russian and English): 1) Classical music (categories for symphonies, operas, oratorios, and ballets); 2) Other (folk music, jazz, operettas, drama, children's records, and bird songs). Valuable supplementary coverage for larger collections will be found in *Soviet Long Playing Records* (Moscow: V/O Mezhdunarodnaya, 1955–).

773. Rust, Brian. **Jazz Records, A–Z, 1897-1931**. 2nd ed. Kenton, Middlesex, the Author, 1961. 736p.
Consists mainly of recordings made before 1932. Arranged by composers. Continued by Rust in *Jazz Records, A–Z, 1932-1942* (1965) and by J. P. Jepsen in *Jazz Records, A–Z, 1942-1967* (1968). *Record Research* (New York, 1955–) is devoted to jazz discography.

774. Santella, Jim. "The Common Vibration," **Library Journal** 95 (Nov. 15, 1970): 3967-70.
Includes "a list of rock and roll records which should prove useful in tracing rock from its early beginnings to the present."

775. Tudor, Dean. "A Discography of the Real Blues," **Library Journal** 97 (Feb. 15, 1972): 633-49.

776. U.S. Library of Congress. Music Division. **A List of American Folksongs Currently Available on Records** ... Washington, D.C.: Library of Congress, 1953. 176p.

Music Periodicals

777.   **Acta Musicologica**, 1928– . Quarterly. Bärenreiter-Verlag, Neuweilerstr.
       15, Ch 400 Basel 15, Switzerland.
Indexed in: *Music Index*. Fully documented research papers, often with valuable
bibliographies. Official publication of Société Internationale de Musicologie.
Papers are in languages chosen by the authors.

778.   **American Music Teacher**, 1951– . Bi-monthly. Music Teachers National
       Association, 1831 Carew Tower, Cincinnati, Ohio 45202.
Indexed in: *Education Index* and *Music Index*. Contains articles on and reviews
of keyboard, vocal, organ, and string music. Written to assist teachers.
Occasional bibliographies.

779.   American Musicological Society. **Journal**, 1948– . 3 per year. William
       Byrd Press, 2901 Byrdhill Road, Richmond, Virginia 23205.
Indexed in: *Music Index* and *Répertoire international de la littérature musicale*.
Scholarly articles, usually with bibliographies. Extensive book reviews and
information on new editions of music and recordings. Reports on doctoral
dissertations and abstracts of papers presented at various meetings of the
Society.

780.   **American Record Guide: Incorporating the American Tape Guide**.
       (Formerly **The American Music Lover**), 1934– . Monthly. James
       Lyons, Box 319, Radio City Station, New York, N.Y. 10019.
Indexed in: *Music Index* and *Reader's Guide*. Excellent review medium for
recordings and tapes. Compares new releases with older recordings. One major
artist's work is studied each month. Sometimes two reviewers will present
opposing views on one recording.

781.   **Audio**, 1947– . Monthly. North American Publishing Co., 134 N.
       13th St., Philadelphia, Pa. 19107.
Indexed in: *Music Index*, *Applied Science and Technology Index*, *Engineering
Index*. Emphasizes new products, installation, maintenance. Reviews are
analytical. There are articles on the theory of sound and reviews of records—
classical, popular, and jazz. More emphasis on equipment than in *Hi-Fi/Stereo
Review* and *High Fidelity*.

782.   **Billboard**, 1894– . Weekly. Billboard Publishing Co., 165 W. 46th St.,
       New York, N.Y. 10006.
Indexed in: *Music Index*. Subtitle: "International Music Record News-Weekly."
A newspaper that focuses on publishing, recording, and selling music. Informa-
tion on new albums, tapes, performers, and pop music, plus sections on country,
gospel, and classical music; musical instruments; audio retailing; and "Hits of the
World" arranged by country.

783.   **Crawdaddy**, 1966– . Bi-weekly. Superstar Productions, Inc., 232
       Madison Ave., New York, N.Y. 10016.

Subtitle: "The Magazine of Rock." Not indexed. Illustrated articles on personalities, music, concerts, and teenage songs. Emphasis on analysis and social issues. Each number has an interview with a leading musical figure.

784. **Down Beat**, 1934– . Fortnightly. Maher Publications, 222 W. Adams St., Chicago, Ill. 60606.

Indexed in: *Music Index*. Devoted to personalities, music, scenes, and recording of jazz. Reviews of books, concerts, recordings. Teenagers may prefer rock magazines like *Crawdaddy* or *Rolling Stone*. Available in microform.

785. **Gramophone**, 1923– . Monthly. General Gramophone Publications, Ltd., 177 Kenton Road, Kenton, Middlesex, HA3 0HA, England.

Long, critical reviews of classical recordings in the United Kingdom. Also articles on music and audio equipment, and "Gramophone Long Playing Record Catalog."

786. **High Fidelity**, 1951– . Monthly. Billboard Publishing Co., 165 W. 46th St., New York, N.Y. 10036.

Indexed in: *Reader's Guide, Abridged Reader's Guide, Music Index*. For the informed hi-fi enthusiast. Published in several regional editions and also in a "Musical America" edition with extra pages on current music performances, music centers, and performing artists. Articles on music, musicians, and audio and video home equipment. Critical reviews of recordings, with special emphasis on classical.

787. **JEMF Quarterly**, 1965– . Quarterly. John Edwards Memorial Foundation, Folklore and Mythology Center, University of California, Los Angeles, Calif. 90024.

Specializes in country, western, country-western, hillbilly, bluegrass, mountain, cowboy, old-time, and sacred music. The Foundation also preserves material on race, blues, and gospel.

788. **Journal of the Association for Recorded Sound Collections**, 1968(?)– . 3 per year. Association for Recorded Sound Collections, c/o Rogers and Hammerstein Archives, 111 Amsterdam Ave., New York, N.Y. 10023.

The professional journal of those charged with responsibility for organizing and servicing sound collections.

789. **Keyboard, Jr.**, 1943– . Monthly (Oct.–May). Keyboard, Jr., Publications, 1346 Chapel St., New Haven, Conn. 06511.

Indexed in: *Subject Index to Children's Magazines*. Music appreciation bulletin for use in junior and senior high. Each issue has an article on a composer, musician, piece of music, orchestra, or type of composition. Same publisher also issues *Young Keyboard* (1946–) for grades 4-6.

790. **Music and Letters**, 1920– . Quarterly. Music and Letters, Ltd., 44 Conduit St., London, W1R 0DE, England.

Indexed in: *British Humanities Index* and *Music Index*. International coverage of classical music and musicians. Scholarly. Long articles on styles, outstanding musicians, and subjects of historical importance. Critical reviews of books and new music. British emphasis.

791.   **Music and Musicians**, 1952– . Monthly. Hansom Books, Ltd., Artillery Mansions, 75 Victoria St., London, S.W.1, England.

Indexed in: *Music Index*. Issued in England but international in scope. Performances, performers, musical styles, and calendar of events. Survey of current recordings emphasizes English and Continental European releases. Excellent illustrations.

792.   **Music Educators Journal**, 1941– . Monthly (Sept.–June). Music Educators National Conference, 1201 16th St., N.W., Washington, D.C. 20036.

Indexed in: *Education Index, Music Index*. Major periodical in field, covering grade school through university. Topics include teaching suggestions, plus developments, research, awards, competitions, etc.

793.   **The Musical Quarterly**, 1915– . Quarterly. G. Schirmer, Inc., 609 Fifth Ave., New York, N.Y. 10017.

Indexed in: *Music Index, Social Sciences and Humanities Index, Répertoire international de la littérature musicale*. Publishes research results in field of serious music. A section of about 25 pages called "current chronicle" covers events in the United States and abroad. Signed, critical book reviews. Also, a quarterly booklist—not annotated—which covers international publications. Record reviews report in depth and include bibliographies.

794.   **The Musical Times**, 1844– . Monthly. Novello & Co., Ltd., 27 Soho Square, London, W.1, England.

Indexed in: *British Humanities Index, Music Index, Répertoire international de la littérature musicale*. For students and teachers. Long articles on music, musicians, concerts, instruments, and education, usually based on original research. News stories, and reviews of books, records, new music, and concerts.

795.   **Notes: The Quarterly Journal of the Music Library Association**, 1931– . 2nd Series, 1948– . Quarterly. Music Library Association, Inc., 104 W. Huron St., Room 329, Ann Arbor, Mich. 48108.

Indexed in: *Music Index, Library Literature*. Devoted primarily to book and record reviews done by key people in music librarianship. Digest and index to record reviews, which usually covers over 200 tapes and discs reviewed in 19 journals. Also lists of books and music received. Scholarly but comprehensive. Articles on topics of interest to librarians and musicians.

796.   **Opera News**, 1936– . Monthly (irreg. in season). Metropolitan Opera Guild, 1965 Broadway, New York, N.Y. 10023.

Indexed in: *Music Index, Reader's Guide*. During the Metropolitan Opera season, it appears more frequently and deals with the operas to be performed each week—plot, cast, historical notes, photographs of characters, and staging.

Monthly issues are more likely to have articles on history and personalities. Reports on music centers in the United States and abroad. Chief periodical in the United States devoted to opera.

797.   **Phonographic Bulletin**. International Association of Sound Archives, 1971– .
Official organ of the International Association of Sound Archives. Concerned with improving bibliographical control.

798.   **Rolling Stone**, 1967– . Bi-weekly. Straight Arrow Publishers, Inc., 625 Third St., San Francisco, Calif. 94107.
A newspaper-format magazine devoted to rock. Articles on the meaning of music for teenagers as well as coverage of current figures. Articles are well illustrated. Record reviews. Should be included, along with *Crawdaddy*, if a library serves patrons interested in rock.

799.   **Sing Out**, 1950– . Bi-monthly. 33 W. 60th St., New York, N.Y. 10023.
Indexed in: *Music Index*. Covers all aspects of folk music. Interviews with singers, song writers, teachers. Articles on guitar, banjo, etc. News and notes. Attractive to players because each issue has several folk songs, with words, music, and guitar chords.

800.   **Stereo Review**, 1958– . Monthly. Formerly called **Hi-Fi/Stereo Review**. Ziff-Davis Publishing Co., 1 Park Ave., New York, N.Y. 10016.
Indexed in: *Music Index*. Covers both equipment and recordings. Includes well-illustrated general articles on music, advertisements, test reports and reports on new products, general equipment surveys, and a question-and-answer section. Excellent section of reviews for all types of recordings.

801.   **World of Music**, 1959– . Quarterly. B. Schott's Sohne, D-65, Mainz, Weihergarten, P.O.B. 3640, West Germany.
Indexed in: *Music Index*. General music magazine published in three languages (English, German, French). Each issue has major articles on world music and information on world music festivals, recordings, books, first performances, etc. Especially valuable for coverage of Oriental, African, and other non-Western music. Supported by Unesco through the International Music Council and published in cooperation with the International Institute for Comparative Music Studies.

DANCE

Introductory Works and Bibliographic Guides

802.   Bowers, Faubion. **Theatre in the East: A Survey of Asian Dance and Drama**. New York: Nelson, 1956. 374p.
A well-illustrated book that gives history of the dance and describes folk, traditional, and modern forms. The 14 chapters cover the following countries:

India, Ceylon, Burma, Thailand, Cambodia, Laos, Malaya, China, Indonesia, Philippines, Vietnam, Hong Kong, Okinawa, and Japan.

803. DeMille, Agnes. **The Book of the Dance**. New York: Golden Press, 1963. 252p.

Encyclopedic coverage of all periods and many countries. Definitions. Types and methods of choreography. Brief biographies of performers. Excellent illustrations, many in color. Lists of major ballets and choreographers. Index.

804. Martin, John Joseph. **Book of the Dance**. New York: Tudor, 1963. 192p.

Opens with brief treatment of basic dance movements and primitive dances. Main part of book is a detailed history of classic ballet and modern dance, especially contemporary American. Excellent illustrations. Name and subject index.

805. Shaw, Lloyd. **Cowboy Dances: A Collection of Western Square Dances**. With a Foreword by Sherwood Anderson. Caldwell, Idaho: Caxton Printers, 1949. 411p.

History, description, directions, and calls. Glossary of terms. Illustrated. Appendix of cowboy dance tunes.

Bibliographies

806. Beaumont, Cyril William, comp. **A Bibliography of Dancing**. New York: Blom, 1963. 228p.

Based on items in the British Museum, this bibliography consists of 422 annotated entries arranged alphabetically by author. Subject index.

807. Forrester, Felicitée Sheila. **Ballet in England: A Bibliography and Survey, c.1700–June 1966**. London: Library Association, 1968. 224p.

Classified, annotated bibliography of 664 items. Appendices include exhibitions and a guide for further study. Analytical index of names, titles, and subjects.

808. Leslie, Serge. **A Bibliography of the Dance Collection of Doris Niles and Serge Leslie**. Annotated by Serge Leslie. Ed. by Cyril Beaumont. London: Beaumont, 1966-68. 2 vols.

Coverage centers on ballet, although folk dancing and social dances are included. Arrangement is alphabetical by author (Vol. 1, A–K; Vol. 2, L–Z). Each volume has a subject index. About 2,000 entries.

809. Magriel, Paul David. **A Bibliography of Dancing: A List of Books and Articles on the Dance and Related Subjects**. New York: H. W. Wilson, 1936. 229p. Supp., 1941. 104p. Reprinted New York: Blom, 1966.

About 1,000 items, including folk dances and ballet. Locations for rare and out-of-print books. Author and subject index.

810.   Tanzbibliographie: Verzeichnis der in deutscher Sprache veroffent-
       lichen Schriften und Aufsatze zum Buhnen; Besellschafts, Kinder-,
       Volks- und Turniertanz sowie zur Tanzwissenschaft, Tanzmusik und
       zum Jazz. Hrsg. vom Institut für Volks Kunstforschung beim Zentral-
       haus für Kulturarbeit, Leipzig. Leipzig: VEB Bibliographisches Institut,
       1966– .
"A classified bibliography of books and periodical articles in German on
theatrical, social, children's, folk and competition dancing as well as on the
science of dancing, dance music and jazz" [A. J. Walford, *Guide to Reference
Material* (3 vols., 2nd ed. London: Library Association, 1966-70), Vol. III,
p. 390].

811.   United Nations Educational, Scientific and Cultural Organization.
       Catalogue: Ten Years of Films on Ballet and Classical Dance,
       1956-1965. Paris: Unesco, 1968. 104p.
Lists 190 films from 23 countries. Basic arrangement is alphabetical by country
and then by title. Entries give information about production, music, choreography, costumes, dancers, etc. Three indexes: countries, choreographers, and
composers.

Indexes, Abstracts, and Current Awareness Services

812.   Guide to Dance Periodicals, Vols. 1-10(?), 1931/35–1961/62(?).
       Gainesville: University of Florida Press, 1948-59. New York: Scarecrow
       Press, 1959(?)–1963(?).
Quinquennial coverage of years from 1931/35 through 1946/50. Biennial after
1951/52. Irregular and often late in appearance, but the indexing of 19
periodicals by subject and author (with separate index for illustrations) won high
praise for its thoroughness. Compiled by S. Yancey Belknap. Now incorporated
in *Guide to the Performing Arts* (unable to verify exact date of change).

813.   Minneapolis Public Library. Music Department. An Index to Folk
       Dances and Singing Games. Chicago: American Library Association,
       1936. 202p. Supp. 1949. 98p.
Together, the two volumes cover 178 books on folk dancing, singing games,
classic dances, tap and clog dances, and some square dances.

Dictionaries and Encyclopedias

814.   Baril, J. Dictionnaire de la danse. Paris: Editions du Seuil, 1964. 273p.
Has approximately 1,500 entries, including definitions of more than 200
technical terms and notes on 845 dances and 530 ballets. There are 450
illustrations.

815.   Beaumont, Cyril William, comp. A French-English Dictionary of
       Technical Terms Used in Classical Ballet. Rev. ed. London: the Author,
       1939. 44p.
Some 140 French terms, with explanations in English.

816.   Chujoy, Anatole, and Phyllis Winifred Manchester. **The Dance Encyclopedia**. Rev. and enl. ed. New York: Simon and Schuster, 1967. 992p.

The revised edition of this standard work (first published in 1949) is nearly double the size of the previous edition; it contains about 5,000 entries on the dance, especially ballet. About 40 of the longer articles are signed. Brief definitions. Entries for individual ballets include synopses, names of choreographers, designers, composers, original casts, and performance dates. Coverage includes virtually everything from biographies to techniques and education. Especially strong for American ballet.

817.   **A Dictionary of Modern Ballet**. Gen. eds.: Francis Gadan and Robert Maillard. With the assistance of Ronald Crichton and Mary Clarke. London: Methuen, 1959. 359p.

Originally published in France, coverage includes France, Britain, USSR, USA, Denmark, Sweden, Italy, and Spain. About 650 articles on artists, performers, ballets, and institutions of the twentieth century. Does not include definitions of terms.

818.   Grant, Gail. **Technical Manual and Dictionary of Classical Ballet**. 2nd ed. New York: Dover Publications, 1967. 127p.

Technical terms and pronunciations. Small line drawings. Brief bibliography.

819.   Kersley, Leo, and Janet Sinclair. **A Dictionary of Ballet Terms**. 2nd ed. New York: Pitman Publishing Corp., 1964. 112p.

Includes some 500 entries and cross references, illustrated with 127 line drawings.

820.   Mara, Thalia. **The Language of Ballet: An Informal Dictionary**. Cleveland: World, 1966. 120p.

Definitions and pronunciations. Includes some entries not readily found elsewhere.

821.   Raffé, Walter George, and M. E. Purdon. **Dictionary of the Dance**. New York: Barnes, 1964. 583p.

Definitions for 2,500 terms. Especially strong on folk and ethnic. No biographies. International coverage. Bibliography. Geographical and subject indexes.

822.   Wilson, George Buckley. **A Dictionary of Ballet**. Rev. ed. London: Cassell, 1961. 313p.

Some 2,500 entries dealing with such aspects of classical and operatic ballet as technical terms, individual ballets, biographies, companies, etc. Good cross references. Illustrated.

Directories and Annuals

823.   **The Ballet Annual: A Record and Year-Book of the Ballet**. London: Black, 1947-63. 18 vols.

Discontinued at the end of Vol. 18 (1963); coverage was then incorporated into the monthly periodical *Dancing Times*.

824.   **Dance World**. New York: Crown, 1966– . Annual.
Pictorial survey of New York dance season, personnel of companies, repertoires, etc. Some coverage outside New York. Biographies.

Histories

825.   Sachs, Curt. **World History of the Dance**. New York: Norton, 1973. 469p.
Originally published in Germany. Translated by Bessie Schonberg.

826.   Sorell, Walter. **The Dance through the Ages**. New York: Grosset & Dunlap, 1967. 304p.

827.   Terry, Walter. **The Dance in America**. Rev. ed. New York: Harper & Row, 1971. 272p.
First published in 1956. New edition adds chapters on the black dance, the regional ballet movement, and new or expanded dance companies.

Biographies

The following works (described in the section **Dictionaries and Encyclopedias**) are useful: Chujoy's *The Dance Encyclopedia: A Dictionary of Modern Ballet* and Wilson's *A Dictionary of Ballet*.

Ballet Digests

828.   Balanchine, G. **Balanchine's Complete Stories of the Great Ballets**. Ed. by Francis Mason. Drawings by Mara Becket. Garden City, N.Y.: Doubleday, 1954. 615p.
Main part (stories and reviews) is arranged alphabetically by title, followed by sections on history, careers, etc. Includes an illustrated glossary, an annotated selection of ballet records, and a bibliography. The analytical index is unusually detailed.

829.   Beaumont, Cyril William. **Complete Book of Ballets: A Guide to the Principal Ballets of the Nineteenth and Twentieth Centuries**. Rev. ed. London: Putnam, 1951. 1106p. Supplements: 1945 (reprinted 1952), 212p.; 1954, 250p.; 1955, 259p.
Covers 198 ballets chronologically by birth dates of choreographers. Gives synopsis, author, designer, composer, choreographer, date and cast of first production, and criticism. Supplement on Soviet ballet. Very detailed index.

830.   Brinson, Peter, and Clement Crisp. **The International Book of Ballet**. New York: Stein and Day, 1971. 304p.
Includes 115 ballets of 38 choreographers from 1653 to 1969. Gives synopsis, original dnacers, and criticism. Well illustrated.

831.   Drew, D., ed. **The Decca Book of Ballet**. London: Muller, 1958. 572p. Opens with a brief history. Main section, which describes 198 ballets, is alphabetical by composer. Other parts deal with dancers, choreographers, and major ballet companies.

832.   Lawrence, Robert. **The Victor Book of Ballets and Ballet Music**. New York: Simon and Schuster, 1950. 531p.
Covers 71 ballets with musical examples. Three indexes: choreographers, composers, and general index. Selective discography of RCA Victor records.

Periodicals

833.   **Dance and Dancers**, 1950– . Monthly. Hansom Books, Artillery Mansions, 75 Victoria Street, London, SWIH OHZ, England.
International coverage of ballet and modern dance, including a range of topics from education to reviews of records and recitals. Well illustrated.

834.   **Dance Magazine**, 1926– . Monthly. Danad Publishing Co., 10 Columbus Circle, New York, N.Y. 10010.
Indexed in: *Reader's Guide*. International coverage of all aspects of the subject. Information on performers, tours, schools, costumes, dance companies, etc. Annual directory. Excellent photographs.

835.   **Dance Perspectives**, 1959– . Quarterly. Dance Perspectives Foundation, 29 E. Ninth St., New York, N.Y. 10003.
Indexed in: *Music Index*. Critical and historical articles. Usually each issue is devoted to one topic; it may consist of several articles by different authorities or a monograph by one. Attractive format.

836.   **Square Dancing: The Official Magazine of the Sets in Order American Square Dance Society**, 1948– . Monthly. American Square Dance Society, 462 N. Robertson Blvd., Los Angeles, Calif. 90048.
For teachers, callers, and dancers. Includes information on dances and calls, record reviews, news items, etc.

THEATER

Introductory Works and Bibliographic Guides

837.   Cheshire, David F. **Theatre: History, Criticism and Reference**. London: Bingley, 1967. 131p.
An extended bibliographic essay written by a librarian for librarians. Chapters include: general reference works; histories; dramatic criticism; biographies and autobiographies; theory; current periodicals. Extensive author, subject, and title index. Coverage international, but from a British viewpoint.

838.   Drury, Francis Keese Wynkoop. **Drury's Guide to Best Plays**. 2nd ed. by James M. Salem. Metuchen, N.J.: Scarecrow Press, 1969. 512p.
Guide for locating plays most often used by amateur and educational theater groups. Alphabetical by author. Main entries give publishers, cast breakdown, setting, plot synopsis, current holder of play, and royalty fee. Indexes provide listings under co-authors, lists of plays most popular among producing groups, and lists of play publishers.

839.   Howard, Vernon Linwood. **The Complete Book of Children's Theater**. Garden City, N.Y.: Doubleday, 1969. 544p.
Contains more than 350 non-royalty plays, skits, and monologues for home, youth group, and classroom use, plus suggestions for beginning students on such topics as conveying emotions, conducting rehearsals, and overcoming stage fright.

840.   New York Public Library. The Research Libraries. **Theatre Subject Headings**. 2nd ed. New York: New York Public Library, 1966. 386p.

841.   Plummer, Gail. **Dramatists' Guide to Selection of Plays and Musicals**. Dubuque, Iowa: Brown, 1963. 144p.
Of particular value for amateur theatrical groups.

Bibliographies

842.   Adelman, Irving, and Rita Dworkin. **Modern Drama: A Checklist of Critical Literature on 20th Century Plays**. Metuchen, N.J.: Scarecrow Press, 1967. 370p.
An exceedingly useful guide to sources of criticism and interpretation.

843.   Baker, Blanch (Merritt). **Theatre and Allied Arts: A Guide to Books Dealing with the History, Criticism, and Technic of the Drama and Theatre, and Related Arts and Crafts**. 2nd ed. New York: H. W. Wilson, 1952. Reprinted New York: Blom, 1966. 536p.
Classified, annotated bibliography of some 6,000 items, mainly in English and with an American emphasis, published between 1885 and 1945. Author and subject indexes. Covers costume, puppet plays, and the dance, but *not* radio, motion pictures, opera, or television.

844.   British Drama League. Library. **The Player's Library: The Catalogue of the Library of the British Drama League**. 2nd ed. London: Faber and Faber, 1950. 1115p. Supps. 1951, 128p.; 1954, 256p.; 1956, 256p.
Some 14,500 plays are listed under authors, with brief information on number of acts, cast setting, period, and costume. Title index of plays. Author index of books on the theater. Most comprehensive bibliography of English plays and books about the drama.

845.   Coleman, Arthur, and Gary R. Tyler. **Drama Criticism**. Denver: Alan Swallow, 1966-69. 2 vols.

Vol. 1, *A Checklist of Interpretation since 1940 of English and American Plays* (1966); Vol. 2, *A Checklist of Interpretation since 1940 of Classical and Continental Plays* (1969). Basic arrangement is alphabetical by authors and then by titles of plays.

846.   Greg, Walter Wilson. **A Bibliography of the English Printed Drama to the Restoration**. London: Bibliographical Society, 1939-59. 4 vols.

Arranged chronologically. Gives locations in European and American libraries. Contents: Vol. 1, *Stationers' Records: Plays, to 1616, Nos. 1-349* (1939); Vol. 2, *Plays, 1617-1689, Nos. 350-386; Latin Plays; Last Plays* (1951); Vol. 3, *Collections; Appendix; Reference Lists* (1958); Vol. 4, *Introduction; Additions; Corrections; Index of Titles* (1959).

847.   Hatch, James Vernon, ed. **Black Image on the American Stage: A Bibliography of Plays and Musicals, 1770-1970**. New York: DBS, 1970. 162p.

If a play (one-act, musical, revue, or opera) includes a black character, has black authorship, or a black theme, and if it was produced in America, it is included. Good introduction. Author and title indexes. Bibliography. Suggestions for research. Manuscripts have library locations if the plays are available only in this form.

848.   Houle, Peter J. **The English Morality and Related Drama: A Bibliographical Survey**. Hamden, Conn.: Archon Books, 1972. 195p.

849.   Litto, Fredric M. **American Dissertations on Drama and the Theatre: A Bibliography**. Kent, Ohio: Kent State University Press, 1969. 519p.

Lists all dissertations up to 1965. Compiler plans five-year supplements. Finding index by author, key word, and subject.

850.   New York Public Library. The Research Libraries. **Catalog of the Theatre and Drama Collections**. New York: New York Public Library, 1967. 21 vols.

Covers more than 120,000 plays (excluding children's and Christmas plays) and works about the theater in the broadest sense. In three parts: Part I, Drama Collection: Listing by Cultural Origin; Part II, Drama Collection: Author Listing; Part III, Theatre Collection: Books on the Theatre.

851.   Palmer, Helen H., and Anne Jane Dyson. **American Drama Criticism**. Hamden, Conn.: Shoe String Press, 1967. 239p. Supp. 1970. 101p.

A bibliography of criticisms of American drama published between 1890 and 1969 in books, periodicals, and monographs. All playwrights from the earliest days of the United States are covered. Arrangement is alphabetical by playwright and then by play. Alphabetical author and title index, with author capitalized.

852.   Palmer, Helen H., and Anne Jane Dyson. **European Drama Criticism**. Hamden, Conn.: Shoe String Press, 1968. 400p. Supp. 1970. 243p.

Includes criticisms of dramatic works by outstanding European playwrights past and present. Covers published criticism from 1900 to 1970. Emphasis is on English-language materials. Arrangement is alphabetical by playwright. Index of playwrights, pseudonyms, and play titles. Companion to the compilers' *American Drama Criticism* (1967).

853.　Ryan, Pat M., comp. **American Drama Bibliography: A Checklist of Publications in English**. Fort Wayne, Ind.: Public Library, 1969. 240p.
Checklist of English language books, articles, and pamphlets on significant American plays from Colonial times to the present. Section on individual authors better than section on general background.

854.　Salem, James M. **A Guide to Critical Reviews**. Metuchen, N.J.: Scarecrow Press, 1966-71. 4 parts in 5 vols.
Contents: I, American Drama from O'Neill to Albee; II, The Musical from Rodgers-and-Hart to Lerner-and-Loewe; III, British and Continental Drama from Ibsen to Pinter; IV, The Screenplay from The Jazz Singer to Dr. Strangelove.

855.　Stratman, Carl Joseph. **A Bibliography of British Dramatic Periodicals, 1720-1960**. New York: New York Public Library, 1962. 58p.
Covers 674 titles in a chronological arrangement and gives locations of complete files in American and British libraries.

856.　Stratman, Carl Joseph. **Bibliography of English Printed Tragedy, 1565-1900**. Carbondale: Southern Illinois University Press, 1966. 843p.
Basic arrangement is alphabetical by author. Gives locations in libraries. Has an appendix of manuscript locations, a list of anthologies and collections, a chronological table, and a title index.

857.　Stratman, Carl Joseph. **Bibliography of Medieval Drama**. 2nd ed. rev. and enl. New York: Frederick Ungar, 1972. 2 vols.
Classified bibliography of the drama of medieval Europe. Wide range of topics. References to reviews of major books.

858.　Stratman, Carl Joseph. **Bibliography of the American Theatre, Excluding New York City**. Chicago: Loyola University Press, 1965. 397p.
Coverage includes books, periodical articles, theses and dissertations on the American theater (including ballet, opera, and children's theater). Arranged by state and then by city. Indicates locations for books. Author and subject index.

859.　Stratman, Carl Joseph, and others, eds. **Restoration and Eighteenth Century Theatre Research: A Bibliographical Guide, 1900-1968**. Carbondale: Southern Illinois University Press, 1971. 811p.
Over 6,000 entries under 780 subject headings in alphabetical order (432 are names and 348 are general subjects). Over 5,000 of the entries are annotated. Name and subject index (pp. 783-811) consists of three columns per page of very small type.

860.   "Theatre." In **Bulletin signalétique**. C(19-24): **Sciences humaines; Section 23: Littérature et arts du spectacle**, 1961– . Quarterly. Paris: Centre National de la Recherche Scientifique.

Classified arrangement. Bibliographical information and brief descriptive abstracts.

Indexes, Abstracts, and Current Awareness Services

861.   Breed, Paul F., and Florence M. Sniderman. **Dramatic Criticism Index: A Bibliography of Commentaries on Playwrights from Ibsen to the Avant-Garde**. Detroit: Gale, 1972. 1022p.

Compilers used about 630 books and over 200 periodicals. Work includes some 12,000 entries in English on about 300 playwrights, both American and foreign. Basic arrangement is alphabetical by playwright, subarranged by titles of plays. Indexed by play title and by critic. List of books indexed.

862.   **Chicorel Theater Index to Plays in Anthologies, Periodicals, Disc and Tapes**. Ed. by Marietta Chicorel and Veronica Hall. New York: Chicorel Library Publishing Co., 1970– .

Includes books (mostly in print) and periodicals, in English only. Excellent, easy-to-use format. Carefully researched. Gives complete bibliographic data. Authors, editors, and titles (of plays and anthologies) are in one alphabet. Appended are lists of authors, editors, and titles of plays. Supplements, but does not supersede, Ottemiller's *Index to Plays in Collections* and Firkins' *Play Index*.

863.   **Cumulated Dramatic Index, 1909-1949**. Boston: G. K. Hall, 1965. 2 vols.

Cumulates the 41 annual volumes of the *Dramatic Index*, including the three appendices: Author List of Books about the Drama; Title List of Published Play Texts; and Author List of Published Play Texts. Subject index to articles about the drama, the theater, actors and actresses, playwrights, librettists, managers, etc.; reviews; stage and dramatic portraits; scenes from plays and other theatrical illustrations; texts of plays.

864.   Firkins, Ina Ten Eyck, comp. **Index to Plays, 1800-1926**. New York: H. W. Wilson, 1927. 307p. Supp., 1927-34. 1935. 140p.

More than 10,000 plays. Shows where texts can be found in collections or other sources. Covers only plays in English but does include translations. Two parts: 1) author index, with full bibliographical information and often number of acts, brief characterization (comedy, tragedy, social, domestic, etc.); 2) title and subject index, referring to the author list.

865.   Guernsey, Otis L., Jr., comp. and ed. **Directory of the American Theater, 1894-1971: Index to the Complete Series of Best Plays Theater Yearbooks: Titles, Authors and Composers of Broadway, Off-Broadway, and Off-Off Broadway Shows and Their Sources**. New York: Dodd, Mead, 1971. 343p.

Divided into two sections: 1) playwrights, librettists, composers, lyricists, etc.; 2) titles.

866.   Ireland, Norma (Olin). **Index to Full Length Plays 1944-1964**. Boston: Faxon, 1965. 296p.

Companion volume to Ruth Thomson's *Index to Full Length Plays*. Instead of separate author, subject, and title indexes (as was done by Thomson), all three types are combined in one alphabet.

867.   Keller, Dean H. **Index to Plays in Periodicals**. Metuchen, N.J.: Scarecrow Press, 1971. 558p. Supp., 1973. 263p.

Indexes over 5,000 plays in 100 periodicals. Divided into two parts. Main entry is under author and includes full name and dates; title of play; number of acts; brief description; citation; name of translator or adaptor; title in original (if translated). The second part is a title index, which refers to the item number of the main entry.

868.   Kreider, Barbara. **Index to Children's Plays in Collections**. Metuchen, N.J.: Scarecrow Press, 1972. 138p.

869.   Logasa, Hannah. **An Index to One-Act Plays**. Boston: Faxon, 1924-66. 6 vols.

Basic volume, 1924; first supplement, 1924-31; second supplement, 1932-40; third supplement, 1941-48; fourth supplement, 1948-57; fifth supplement, 1956-64. Title, author and subject indexes to one-act plays in collections and separately published pamphlets. The third supplement includes radio plays, while the fourth and fifth also include television. Intended primarily for children and young people.

870.   Ottemiller, John H. **Ottemiller's Index to Plays in Collections: An Author and Title Index to Plays Appearing in Collections Published between 1900 and Mid-1970**. By John M. Connor and Billie M. Connor. 5th ed. rev. and enl. Metuchen, N.J.: Scarecrow Press, 1971. 452p.

Includes plays from ancient to modern times. Does *not* include children's plays, amateur plays, or one-act plays, unless they appear in one of the collections indexed. Contents: 1) author index, giving name and date, title of play, date of first production, references from original titles, variant translated titles, joint authors, translators, etc.; 2) list of collections and key to symbols; 3) title index.

871.   Patterson, Charlotte A. **Plays in Periodicals**. Boston: G. K. Hall, 1970. 240p.

Contains more than 4,000 plays published in 97 English-language periodicals between 1900 and 1968. For comprehensive search, one should also consult *Index to Plays in Periodicals*, by Dean H. Keller.

872.   **Play Index**, 1949-1952– . New York: H. W. Wilson, 1953– .

Vol. 1, 1949-52, edited by Dorothy West and Dorothy Peake; Vol. 2, 1953-60, edited by Estelle Fidell and Dorothy Peake; Vol. 3, 1961-67, edited by Estelle Fidell; Vol. 4, 1968-72, edited by Estelle Fidell. Each volume has four parts: 1) main list, arranged by author, title, and subject; 2) cast analysis, listing each play under type of cast (male, female, mixed, puppet); 3) list of collections indexed; 4) directory of publishers.

873. **Theatre/Drama & Speech Index**, 1974– . 3 per year and cumulations. Theatre/Drama & Speech Information Center, 1115 Crestline, Crete, Neb. 68333.

To be issued in April, September, and December, with an annual cumulation. Two main sections: Theatre/Drama, and Speech Communication. In both sections main entries are in a classified arrangement. Supplementary access to the Theatre/Drama section is provided through: author index, subject index, play-in-text index, name-in-text index, illustration index. The Speech section has three indexes: author, subject, and name-in-text.

874. Theatre Magazine (indexes). **A Selective Index to Theatre Magazine**. By Stan Coryn. New York: Scarecrow Press, 1964. 289p.

About 45,000 references covering the period from 1900 to 1930.

875. Thomson, Ruth. **Index to Full Length Plays**. Boston: Faxon, 1946-56. 2 vols.

Contents: Vol. 1, 1895-1925; Vol. 2, 1926-1944. Each volume places the main entry under title and gives detailed information on number of acts, characters, etc. Author and subject indexes. Bibliography.

Dictionaries and Encyclopedias

Dictionaries

876. Band-Kuzmany, Karin R. M., comp. **Glossary of the Theatre: In English, French, Italian and German**. New York: Elsevier, 1969. 130p.

Includes slang phrases as well as standard theater terminology. Well supplied with cross references. Compiled by an expert in theater history.

877. Bowman, Walter Parker, and Robert Hamilton Ball. **Theatre Language: A Dictionary of Terms in English of the Drama and Stage, from Medieval to Modern Times**. New York: Theatre Arts Books, 1961. 428p.

About 5,000 concise definitions of technical terms.

878. Granville, Wilfred. **The Theater Dictionary: British and American Terms in the Drama, Opera and Ballet**. New York: Philosophical Library, 1952. 227p.

Defines about 3,000 terms. British edition entitled *A Dictionary of Theatrical Terms*.

879. Rae, Kenneth, ed. **An International Vocabulary of Technical Theatre Terms in Eight Languages: American, Dutch, English, French, German, Italian, Spanish, Swedish**. Paris: Elsevier, 1959. 139p.

880. Taylor, John Russell. **The Penguin Dictionary of the Theatre**. London: Methuen, 1967. 295p.

Includes playwrights, actors, theaters, movements.

Encyclopedias

881.   **Crowell's Handbook of Contemporary Drama**. By Michael Anderson and others. New York: Crowell, 1971. 505p.
Short articles (in one alphabetical sequence) on dramatists, outstanding dramatic works, theater companies, and the drama in Europe and the Americas. Especially strong on avant-garde.

882.   **Enciclopedia dello spettacolo**. Roma: Maschere, 1954-62. 9 vols. Aggiornamento, 1955-65. Roma: Unione Editoriale, 1966.
Similar in format and profusion of illustrations to *Enciclopedia Italiana*. Covers period from antiquity to present, including theater, opera, ballet, motion pictures, vaudeville, the circus, etc. It treats performers, authors, composers, directors, designers; types of entertainment; dramatic themes; historical and technical subjects; organizations and companies; and pertinent place names. The supplement is devoted priarmily to biographical sketches of figures not in the basic set. A supplement on the cinema, published in 1963, is now superseded except for the illustrations.

883.   Gassner, John, and Edward Quinn, eds. **The Reader's Encyclopedia of World Drama**. New York: Crowell, 1969. 130p.
Covers drama of five continents from earliest times to the present. Emphasizes drama as literature, with biography and criticism of playwrights, plots of plays, articles on genres, and historical surveys of national drama. Some articles give references to best editions, translations, and sources of added information, and there are some pictures of playwrights and scenes from plays. Generally very good.

884.   Hartnoll, Phyllis. **The Oxford Companion to the Theatre**. 3rd ed. New York: Oxford University Press, 1967. 1088p.
International in scope. Covers all periods of history. Emphasizes popular rather than literary theater, and actors rather than dramatists. Opera and ballet are each treated in a single article. Cinema is omitted. Short articles, alphabetically arranged. "Select List of Theatre Books" (pp. 1029-74); 175 illustrations, with notes, at end.

885.   **McGraw-Hill Encyclopedia of World Drama**. New York: McGraw-Hill, 1972. 4 vols.
Attempts world coverage. Includes biographies of 910 dramatists, definitions of terms and about 60 articles on schools and movements. Listing of works of major playwrights includes dates of writing, first performance, and first publication. There are about 2,000 illustrations.

886.   Matlaw, Myron. **Modern World Drama: An Encyclopedia**. New York: Dutton, 1972. 960p.
Includes geographical entries (theater in various countries and regions), biographical entries (playwrights of the twentieth century), and technical terms (limited to modern ones describing movements and trends), all in one

alphabetical sequence. Many cross references. Short bibliographies at ends of
many entries, plus a general bibliography. There is a "Character Index"
(pp. 859-83) as well as a general index (pp. 887-960).

887.   Melchinger, Siegfried. **The Concise Encyclopedia of Modern Drama**.
        Tr. by George Wellwarth. Ed. by David Popkin. New York: Horizon
        Press, 1964. 288p.
European and American coverage since about 1900. Divided into the following
parts: Introduction to the Modern Drama; Documents on Contemporary
Playwriting; Glossary of Modern Dramatic Theory; Biographies of Playwrights;
Chronology of First Performances; Bibliography. Has 64 pages of production
photographs.

888.   Sobel, Bernard, ed. **The New Theatre Handbook and Digest of Plays**.
        8th ed. New York: Crown, 1959. 749p.
Contains about 3,500 entries on topics ranging from general subjects to
individual plays, actors, playwrights, producers, theaters, etc. Short bibliography. No index.

Directories and Annuals

889.   **Broadway's Best: The Complete Record of the Theatrical Year**,
        1957– . Garden City, N.Y.: Doubleday, 1957– .
Typical contents: A View of the Season; Best of Broadway (i.e., summaries of
top hit plays and musicals); Prize Plays; The Longest Runs; The Holdovers; The
Season in Full; Books about the Theatre Published during the Season;
Obituaries; Index.

890.   **"The Stage" Year Book**, 1908– . Annual. London: Carson and
        Comerford, 1908– .
Traditionally a directory of theaters and survey of theatrical events, this
publication has broadened its scope in recent years to include television.

891.   **Theatre**, 1954/55– . Annual. London: M. Reinhardt, 1955– .
Covers Great Britain, with particular emphasis on London.

892.   **The Theatre Annual . . . a Publication of Information and Research in
        the Arts and History of the Theatre**, 1942– . New York: Theatre
        Library Association, 1943– .

893.   **Theatre World**, 1944/45– . Annual. Philadelphia: Chilton, 1945– .
Productions, openings, closings, casts, obituaries, biographies. Edited by Daniel
Blum.

894.   Young, William C. **American Theatrical Arts: A Guide to Manuscripts
        and Special Collections in the United States and Canada**. Chicago:
        American Library Association, 1971. 166p.
Covers collections in 138 institutions. Part I is arranged alphabetically by state

or province, subarranged by institution and (if necessary) by name of collection. Part II is an analytical index by person and subject.

Histories

General

895. Berthold, Margot. **A History of World Theater**. Tr. from German by Edith Simmons. New York: Ungar, 1972. 733p.
The author teaches theater history at the University of Munich. "The book includes an extensive index, separate bibliographies for each historical period, and over 400 illustrations" (review by Louis A. Rachow, *Library Journal*, Oct. 15, 1972, p. 3330).

896. Brockett, Oscar G. **History of the Theatre**. Boston: Allyn and Bacon, 1968. 741p.
Covers entire period from ancient Egypt to the present. Very favorably reviewed. One critic thought it the best one-volume history available and another said that it superseded Sheldon Cheney's *The Theater*, a judgment that might need revision with the 1972 appearance of a revised edition of Cheney's book.

897. Cheney, Sheldon. **The Theatre: Three Thousand Years of Drama, Acting and Stagecraft**. Rev. and reset illus. ed. New York: McKay, 1972. 710p.
Originally published in 1929. Revised edition contains about 60 new illustrations, some changes of text, about 50 pages of new text, and a new bibliography.

898. Freedley, George, and John A. Reeves. **A History of the Theatre**. 3rd ed. New York: Crown, 1968. 1008p.
Covers the entire period from ancient Egypt to the present and deals with all aspects of the theater. Well illustrated. Bibliography.

899. Gascoigne, Bamber. **World Theatre: An Illustrated History**. Boston: Little, Brown, 1968. 335p.
Includes 31 color plates and 290 black and white illustrations.

900. Geisinger, Marion. **Plays, Players, and Playwrights: An Illustrated History of the Theatre**. New York: Hart Publishing Co., 1971. 767p.

901. Hartnoll, Phyllis. **A Concise History of the Theatre**. New York: Abrams, 1968. 288p.

902. **Histoire des spectacles**. Volume publié sous la direction de Guy Dumur. Paris: Gallimard, 1965. 2011p.
Encyclopédie de la pléiade, 19. Historical articles by specialists covering a wide range of topics. Detailed name index. Title index.

903.   Kindermann, Heinz. **Theatergeschichte Europas**. Salzburg: Muller, 1957– .
1) *Das Theater der Antike und des Mittelalters* (1957); 2) *Das Theater der Renaissance* (1959); 3) *Das Theater der Barockzeit* (1959); 4, 5) *Von der Aufklärung zur Romantik* (1961/62); 6) *Romantik* (1964); 7) *Realismus* (1965); 8) *Naturalismus und Impressionismus; Part I, Deutschland, Osterreiche, Schweiz* (1968).

Particular Topics and Countries

904.   Abramson, Doris E. **Negro Playwrights in the American Theatre, 1925-1959**. New York: Columbia University Press, 1969. 335p.

905.   Bentley, Gerald Eades. **The Jacobean and Caroline Stage**. Oxford: Clarendon Press, 1941-68. 7 vols.
Contents: Vols. 1, 2, *Dramatic Companies and Players* (1941); Vols. 3, 4, and 5, *Plays and Playwrights* (1955); Vol. 6, *Theatres* (1968); Vol. 7, *Appendices to Vol. 6 and General Index* (1968). Covers period from death of Shakespeare in 1616 to closing of theaters in 1642. Entries in volumes 3 to 5 are alphabetical by playwright and give brief biographical information, manuscripts and important editions of plays, and a bibliography about the plays and their performance. Continuation of *The Elizabethan Stage*, by E. K. Chambers.

906.   Blum, Daniel C. **A Pictorial History of the American Theatre, 1860-1970**. New 3rd ed. enl. and rev. New York: Crown, 1969. 416p.
Adds 30 pages of pictures to the previous edition. Continues to be a major source of pictorial and other information about the American stage (especially New York). Excellent index to plays and players.

907.   Brockett, Oscar G., and Robert R. Findlay. **Century of Innovation: A History of European and American Theatre and Drama since 1870**. Englewood Cliffs, N.J.: Prentice-Hall, 1973. 826p.

908.   Chambers, Edmund Kerchiver. **The Elizabethan Stage**. Oxford: Clarendon Press, 1923. Reprinted with corrections, 1951 and 1965. 4 vols.
Still the standard work, though parts have been updated in other studies. Topics covered include: the Court and control of the stage; companies and playhouses; staging at Court and in the theaters; plays and authors. At the end of Vol. 4 are anonymous works, appendices of original documents, and the indexes (plays, persons, places, subjects). Chambers also wrote a companion work entitled *William Shakespeare: A Study of Facts and Problems* (Oxford: Clarendon Press, 1930). These two works have been indexed by Beatrice White in *Index to "The Elizabethan Stage" and "William Shakespeare"* (Oxford: Clarendon Press, 1934; reprinted New York: Blom, 1964).

909.   Chambers, Edmund Kerchiver. **The Mediaeval Stage**. Oxford: Clarendon Press, 1903. 2 vols.
Contents: Vol. 1, Minstrelsy. Folk Drama; Vol. 2, Religious Drama. The

Interlude. Appendices. Subject Index. Most comprehensive and authoritative account of the period from the fall of the Roman Empire to early Tudor England.

910.　Genest, John. **Some Account of the English Stage, from the Restoration in 1660 to 1830**. Bath: H. E. Carrington, 1832. 10 vols.
Arrangement is chronological. Vol. 10 deals with Ireland but also includes additions, corrections, and the index to the set.

911.　Harbage, Alfred. **Annals of English Drama, 975-1700: An Analytical Record of All Plays, Extant or Lost, Chronologically Arranged and Indexed by Authors, Titles, Dramatic Companies, etc.** Rev. by S. Schoenbaum. London: Methuen, 1964. 321p.

912.　Hughes, Glenn. **A History of the American Theatre, 1700-1950**. New York: S. French, 1951. 502p.

913.　**The London Stage, 1660-1800: A Calendar of Plays, Entertainments and Afterpieces, together with Casts, Box Receipts and Contemporary Comment**. Comp. from the playbills, newspapers and theatrical diaries of the period. Carbondale: Southern Illinois University Press, 1960– .
Each volume covers part of the period. To be completed in 10 to 12 volumes. Day-by-day chronology of performances. Information about each play includes cast, incidental comments, and supporting references.

914.　Mitchell, Lofton. **Black Drama: The Story of the American Negro in the Theatre**. New York: Hawthorn, 1967. 248p.

915.　Nicoll, Allardyce. **A History of English Drama, 1660-1900**. Cambridge: Cambridge University Press, 1952-59. 6 vols.
Vols. 1 through 5 follow the same general pattern: an historical section followed by appendices covering such topics as lists of theaters, handlists of plays, etc. Vol. 6 serves as an index to the set, although it is much more than that. Contents: Vol. 1, *Restoration Drama, 1660-1700*; Vol. 2, *Early Eighteenth Century Drama, 1700-1750*; Vol. 3, *Late Eighteenth Century Drama, 1750-1800*; Vol. 4, *Early Nineteenth Century Drama, 1800-1850*; Vol. 5, *Late Nineteenth Century Drama, 1850-1900*; Vol. 6, *A Short-Title Alphabetical Catalogue of Plays Produced or Printed in England from 1600 to 1900*.

916.　Wickham, Glynne William Gladstone. **Early English Stages, 1300 to 1660**. New York: Columbia University Press, 1959– .
Vol. 1, 1300 to 1576 (1959); Vol. 2, 1576 to 1660, Part 1 (1963). Planned for completion in three volumes. It is expected that Vol. 2, Part 2, and Vol. 3 will cover theater buildings and performances. Vol. 1 covers outdoor and indoor entertainment and dramatic theory. Vol. 2, Part 1, covers emblems and images. Illustrated.

917.   Williams, Raymond. **Drama from Ibsen to Brecht**. New York: Oxford, 1969. 352p.
The 1953 edition was published under the title "Drama from Ibsen to Eliot." Includes bibliographical references.

Biographies

918.   **A Biographical Dictionary of Actors, Actresses, Musicians, Dancers, Managers and Other Stage Personnel in London, 1660-1800**. Comp. and ed. by Philip H. Highfill, Jr., Kalman A. Burnim, and Edward A. Langhams. Carbondale: Southern Illinois University Press, 1972– .
Alphabetical by surnames. To be published in 12 volumes. Vol. 1, *Abaco to Bertie* (1972); Vol. 2, *Bertin to Byzard* (1972).

919.   Fleay, Frederick Gard. **A Biographical Chronicle of the English Drama, 1559-1642**. London: Reeves and Turner, 1886. Reprinted New York: AMS Press, 1970. 2 vols.
Arrangement is alphabetical by author with appendices at end of Vol. 2 on anonymous plays and masques, university plays, and translations.

920.   Kosch, Wilhelm. **Deutsches Theater-Lexikon: biographisches und bibliographisches Handbuch**. Klagenfurt: F. V. Kleinmayr, 1951– .
Covers theater and drama in Germany, including movements, actors, playwrights, and critics, with lists of works. To be completed in approximately 20 parts.

921.   Lewis, Allan. **American Plays and Playwrights of the Contemporary Theatre**. Rev. ed. New York: Crown, 1970. 270p.
First published in 1962, the new edition has added material on the contemporary English and American theater as well as the German theater since World War II.

922.   Rigdon, Walter, ed. **Biographical Encyclopedia and Who's Who of the American Theatre**. New York: Heineman, 1965. 1101p.
Opening sections cover New York productions from 1900 to 1964, theater playbills after 1959, and premieres of American plays abroad. Main part consists of 3,500 detailed biographies of Americans and others connected with the American theater. Following these biographies are sections on theater group biographies, New York theater buildings, bibliography, discography, and necrology. An excellent reference work.

923.   **Who's Who in the Theatre: A Biographical Record of the Contemporary Stage**. New York: Pitman, 1912– .
Fifteenth edition, 1972. Published at irregular intervals. Contents typically include an index to London playbills, biographies of about 2,000 actors (mainly British), major productions and long runs in London and New York, centers for theater research, etc.

Anthologies and Digests of Plays

924.   **Best American Plays**, 1939– . New York: Crown.
The title has varied. For the first series it was *Twenty Best Plays of the Modern American Theatre*. A supplementary volume, edited by John Gassner and covering the years 1918 to 1958, was published in 1961.

925.   **Best Plays of 1894/99– and Yearbook of the Drama in America**. Boston: Small, Maynard, 1920-25; New York: Dodd, Mead, 1926– . Annual.
A complicated bibliographical situation was created by attempts at retrospective coverage of the years 1894 to 1920. This was accomplished in three basic volumes edited by Burns Mantle, which covered 1909/19 (1933), 1899/1909 (1944), and 1894/99 (1955). A typical annual volume contains: digests and criticisms of selected plays; title list of New York productions; plays produced outside New York; Shakespeare festivals; statistics of runs; list of actors; prizes and awards; indexes of authors, plays, and casts and of producers, directors, and designers. Used in conjunction with Odell's *Annals of the New York Stage*, it will provide continuous coverage from 1699 to the present. Two index volumes to *Best Plays* were published: 1899-1950 (1950); 1949-1960 (1961). These have now been superseded by *Directory of the American Theater 1894-1971*.

926.   Cartmell, Van Henry, ed. **Plot Outlines of 100 Famous Plays**. New York: Barnes and Noble, 1952 (c.1945). 390p.

927.   Gassner, John, comp. **Best Plays of the Early American Theatre: From the Beginning to 1916**. New York: Crown, 1967. 716p.
A collection of representative plays.

928.   Gassner, John, comp. **A Treasury of the Theatre**. 3rd ed. rev. and enl. New York: Simon and Schuster, 1967. 3 vols.
Main part is an anthology of plays arranged by periods, with brief period introductions. There is also a selection of additional plays, grouped topically, with brief introductions to the topical sections. About 40 of the world's most famous plays are reproduced in full. There is "A Representative List of Plays to 1875" and a bibliography. No index, but a detailed table of contents.

929.   Gassner, John, ed. **Twenty Best European Plays on the American Stage**. New York: Crown, 1957. 733p.

930.   Goldman, Mark, comp. **The Drama: Traditional and Modern**. Boston: Allyn and Bacon, 1968. 690p.
Includes introductions to periods and types as well as representative plays with notes. Bibliographical references are also given. Covers a relatively small selection of landmark plays, with emphasis on the modern period.

931.   Laufe, Abe. **Broadway's Greatest Musicals**. 2nd ed. New York: Funk and Wagnalls, 1973. 502p.

Covers period from 1880s to early 1970s, giving information on plots, criticism, etc. Illustrated. New edition does not revise the 1969 edition very much but simply adds about 45 pages on newer developments.

932.   Lovell, John. **Digests of Great American Plays: Complete Summaries of More Than 100 Plays from the Beginnings to the Present**. New York: Crowell, 1961. 452p.

Basic arrangement is chronological, with author and title indexes and some supplementary lists of songs, famous actors, etc. Information given about each play includes plot summary and cast.

933.   Odell, George. **Annals of the New York Stage**. New York: Columbia University Press, 1927-49. 15 vols.

Covers period from 1699 to 1894. Each volume covers a specified part of the period (Vol. 1, to 1798; Vol. 2, 1798 to 1821; etc.). Extremely detailed. Each volume has many illustrations and an analytical index. Access to the illustrations is facilitated by *Index to Portraits in Odell's "Annals of the New York Stage"* (New York: American Society for Theatre Research, 1963). Coverage from 1894 to the present is provided by the Best Plays series.

934.   **One-Act Plays for Stage and Study**. New York: S. French, 1925– .

Contemporary plays by English, Irish, American and other writers.

935.   Patterson, Lindsay, comp. **Anthology of the American Negro in the Theatre: A Critical Approach**. 2nd ed. New York: Publishers Co., 1968. 306p.

936.   Patterson, Lindsay. **Black Theater: A 20th Century Collection of the Work of Its Best Playwrights**. New York: Dodd, Mead, 1971. 493p.

937.   Richards, Stanley, comp. **Best Plays of the Sixties**. Ed., with an introductory note and prefaces to the plays, by Stanley Richards. Garden City, N.Y.: Doubleday, 1970. 1036p.

938.   Shank, Theodore, Jr., ed. **A Digest of 500 Plays: Plot Outlines and Production Notes**. New York: Crowell-Collier, 1963. 415p.

Classified arrangement (by country and period) with author and title index.

939.   Shipley, Joseph T. **Guide to Great Plays**. Washington: Public Affairs Press, 1956.

For each play chosen the following information is given: 1) name of author, country, date, etc.; 2) a brief synopsis; 3) important aspects of the play's history; 4) analysis; 5) opinions of critics and reviewers; 6) prominent actors who acted in it. Arranged alphabetically by authors.

940.   Sprinchorn, Evert, ed. **20th-Century Plays in Synopsis**. New York: Crowell, 1966. 493p.

Act-by-act summaries of 133 plays.

Reviews

941. **New York Theatre Critics Reviews**, 1940– . 30 per year. New York Theatre Critics Reviews, 4 Park Ave., Suite 21D, New York, N.Y. 10016.

Complete Broadway theater reviews from the *Daily News, New York Post, Newsweek, Time, Wall Street Journal, Women's Wear Daily*, CBS-TV, and WNBC-TV.

942. **New York Times Theater Reviews, 1920-1970**. New York: New York Times, 1971. 10 vols.

Reviews are arranged chronologically in Vols. 1 through 8. Vol. 9 has an appendix of theater awards and summaries of productions and runs, by season, as well as indexes by titles and production companies. Vol. 10 is an index of personal names.

Production and Direction

943. Albright, Hardie. **Stage Direction in Transition**. Encino, Calif.: Dickenson Publ. Co., 1972. 340p.

944. Bailey, Howard. **The ABC's of Play Producing: A Handbook for the Nonprofessional**. New York: McKay, 1955. 276p.

Covers such topics as selection, casting, rehearsing, scenery, and lighting.

945. Baker, Hendrik. **Stage Management and Theatrecraft: A Stage Manager's Handbook**. New York: Theatre Arts Books, 1968. 304p.

Contents: 1) History of the Stage; 2) "Can You Mark a Script?" 3) Rehearsals; 4) The Stage Staff; 5) The Stage; 6) Scenery; 7) Properties; 8) Lighting; 9) The Wardrobe; 10) The Dress Rehearsals; 11) The First Night and Running the Play. Appended are a glossary of theatrical terms, an index, and suggestions for further reading. The book is illustrated with line drawings and black and white photographs.

946. Clurman, Harold. **On Directing**. New York: Macmillan, 1972. 308p.

Part I (Chapters 1-11), deals with the process from the selection of a script through the dress rehearsal. Part II (Chapters 12-14) deals with acting methods and audience reactions. Parts III and IV are devoted to the director's notes on specific modern plays. Brief name and title index.

947. Downs, Harold, ed. **Theatre and Stage: An Encyclopaedic Guide to the Performance of All Amateur Dramatic, Operatic and Theatrical Work**. London: Pitman, 1951. 2 vols.

Deals with techniques—acting, lighting, etc. Articles, arranged alphabetically, run to some length and are signed. Copious illustrations, some in color.

948. Farber, Donald C. **From Option to Opening: A Guide for the Off-Broadway Producer**. 2nd ed. New York: DBS Publications, 1970. 134p.

Contents: 1) Optioning a Property; 2) Co-Production Agreements; 3) The Producing Company; 4) Raising the Money; 5) Obtaining a Theatre; 6) Cast, Crew and Personnel; 7) Musicals; 8) Rehearsals, Open, Run or Close; 9) Repertories, Children's Theatre and Off-Off; 10) Vitally Important Odds and Ends. No index.

949.　Fernald, John. **Sense of Direction: The Director and His Actors**. New York: Stein and Day, 1968. 189p.

950.　Gassner, John. **Producing the Play, with the New Scene Technician's Handbook, by Philip Barber**. Rev. ed. New York: Dryden, 1953. 915p.
Covers all phases of play production.

951.　Heffner, Hubert C., Samuel Selden, and Hanton D. Sellman. **Modern Theatre Practice: A Handbook of Play Production**. 4th ed. New York: Appleton-Century-Crofts, 1959. 662p.
An authoritative text covering all phases of the subject and including glossaries, an annotated bibliography, and an index.

952.　Hodge, Francis. **Play Directing: Analysis, Communication and Style**. Englewood Cliffs, N.J.: Prentice-Hall, 1971. 394p.

953.　Lounsbury, Warren C. **Theatre: Backstage from A to Z**. Seattle: University of Washington Press, 1967. 172p.
Intended for those concerned with technical aspects of production—lighting, scenery, etc.

954.　Smith, Milton. **Play Production for Little Theatres, Schools, and Colleges**. New York: Appleton, 1948. 482p.
Noted for its practicality, especially for amateur groups.

955.　Welker, David Harold. **Theatrical Direction: The Basic Techniques**. Boston: Allyn and Bacon, 1971. 419p.

Periodicals

956.　**Drama: The Quarterly Theatre Review**, 1919– . British Drama League, 9 Fitzroy Square, London W.1, England.
Indexed in: *British Humanities Index*, *Abstracts of English Studies*, *Social Sciences and Humanities Index*. Covers all aspects of the theater. Many excellent book reviews.

957.　**Educational Theatre Journal**, 1949– . Quarterly. American Educational Theatre Association, 1317 F St., N.W., Washington, D.C. 20004.
Indexed in: *Education Index*, *Social Sciences and Humanities Index*, *Abstracts of English Studies*. Planned for teachers and students. Survey of contemporary scholarship, reviews of college productions, and bibliographies.

958. **Plays: The Drama Magazine for Young People**, 1941– . Monthly (Oct.–May). Plays, Inc., 8 Arlington St., Boston, Mass. 02116.
Indexed in: *Index to Children's Magazines, Reader's Guide*. A typical issue will contain eight to ten plays suitable for elementary, junior, or senior high school performances. Book reviews.

959. **Revue de la Société d'Histoire du Théâtre** 1948/49– . Quarterly. Société d'Histoire du Théâtre, 98 Blvd. Kellerman, Paris 13e, France.
The first three issues each year contain articles on theater history. The fourth issue is a classified bibliography of 4,000 to 5,000 items.

960. **Scripts: A Monthly of Plays and Theater Pieces**, 1971– . Monthly. Sahkespeare Festival Public Theatre, 425 Lafayette St., New York, N.Y. 10003.
Wide selection of new plays (entire texts) to aid producers, directors, and actors.

961. **Theatre Design and Technology**, 1965– . Quarterly. U.S. Institute for Theatre Technology, 245 W. 52nd St., New York, N.Y. 10010.
Articles on construction, design, lighting, sound, etc. Bibliographies.

961a. **Theatre Documentation**, 1968– . Semi-annual. Theatre Library Association, 111 Amsterdam Ave., New York, N.Y. 10023.

FILM

Introductory Works and Bibliographic Guides

962. Arnheim, Rudolf. **Film as Art**. Berkeley: University of California Press, 1957. 230p.
A work of fundamental importance by a distinguished scholar in the philosophy and psychology of art. Simply and clearly written. The book is not outdated, even though the examples are from films released prior to 1938, and the author's preference for the silent film as an art form may be open to question.

963. Bukalski, Peter J., comp. **Film Research: A Critical Bibliography with Annotations and Essay**. Boston: G. K. Hall, 1972.
An introductory essay on film research is followed by a classified, annotated bibliography and a separate section on films, distributors, and rental agencies.

964. Eisenstein, Sergei Mikhailovich. **Film Form, and The Film Sense: Two Complete and Unabridged Works**. Ed. and tr. by Jay Leyda. New York: Meridian Books, 1957. 296p.
Two classic works by a world-famous Russian film director who died in 1948. Generally regarded by the critics as among the very few really significant books on this subject. More recently, Leyda has translated and edited another collection of essays, also widely priased, entitled *Film Essays and a Lecture* (New York: Praeger, 1970).

965.   Gottesman, Ronald, and Harry M. Geduld. **Guidebook to Film: An Eleven-in-One Reference**. New York: Holt, 1972. 230p.

A good starting point for a variety of searches. Contents: Books and Periodicals; An Annotated List; Theses and Dissertations; Museums and Archives; Film Schools; Equipment and Supplies; Distributors; Bookstores, Publishers, and Sources for Stills; Film Organizations and Services; Festivals and Contests; Awards; Terminology in General Use.

966.   Huss, Roy Gerard, and Norman Silverstein. **The Film Experience: Elements of Motion Picture Art**. New York: Harper & Row, 1968. 172p.

Well written and illustrated, with examples from all periods of the cinema and from most film-producing countries.

967.   Kracauer, Siegfried. **Theory of Film: The Redemption of Physical Reality**. New York: Oxford University Press, 1960. 364p.

Although fiercely assailed by some reviewers, this work attracted wide attention as a scholarly effort to deal, not always successfully, with a theme of great importance.

968.   Limbacher, James L. **A Reference Guide to Audiovisual Information**. Ann Arbor, Mich.: R. R. Bowker, 1972. 197p.

Annotated bibliography of 400 reference works and 100 periodicals. Glossary. Subject index.

969.   Manoogian, Haig P. **The Film-Maker's Art**. New York: Basic Books, 1966. 340p.

A book on production for reviewers and filmmakers with some blending of theory and technique. Praised for its lucidity and practicality.

970.   Rufsvold, Margaret, and Carolyn Guss. **Guides to Educational Media: Films, Filmstrips, Kinescopes, Phonodiscs, Phonotapes, Programmed Instruction Materials, Slides, Transparencies, Videotapes**. 3rd ed. Chicago: American Library Association, 1971. 116p.

Bibliographies

971.   **Bibliographie internationale du cinéma et de la télévision**. Etabli par Jean Mitry. Paris: Institut des Hautes Etudes Cinématographiques, 1966– .

Contents: 1) France et pays de langue française (4 vols., 1966/67); 2) Italie (2 vols., 1967); 3) Espagne, Portugal et pays de langue espagnol et portuguaise (1968).

972.   California. University. Los Angeles. Theatre Arts Library. **Motion Pictures: A Catalog of Books, Periodicals, Screen Plays and Production Stills**. Boston: G. K. Hall, 1973. 2 vols.

A rich collection of primary and secondary sources, including personal papers and over 3,000 unpublished scripts of American, British, and foreign films.

973. McCarty, Clifford. **Published Screenplays: A Checklist**. Kent, Ohio: Kent State University Press, 1971. 127p.

974. Rehrauer, George. **Cinema Booklist**. Metuchen, N.J.: Scarecrow Press, 1972. 473p.

Primarily an annotated bibliography. Designed for the general reader as an aid in locating information and for the librarian as a guide in collection development. Over 1,500 items are included. Arrangement is alphabetical by title. Entries are given consecutive numbers. Basic arrangement is supplemented by lists of classic film scripts; modern film scripts; film periodicals; study guides. There is an author index and a selective subject index. Lists and indexes refer back to main part by item number.

975. Schuster, Mel. **Motion Picture Performers: A Bibliography of Magazine and Periodical Articles, 1900-1969**. Metuchen, N.J.: Scarecrow Press, 1971. 702p.

A time-saver for obscure figures (despite the formidable "omissions list" of people about whom nothing could be found) and for relatively complete access to sources for better known ones. Arrangement is alphabetical by performer's surnames. Coverage limited to English language publications (primarily American).

976. U.S. Library of Congress. **Library of Congress Catalog: Motion Pictures and Filmstrips**, 1953– .

Quarterly, with annual and five-year cumulations. Basic arrangement is by title, with a subject index. Many cross references. Good bibliographic detail.

977. Writers' Program. New York. **The Film Index, a Bibliography: Vol. 1, The Film as Art**. New York: Museum of Modern Art Film Library and H. W. Wilson Co., 1941. Reprinted New York: Arno Press, 1966. 723p.

Classified, annotated bibliography. Part I deals with "History and Technique," while Part II covers "Types of Film." A detailed index includes authors, titles of books and films, names of persons listed in production credits, names of important persons discussed in digests and titles of classifications.

Indexes, Abstracts, and Current Awareness Services

978. **American Film Institute Catalog of Motion Pictures Produced in the United States**. Ed. by K. W. Munden. New York: R. R. Bowker, 1971– .

A multi-volume set, planned to include all films produced from 1893 to 1970. Three major classifications: feature films, short films, and newsreels. Entries are alphabetical by title and give production and original distributing companies; dates of release or premiere; synopses; cast and technical credits; literary or dramatic sources; genre. Subject index to corporate and individual names.

979. Dimmitt, Richard Bertrand. **An Actor Guide to the Talkies: A Comprehensive Listing of 8,000 Feature-Length Films from January, 1949, until December, 1964**. Metuchen, N.J.: Scarecrow Press, 1967-68. 2 vols.

Vol. I is by film titles, with listings of casts. Vol. II is a name index to the thousands of actors mentioned in Vol. I.

980. Dimmitt, Richard Bertrand. **A Title Guide to the Talkies: A Comprehensive Listing of 16,000 Feature-Length Films from October, 1927, until December, 1963**. Metuchen, N.J.: Scarecrow Press, 1965. 2 vols.

Chief purpose is to help reference librarians meet the needs of patrons who have seen the movies and want to read the novels, plays, poems, short stories, or screen stories on which the movies were based.

981. Enser, A. G. S. **Filmed Books and Plays: A List of Books and Plays from Which Films Have Been Made, 1928-1967**. Rev., and with a supplementary list for 1968 and 1969. London: Andre Deutsch, 1971. 509p.

Compiled by a British librarian, this book takes 1928 as the starting point because most films from that time forward have been talking pictures. Main work and supplement have three parts: film title index, author index, and change of original title index.

982. **Film Review Index**, 1970– . Monterey Park, Calif.: Audio Visual Associates.

983. Gifford, Denis. **The British Film Catalogue 1895-1970: A Guide to Entertainment Films**. Newton Abbot, England: David & Charles, 1973. c.1000 unnumbered pages.

984. Wall, C. Edward, ed. **Multi Media Reviews Index**, 1970– . Ann Arbor, Mich.: Pierian Press. Annual.

Vol. I (1970) has about 12,000 entries from 70 sources; Vol. II (1971) has about 20,000 entries from 130 periodicals.

985. Weaver, John T. **Forty Years of Screen Credits, 1929-1969**. Metuchen, N.J.: Scarecrow Press, 1970. 2 vols.

Basic arrangement is alphabetical by surnames of actors and actresses and then chronological, with years and titles of movies each year.

986. Weaver, John T. **Twenty Years of Silents, 1908-1928**. Metuchen, N.J.: Scarecrow Press, 1971. 514p.

Part I is entitled "The Players." The heart of this section is "Screen Credits," arranged alphabetically by actor, then chronologically with years and titles of movies. A similar plan is followed in Part II, "The Directors and Producers." Both parts also have separate sections on "vital statistics." Part III deals with corporations and distributors.

Dictionaries and Encyclopedias

987. Bessy, Maurice, and Jean-Louis Chardans. **Dictionnaire du cinéma et de la télévision**. Paris: Jean-Jacques Pauvert, 1965– . 5 vols.

An important set, especially good on the history and technology of the movies, but less consistent on television. Final volume is to include a list of film titles. Profusely illustrated with small black and white photographs.

988.   Boussinot, Roger. **L'Encyclopédie du cinéma**. Paris: Bordas, 1967. 1550p.
Encompasses all aspects in one volume. One alphabetical listing includes individuals, films, techniques, organizations, and countries. No bibliographies. Articles unsigned. International in scope.

989.   Graham, Peter John. **A Dictionary of the Cinema**. Rev. ed. New York: A. S. Barnes, 1968. 175p.
Over 600 short biographies, a brief guide to technical terms, and an index to 7,500 film titles.

990.   Halliwell, Leslie. **The Filmgoer's Companion**. 3rd ed. London: MacGibbon & Kee, 1970. 1072p.
For the general public. Entries for actors, directors, producers, photographers, technical terms, general topics, and outstanding individual films. Expanded edition adds many biographical articles and short articles on new topics. Many short entries in one alphabet, thus avoiding need for an index.

991.   **The International Encyclopedia of Film**. Gen. ed.: Roger Manvell. American advisory ed.: Lewis Jacobs. New York: Crown, 1972. 574p.
Nearly 1,300 entries. Good bibliography, and many illustrations.

992.   Jordan, Thurston C. **Glossary of Motion Picture Terminology**. Menlo Park, Calif.: Pacific Coast Publishers, 1968. 63p.
A small book of brief and simple definitions.

993.   Sadoul, Georges. **Dictionary of Films**. Tr. and updated by Peter Morris. Berkeley: University of California Press, 1972. 432p.
International, selective coverage. Lists about 1,200 films by title, providing the following types of information: country, date, credits, cast, plot, criticism.

Directories and Annuals

994.   **International Motion Picture Almanac**, 1929– . Annual. New York: Quigley.
Contents: index of subjects; index of advertisers; statistics; the great hundred (best of all time); awards and polls; who's who; pictures; corporations; theater circuits; buying and booking; drive-in theaters; equipment; services; talent and literary agencies; the industry in Great Britain and Ireland; non-theatrical motion pictures; the world market; organizations; the press; codes and censorship. Another publication to be considered is *International Film Guide* (London: Tantivy Press, 1963–).

995. Limbacher, James L., comp. and ed. **Feature Films on 8mm and 16mm: A Directory of Feature Films Available for Rental, Sale and Lease in the United States**. 3rd ed. New York: R. R. Bowker, 1971. 269p.

Alphabetical by title, with index of directors and their films. Does not give prices.

Histories

996. Bardèche, Maurice, and Robert Brasillach. **The History of Motion Pictures**. Tr. and ed. by Iris Barry. New York: Arno Press, 1970 (c.1938). 412p.

Covers period from 1895 to 1935. Published in 1938 as *History of the Film*, it is now regarded as a classic.

997. Cowie, Peter, ed. **A Concise History of the Cinema**. New York: Barnes, 1971. 2 vols.

Vol. I covers the period to World War II; Vol. II brings the coverage to 1970.

998. Hampton, Benjamin. **A History of the Movies**. New York: Arno Press, 1970 (c.1931). 456p.

Originally published as *History of the American Film Industry from the Beginning to 1931*; long regarded as a major contribution.

999. Jacobs, Lewis. **The Rise of the American Film: A Critical History**. New York: Columbia University Teachers College Press, 1968. 631p.

Covers period to 1939.

1000. Knight, Arthur. **The Liveliest Art**. New York: New American Library, 1959. 352p.

Covers period from 1895 to 1955. Very popular. Often used as a text.

1001. Ramsaye, Terry. **A Million and One Nights**. New York: Simon & Schuster, 1964 (c.1926). 868p.

Covers period to 1925. Standard history for early period. Detailed index.

1002. Seldes, Gilbert. **The Movies Come from America**. New York: Scribner's, 1937. 120p.

Well written. Excellent illustrations and index.

Biographies

1003. **Filmlexikon degli autore e della opere**. Firenze: Edizioni de Bianco e Negro, 1958-67. 7 vols.

Over 50,000 entries in this international, illustrated biographical dictionary of actors, authors, directors, writers, producers, cameramen, composers, costume designers, and art directors. A second series, with more general encyclopedic coverage, is planned.

1004.   Sadoul, Georges. **Dictionary of Film Makers**. Tr. and updated by Peter Morris. Berkeley: University of California Press, 1972. 288p.

International biographical dictionary of over 1,000 producers, directors, scriptwriters, cinematographers, art directors, composers, and inventors. Does *not* include actors or actresses.

Reviews

1005.   **The New York Times Directory of the Film**. Intro. by Arthur Knight. New York: Arno Press and Random House, 1971. 1243p.

Collection of reviews from *The New York Times*. Contents: I, Listings of Awards; The Times "10 Best"; The New York Film Critics Awards; The Academy Awards; II, Reprints of Reviews (by year, and then alphabetically by title); III, Portrait Gallery (2,000 stars, grouped by sex and then by name); IV, Index. The index covers all reviews from 1913 to 1968; it is divided into two parts: Personal Name Index and Corporate Index. The former lists every performer, producer, director, screen writer, etc., and runs to nearly 900 pages. The latter, which runs to 70 pages, covers producing, participating, and other companies mentioned in the reviews. Both are computer-produced and remarkably detailed.

1006.   **New York Times Film Reviews, 1913-1968**. New York: New York Times and Arno Press, 1970. 6 vols.

Facsimile of newsprint. Vol. 6, Appendix and Index. Over 17,000 reviews, as well as articles on outstanding films of the year. Reviews are arranged chronologically. Appendix includes overlooked reviews, New York Film Critics Awards, Academy Awards, and pictures of 2,000 actors and actresses. Index has 250,000 entries. Separate sections for movie titles, people, and corporations.

Periodicals

1007.   **Cahiers du cinéma**, 1951– . Monthly. J. L. Comolli and J. L. Ginibre, 39 rue Cognillierè, Paris, France.

Emphasis on French filmmaking. Ratings. Information about awards. Avant-garde in tone, somewhat political in recent years. Reviews of film journals and books.

1008.   **Film Comment**, 1962– . Quarterly. Film Comment Publishing Co., 100 Walnut Place, Brookline, Mass. 02146.

Critical commentary that relates the film to pressing social issues. Good section of book reviews.

1009.   **Film Culture**, 1955– . Irregular. Jonas Mekas, Box 1499, New York, N.Y. 10001.

Avant-garde and imaginative. Includes interviews with filmmakers, news of film festivals, and bibliography of books received.

1010.   **Film Library Quarterly**, 1967– . Film Library Information Council, 17 W. 60th St., New York, N.Y. 10023.
Reviews and information on 16mm films for use in public and academic libraries. Good book reviews.

1011.   **Film Quarterly**, 1945– . University of California Press, Berkeley, Calif. 94720.
Indexed in: *Reader's Guide, Art Index, Social Sciences and Humanities Index*. Good reputation for scholarly reviews of films and for lengthy articles on historical or biographical topics. Book reviews stress academic titles.

1012.   **Film World**, 1946– . 5 per year. Film World International Publications Prive, Ltd., A-15, Anand Nager, Juhu Tara Road, Bombay 400 054, India.
International coverage, with single issues on particular countries. Articles are in English.

1013.   **Soviet Film**, 1957– . Monthly. V/0 Sovexportfilm 14, Kalashny Pereulok, Moscow K-9, U.S.S.R.
Covers wide range of topics relating to the cinema in the Soviet Union. Editions are published in English, French, German, Spanish, Arabic, and Russian.

LANGUAGE
AND
LITERATURE

15　TRENDS IN LITERATURE AND CRITICISM

Poetry (especially epic poetry) preceded the invention of writing in many cultures. Other forms of literature evolved over a period of time; the standard divisions of *belles-lettres* (drama, essays, poetry, fiction) are of relatively recent origin, though their antecedents can be traced to antiquity.

FROM 3000 B.C. TO 1700

Some fragments of Egyptian literature from the third millenium B.C. have survived. From the Middle East, the *Gilgamesh* epic (c.2000 B.C.) is the earliest surviving example of this form. Indian poetry from the *Vedas* and the *Mahabharata* should be noted, as well as the more literary portions of the Bible. Outside the field of religion, a major piece of Indian literature is the *Panchantantra* (c.200 B.C.). Much of the rest of the literature that has survived from antiquity belongs to Greece and Rome. Homer's *Iliad* and *Odyssey* date from the ninth century B.C., while in the fifth century B.C. the lyric odes of Pindar and the dramatic odes of Aeschylus and Sophocles were the major literary productions. Roman literature tended toward satire, as in the *Satyricon* of Petronius (d.66 A.D.) and the *Metamorphoses* of Apuleius (fl. 155 A.D.). (One of the latter has been frequently translated into English as *The Golden Ass*.) Lucretius' *De Rerum Natura* is noteworthy as poetry in addition to its place in the history of philosophy. Virgil's *Aeneid* (19 B.C.) is comparable to the epics of Homer.

In the early Middle Ages, literature was centered around the concerns of the Church. Shortly, however, other forms again emerged. *Beowulf* (eighth century) celebrates heroic defense against the monster Grendel. *The Song of Roland* (eleventh century) deals with the defeat of Charlemagne's rear guard at Roncesvalles in 778. *Poem of the Cid* (twelfth century) commemorates the Spanish hero Rodrigo Diaz de Vivar. In Germany, heroic poetry was represented by the *Nibelungenlied* (twelfth century). English romances of the late Middle Ages included *Sir Gawain and the Green Knight* and Sir Thomas Malory's *Le Morte Darthur*. Geoffrey Chaucer's *Canterbury Tales* are transitional.

Among the most famous works of the Renaissance period is *Don Quixote*, by Cervantes (1547-1616), which some regard as the first modern novel. The poetry of Petrarch was widely read and imitated. Epic poetry was represented by Camões' *Lusiads*, which dealt with Vasco da Gama's voyage around the Cape of Good Hope in 1497. Other epics of the period included Ariosto's *Orlando furioso* (1532), Edmund Spenser's *The Faerie Queene* (1596), and Torquato Tasso's *Jerusalem Delivered* (1580). Probably the greatest epic was *Paradise Lost*, written by John Milton in the next century (1667). In France, François Rabelais was writing his famous satires *Gargantua* and *Pantagruel*. English literature showed pastoral and chivalric influences in Sir Philip Sidney's *Arcadia*, while moral and spiritual concerns were reflected in John Bunyan's *Pilgrim's Progress* (1678).

EIGHTEENTH CENTURY

In the eighteenth century the novel emerged as a distinct literary genre. *Robinson Crusoe* (1719) and *Moll Flanders* (1722), by Daniel Defoe, were important, but works by Samuel Richardson like *Pamela* (1740), *Clarissa Harlowe* (1747048) and *Sir Charles Grandison* (1753-54) were even more influential. Henry Fielding is chiefly remembered for *The History of Tom Jones, a Foundling* (1749) and his disciple, Tobias George Smollett, for *The Expedition of Hymphrey Clinker*. Laurence Sterne's *The Life and Opinions of Tristram Shandy, Gentleman* (1759-67) and Horace Walpole's Gothic novel, *The Castle of Otranto*, were other landmarks.

In France, Voltaire's *Candide* (1759) became a household word, while Jean-Jacques Rousseau wrote *La nouvelle Héloise* (1761) and *Emile* (1762). More than 200 works were written by Nicolas-Anne-Edmé Restif de la Bretonne (1734-1806), while the writings of the Marquis de Sade (1740-1814) have been revived in the twentieth century.

The century produced such diverse poets as Alexander Pope, Thomas Gray, Robert Burns, and William Blake. Noteworthy German writers included Gotthold E. Lessing, Friedrich von Schiller, and Johann Wolfgang von Goethe.

NINETEENTH CENTURY

The nineteenth century opened with the romantic movement, progressed to realism and naturalism, and closed with great interest in symbolism. Romantic poetry placed fresh emphasis on the lyrical. Johann Paul Friedrich Richter in Germany and William Wordsworth, John Keats, Samuel Taylor Coleridge, and Percy Bysshe Shelley in England were among the leaders. A satirical element entered the work of George Gordon, Lord Byron, who was one of the great romantic figures of the era. Alfred Lord Tennyson, Robert Browning, and Matthew Arnold were the leading poets of Victorian England, while their more original contemporary, Gerard Manley Hopkins, had to wait until the twentieth century for recognition.

In France, Alphonse de Lamartine was noted for his lyrics and Alfred de Vigny for more philosophical poems, while Alfred de Musset and Gérard de Nerval represented a late flowering of romanticism. Towering above them all, both as poet and as novelist, was Victor Hugo. Lyric poetry continued to flourish in France in the second half of the nineteenth century in the work of Charles Baudelaire, Paul Verlaine, and Arthur Rimbaud.

In Russia, Alexander Pushkin was noted for plays and poems. Later in the century, Count Aleksei K. Tolstoy wrote nonsense verse, lyrics, and dramas, and Nikolai A. Nekrasov wrote powerful narrative poems of social protest. The novel reached a high point in nineteenth century Russia. Fyodor Dostoyevsky is remembered for *Crime and Punishment, The Idiot, The Possessed,* and *The Brothers Karamazov.* Leo Tolstoy's *War and Peace* is of monumental proportions. Ivan Turgenev's *Fathers and Sons* is noted for its sensitive portrayal of feelings.

The nineteenth century novel in Britain was represented by Jane Austen's *Sense and Sensibility, Pride and Prejudice, Mansfield Park,* and *Emma,* while Sir Walter Scott was capturing the heroic past in *Ivanhoe, Quentin Durward,* and *Talisman.* In midcentury, William Makepiece Thackeray produced *Vanity Fair, The History of Pendennis,* and *The Newcomes,* while Charles Dickens reflected another side of English life in *David Copperfield, The Pickwick Papers, Oliver Twist, Bleak House,* and *A Tale of Two Cities.* Anthony Trollope's *Barchester Towers* gave realistic and satiric glimpses of the Victorian era. George Eliot's *Adam Bede, The Mill on the Floss, Silas Marner,* and *Middlemarch* brought her wide acclaim. Thomas Hardy's pessimism was reflected in his poetry and in such novels as *The Return of the Native, Tess of the D'Urbervilles,* and *Jude the Obscure.*

In the United States, James Fenimore Cooper's *The Last of the Mohicans, The Prairie, The Pathfinder,* and *The Deerslayer* were popular evocations of the early colonial period. The moral tales of Nathaniel Hawthorne (*The Scarlet Letter, The House of Seven Gables,* and *The Marble Faun*) received less immediate recognition. Herman Melville's allegorical sea-story, *Moby Dick,* remained virtually undiscovered until the 1920s. Samuel L. Clemens (Mark Twain) achieved lasting fame for *The Adventures of Tom Sawyer* and *The Adventures of Huckleberry Finn.* William Dean Howells' works (*The Rise of Silas Lapham,* for example) and those of Henry James (*The Wings of the Dove, The Ambassadors,* and *The Golden Bowl*) are transitional.

Meanwhile, Honoré de Balzac set a realistic direction for the novel in France in 85 novels projected to form part of the unfinished 137-volume series entitled *La comédie humaine.* His contemporary, Stendhal (Henri Beyle), wrote psychological novels of great perceptiveness, notably *Le rouge et le noir* and *La chartreuse de Parme.* Gustave Flaubert, who stressed craftsmanship in writing, exemplified this in *Madame Bovary* and *L'éducation sentimentale.*

TWENTIETH CENTURY

Trends in the twentieth century are even more difficult to define precisely than in the nineteenth. It may be useful to provide separate discussions of the development of poetry and of the novel.

Poetry

W. B. Yeats began writing in the late nineteenth century, but his mature work appeared in the 1930s; examples of his poetry and drama can be found in *Poems* (1957) and the *Variorum Edition of the Plays of W. B. Yeats* (1966). T. E. Hulme was influential prior to World War I as a poet and philosopher of poetry. Ezra Pound (*Hugh Selwyn Mauberly, The Cantos*, etc.) was influenced by Hulme's ideas, as was T. S. Eliot (*The Waste Land, The Hollow Men, Ash Wednesday, Four Quartets*). A. E. Housman, W. H. Auden, C. Day Lewis, Stephen Spender, and Louis MacNiece were influenced in varying degrees by Eliot. The poetry of Dylan Thomas celebrated both vitality and death. More recently, Roy Fuller, Philip Larkin, Donald Davie, Thom Gunn, and Ted Hughes have achieved prominence in England.

American poets of the twentieth century include Amy Lowell (*Men, Women and Ghosts*), William Carlos Williams (*Pictures from Breughel*), Vachel Lindsay (*The Congo and Other Poems*), Edgar Lee Masters (*Spoon River Anthology*), Carl Sandburg (*Chicago Poems*), Edwin Arlington Robinson (*The Town down the River*), Edna St. Vincent Millay (*The Ballad of the Harp-Weaver*), Wallace Stevens (*The Man with the Blue Guitar*), e. e. cummings (*is 5, 95 Poems*), Hart Crane (*The Bridge*), Marianne Moore (*What Are Years, Collected Poems*), Karl Shapiro (*Poems of a Jew*), Robert Lowell (*Lord Weary's Castle, Near the Ocean*), John Ciardi (*In Fact*), Archibald MacLeish (*Collected Poems*), Theodore Roethke (*The Far Field*), and Robert Frost (*Mountain Interval, West-Running Brook, A Further Range, A Masque of Reason*, and *In the Clearing*).

Among French poets, Paul Claudel (*Connaissance de l'est, Cinq grandes odes*) is regarded as outstanding, along with St. John Perse and Paul Valéry (*La Jeune parque, Le cimetière marin*).

Russian poetry in the early years of the century was predominantly symbolist, as exemplified in the writings of Aleksandr A. Blok (*Verses about the Beautiful Lady, The Twelve*). After 1917, Vladimir V. Mayakovsky dominated the scene with long, narrative poems like *150,000,000, Vladimir Ilich Lenin*, and *Well and Good*. One of the best-known poets since World War II is Yevgeni Yevtushenko (*Zima Station, Babi Yar, Third Snow, Promise, Apple, Tenderness, The Power Station of Bratsk*). Others include Joseph Brodsky (*Poems, Halt in the Wilderness*), Bulat Okudzhava (*Johnny Morozov, The Paper Soldier, From a Traveller's Diary*), Nikolai A. Zabolotsky (*Old Tale, Flight into Egypt, Poem of Spring*) and Boris Slutsky (*When They Killed Beloyannis, A Quarter to Nine, Physicists and Lyricists, In the State There Is the Law*).

Novel

Experimental approaches, internationalism, and competition from motion pictures have all affected the novel in the twentieth century. Among the major innovators were Marcel Proust (*The Remembrance of Things Past*) and Franz Kafka (*Amerika, The Trial, The Castle*). But perhaps the most revolutionary figure of all was James Joyce (*A Portrait of the Artist as a Young Man, Ulysses, Finnegan's Wake*). More traditional novelists included John

Galsworthy (*The Forsyte Saga*) and Arnold Bennett (*The Old Wives' Tale*). Joseph Conrad (*Nostromo, The Secret Agent, Under Western Eyes, Chance, Heart of Darkness, The Nigger of the Narcissus, Victory, Lord Jim*) provided a series of studies of human corruption. Stream-of-consciousness techniques were used by Virginia Woolf (*Mrs. Dalloway, To the Lighthouse*). D. H. Lawrence (*Sons and Lovers, Lady Chatterly's Lover*) was surrounded by controversy because of his unorthodox views of the nature and role of sex in life and in fiction. Aldous Huxley wrote novels satirizing many aspects of modern British society, including artists and intellectuals (*Crome Yellow, Point Counter Point, Brave New World*). George Orwell (*Animal Farm, 1984*) was basically a journalist and essayist; his novels reflected a determined opposition to totalitarian government. Graham Green (*The Power and the Glory, The Heart of the Matter, The End of the Affair*) exemplified the Catholic novel in English, and Muriel Spark (*Memento Mori, The Prime of Miss Jean Brodie*) also writes from a Catholic viewpoint. Joyce Cary (*Herself Surprised, To Be a Pilgrim, The Horse's Mouth*) and E. M. Forster (*Passage to India*) should also be noted. Iris Murdock (*Under the Net, The Bell, A Severed Head, The Unicorn*) reflects existential philosophy in her novels. William Golding (*Lord of the Flies, The Inheritors*) deals with problems of degeneration. Samuel Beckett, an Irishman living in Paris, writes in French and then translates his work into English (*Molloy, Malone Dies*).

Among French novelists, André Gide (*The Counterfeiters, The Immoralist, Pastoral Symphony*) held a prominent position early in the century. Other novelists between the wars included: Jules Romains (*Men of Good Will*); Louis-Ferdinand Céline (*Journey to the End of Night*); and André Malraux (*Man's Fate*). Existentialist writers include Jean-Paul Sartre (*The Roads to Freedom, Nausea*) and Albert Camus (*The Stranger, The Plague, The Fall*). Two novelists with a predominantly Catholic outlook are François Mauriac (*The Family, The Desert of Love, Thérèse, Vipers' Tangle*) and George Bernanos (*Diary of a Country Priest, The Star of Satan*). Among the so-called "anti-novelists" of the 1950s and 1960s are: Alain Robbe-Grillet (*The Seer, The Gurus, Jealousy, In the Labyrinth*), Michel Butor (*Change of Heart, Passage to Milan, Passing Time*), and Nathalie Sarraute (*Portrait of a Man Unknown*).

In the United States, the early part of the century saw publication of novels by Theodore Dreiser (*Sister Carrie, The Financier, The Titan, An American Tragedy*). Willa Cather wrote of the lives of immigrants and settlers in the West and in the Great Plains (*Death Comes for the Archbishop, Shadows on the Rock, My Antonia*). Edith Wharton published novels that showed the influence of Henry James (*Ethan Frome, The Custom of the Country, The Age of Innocence*).

The period after World War I was highlighted by Sherwood Anderson (*Winesburg, Ohio*) and Sinclair Lewis (*Babbitt, Main Street*), among others. F. Scott Fitzgerald exemplified the "Jazz Age" of the 1920s in his life as well as his writings (*This Side of Paradise, The Great Gatsby, Tender Is the Night*). Urban themes and structural experimentation were at the heart of John Dos Passos' works, including his trilogy, *U.S.A.* James T. Farrell (*Studs Lonigan*) and John Steinbeck (*The Grapes of Wrath*) both explored the dehumanizing effect of modern society.

A new economy of language characterized the works of Ernest Hemingway (*The Sun Also Rises, A Farewell to Arms, For Whom the Bell Tolls*). William Faulkner (*The Sound and the Fury, As I Lay Dying, Light in August, Absalom! Absalom!, The Hamlet, Intruder in the Dust*) created the universe of Yoknapatawpha County, using a complex and involuted style. Thomas Wolfe wrote massive and sprawling novels that were largely autobiographical (*Look Homeward, Angel, Of Time and the River, The Web and the Rock, You Can't Go Home Again*).

Other American writers include Eudora Welty, a Mississippian who captured the South and its people in her short stories and in her novels *The Ponder Heart* and *Losing Battle*; James Gould Cozzens (*Guard of Honor, By Love Possessed*); Robert Penn Warren, a poet and novelist who was one of the Fugitive group at Vanderbilt University in the 1920s (*All the King's Men, World Enough and Time*); and Carson McCullers (*The Heart Is a Lonely Hunter, Member of the Wedding, Clock without Hands*). Among novelists prominent today are J. D. Salinger, whose *Catcher in the Rye* has become a classic depiction of adolescence, and William Styron (*Lie Down in Darkness, Set This House on Fire*, and *The Confessions of Nat Turner*). Kurt Vonnegut (*Cat's Cradle, Slaughterhouse Five*) uses a science fiction approach to satirize both religion and science. Finally, Wallace Stegner (*The Big Rock Candy Mountain, Wolf Willow, All the Little Things*, and the Pulitzer Prize-winning *Angle of Repose*) writes about the West and the Great Plains and the people who settled there.

In the Soviet Union, heavy censorship has inhibited novelists since 1917. Among those who have achieved international fame are Mikhail A. Sholokhov (*And Quiet Flows the Don, The Don Flows Home to the Sea*), and Boris Pasternak (*Doctor Zhivago*). A tribute to and reminder of those who perished in governmental purges is the continuing effort of Aleksandr Solzhenitsyn (*One Day in the Life of Ivan Denisovich, Cancer Ward, The First Circle, August 1914*, and *Gulag Archipelago*).

The figure of Thomas Mann towers above all other German novelists (*Buddenbrooks, Royal Highness, The Magic Mountain, Joseph and His Brethren, The Beloved Returns, Doctor Faustus, Felix Krull*). Hermann Hesse (*Steppenwolf*) has enjoyed a revival in popularity. Gunter Grass (*The Tin Drum, Stiller*) and Heinrich Böll (*Where Wert Thou Adam?, House without Protectors, Group Portrait with Lady*) are prominent among the novelists who have emerged since World War II.

LITERARY CRITICISM

Literary criticism in the twentieth century has nearly become an art form in its own right, with the development and exposition of general aesthetic theories in addition to criticism of specific poems, novels, etc. Various schools of thought have competed at the same time—in contrast to previous centuries, when changes were more likely to be associated with historical periods. Five major schools have been identified: impressionistic criticism; the new humanism; psychological criticism; sociological and Marxist criticism; and the new criticism.

Impressionistic criticism is practiced by those who seek to avoid bringing to literary criticism a particular method or principle. Instead, an effort is made to appreciate excellence in literature whatever its form or technique. Each work is judged by the impression it makes upon the critic, who generally tries to give an author or work a personal assessment and often seeks to widen the circle of appreciation. Jules Lemaitre, Rémy de Gourmont, Benedetto Croce, James Gibbons Huneker, and H. L. Mencken have been cited as critics of this school.

The new humanism was one of the most important critical movements of the early part of the century, even though its influence was largely confined to the United States. It was an attempt to apply to American literature the principles of ancient and modern classicism. Emphasis was placed on balance, order, and reason, as opposed to the emotionalism and individuality found in romanticism and to the violation of decorum and lack of form found in naturalism. These critics placed strong emphasis on discipline, whether the formal discipline of technique or the moral discipline of content. They supported religion—not from theological belief but from their perception of its role as a stabilizing, conservative force in society. Leading exponents included Paul Elmer More, Irving Babbitt, Stuart P. Sherman, and Norman Forster.

The psychological critics exhibited significant differences but shared a common belief in the importance of a psychological approach. In general, they believed that art and literature are born in the subconscious, later acquiring outward structure and texture in the conscious mind of the artist. The psychological critic views the artist essentially as a neurotic personality; he differs from the ordinary neurotic, however, in that his heightened sensitivity makes it possible to translate frustration into art. Thus, art is most successful when it seeks to portray the subconscious processes of the mind, something that may be achieved without theoretical knowledge of psychology. Literature at its best, in this view, demonstrates the universal mythology and symbolism that psychology has discovered. In the United States and England, psychological critics attacked Puritanism for its repression of sexual activity. Critics of this persuasion included Floyd Bell, Waldo Frank, and Herbert Read.

The sociological and Marxist critics regarded literature as a reflection of history, economics, technology, and class relations. For them, sound characterization in literature would portray the individual as motivated mainly by his environment rather than by his internal will, with a destiny determined by economic, social, industrial, and political processes. V. F. Calverton and V. L. Parrington were non-Marxist sociological critics. The Marxists tended to view history chiefly in terms of class struggle and to believe that social progress could be achieved only through class warfare and revolution. Thus, the heroic individual would work to intensify the class war. Literature should be judged in terms of its effectiveness in inspiring class consciousness and preparing the proletariat for revolution. Michael Gold and Philip Rahv were critics of this school. For a time, Edmund Wilson and Granville Hicks were also influenced by it.

The so-called "new criticism" began to emerge in the 1930s and dominated the 1940s and 1950s. Critics of this school were generally influenced by the findings of the semanticists and by the analytical movement in philosophy. They tended to be hostile to traditional criticism and to literary history, feeling that too much emphasis was usually placed on period and social milieu. The "new critics" felt that each work of art should be taken by itself and treated purely as a work of art, regardless of origin. These critics believed that their predecessors had been too much preoccupied with the moral element in literature and argued that a good poem could be built around a bad idea. Their emphasis, therefore, was chiefly on technique (style, language, structure, meter, and metaphor). They viewed poetry (and many were practicing poets) as a craft to be learned for itself and not as a vehicle for philosophical, religious, or political ideas. A typical passage of such criticism would be a detailed, line-by-line analysis of a poem, considering the effectiveness of each literary device, with special attention paid to levels of meaning, symbolism, allegory, and psychological associations. In addition, they regarded literary criticism as an art comparable to poetry or painting—i.e., a branch of literature, rather than a subsidiary field. Critics of this school included I. A. Richards, William Empson, T. S. Eliot, John Crowe Ransom, Allen Tate, Ivor Winters, and Cleanth Brooks. During the 1940s they dominated periodicals like the *Kenyon Review* and the *Sewanee Review*.

16 ACCESSING INFORMATION IN LANGUAGE AND LITERATURE

MAJOR DIVISIONS OF THE FIELD

Both of the two basic approaches to the division of literature—by language and by form—are usually taken into account in customary divisions of the field.

Division of literature on the basis of the language in which it is written may require some refinements and modifications. For example, the volume of literature written in English is so large that further subdivision is desirable. In this case, the term "English literature" is restricted to the literary output of the United Kingdom that appears in English, or even to the literature of England alone. Separate provision is customarily made for American literature, Australian literature, etc. At the other extreme, some of the world's smallest literatures may be grouped together under a parent language.

The two basic forms of literature are prose and poetry. Prose is normally divided into novels, short stories, and essays. Poetry is normally treated as a unit, but it may be further subdivided by type (lyric poems, epic poems, etc.). The drama, as a literary record of what is to be performed on stage, has an independent life of its own and is also considered to be one of the major literary forms. Modern drama is ordinarily in prose, but it may also be in verse or may consist of both poetry and verse.

Another approach to the organization of literature is by historical periods or literary movements, often in combination with the basic schemes described above.

MAJOR CLASSIFICATION SCHEMES

Dewey and LC are the two schemes most widely encountered in American libraries. The major features of each in the classification of library materials in language and literature will be described in the paragraphs that follow.

One of the characteristics of Dewey is the wide separation of language (400-499) from literature (880-899). Many libraries attempt to compensate for this by shelving the 400s adjacent to the 800s.

A representative sampling of the basic divisions for language is given below:

400	Language
410	Linguistics
411	Notations
412	Etymology
413	Polyglot dictionaries
414	Phonology
415	Structural systems (Grammar)
416	Prosody
417	Dialectology & Paleography
418	Usage (Applied linguistics)
419	Verbal language not spoken or written
420	English & Anglo-Saxon languages
430	Germanic languages, German
440	French, Provençal, Catalan
450	Italian, Romanian, Rhaeto-Romanic
460	Spanish & Portuguese languages
470	Italic languages. Latin
480	Hellenic languages. Classical Greek
490	Other languages
491	East Indo-European & Celtic
492	Afro-Asiatic (Hamito-Semitic)
493	Hamitic & Chad languages
494	Ural-Altaic, Paleosiberian, Dravidian
495	Of East and Southeast Asia
496	African languages
497	North American aboriginal
498	South American aboriginal
499	Other languages

There is also a table of subdivisions of individual languages, which closely parallels the divisions given above under "Linguistics" and which can be used if divisions are not already contained in the schedules.

The following numbers provide a representative sampling of the literature divisions, showing some parallels with language:

800	Literature (Belles-lettres)
810	American literature in English
811	American poetry
812	American drama
813	American fiction
814	American essays
815	American speeches
816	American letters
817	American satire & humor
818	American miscellaneous writings
819	(Some libraries use for Canadian literature in English)
820	English & Anglo-Saxon literature
830	Literatures of Germanic languages
840	French, Provençal, Catalan
850	Italian, Romanian, Rhaeto-Romanic
860	Spanish & Portuguese literatures
870	Italic languages literature. Latin
880	Hellenic languages literature
890	Literatures of other languages (like 490-499)

There is also a table of subdivisions of individual literatures, which closely follows the divisions given above under "American Literature in English" but which expands to give considerably more depth and detail.

LC brings languages and literatures together in the framework of Class P, but with some combinations and some separations as noted in the synopsis below:

PHILOLOGY. LINGUISTICS

P	Comparative philology. Linguistics. Indo-European comparative philology. Extinct languages of doubtful relationship.
PA	Classical philology and literature
PB	Modern languages. General. Celtic.
PC	Romanic.
PD-PF	Germanic
PD	General. Gothic. Scandinavian.
PE	English.
PF	Dutch. Friesian. German.
PG	Slavic. Balto-Slavic. Albanian.
PH	Finnish. Hungarian. Basque.
PJ-PL	Oriental
PJ	General. Hamitic. Semitic.
PK	Indo-Iranian. Indo-Aryan. Armenian. Caucasian.
PL	Altaic. Eastern Asia. Oceanica. Africa.
PM	Hyperborean. Indian. Artificial languages.

LITERARY HISTORY. LITERATURE.

PN	General.
(PP)	Classical, see PA.
PQ	Romanic.
PR	English.
PS	American.
PT	German. Dutch, Scandinavian.
(PV)	Slavic, see PG.
(PX)	Oriental, see PJ-PL.
PZ	Fiction and juvenile literature.

Under PR, LC includes literature in English from the Commonwealth as well as that written in Great Britain.

Other key points about LC's treatment of literature are very ably summarized in John Phillip Immroth's *A Guide to the Library of Congress Classification* (2d ed., Littleton, Colo.: Libraries Unlimited, Inc., 1971), p. 190:

> Within this schedule the recurring plan or pattern for each literature appears for the first time. This pattern is the following:
> 1) History and criticism;
> 2) Collections or anthologies of more than one author;
> 3) Individual authors; and
> 4) Non-national literature if appropriate.

The third element, individual authors, is a most important characteristic of the Library of Congress Classification. The complete literary work by and about an author is arranged in a single group, as demonstrated in Chapter 4. Subdivision by literary form, common in the *Decimal Classification*, does not occur under individual authors in the Library of Congress Classification, with the exception of Elizabethan drama in Subclass PR, English literature, which is treated as a separate form.

SUBJECT HEADINGS FREQUENTLY USED

Once again, LC is used by an overwhelming majority of libraries in the United States. The following excerpts dealing with languages and literatures will alert the reference librarian to possible combinations and arrangements of search terms.

Language and languages
Here are entered works on language and languages in general, also works on the origin and history of language. Works on the philosophy and psychology of language are entered under Languages–Philosophy, and Languages–Psychology, respectively.
sa Bilingualism
Children–Language
Communication . . .
Literature . . .
Philology . . .
Semantics . . .
Translating and interpreting . . .
also names of particular languages or groups of cognate languages, e.g., English language, Semitic languages; *and subdivision* Languages *under names of continents, countries, cities, etc., e.g.,* Europe–Languages; U.S.–Languages; *and subdivision*

Language (New words. slang, etc.)
under classes of persons, names of schools and colleges, names of wars, etc. e.g., Cowboys–Language (New words, slang, etc.); Phillips Exeter Academy–Language (New words, slang. etc.); World War. 1939-1945–Language (New words. slang, etc.)
x Comparative linguistics
Dialects
Linguistics . . .
–Grammar, Comparative
see Grammar, comparative and general . . .
–Inflection
see Grammar. Comparative and general–Inflection Languages. Modern–Inflection *and subdivision* Inflection *under names of languages and groups of languages* . . .
Language question in the church (Direct). . .
Languages, Artificial . . .
sa Esperanto . . .

Some key terms and combinations for searches in the field of literature would be:

Literature
Here are entered works dealing with literature in general, not limited to aesthetic. philosophy, history, or any one aspect.
sa America–Literatures
Anthologies
Art and literature . . .
Negro literature . . .

also Agnosticism in literature; Australia in literature; Bible in literature . . . *and similar headings; also national literatures, e.g.* English literature. French literature . . .
–Bibliography
–Early
For bibliographies issued before 1800. First editions . . .

−History and criticism
  Here are entered histories of
  literature and works evaluating
  the character and qualities of
  works of literature. Works on
  the principles of literary
  criticism are entered under the
  heading Criticism . . .
Literature, Comparative
  Subdivided by nationality of
  literatures compared, with
  duplicate entry, e.g., 1. Literature, Comparative−English and
  German. 2. Literature, Compara-
  tive−German and English.
  x Comparative literature
  xx Philology
  −Themes, motives
    For typical plots, motives, etc.
  sa Fairy tales−Classification . . .

American Literature
  sa America−Literatures
  also German−American literature;
    Spanish-American literature; Swedish-
    American literature; *and similar*
    headings . . .
  −Colonial period
  −Revolutionary period
  −19th century
  −Early 19th century
  −20th century . . .
American literature (French)
  Duplicate entry is made under French
    literature−American authors.
  sa French−Canadian literature . . .
American poetry
  sa Negro poetry (American)
    Political poetry, American
  also German-American poetry; Spanish-
    American poetry; *and similar*
    headings . . .

MAJOR ORGANIZATIONS, INFORMATION CENTERS,
AND SPECIAL COLLECTIONS

Languages

The oldest, largest, and best-known of the organizations that promote
the study and teaching of languages in this country is the Modern Language
Association of America (62 Fifth Ave., New York, N.Y. 10011). Founded in
1883, it has more than 30,000 members, primarily college and university
teachers, and it conducts an immense range of programs and activities.
Publications include: *MLA Newsletter* (7 per year); *PMLA* (quarterly); *Job
Information List−English* (quarterly); *Job Information List−Foreign Languages*
(quarterly); *Directory* (annual); and *MLA International Bibliography* (annual).

The American Council on the Teaching of Foreign Languages was
founded by MLA in 1966 and shares office space and staff of the parent
organization. Its publications include: *Foreign Language Annals* (quarterly);
Accent on ACTFL (quarterly); *Annual Review of Research*; and *Focus Reports*.

The International Association for the Study and Promotion of
Audio-Visual and Structuro-Global Methods (Avenue Georges Bergmann 109,
1050 Bruxelles, Belgium) was founded in 1964 to promote the use of
audiovisual methods in teaching languages. Publications include: *Degrés* (3 per
year); *Linguistique appliquée* (3 per year); *Techniques audio-visuelles* (3 per
year); and *Procès-verbal d'assemblée générale* (annual).

The International Federation of Modern Language Teachers (D-355
Marburg/Lahn, Liebigstrasse 37, Germany) is made up of multilingual and
unilingual associations. It corresponds at the international level to the National
Federation of Modern Language Teachers (212 Crosby Hall, State University of
New York at Buffalo, Buffalo, N.Y. 14214), a federation of national, regional,
and state associations in this country that publishes *Modern Language Journal*
(8 per year).

The National Association of Language Laboratory Directors (Box 623, Middlebury, Vt. 05753) conducts workshops and seeks to improve the liaison between manufacturers and users of language lab equipment. It publishes *NALLD Journal* (quarterly).

The American Association of Language Specialists (Suite 9, 1000 Connecticut Ave., N.W., Washington, D.C. 20036) is a small group of interpreters, editors, and translators. The International Committee for Breaking the Language Barrier (268 W. 12th St., New York, N.Y. 10014) develops international signs and other aids to facilitate communication and offers consulting services to businesses and governmental agencies.

Literature

The International Comparative Literature Association (17, place Guy d'Arezzo, 1060 Bruxelles, Belgium) promotes the worldwide study of comparative literature and is preparing to publish a *Dictionary of International Literary Terms* and a *Comparative History of Literatures in European Languages*.

The International Institute for Children's Literature and Reading Research (Fuhrmannsgasse 18a, 1080 Vienna, Austria) promotes and evaluates international research in children's literature. Its publications are *Jugend und Buch* (quarterly), and *Bookbird* (quarterly).

Grants from the National Endowment for the Arts (matched by private gifts) have enabled the Coordinating Council of Literary Magazines (80 Eighth Ave., Room 1101, New York, N.Y. 10011) to assist "little" magazines in a variety of ways.

The American Comparative Literature Association (Department of Comparative Literature, State University of New York, Binghamton, N.Y. 13901) promotes study and teaching of comparative literature in American universities, publishes *ACLAN* (newsletter), co-sponsors *Yearbook of Comparative and General Literature*, and assists in the publication of two quarterly journals: *Comparative Literature* and *Comparative Literature Studies*.

Regional interests within the United States are served by such groups as the Society for the Study of Southern Literature (Department of English, University of North Carolina at Chapel Hill, Chapel Hill, N.C. 27514) and the Western Literature Association (English Department, Colorado State University, Fort Collins, Colo. 80521).

Information Centers in Language and Literature

The identification of information centers as distinct from professional organizations, on the one hand, and from special collections, on the other, is not a clearcut and simple matter. Many (but by no means all) professional organizations conduct programs of research and information dissemination. Many libraries holding special collections do the same. Nevertheless, mention should be made here of a few noteworthy examples.

The first is the Folger Shakespeare Library (201 E. Capitol St., Washington, D.C. 20003), which has an active research and publication program in British civilization of the Tudor and Stuart periods and theatrical history as these relate to Shakespeare.

The Center for Hellenic Studies (3100 Whitehaven St., Washington, D.C. 20003) is an international center associated with Harvard University. It conducts research in such areas as classical Greek literature, philosophy, and history.

The Center for Textual Studies (323 Main Library, Ohio State University, Columbus, Ohio 43210) conducts research on definitive texts of nineteenth and twentieth century authors, including the publication of definitive editions of Hawthorne and Emerson.

Special Collections in Language and Literature

The number of special collections in language and literature is so vast that mentioning names beyond the obvious giants like the Library of Congress, the British Library, the Bibliothèque Nationale, the New York Public Library, and Harvard University could easily run to several pages. Lee Ash's *Subject Collections: A Guide to Special Book Collections in Libraries* (4th ed. New York: R. R. Bowker, 1974) covers some 45,000 subject collections in all areas of knowledge from nearly 2,000 museums and over 15,000 academic libraries. The number of entries under "Literature" tends to be relatively small, but there are numerous cross references to more specific headings such as "Children's Literature" or "English Literature." Direct search under the names of individual authors (e.g., "Eliot, Thomas Stearns") will often be most fruitful.

Once again, Lewanski's *Subject Collections in European Libraries* will occasionally prove useful. Volume 2 of the *ASLIB Directory* has an exceedingly helpful index for literature in general and for the various specialized branches. Sometimes the index can be used for individual authors (e.g., "Dickens, Charles").

17 PRINCIPAL INFORMATION SOURCES IN LANGUAGE AND LITERATURE

CHAPTER OUTLINE

Language
 Introductory Works and Bibliographic Guides
 Bibliographies
 Indexes, Abstracts, and Current Awareness Services
 Dictionaries
 Histories
 Periodicals
General Literature
 Introductory Works and Bibliographic Guides
 Bibliographies
 Indexes, Abstracts, and Current Awareness Services
 Dictionaries and Encyclopedias
 Anthologies and Digests
 Theory and Criticism
 Serials
Literature in English
 Introductory Works and Bibliographic Guides
 Bibliographies
 Indexes, Abstracts, and Current Awareness Services
 Encyclopedias, Dictionaries and Handbooks
 Biographies
 Reference Histories
 Recommended Collections
 Poetry
  Introductory Works and Bibliographic Guides
  Bibliographies
  Indexes, Abstracts and Current Awareness Services
  Biographies
  History and Criticism
 Fiction
  Introductory Works and Bibliographic Guides
  Bibliographies of Fiction
  Bibliographies of Fiction Criticism
  Indexes, Abstracts, and Current Awareness Services
  Biographies
  History and Criticism
 Serials

Literature in Other Languages
Greek and Latin
Romance Languages
Germanic Languages
Slavonic Languages
Oriental Languages
African Languages

LANGUAGE

Introductory Works and Bibliographic Guides

1014.   DeBray, Reginald George Arthur. **Guide to the Slavonic Languages**. 2nd
ed. New York: Dutton, 1969. 798p.
Separate section for each language: history; alphabet; pronunciation; morphology; word order; special characteristics; brief literary quotations. Bibliography.
Detailed table of contents but no index.

1015.   **The Great Languages**. Gen. ed.; L. R. Palmer. London: Faber and
Faber, 1934– .
Each volume covers a major language or group of languages comprehensively and
is written by a subject specialist. LC catalogs and classifies separately. Some
libraries make a series added entry. For a list of titles published and planned, see
A. J. Walford's *Guide to Reference Material* (2nd ed., 3 vols. London: Library
Association, 1966-70), III, 177.

1016.   Jespersen, Otto. **A Modern English Grammar on Historical Principles**.
Copenhagen: E. Munksgaard, 1949. 7 vols.

1017.   Meillet, Antoine, and M. Cohen, eds. **Les Langues du monde, par un
groupe de linguistes**. Nouv. éd. Paris: Centre Nationale de la Recherche
Scientifique, 1952. 1294p.
Main reference work in this field. Coverage of some 10,000 languages and
dialects. Includes a pocket atlas with 21 maps.

1018.   Palmer, Leonard R. **Descriptive and Comparative Linguistics: A Critical
Introduction**. New York: Crane, Russak, 1972. 430p.
Rated highly successful as an introduction and state-of-the-art review.

1019.   Rice, Frank A., and Allene Guss, eds. **Information Sources in
Linguistics: A Bibliographical Handbook**. Washington, D.C.: Center for
Applied Linguistics, 1965. 42p.
Covers virtually all areas except individual languages, which are covered in
Bibliographie linguistique. Rice has also compiled *Study Aids for Critical
Languages* (Rev. ed. Washington, D.C.: Center for Applied Linguistics, 1968).

Bibliographies

1020.   Alston, Robin C. **A Bibliography of the English Language from the Invention of Printing to the Year 1800**. Leeds: E. J. Arnold and Son, 1965– .
To be published in 20 volumes, about half of which have appeared to date. Will eventually supersede Kennedy for the period before 1800. LC catalogs separately but classifies as a set and provides a series entry.

1021.   **Bibliographie linguistique**, 1939/47– . Utrecht: Permanent International Committee of Linguists, 1949– .
Comprehensive, annual bibliography of books, reviews, and articles. International and multilingual in coverage. Separate sections on individual languages.

1022.   Brenni, Vito Joseph, comp. **American English: A Bibliography**. Philadelphia: University of Pennsylvania Press, 1964. 221p.
Classified, annotated bibliography of books, articles, and dissertations.

1023.   Kennedy, Arthur Garfield. **Bibliography of Writings on the English Language from the Beginning of Printing to the End of 1922**. Cambridge: Cambridge University Press, 1927. Reprinted New York: Hafner, 1961. 517p.
The standard work for many years. Now in the process of being superseded for the period before 1800 by R. C. Alston's *A Bibliography of the English Language from the Invention of Printing to the Year 1800*.

1024.   Lewanski, Richard Casimir. **A Bibliography of Slavic Dictionaries**. New York: New York Public Library, 1959-63. 3 vols.
Contents: Vol. 1, Polish; Vol. 2, Belorussian, Bulgarian, Czech, Kashubian, Lusatian, Old Church Slavic, Macedonian, Polabian, Serbocroatian, Slovak, Slovenian, Ukrainian; Vol. 3, Russian. Quarterly checklist. International index of current books, monographs and separates.

1025.   **Quarterly Check-List of Linguistics**, 1958– . Quarterly. American Bibliographic Service, Darien, Conn. 06820.

1026.   Wawrzyszko, Aleksandra K. **Bibliography of General Linguistics: English and American**. Hamden, Conn.: Archon/Shoestring, 1971. 120p.
Classified, annotated bibliography of 344 books and periodicals. Especially useful for graduate students.

Indexes, Abstracts, and Current Awareness Services

1027.   **LLBA: Language and Language Behavior Abstracts**, 1967– . Quarterly. New York: Appleton-Century-Crofts, 1967– .
A collaborative effort of the University of Michigan Center for Research on Language and Language Behavior and the Bureau pour l'Enseignement de la

Langue et de la Civilisation Française à l'Etranger, Paris. Covers about 600 journals for four main areas: linguistics; psychology; communication sciences; hearing. Annual author index.

1028.   **Language-Teaching Abstracts**, 1968– . Quarterly. London: Cambridge University Press.
Compiled by the English-Teaching Information Centre of the British Council and Centre for Information on Language Teaching. Abstracts articles from over 300 periodicals and includes notes on new books.

Dictionaries

1029.   Baldinger, Kurt. **Dictionnaire étymologique de l'ancien français**. Quebec: Les Presses de l'Université Laval, 1971– . (In progress).
Covers the period from the middle of the ninth to the middle of the fourteenth centuries.

1030.   Bliss, Alan Joseph. **A Dictionary of Foreign Words and Phrases in Current English**. New York: Dutton, 1966. 389p.
Over 5,000 entries. Extensive information about sources and original meanings, as well as current definitions and pronunciations. Advice on spelling, transliteration, grammatical handling, etc. A table shows what was borrowed when.

1031.   Bosworth, Joseph. **An Anglo-Saxon Dictionary**. Ed. and enlgd. by T. Northcote Toller. Oxford: Clarendon Press, 1898. 1302p. Supplement, 1921. 768p.
The most comprehensive source yet available. Many quotations, with citations of manuscripts and printed sources.

1032.   Chantraine, Pierre. **Dictionnaire étymologique de la langue grecque: histoire des mots**. Paris: Editions Klincksieck, 1968– . t. 1– . (In progress).
Compiler has relied on standard earlier works except when modern scholarship requires a different interpretation. Concentrates on the use of words from about 2000 B.C. to modern Greek. Citations to classical authors and inscriptions are provided. Derivations and compounds are listed. References are made to linguistic and philological studies in books and journals.

1033.   Dalbiac, Lilian. **Dictionary of Quotations (German) with Author and Subject Indexes**. New York: Macmillan, 1906. Reprinted New York: Frederick Ungar, 1958. 485p.
About 3,000 German quotations are arranged in alphabetical order, with English translations. Subject indexes are in both German and English.

1034.   de Gama, Tana, ed. **Simon and Schuster's International Dictionary: English/Spanish, Spanish/English**. New York: Simon and Schuster, 1973. 1605p.
Contains 200,000 entries ranging from scientific and technical terms to

regionalisms and colloquialisms. Uses International Phonetic Alphabet to explain English pronunciations. General guide to Spanish pronunciation, but no pronunciations for individual words. Good definitions, typography, and layout.

1035.   Gluski, Jerzy, comp. and ed. **Proverbs: A Comparative Book of English, French, German, Italian, Spanish, and Russian Proverbs with a Latin Appendix**. New York: Elsevier, 1971. 448p.

1036.   Grimm, Jakob Ludwig Karl, and Wilhelm Grimm. **Deutsches Wörterbuch**. Hrsg. von der Deutschen Akademie der Wissenschaften zu Berlin in Zusammenarbeit mit der Akademie der Wissenschaften zu Gottingen, Neubearbeitungen. Leipzig: Hirzel, 1965– .

A new edition of this pioneer work which first promoted the idea of a dictionary compiled on historical principles and which influenced Littré and the *Oxford English Dictionary*.

1037.   Guterman, Norbert. **A Book of French Quotations with English Translations**. Garden City, N.Y.: Doubleday, 1963. 442p.

Chronological arrangement. About 2,000 French and English quotations on opposite pages. Indexes: authors; first lines in French; first lines in English.

1038.   Harbottle, Thomas Benfield. **Dictionary of Quotations (Classical)**. 3rd ed. London: Sonnenschein, 1906. Reprinted New York: Frederick Ungar, 1958. 678p.

Separate sections for Latin and Greek. Arrangement is alphabetical by first word. Sources are cited and English translations are given. Indexes: authors; subjects, Latin; subjects, Greek; subjects, English.

1039.   Harbottle, Thomas Benfield, and P. H. Dalbiac. **Dictionary of Quotations (French and Italian)**. New York: Macmillan, 1901. Reprinted New York: Frederick Ungar, 1958. 565p.

Under each language, arrangement is alphabetical by first word of quotation. Index of authors and subjects.

1040.   **Harrap's Standard German and English Dictionary**. Ed. by Trevor Jones. London: Harrap, 1963– .

To be completed in eight volumes. Part I (German-English) is now appearing, and Part II (English-German) will follow.

1041.   Hartmann, R. R. K., and F. C. Stork. **Dictionary of Language and Linguistics**. New York: Wiley, 1972. 302p.

Concentrates on technical terms not adequately defined in general dictionaries. Cross references are indicated by arrows. Appendix I is a list of languages with over one million speakers. Appendix II is a classified bibliography (pp. 277-302).

1042.   Major, Clarence. **Dictionary of Afro-American Slang**. New York: International Publishers, 1970. 127p.

1043.   Mansion, J. E. **Harrap's New Standard French and English Dictionary. Part 1, French-English**. New York: Scribner's, 1972. 2 vols.
Earlier standards of excellence have been maintained in this new edition. Large vocabulary. Good definitions. Clear indications of pronunciation. Many new terms have been added.

1044.   **Middle English Dictionary**. Hans Kurath, ed. Sherman M. Kuhn, assoc. ed. Ann Arbor: University of Michigan Press, 1952– .
Covers period from 1100 to 1475. Most comprehensive work to date. Uses quotations assembled for the *OED* as well as thousands more gathered for this set. Projected for publication in about 65 parts (of which approximatley half have appeared); it will run to some 10,000 pages.

1045.   **Oxford Latin Dictionary**. Oxford: Clarendon Press, 1968– . Fasc. 1– . (In progress).
Planning underway since 1931. Covers classical Latin from its beginnings to the end of the second century A.D., with an effort to treat all known words from whatever source—literary or non-literary. Proper names included if important. Similar in layout and organization to *OED*. Quotes to show usage are in chronological order; notes on etymology are brief. Seven more fascicles are to be published at two-year intervals. Promises to become standard in all academic libraries.

1046.   Robert, Paul. **Dictionnaire alphabétique et analogique de la langue française: les mots et les associations d'idées**. Paris: Société du Nouveau Littré, 1970. 6 vols. Supplément. Rédaction dirigée par Alain Rey et Josette Rey-Debove. 1970. 514p.
A major modern French-language dictionary compiled on historical principles. Published with the approval of the Académie Française. A worthy complement and successor to E. Littré's *Dictionnaire de la langue française* (7 vols. Paris: Pauvert, 1956-58), which is still especially good for examples from the ninth to the seventeenth centuries.

1047.   Smith, William George. **Oxford Dictionary of English Proverbs**. 2nd ed. New York: Oxford University Press, 1948. 740p.

1048.   Taylor, Archer, and Bartlett Jere Whiting. **A Dictionary of American Proverbs and Proverbial Phrases, 1820-1880**. Cambridge: Harvard University Press, 1958. 418p.

1049.   Tilley, Morris Palmer. **A Dictionary of the Proverbs of England in the 16th and 17th Centuries**. Ann Arbor: University of Michigan Press, 1950. 854p.

1050.   Wall, C. Edward, and Edward Przebienda, comps. **Words and Phrases Index: A Guide to Antedatings, New Words, New Compounds, and Other Published Scholarship Supplementing the Oxford English Dictionary, Dictionary of American English and Other Major Dictionaries**

of the English Language. Ann Arbor: Pierian Press, 1969. 390p.
Has over 60,000 citations to words and phrases from *American Notes and Queries*, *American Speech*, *Notes and Queries*, etc. Computer-produced, it serves as a valuable supplement to such classic works as Sir James A. H. Murray's *Oxford English Dictionary* (13 vols. Oxford: Clarendon Press, 1933. Supplement, 1972) and *Dictionary of American English on Historical Principles*, by Sir William Alexander Craigie and James R. Hulbert (4 vols. Chicago: University of Chicago Press, 1938-44).

1051.   Whiting, Bartlett Jere. **Proverbs, Sentences and Proverbial Phrases: From English Writings Mainly before 1500**. Cambridge: Harvard University Press, 1968. 733p.
Over 40 years were devoted to this compilation, which is based on historical principles. Key word entries; cross references; general index; separate index for proper nouns.

Histories

1052.   Baugh, Albert Croll. **A History of the English Language**. 2nd ed. New York: Appleton-Century-Crofts, 1959. 506p.
Planned as a text for college students but useful for reference work in language and literature departments. Chapter on English language in America. Analytical index. Evaluative chapter bibliographies.

1053.   Brunot, Ferdinand. **Histoire de la langue française, des origines à nos jours**. Préface de la nouvelle édition par Gérald Antoine. Paris: A. Colin, 1966– .
A major scholarly work that is still in progress. Volumes cover specific chronological periods. The earlier edition was begun in 1905.

Periodicals

1054.   **American Speech: A Quarterly of Linguistic Usage**, 1925– . Quarterly. Columbia University Press, 440 W. 110th St., New York, N.Y. 10025.
Indexed in: *Social Sciences and Humanities Index*.

1055.   **Anglia: Zeitschrift für englische Philologie**, 1878– . 4 per year. Max Niemeyer Verlag, Pfrondorder Str. 4, 74 Tübingen, West Germany.
Covers all periods from Old English to the twentieth century. English and American language and literature.

1056.   **Etc.: A Review of General Semantics**. 1943– . 4 per year. International Society for General Semantics, Box 2469, San Francisco, Calif. 94126.
Indexed: *Psychological Abstracts*. Deals with role of language and other symbols in human activities.

1057.   **Foundations of Language: International Journal of Language and Philosophy**, 1965– . Quarterly. D. Reidel Publishing Co., Box 17, Dordrecht, Netherlands.

Indexed in: *Language and Language Behavior Abstracts, Philosopher's Index, Science Abstracts*.

1058. **Journal of English and Germanic Philology**, 1897– . Quarterly. University of Illinois Press, Urbana, Ill. 61801.
Indexed in: *Current Contents, Social Sciences and Humanities Index*. Coverage of German, English, and Scandinavian languages and literatures.

1059. **Lingua: International Review of General Linguistics**, 1947– . 6 per year. North-Holland Publishing Co., P.O. Box 211, Amsterdam, Netherlands.
Text in English, French, and German. Long, critical reviews of major books.

1060. **Modern Language Quarterly**, 1940– . Parrington Hall, University of Washington, Seattle, Wash. 98105.
Indexed in: *Social Science and Humanities Index*. Covers American, English, Germanic, and Romance languages. Excellent book reviews.

1061. **Modern Language Review**, 1905– . Quarterly. Modern Humanities Research Association, Downing College, Cambridge, England.
Indexed in: *British Humanities Index, Social Sciences and Humanities Index*. Large proportion of space given over to book reviews.

1062. **Studies in Philology**, 1906– . 5 per year. University of North Carolina Press, Box 510, Chapel Hill, N.C. 27514.
Indexed in: *Social Sciences and Humanities Index*. Covers both classical and modern languages and literatures.

GENERAL LITERATURE

Introductory Works and Bibliographic Guides

1063. Altick, Richard Daniel. **The Art of Literary Research**. New York: Norton, 1963. 240p.
Still useful for discussion of such topics as research methodology, textual study, authorship, origins, reputation, and influence.

1064. Fisher, John H., ed. **The Medieval Literature of Western Europe: A Review of Research, Mainly 1930-1960**. New York: Modern Language Association, 1966. 432p.

1065. **Modern Literature**. Englewood Cliffs, N.J.: Prentice-Hall, 1966-68. 2 vols.
Part of a larger series entitled "The Princeton Studies: Humanistic Scholarship in America." Contents: Vol. 1, *The Literature of France*, by H. Peyre; Vol. 2, *Italian, Spanish, German, Russian, and Oriental Literature*.

1066.   Pellowski, Anne. **The World of Children's Literature**. New York: R. R. Bowker, 1968. 538p.
Lists, with critical annotations, 4,495 books, journals, and articles on children's books and library services. Gives brief summaries, also, for 106 countries. Helps to stimulate an international approach.

1067.   Scherf, Walter. **The Best of the Best. Die Besten der Besten**. 2nd ed. New York: R. R. Bowker, 1973. 189p.
Also published in Germany. About 1,500 selected children's books from over 50 countries for ages 3 to 15. Arranged by country and author.

1068.   Seymour-Smith, Martin. **Funk & Wagnalls Guide to Modern World Literature**. New York: Funk & Wagnalls, 1973. 1206p.
Attempts to survey world literature in the twentieth century, with chapters devoted to individual countries or to regions; trends, leading writers, and major works are discussed. Select bibliography and detailed index.

1069.   U.S. Library of Congress. Children's Book Section. **Children's Literature: A Guide to Reference Sources**. Prep. under the direction of Virginia Haviland. Washington, D.C.: Library of Congress, 1966. 341p.

Bibliographies

1070.   Baldensperger, Fernand, and Werner P. Friederich. **Bibliography of Comparative Literature**. Chapel Hill: University of North Carolina Press, 1950. Reprinted New York: Russell and Russell, 1960. 701p.
Very extensive coverage of literary influences from ancient to modern times. Arranged in four books: 1 and 3 deal with themes, motifs, genres, international literary relations, etc.; 2 and 4 cover specific literatures, according to country or author exerting influence. Detailed table of contents but no index. For current updatings, see the "Annual Bibliography" section of *Yearbook of Comparative and General Literature* (Bloomington: Indiana University, 1952–).

1071.   **Goldentree Bibliographies in Language and Literature**. Ed. by O. B. Harbison, Jr. New York: Appleton-Century-Crofts, 1966– .
Selective bibliographies on periods, genres, major authors, etc. They do *not* include dissertations or book reviews. Planned for undergraduates. LC catalogs separately with no series entry. For a list, see the publisher's latest catalog.

1072.   Milic, Louis Tonka. **Style and Stylistics: An Analytical Bibliographys,**. New York: Free Press, 1967. 199p.

1073.   Modern Language Association of America. **MLA International Bibliography**, 1921– . Published as supplements to **PMLA**, Vol. 39– . Annual.
From 1921 to 1955 was entitled *American Bibliography* and was limited to writings by Americans on the literature of the various countries. From 1956 to 1962, the coverage varied. Since 1963 it has had its present title and includes

writers in other languages. Coverage is mainly American and European. Classified arrangement, with author index. No cumulations.

1074.   **Quarterly Check-List of Literary History (English, American, French, German)**, 1958– . Quarterly. American Bibliographic Service, Darien, Conn. 06820.

Indexes, Abstracts, and Current Awareness Services

1075.   Modern Language Association of America. **MLA Abstracts of Articles in Scholarly Journals**, 1970?– . Annual. New York: Modern Language Association of America, 1970– .
Classified arrangement in three volumes (bound together in "Library Edition"). Arrangement parallels that of *MLA International Bibliography*, for which it is a supplement and with which it must be used because *MLA Abstracts* does not yet have cross references or author indexes.

Dictionaries and Encyclopedias

1076.   Benet, William Rose. **The Reader's Encyclopedia**. 2nd ed. New York: Crowell, 1965. 1118p.
Alphabetically arranged brief articles on writers, scientists, etc., of all periods. Allusions, literary expressions and terms. Literary schools and movements. Plots and characters. Descriptions of musical compositions and works of art. The second edition covers world literature, with emphasis on areas of growing interest–e.g., Orient, Soviet Union, Latin America, Near East.

1077.   Clapp, Jane. **International Dictionary of Literary Awards**. New York: Scarecrow Press, 1963. 545p.
More recent coverage will be found in the latest edition of *Literary and Library Prizes* (New York: R. R. Bowker, 1935–).

1078.   **Columbia Dictionary of Modern European Literature**. Ed., Horatio Smith. New York: Columbia University Press, 1947. 899p.
Alphabetical arrangement. Scholarly biographical sketches and critical evaluations (signed) covering major writers of Europe in the twentieth century. Also contains survey articles, with bibliographies, for 31 literatures of Europe. The 1,167 articles were written by 239 specialists. Good balance in coverage. Careful editing.

1079.   Deutsch, Babette. **Poetry Handbook: A Dictionary of Terms**. 3rd ed. New York: Funk & Wagnalls, 1969. 201p.
Useful for both browsing and reference. Alphabetized definitions–often subjective, but supported by examples. Emphasis is on classical and French poetry, but this edition shows more interest in German poetry than did the earlier ones.

1080.   **Dizionario letterario Bompiani degli autori, di tutti i tempi e de tutte le letterature**. Milano: Bompiani, 1956-57. 3 vols.
Supplements the Bompiani work that follows. Contains biographical and critical sketches of 6,000 authors, from all periods and countries. Lists their important works, but not works about them. Noted for its many handsome illustrations, a large proportion of which are in color.

1081.   **Dizionario letterario Bompiani delle opere e dei personaggi de tutti i tempi e di tutte le letterature**. 5th ed. Milano: Bompiani, 1947-50. 9 vols. Supplement, 1964-66. 2 vols.
Contents: Vols. 1-7, literary works, A–Z; Vol. 8, dictionary of literary characters; Vol. 9, indexes. A dictionary, listing and describing the works of all times and countries in literature, art, and music. Main emphasis on literature, but musical works and many famous pictures are described. Lavishly illustrated, with many colored plates and black and white illustrations.

1082.   **Dizionario universale delle letteratura contemporanea**. Milano: Mondadori, 1959-63. 5 vols.
An encyclopedia of world literature covering 1870 to 1960 and supplementing Bompiani. Arranged alphabetically, it includes authors, literary movements, periodicals, national literatures, etc. Bibliographies usually include works by and about an author. Extensively illustrated in black and white and color. Vol. 5 includes chronological tables and various indexes.

1083.   **Encyclopedia of Poetry and Poetics**. Ed. by Alex Preminger. Princeton, N.J.: Princeton University Press, 1965. 906p.
Includes about 1,000 individual entries, ranging in length from 20 to 20,000 words. History, theory, techniques and criticism of poetry from earliest times to the present. Most articles are signed with initials and most have bibliographies. International in scope. Special articles on poetry of various nationalities and ethnic groups. Authoritative and scholarly, it is for university libraries and other libraries with large poetry collections.

1084.   **Encyclopedia of World Literature in the 20th Century**. Gened.: Wolfgang Bernard Fleischmann. New York: Frederick Ungar, 1967-71. 3 vols.
Material translated or adapted from *Lexikon der Weltliteratur im 20 Jahrhundert*. Has a distinguished Board of Advisers in the United States. The 1,400 articles cover world literature on a truly global scale in the twentieth century, with survey articles on individual literatures, literary movements, and major genres, plus articles on individual authors of importance. Dictionary-type arrangement. Some photographs of authors. Details of inclusions, omissions, fine points of arrangement explained in the introduction.

1085.   Eppelsheimer, Hanns Wilhelm. **Handbuch der Weltliteratur von der Anfangen bis zur Gegenwart**. 3rd rev. and enl. ed. Frankfurt: Klosterman, 1960. 808p.
Covers literature of East Asia, India, ancient Near East, Islam, Greece and Rome,

the Middle Ages, and Europe, the latter arranged by century and then by country. Each section has a brief introduction, followed by a bibliography, with biographical sketches of authors that give editions, translations, criticism, etc.

1086.   Hargreaves-Mawdsley, William N. **Everyman's Dictionary of European Writers**. New York: Dutton, 1968. 561p.
Both current and retrospective, prominent and obscure (the latter if they influenced prominent writers or helped start a movement).

1087.   Holman, Clarence Hugh. **A Handbook to Literature**. Based on the original by William Flint Thrall and Addison Hibbard. 3rd ed. Indianapolis: Odyssey Press, 1972. 646p.
Explanations of terms, concepts, schools, and movements. Best in field since first edition appeared in 1936. New edition thoroughly revised and updated. Over 1,360 entries. Cross references indicated by small capitals in text of entries. Special features include "Outline of Literary History, English and American" (pp. 561-621), which covers leading events and works by periods from 55 B.C. to 1971 A.D. and lists of National Book Awards for Fiction, Poetry, Arts and Letters; Nobel Prizes for Literature; and Pulitzer Prizes for Fiction, Poetry, and Drama.

1088.   **International Literary Market Place**. European ed. New York: R. R. Bowker, 1965– .
Lists between 1,500 and 2,000 firms, often with number of titles published in preceding year, titles in stock, subject specialties, date of founding, foreign representatives, subsidiaries, distributors, and names of bookstores or book clubs owned by firms. Indexes to firms, book clubs, and advertisers, but no index to subject specialties.

1089.   **International Who's Who in Poetry**. Ed. by Ernest Kay. 3rd ed., 1972/73. New York: Rowman and Littlefield, 1972. 696p.
Includes biographical information on 3,000 poets around the world. Information on poetry groups in various countries, little magazines, publishers, prizes, and recordings. Edited and published in England. First edition appeared in 1958, and second in 1970.

1090.   **Kindlers Literatur Lexikon**. Zurich: Kindler Verlag, 1965-70. 7 vols.
Covers some 150 literatures of the world, with entries by titles (usually in original languages). Many color plates. Each volume has an index; Vol. 7 is the index for the set.

1091.   Magill, Frank N. **Cyclopedia of Literary Characters**. New York: Harper & Row, 1963. 1280p.
Sometimes appears under the title *Masterplots Cyclopedia of Literary Characters*. Over 16,000 characters from 1,300 novels, dramas, and epics. International coverage from ancient times to the present. Basic arrangement is alphabetical by title of work, with information about author, time of action, date of publication, and principal characters. Supplemented by an author index and an alphabetical character index.

1092.   Magill, Frank N. **Masterplots Cyclopedia of World Authors**. New York: Salem Press, 1958. 2 vols.

Short biographies of more than 750 authors whose works are used in the Masterplots series. Also gives principal works and bibliographical references. Title is sometimes shortened to *Cyclopedia of World Authors*.

1093.   **Penguin Companion to Literature**. New York: McGraw-Hill, 1969-71. 4 vols.

Contents: Vol. 1, English, edited by David Daiches; Vol. 2, European, edited by A. Thorlby; Vol. 3, American, edited by M. Bradbury and others; Vol. 4, Classical and Byzantine, Oriental and African, edited by D. R. Dudley and D. M. Lang. Biographical and bibliographical information about authors. Some volumes have supplementary information such as guides to entries by language and country and lists of general articles. The volume on American literature includes a section on Latin America.

1094.   Shaw, Harry. **Dictionary of Literary Terms**. New York: McGraw-Hill, 1972. 402p.

Includes literary terms, references and allusions drawn from books, periodicals, films, plays, television programs, and speeches. Gives examples. Includes phrases (e.g., "Theater of the Absurd") as well as individual words. Planned for the beginning student and the general reader.

1095.   Ward, A. C. **Longman Companion to Twentieth Century Literature**. New York: Longman, 1973. 593p.

First published in England in 1970. International coverage is attempted, but concentration is on British writers. In addition to biographical articles, there are definitions of terms, summaries of famous works, and descriptions of fictional characters.

Anthologies and Digests

1096.   Cowley, Malcolm, and Howard E. Hugo, eds. **The Lesson of the Masters: An Anthology of the Novel from Cervantes to Hemingway**. New York: Scribner's, 1971. 514p.

1097.   Haydn, Hiram, and Edmund Fuller, eds. **Thesaurus of Book Digests: Digests of the World's Permanent Writings from the Ancient Classics to Current Literature**. New York: Crown, 1949. 831p.

Arranged by title. Author index. Index of characters.

1098.   Keller, Helen Rex, ed. **Reader's Digest of Books**. Rev. ed. New York: Macmillan, 1929. 1447p.

Synopses of fiction and nonfiction from many countries and periods. Note that the material added in the 1929 edition is in a separate section and has its own index.

1099.   Magill, Frank N., ed. **Magill's Quotations in Context**. New York: Harper, 1966. 2nd series, 1969. 2 vols.

An attempt to go beyond merely identifying the source and to provide background remarks or summary of context to clarify meaning. About 2,000 quotations in alphabetical arrangement, with key word and author indexes. Chiefly useful as a supplement to standard books because of the limited number of quotes.

1100.   Magill, Frank N., ed. **Masterpieces of World Literature in Digest Form**. New York: Harper, 1952. 2nd series, 1956. 3rd series, 1960. 4th series, 1969.

Published in 1949 under the title *Masterplots*. Useful digests, despite the temptation to substitute these for reading the originals. Cumulated as *Masterplots Comprehensive Library Edition: The Four Series in Eight Volumes* (New York: Salem Press, 1968). Updated by *Masterplots Annual/Magill's Literary Annual* (New York: Salem Press, 1954–).

Theory and Criticism

1101.   Frye, Northrop. **Anatomy of Criticism: Four Essays**. Princeton, N.J.: Princeton University Press, 1957. 383p.

Cited by numerous authors as a landmark work in the development of critical theory.

1102.   Frye, Northrop. **The Critical Path: An Essay on the Social Context of Literary Criticism**. Bloomington: Indiana University Press, 1971. 174p.

1103.   **In Search of Literary Theory**. Ed. by Morton W. Bloomfield. Ithaca, N.Y.: Cornell University Press, 1972.

Essays by major literary critics: M. H. Abrams, E. D. Hirsch, Morton W. Bloomfield, Northrop Frye, Geoffrey Hartman, and Paul de Man.

1104.   Saintsbury, George B. **History of Criticism and Literary Taste in Europe**. 4th ed. London: Blackwood, 1922-29. 3 vols.

A pioneer effort. Although it is very readable, it has been somewhat discounted in the light of more recent studies.

1105.   Wellek, René. **Concepts of Criticism**. Ed. with an intro. by Stephen G. Nichols, Jr. New Haven: Yale University Press, 1963. 403p.

Reflections on this subject by one of the foremost contemporary scholars.

1106.   Wellek, René. **Discriminations: Further Concepts of Criticism**. New Haven: Yale University Press, 1970. 387p.

1107.   Wellek, René. **A History of Modern Criticism: 1750-1950**. New Haven: Yale University Press, 1955– .

A landmark work in this field. Contents: Vol. 1, *The Later Eighteenth Century*; Vol. 2, *The Romantic Age*; Vol. 3, *The Age of Transition*; Vol. 4, *The Later Nineteenth Century*; Vol. 5, *The Twentieth Century*.

1108.   Wellek, René, and Austin Warren. **Theory of Literature**. 3rd ed. New York: Harcourt, Brace and World, 1956. 374p.
Contents: Definitions and Distinctions; Preliminary Operations; The Extrinsic Approach to the Study of Literature; The Intrinsic Approach to the Study of Literature; The Academic Situation; Notes; Chapter Bibliographies; Index.

1109.   Wimsatt, William Kurtz, and Cleanth Brooks. **Literary Criticism: A Short History**. New York: Knopf, 1957. 755p.
A survey of critical approaches from antiquity to the twentieth century. Analytical index. Extensive bibliographies.

Serials

1110.   **Books Abroad: An International Literary Quarterly**, 1927– . Quarterly. University of Oklahoma Press, Norman, Okla. 73069.
Indexed in: *Book Review Index, Social Sciences and Humanities Index*. Attempts to keep abreast of foreign literature and interpret it for American readers.

1111.   **Comparative Literature**, 1949– . Quarterly. University of Oregon, Eugene, Ore. 97403.
Indexed in: *Social Sciences and Humanities Index*. Text mainly in English, but occasionally in French, German, Italian, or Spanish.

1112.   **Comparative Literature Studies**, 1963– . Quarterly. Lincoln Hall, University of Illinois, Urbana, Ill. 61801.
Indexed in: *Abstracts of English Studies*. Text in English, French, German, Italian, and Spanish.

1113.   **Contemporary Literature**, 1960– . Quarterly. Department of English, Bascom Hall, University of Wisconsin, Madison, Wisc. 53706.
Indexed in: *Social Sciences and Humanities Index, Modern Language Abstracts*.

1114.   **Modern Philology: A Journal Devoted to Research in Medieval and Modern Literature**, 1903/4– . University of Chicago Press, 5750 Ellis Avenue, Chicago, Ill. 60637.
Indexed in: *Social Sciences and Humanities Index*. Literature in English is prime focus, with secondary emphasis on Romance and Germanic literatures.

1115.   **PMLA: Publications of the Modern Language Association of America**, 1884/5– . 6 per year. Modern Language Association of America, 62 Fifth Ave., New York, N.Y. 10011.
Indexed in: *Social Sciences and Humanities Index*. Wide range of scholarly articles on modern languages and literatures.

1116.   **Revue de littérature comparée**, 1921– . Quarterly. Librairie Marcel Didier, 4-6 rue de la Sorbonne, Paris 5e, France.
Cumulative index every 10 years. Text in English, French, German, Italian, and Spanish.

1117.   **Yearbook of Comparative and General Literature**, 1952– . Department of Comparative Literature, Ballantine Hall, Indiana University, Bloomington, Ind. 47401.

Includes articles, news items, biographical sketches, and *Annual Bibliography* designed as supplement to Baldensperger.

LITERATURE IN ENGLISH

Introductory Works and Bibliographic Guides

1118.   Altick, Richard Daniel, and Andrew Wright. **Selective Bibliography for the Study of English and American Literature**. 4th ed. New York: Macmillan, 1971. 164p.

Intended primarily for the use of graduate students. Omits works considered inferior unless coverage would be seriously incomplete. Inclusion generally denotes excellence in the view of the compilers. Evaluative annotations are given only when this is *not* the case. Classified arrangement. Glossary. Name, title, and subject index.

1119.   Bateson, Frederick Wilse. **A Guide to English Literature**. 2nd ed. Chicago: Aldine Publishing Co., 1968. 261p.

Evaluative comments to aid the graduate student. Classified arrangement. Index.

1120.   Bell, Inglis F., and Jennifer Gallup. **A Reference Guide to English, American and Canadian Literature: An Annotated Checklist of Bibliographical and Other Reference Materials**. Vancouver: University of British Columbia Press, 1971. 139p.

Planned for the undergraduate who is majoring in English. The first part is a classified, annotated bibliography of standard research tools. The second part is devoted to bibliographies of individual authors. Indexes: to authors as contributors, and to authors as subjects.

1121.   Bond, Donald F. **A Reference Guide to English Studies**. 2nd ed. Chicago: University of Chicago Press, 1971. 198p.

Classified arrangement. Some brief annotations. Includes some periodical articles. Indexes: persons, subjects.

1122.   Chandler, George. **How to Find Out about Literature**. New York: Pergamon Press, 1968. 224p.

An introductory survey, with exercises. Over 50 facsimile reproductions of title pages, etc.

1123.   Dick, Aliki Lafkidou. **A Student's Guide to British Literature: A Selective Bibliography of 4,128 Titles and Reference Sources from the Anglo-Saxon Period to the Present**. Littleton, Colo.: Libraries Unlimited, 1972. 285p.

Opens with general works, divided by form. Then a period arrangement for the main part, subdivided by authors. Author and subject index. More specialized is *Twentieth Century British Literature: A Bibliography and Reference Guide*, by Ruth Temple and Martin Tucker (New York: Frederick Ungar, 1968).

1124. Jones, Howard Mumford, and Richard M. Ludwig. **Guide to American Literature and Its Backgrounds since 1890**. 4th ed. Cambridge: Harvard University Press, 1972. 264p.

A guide listing works that present the intellectual, sociological, and political backgrounds of American literary history, followed by reading lists on various aspects and schools in American Literature since 1890. Walter Sutton's *Modern American Criticism* (Englewood Cliffs, N.J.: Prentice-Hall, 1963) is a review of American scholarship of the preceding 30 years.

1125. Kennedy, Arthur Garfield, and Donald B. Sands. **A Concise Bibliography for Students of English**. Rev. by William E. Colburn. 5th ed. Stanford: Stanford University Press, 1972. 300p.

Classified bibliography without annotations. Author and subject indexes.

1126. National Council of Teachers of English. Committee on Literary Scholarship and the Teaching of English. **Contemporary Literary Scholarship: A Critical Review**. By Lewis Leary. New York: Appleton-Century-Crofts, 1958. 474p.

Essays on achievements and trends in the study of English literature during the preceding 30 years.

1127. Thompson, James. **English Studies: A Guide for Librarians to the Sources and Their Organization**. Hamden, Conn.: Linnet Books, 1971. 155p.

Bibliographies

1128. Abrash, Barbara. **Black African Literature in English since 1952: Works and Criticism**. New York: Johnson Reprint Corp., 1967. 92p.

Includes citations to general bibliography and criticism, anthologies, individual author bibliographies (works and criticism), a selected list of periodicals, and an author index. Covers both books and periodical articles. Full bibliographic citations.

1129. **Annals of English Literature, 1475-1950: The Principal Publications of Each Year, Together with an Alphabetical Index of Authors with Their Works**. 2nd ed. Oxford: Clarendon Press, 1961. 380p.

A chronological bibliography that provides factual underpinnings for research in literary history.

1130. Blanck, Jacob Nathaniel. **Bibliography of American Literature**. New Haven: Yale University Press, 1955– .

Vol. 1, *Adams to Byrne* (1955); Vol. 2, *Cable to Dwight* (1957); Vol. 3, *Eggleston to Harte* (1959); Vol. 4, *Hawthorne to Ingraham* (1963); Vol. 5, *Irving to Longfellow* (1969). Selective bibliography. Will include about 300 authors from the Federal period to 1930. Excludes authors without literary interest. Material for each author is arranged chronologically. Includes: 1) first editions of books and pamphlets and any other book containing the first appearance of a work; 2) reprints containing textual or other changes; 3) a selected list of biographical, bibliographical, and critical works. Locations are indicated for copies examined. Excludes periodical and newspaper publications, later editions, translations, and volumes with isolated correspondence.

1131.   English Association. **The Year's Work in English Studies**, 1919– .
         London: Oxford University Press, 1921– .
Critical, selective survey of studies in English literature appearing in books and articles published in Britain, Europe, and America. Arranged by periods; indexed by author and subject. Since 1954 it has included a chapter on American literature.

1132.   **English Literature, 1660-1800: A Bibliography of Modern Studies**.
         Princeton, N.J.: Princeton University Press, 1950– .
Photoprints of annual bibliographies in *Philological Quarterly*, 1926– . The four volumes published provide the following coverage: Vol. 1, 1926-38; Vol. 2, 1939-50; Vol. 3, 1951-56; Vol. 4, 1957-60. Vol. 2 includes name, subject, and topical index for Vols. 1 and 2. Vol. 4 has the same for Vols. 3 and 4. Supplementary coverage will be found in *Eighteenth Century English Literature and Its Cultural Background: A Bibliography*, by James Edward Tobin (New York: Fordham University Press, 1939).

1133.   Gohdes, Clarence Louis Frank. **Bibliographical Guide to the Study of the Literature of the U.S.A.** 3rd ed. Durham, N.C.: Duke University Press, 1970. 134p.
Classified arrangement with short, evaluative annotations. Indexes: subjects; names of authors, editors, and compilers. Gohdes has also compiled *Literature and Theatre of the States and Regions of the U.S.A.: An Historical Bibliography* (Durham, N.C.: Duke University Press, 1967). Another major segment of American literature is covered in Louis D. Rubin's *A Bibliographical Guide to the Study of Southern Literature* (Baton Rouge: Louisiana State University Press, 1969).

1134.   Howard-Hill, Trevor Howard. **Index to British Bibliography**. New York: Oxford University Press, 1969– . 3 vols.
Vol. 1, *Bibliography of British Literary Bibliographies* (1969; 570p.); Vol. 2, *Bibliography of Shakespeare Bibliographies*; Vol. 3, *Bibliography of British Bibliography and Textual Criticism*. Appears to complement, rather than supersede, C. S. Northup's *A Register of Bibliographies of the English Language and Literature* (New Haven: Yale University Press, 1925). Focusing on a more restricted period is Elgin W. Mellown's *A Descriptive Catalogue of the Bibliographies of Twentieth Century British Writers* (Troy, N.Y.: Whitston, 1972).

1135. McNamee, Lawrence F. **Dissertations in English and American Literature: Theses Accepted by American, British and German Universities, 1865-1964**. New York: R. R. Bowker, 1968. 1124p. Supplement, 1964-68. 1972. 450p.

Computer-produced, classified listing. Includes sections on English language and linguistics, the teaching of English, comparative literature and "creative" dissertations as well as the usual sections for periods, types, individual authors, etc. If a dissertation deals with more than one literary figure the "cross index of authors" will provide access to those items that do not appear under a given literary figure's name in main body of work. Also includes an index of authors of dissertations. Confined to dissertations submitted in a single department. Though more limited in coverage, *Dissertations in American Literature, 1891-1966*, by James Woodress (Durham, N.C.: Duke University Press, 1968), is somewhat more attractive and easier to use, despite its lack of a good analytical index.

1136. Modern Humanities Research Association. **Annual Bibliography of English Language and Literature**, 1920– . Cambridge: Cambridge University Press, 1921– .

Classified arrangement of books, pamphlets, and articles covering English and American literature. Gives references to reviews. Occasionally a volume will cover two or three years. Language section arranged by subject, literature section chronologically. Name index.

1137. Modern Language Association of America. American Literature Group. Committee on Manuscript Holdings. **American Literary Manuscripts: A Checklist of Holdings in Academic, Historical, and Public Libraries in the United States**. Austin: University of Texas Press, 1960. Reprinted, 1971. 421p.

A valuable finding tool because so few repositories have been able to publish their own catalogs. One particularly fine example of a publication is the New York Public Library's *Dictionary Catalog of the Albert A. and Henry W. Berg Collection of English and American Literature* (Boston: G. K. Hall, 1970. 5 vols.), which gives access to 50,000 manuscripts.

1138. **The New Cambridge Bibliography of English Literature**. Ed. by George Watson. Cambridge: Cambridge University Press, 1969– .

Vol. 1, 600-1600 (not yet published); Vol. 2, 1660-1800 (1971); Vol. 3, 1800-1900 (1969); Vol. 4, 1900– (not yet published); Vol. 5, Index (not yet published). A revision and substantial expansion of *The Cambridge Bibliography of English Literature*, edited by F. W. Bateson (Cambridge: Cambridge University Press, 1940. 4 vols. Supplement, 1957). A work of absolutely fundamental importance. Entries are arranged by literary periods and then by form (poetry, drama, etc.). Within these divisions, there are further subdivisions by special topics and individual authors. *The Concise Cambridge Bibliography of English Literature, 600-1950*, edited by George Watson (2nd ed. Cambridge: Cambridge University Press, 1965), follows the same plan as the basic set but is highly selective.

1139.   Nilon, Charles H. **Bibliography of Bibliographies in American Litera-
          ture**. New York: R. R. Bowker, 1970. 483p.
Has 6,463 entries arranged by author, genre, literary period, and special
categories. Includes an author index and a detailed subject index. Numerous
cross references. On occasion, it will still be useful to consult Nathan
Van Patten's *An Index to Bibliographies and Bibliographical Contributions
Relating to the Work of American and British Authors, 1923-1932* (Stanford:
Stanford University Press, 1934).

1140.   Pollard, A. W., and G. R. Redgrave. **A Short-Title Catalogue of Books
          Printed in England, Scotland and Ireland, and of English Books Printed
          Abroad, 1475-1640**. London: Bibliographical Society, 1926. Reprinted
          Oxford: Oxford University Press, 1946. 609p.
Often cited as STC. The most comprehensive record of English books for this
period. About 26,500 editions. Arranged alphabetically by author and other
main entries. Gives author, brief title, size, printer, date, reference to Stationers'
registers and symbols for libraries (mainly British) that have copies. Tries to
record all known copies of very rare items and a representative sampling of
libraries with commoner titles. Because the main work records holdings of only
15 American libraries, William Warner Bishop compiled *A Checklist of American
Copies of Short Title Catalogue Books* (2nd ed. Ann Arbor: University of
Michigan Press, 1950. 203p.), which records over 26,000 holdings from 120
libraries. P. G. Morrison has prepared *Index of Printers, Publishers and
Booksellers in A. W. Pollard and G. R. Redgrave, "A Short-Title Catalogue..."*
(Charlottesville: Bibliographical Society of Virginia, 1950. 82p.). The books
listed in STC are reproduced on microfilm by University Microfilms, Ann Arbor,
Michigan.

1141.   Severs, Jonathan Burke, ed. **A Manual of the Writings in Middle English,
          1050-1500**. New Haven: Connecticut Academy of Arts and Sciences,
          1967– .
Two volumes have appeared. The first is on the romances. The second deals with
the *Pearl* poet, Wyclif and followers, Bible and religious works. Contains
information about critical commentaries and manuscripts of original works.
Scholarly. Makes heavy use of abbreviations that may not be familiar to
librarians. The work has been prepared by the Middle English Group of the
Modern Language Association of America. When completed, it will be an
examination and updating of *A Manual of the Writings in Middle English,
1050-1400*, by John Edwin Wells (New Haven: Yale University Press, 1916.
Supplements 1-9, 1919-45).

1142.   Templeman, William D. **Bibliographies of Studies in Victorian Litera-
          ture for the Thirteen Years, 1932-1944**. Urbana: University of Illinois
          Press, 1945. 450p.
Compiled from annual lists in *Modern Philology*. Cumulations continued by
A. Wright in *Bibliographies of Studies in Victorian Literature for the Ten Years,
1945-1954* (Urbana: University of Illinois Press, 1956. 310p.) and R. C. Slack in
Bibliographies of Studies in Victorian Literature for the Ten Years, 1955-1964

(Urbana: University of Illinois Press, 1967. 461p.). Now continued as "Victorian Bibliography for . . ." in *Victorian Studies*. Supplemental coverage is offered in *Guide to Doctoral Dissertations in Victorian Literature, 1886-1958*, by Richard D. Altick and William R. Matthews (Urbana: University of Illinois Press, 1960), which is a classified bibliography of more than 2,000 items, with an author index.

1143.   Watters, Reginald Eyre. **A Checklist of Canadian Literature and Background Materials, 1628-1960**. 2nd ed. Toronto: University of Toronto Press, 1972. 1085p.
Confined to Canadian literature in English, but the most comprehensive compilation available. Part I covers fiction, drama, and poetry. Part II deals with background materials. Library locations are given. One segment is given selective, in-depth coverage by Sheila Egoff in *The Republic of Childhood: A Critical Guide to Canadian Children's Literature in English* (Toronto: Oxford University Press, 1967).

1144.   Wing, Donald. **Short Title Catalogue of Books Printed in England, Scotland, Ireland, Wales and British America, and English Books Printed in Other Countries, 1641-1700**. New York: Index Society, 1945-51. 3 vols.
Continuation of STC (entry 1140) by Pollard and Redgrave. Items are located in 200 libraries (for common titles, five in Britain, five in the United States). Tries to have geographical distribution. Not a census of copies. Location symbols are *not* the same as those in STC or NUC, but were devised by Wing. Supplemented by P. G. Morrison's *Index of Printers, Publishers, and Booksellers in Donald Wing's "Short-Title Catalogue . . ."* (Charlottesville: Bibliographical Society of the University of Virginia, 1955. 217p.). Books listed in Wing are being reproduced on microfilm by University Microfilms, Ann Arbor, Michigan.

Indexes, Abstracts, and Current Awareness Services

1145.   **Abstracts of English Studies**. Champaign, Ill.: National Council of Teachers of English, 1958– . 10 per year.
Covers 400 periodicals. Abstracts are grouped under journal title. Monthly and annual subject indexes; annual author-title index. American and foreign periodicals on English, Commonwealth and American literature and English philology.

1146.   **American Literature Abstracts: A Review of Current Scholarship in the Field of American Literature**. San Jose, Calif.: Department of English, San Jose State College, 1967– . Semi-annual.
Available in microform.

1147.   Combs, Richard E. **Authors: Critical and Biographical References: A Guide to 4,700 Critical and Biographical Passages in Books**. Metuchen, N.J.: Scarecrow Press, 1971. 221p.
Uses double-column page and letter symbols similar to Granger. Covers 1,400

authors from about 500 books. Both duplicates and complements *Essay and General Literature Index*.

1148.   Eastman, Mary Huse. **Index to Fairy Tales, Myths, and Legends**. 2nd ed. Boston: F. W. Faxon, 1926. 610p. Supplement, 1937. 566p. 2nd Supplement, 1952. 370p.

Main entry is under best-known title, with cross references from variant titles. Continued by Norma O. Ireland's *Index to Fairy Tales, 1949-1972*.

1149.   **Essay and General Literature Index, 1900-1933: An Index to About 40,000 Essays and Articles in 2,144 Volumes of Collections of Essays and Miscellaneous Works**. Ed. by Minnie Earl Sears and Marian Shaw. New York: H. W. Wilson, 1934. 1952p. Supplements, 1934– .

Kept up to date by semi-annual, annual, and quinquennial supplements. Some of the earlier ones followed a seven-year pattern of cumulation. Dictionary arrangement (authors, titles, and subjects all in one alphabet) with numerous cross references. A vital reference tool—especially in libraries serving students who may need to read a particular essay in a limited period of time. Also supplemented by *Works Indexed, 1900-1969* (New York: H. W. Wilson, 1973).

1150.   Havlice, Patricia Pate. **Index to American Author Bibliographies**. Metuchen, N.J.: Scarecrow Press, 1971. 204p.

"This index duplicates information readily available on standard American authors, especially fiction writers; but it will be particularly valuable in locating bibliographies of minor American authors . . ." (Carolyn A. Hough, *Library Journal*, June 1, 1972, pp. 2075-76).

1151.   Houghton, Walter Edwards, ed. **The Wellesley Index to Victorian Periodicals, 1824-1900**. Toronto: University of Toronto Press, 1966– .

Provides subject, book review, and author index. Particularly valuable for contemporary criticism of Victorian authors.

1152.   **Index to Commonwealth Little Magazines**, 1964/65– . Biennial. New York: Johnson Reprint Corp., Vols. 1 and 2. Troy, N.Y.: Whitston Publishing Co., Vols. 3– .

Edited by Stephen H. Goode. Somewhat slow in appearing. Vol. 4 (1970/71) announced for Spring 1973. Plans were announced for a series of volumes giving retrospective coverage.

1153.   **Index to Little Magazines**, 1948– . Denver and Chicago: Swallow Press. Of importance because of the number of major writers who began by having creative works published in this way. Over the years, the various editors have tried to concentrate on publications likely to have some permanent value. Retrospective coverage is achieved through *Index to Little Magazines, 1943-1947* (Denver: Alan Swallow, 1965), *Index to Little Magazines, 1940-1942* (New York: Johnson Reprint Corp., 1966), *Index to American Little Magazines, 1920-1939* (Troy, N.Y.: Whitston Publishing Co., 1970), and *Index to American Little Magazines, 1900-1919* (Troy, N.Y.: Whitston Publishing Co., 1972).

1154.   Ireland, Norma (Olin). **Index to Fairy Tales, 1949-1972, Including Folklore, Legends and Myths in Collections**. Boston: F. W. Faxon, 1973. 741p.
Analyzes over 400 collections of fairy tales, folklore, legends, and myths. Updates Eastman's *Index to Fairy Tales* and its supplements, but with titles and subjects in one alphabet.

1155.   Johnson, Robert Owen. **An Index of Literature in The New Yorker**. Metuchen, N.J.: Scarecrow Press, 1969– . Vol. 1, Volumes I-XV, 1925-1940. 1969. 543p. Vol. 2, Volumes XVI-XXX, 1940-1955. 1970. 477p.
A series covering imaginative work, profiles, "Talk of the Town," theater and film criticism, and book reviews. Title arrangement with author index. Also a list of initials, pseudonyms and abbreviations of names. Useful though not exhaustive. Compiler has indicated whether New York or out-of-town edition is cited. Preface explains very well how best to use this index.

1156.   Leary, Lewis Gaston. **Articles on American Literature, 1900-1950**. Durham, N.C.: Duke University Press, 1954. 437p.
Based primarily on bibliographies published in *American Literature* and *PMLA*. Classified arrangement. Largest section devoted to individual authors, followed by sections on biography, fiction, etc. Supplemented, updated, and corrected in *Articles on American Literature, 1950-1967* (Durham, N.C.: Duke University Press, 1970. 751p.).

1157.   **Reader's Index to the Twentieth Century Views of Literary Criticism Series, Volumes 1-100**. Englewood Cliffs, N.J.: Prentice-Hall, 1973. 682p.
Fills an important need because the individual volumes in this series have lacked indexes.

Encyclopedias, Dictionaries and Handbooks

1158.   **Contemporary Literary Criticism**. Ed. by Carolyn Riley. Detroit: Gale Research Co., 1973– .
Complements the *Contemporary Authors* series by providing extracts of criticism drawn from various reviewing media. Each volume in the series is planned to cover about 200 authors in 600 to 700 pages. Cumulative author and critic indexes are planned.

1159.   **The Critical Temper: A Survey of Modern Criticism on English and American Literature from the Beginnings to the Twentieth Century**. Martin Tucker, gen. ed. New York: Frederick Ungar, 1969. 3 vols.
Supplements Moulton by providing extracts from twentieth century criticism of authors prior to the twentieth century.

1160.   Curley, Dorothy Nyren, comp. **Modern American Literature**. 4th ed. New York: Frederick Ungar, 1969. 3 vols.

Present edition covers some 300 authors with a bibliography and selection of British and American criticism for each. Formerly entitled: *Library of Literary Criticism, Modern American Literature* (1st ed., 1960. 2nd ed., 1964).

1161.   **The Explicator Cyclopedia**. Ed. by Charles Child Walcutt and J. Edwin Whitesell. Chicago: Quadrangle, 1966-68. 3 vols.

Vol. 1, *Modern Poetry*; Vol. 2, *Traditional Poetry; Medieval to Late Victorian*; Vol. 3, *Prose*. Taken from *The Explicator*, Vols. 1-20, 1942-62, for which it now represents a cumulation. Arrangement is alphabetical by author of poem or prose selection and then by title of poem or prose selection.

1162.   Hart, James David. **The Oxford Companion to American Literature**. 4th ed. New York: Oxford University Press, 1965. 991p.

Alphabetical. Short biographies and bibliographies of American authors, summaries and descriptions of major American novels, stories, essays, poems, and plays. Information on movements, literary societies, magazines, anthologies, literary prizes, book collectors, printers, etc. Not so inclusive as Benet or Burke and Howe, but it has longer articles and is more thorough. Less inclusive, but more scholarly, than *The Reader's Encyclopedia of American Literature* (New York: Crowell, 1962. 1280p.).

1163.   Harvey, Sir Paul. **Oxford Companion to English Literature**. 4th ed. Oxford: Clarendon Press, 1967. 961p.

Brief articles on authors, literary works, characters in fiction, drama, etc., and literary allusions. The fourth edition was revised by Dorothy Eagle, who also revised an abridged version entitled *The Concise Oxford Dictionary of English Literature* (2nd ed. New York: Oxford University Press, 1970).

1164.   Lanham, Richard A. **A Handlist of Rhetorical Terms: A Guide for Students of English Literature**. Berkeley: University of California Press, 1968. 148p.

Until now, such definitions have been scattered in a variety of sources. Of special interest is a section to help the user move from a definition to the term defined or from an example of use to the rhetorical term that describes it. Bibliography.

1165.   Lazarus, Arnold Leslie, and others. **Modern English: A Glossary of Literature and Language**. New York: Grosset, 1971. 462p.

Over 1,000 terms from literary criticism, rhetoric, grammar, and linguistics.

1166.   Leggett, Glenn, C. David Mead, and William Charvat. **Prentice-Hall Handbook for Writers**. 5th ed. Englewood Cliffs, N.J.: Prentice-Hall, 1970. 484p.

Includes a detailed index to contents and an index to grammatical terms.

1167.   Moulton, Charles W. **Library of Literary Criticism of English and American Authors**. Moulton, 1901-1905. 8 vols. Reprinted Gloucester, Mass.: Peter Smith, 1959.

A compilation of quoted material. Covers the period from 680 to 1904. For each author, gives brief biographical data, then selected quotations from criticisms of his work, grouped as 1) personal, 2) individual works, 3) general. Extracts are of some length and have exact references. Can serve both as anthology and index. Continued by works of Dorothy Nyren Curley, Martin Tucker, and Ruth Temple.

1168.   Myers, Robin. **A Dictionary of Literature in the English Language, from Chaucer to 1940**. New York: Pergamon, 1970-71. 2 vols.
Gives brief biographical and bibliographical information on 3,500 authors. Vol. 1 is geographical/chronological index. Brief identifications of periodicals, literary groups, movements, and prizes are also included. Includes scientists, historians, and other writers. Cites other sources of bibliography, some of varying quality. An alphabetical author-title index was published as Vol. 2.

1169.   Story, Norah. **The Oxford Companion to Canadian History and Literature**. New York: Oxford University Press, 1967. 935p.

1170.   Temple, Ruth Zabriskie, and Martin Tucker, eds. **A Library of Literary Criticism: Modern British Literature**. New York: Frederick Ungar, 1966. 3 vols.
Extracts (with citations) from books and articles dealing with over 400 writers of the twentieth century.

1171.   Tucker, Martin. **Africa in Modern Literature: A Survey of Contemporary Writing in English**. New York: Frederick Ungar, 1967. 316p.

1172.   **Webster's New World Companion to English and American Literature**. Arthur Pollard, gen. ed. New York: World Publishing/Times Mirror, 1973. 850p.
Over 1,100 entries for authors, literary genres, etc. Mention is made of some 6,000 individual works. Alphabetical arrangement. Has 92-page appendix listing works of criticism.

Biographies

1173.   Allibone, Samuel Austin. **A Critical Dictionary of English Literature and British and American Authors, Living and Deceased**. Philadelphia: Lippincott, 1858-71. 3 vols. Supp. by John Foster Kirk, 1891. 2 vols.
There are 46,000 authors listed in the basic set, and 37,000 in the supplement. Standard older work, with some inaccuracies.

1174.   **Author's and Writer's Who's Who**. Ed. by L. G. Pine. 6th ed. New York: Hafner, 1971.
Includes not only authors of books, but also editors, feature writers, and other journalists. Limited to writers in the English-speaking world.

1175.   Browning, David Clayton. **Everyman's Dictionary of Literary Biography, English and American**. Comp. after John Cousin by D. C. Browning. Rev. ed. New York: Dutton, 1965. 769p.

Nearly 2,400 biographical sketches on both major and minor writers. Entries are unsigned and vary in length from a few lines to three or four pages.

1176.   Burke, W. J., and W. D. Howe. **American Authors and Books: 1640 to the Present Day**. 3rd ed. Rev. by Irving Weiss and Ann Weiss. New York: Crown, 1972. 719p.

Alphabetical. About 17,000 short articles (with cross references to related subjects) on authors, books, periodicals, newspapers, publishing firms, literary societies, regions, localities, etc. Limited to continental United States. More inclusive than the *Oxford Companion to American Literature*, but the articles are shorter.

1177.   **Contemporary Authors: A Bio-Bibliographical Guide to Current Authors and Their Works**. Ed. by James M. Ethridge. Detroit: Gale Research Co., 1962– .

Semi-annual. Vols. 37-40 include cumulative index to Vols. 1-40. Living authors, mostly writing in English. A selection of entries from *Contemporary Authors*, often revised and extended, has been compiled by Barbara Harte and Carolyn Riley: *200 Contemporary Authors: Bio-Bibliographies of Selected Leading Writers of Today with Critical and Personal Sidelights* (Detroit: Gale Research Co., 1969. 306p.).

1178.   Kunitz, Stanley Jasspon, and Howard Haycraft, eds. **The Junior Book of Authors**. 2nd ed. New York: H. W. Wilson, 1951. 309p.

Has nearly 300 biographical sketches with many portraits. The first edition (1934) is still useful for over 100 authors omitted from the second. Supplementing and updating is provided in *More Junior Authors*, by Muriel Fuller (New York: H. W. Wilson, 1963), and *The Third Book of Junior Authors*, by Doris De Montreville and Donna Hill (New York: H. W. Wilson, 1972). The latter has a cumulative index to the three volumes.

1179.   Kunitz, Stanley Jasspon, and Howard Haycraft, eds. **Twentieth Century Authors: A Biographical Dictionary of Modern Literature; Complete in One Volume, with 1,850 Biographies and 1,700 Portraits**. New York: H. W. Wilson, 1942. 1577p. Supplement, 1955. 1123p.

Provides international coverage, though it favors writers whose works are available in English. Biographies include major works with dates of original publication and sources of further information. Kunitz has provided coverage for earlier periods in such works as *European Authors, 1000-1900* (New York: H. W. Wilson, 1967), *American Authors, 1600-1900* (New York: H. W. Wilson, 1938), *British Authors before 1800* (New York: H. W. Wilson, 1952), and *British Authors of the Nineteenth Century* (New York: H. W. Wilson, 1936).

1180.   Millett, Fred Benjamin. **Contemporary American Authors: A Critical Survey and 219 Bio-Bibliographies**. New York: Harcourt, Brace, 1940. 716p.

A critical survey of more than 200 pages is followed by entries on individual authors. Three indexes: index of authors, divided into 13 types; index of abbreviations of books and periodicals cited; and index of authors also included in *Contemporary British Literature* (3rd ed. London: Harrap, 1935).

1181. Russell, Josiah Cox. **Dictionary of Writers of Thirteenth Century England**. London: Longman, 1936. 210p. Reprinted New York: Burt Franklin, 1971. 220p.
Provides detailed biographical and bibliographical information for 350 authors. Entries are under given names (rather than surnames).

1182. Shockley, Ann A., and Sue P. Chandler. **Living Black American Authors: A Biographical Directory**. New York: R. R. Bowker, 1973. 220p.
Covers novelists, poets, dramatists, broadcasters, educators, athletes, social critics, and theologians. Includes select bibliographies of authors' works.

1183. **Something about the Author**. Detroit: Gale Research Co., 1970– .
Biographical entries typically give personal facts, careers, writings, works in progress, sidelights, and sources of additional information. Many illustrations from children's and young adult books. More selective and critical coverage is given by Miriam Hoffman and Eva Samuels in *Authors and Illustrators of Children's Books* (New York: R. R. Bowker, 1972). Supplemental coverage will be found in *The Who's Who of Children's Literature*, edited by Brian Doyle (New York: Schocken, 1969).

1184. Sylvestre, Guy, Brandon Conron, and Carl F. Klinck, eds. **Canadian Writers: Ecrivains Canadiens: A Bibliographical Dictionary**. New ed. rev. and enl. Toronto: Ryerson Press, 1966. 186p.
Bio-bibliographies of about 300 authors (including many still living). Articles on French-Canadian writers are in French. Chronological table. Index of titles mentioned in articles.

1185. Woodress, James Leslie, ed. **Eight American Authors: A Review of Research and Criticism**. Rev. ed. New York: Norton, 1972. 392p.
Individual scholars have contributed bibliographic essays on: Edgar Allen Poe; Ralph Waldo Emerson; Nathaniel Hawthorne; Henry David Thoreau; Herman Melville; Walt Whitman; Samuel Langhorne Clemens; and Henry James. A similar pattern (for different writers) is followed in *Fifteen Modern American Authors: A Survey of Research and Criticism*, edited by Jackson R. Bryer (Durham, N.C.: Duke University Press, 1969), and *Fifteen American Authors before 1900: Bibliographic Essays on Research and Criticism*, edited by Robert A. Rees and Earl N. Harbert (Madison: University of Wisconsin Press, 1971).

Reference Histories

1186. Baugh, Albert Croll, ed. **A Literary History of England**. 2nd ed. New York: Appleton-Century-Crofts, 1967. 4 vols.
Very highly regarded by scholars in the field. Contents: Vol. 1, The Middle Ages: The Old English Period (to 1100), by K. Malone; The Middle English

Period (1100-1500), by A. C. Baugh; Vol. 2, The Renaissance (1500-1660), by
T. Brooke and M. A. Shaaber; Vol. 3, The Restoration and Eighteenth Century
(1660-1789), by G. Sherburne and D. F. Bond; Vol. 4, The Nineteenth Century
and After (1789-1939), by S. C. Chew and R. D. Altick.

1187.   **Cambridge History of American Literature.** Ed. by William Peterfield
        Trent, John Erskine, Stuart P. Sherman, and Carl Van Doren. New
        York: Putnam, 1917-21. 4 vols. Reprinted in 1933 in 3 vols. without
        bibliographies. Reprint of 1933 ed. in one volume by Macmillan, 1944.
Still a valuable work, especially thorough on early period. Literary forms,
subjects, writers, etc., are treated in great detail. Related topics (explorers,
travelers, colonial newspapers, literary annuals, gift books, children's literature,
oral literature, non-English writings, etc.) are also included.

1188.   **Cambridge History of English Literature.** Ed. by A. W. Ward and A. R.
        Waller. Cambridge: Cambridge University Press, 1907-1927. 15 vols.
The most important general history of English literature, covering earliest times
to the end of the nineteenth century. Each chapter written by a specialist.
Includes extended and very useful bibliographies. Contents: Vol. 1, *From the
Beginnings to the Cycles of Romance*; Vol. 2, *The End of the Middle Ages*;
Vol. 3, *Renaissance and Reformation*; Vol. 4, *Prose and Poetry: Sir Thomas
North to Michael Drayton*; Vols. 5 and 6, *The Drama to 1642*; Vol. 7, *Cavalier
and Puritan*; Vol. 8, *The Age of Dryden*; Vol. 9, *From Steele and Addison to
Pope and Swift*; Vol. 10, *The Age of Johnson*; Vol. 11, *The Period of the French
Revolution*; Vols. 12, 13, and 14, *The Nineteenth Century*; Vol. 15, *Index.*
Reprinted in 1932 without bibliographies.

1189.   Dobrée, Bonamy, ed. **Introductions to English Literature.** London:
        Cresset Press, 1939-58. 5 vols.
Vol. 1, *The Beginnings of English Literature to Skelton, 1509*, by W. L. Renwick
and Harold Orton (3rd ed., rev. by Martyn F. Wakelin, 1966); Vol. 2, *The
English Renaissance, 1510-1688*, by V. de Sola Pinto (3rd rev. ed., 1966);
Vol. 3, *Augustans and Romantics*, by H. V. D. Dyson and John Butt (3rd
rev. ed., 1961); Vol. 4, *The Victorians and After, 1830-1914*, by Edith C. Batho
and Bonamy Dobrée (3rd rev. ed., 1962); Vol. 5, *The Present Age, After 1920*,
by David Daiches (1958). LC classifies and catalogs separately, but provides a
series entry.

1190.   Houtchens, Carolyn W., and Lawrence H. Houtchens. **The English
        Romantic Poets and Essayists: A Review of Research and Criticism.**
        2nd ed. New York: Printed for the Modern Language Association, New
        York University Press, 1966. 395 p.
Planned for graduate students. Chapters on Blake, Lamb, Hazlitt, Scott,
Southey, Campbell, Moore, Landon, Leigh Hunt, DeQuincey, Carlyle.

1191.   Hubbell, Jay Broadus. **The South in American Literature, 1607-1900.**
        Durham, N.C.: Duke University Press, 1954. 987p.
A major historical survey, with an extensive bibliography (pp. 883-974).

1192.   Johnston, Grahame. **Annals of Australian Literature**. New York: Oxford University Press, 1970. 147p.

Covers period from 1789 to 1969. Selective, but principal publications included. Alongside each year's tabulation, the compiler has included marginal notes on such things as founding of newspapers and journals, etc. Indexed by authors but not by titles. Most useful in larger literature and specialized collections. Another important title is Henry Mackenzie Green's *A History of Australian Literature, Pure and Applied: A Critical Review of All Forms of Literature Produced in Australia, from the First Books Published after the Arrival of the First Fleet until 1950, with Short Accounts of Later Publications up to 1960* (Sidney: Angus and Robertson, 1961. 2 vols.).

1193.   Klinck, Carl Frederick, ed. **Literary History of Canada: Canadian Literature in English**. Gen. ed.: Carl F. Klinck; eds.: Alfred G. Bailey and others. Toronto: University of Toronto Press, 1965. 945p.

A broad survey of literature and closely related fields, with chapters by 30 different specialists. Will probably remain the standard work for many years to come. A fresh, individual approach is found in Desmond Pacey's *Creative Writing in Canada: A Short History of English-Canadian Literature* (New ed. rev. and enl. Toronto: Ryerson Press, 1967) and in Margaret Atwood's *Survival: A Thematic Guide to Canadian Literature* (Toronto: Anansi, 1972).

1194.   Legouis, Emile Hyacinthe. **A History of English Literature: The Middle Ages and the Renascence (650-1600)**. By Emile Legouis. Tr. from the French by Helen Douglas Irvine. **Modern Times** (1660-1963) by Louis Cazamian and Raymond Las Vergnas (Book 8). Rev. ed. Bibliographies by Donald Davie and Pierre Legouis. New York: Macmillan, 1964. 1469p.

A standard one-volume history, useful as a text or for reference purposes.

1195.   **Literary History of the United States**. Eds.: Robert E. Spiller and others. 3rd ed. New York: Macmillan, 1963. Bibliography Supplement II, 1972. 3 vols. 1st ed., 1948. 3 vols.

Contents: Vol. 1, History; Vol. 2, Bibliography. First comprehensive history since *Cambridge History of American Literature* (1917-21, 4 vols.). Vol. 1 presents a survey from Colonial times to the present in a series of chapters written by experts and integrated by the editors. No footnotes. Two chapters added in third edition: 1) period between wars; 2) period since 1945. Vol. 2, which consists of bibliographical essays organized to develop treatment of text, is divided into four main sections: 1) Guide to resources; 2) Literature and culture; 3) Movements and influences; 4) Individual authors. Valuable critical comments on editions, biographies, etc. In the revised edition, the first *Supplement* has been added to main bibliography and follows same arrangement. Index now covers both main bibliography and main supplement. Index inadequate. Bibliography Supplement II covers 1958 to 1970, and indexing has been improved.

1196.   Loggins, Vernon. **The Negro Author, His Development in America to 1900**. Port Washington, N.Y.: Kennikat Press, 1964. 480p.
Reprint of 1931 edition.

1197.   Longaker, John Mark, and Edwin C. Bolles. **Contemporary English Literature**. New York: Appleton-Century-Crofts, 1953. 526p.
Valuable for reference purposes because of detailed information about individual authors and their works.

1198.   Mott, Frank Luther. **A History of American Magazines**. Cambridge: Harvard University Press, 1938-68. 5 vols.
A monumental study, with detailed information about the history, editors, and contents of American magazines from the Colonial period to 1930. Vol. 5 contains an index to the complete set.

1199.   **Oxford History of English Literature**. Ed. by Frank Percy Wilson and Bonamy Dobrée. Oxford: Clarendon Press, 1945– .
A long-range project, planned for completion in 12 volumes (some volumes with two parts). Each volume or part is written by a major scholar and includes extensive bibliographies. LC catalogs each volume separately but provides a common classification number and a series added entry. For an update on titles, check the "Series" section of the publisher's catalog. Titles issued to date: Vol. 2, Pt. 1, *Chaucer and the Fifteenth Century*, by H. S. Bennett (1947, 327p.); Vol. 9, *English Literature, 1789-1815*, by W. L. Renwick (1963); Vol. 10, *English Literature, 1815-1832*, by I. Jack (1963, 643p.); Vol. 12, *Eight Modern Writers (Hardy, James, Shaw, Conrad, Kipling, Yeats, Joyce and Lawrence)*, by J. I. M. Stewart (1963).

1200.   Sampson, George. **The Concise Cambridge History of English Literature**. 3rd ed. Rev. by R. C. Churchill. Cambridge: Cambridge University Press, 1970. 976p.
The main portion of this classic work has been thoroughly revised and three essential new chapters have been added, giving fuller coverage to the literature in English from Iceland, India, Pakistan, Ceylon, Malaysia, Canada, Australia, New Zealand, West Indies, South Africa, and the new African states. Another standard history, by a noted scholar, is *A Critical History of English Literature*, by David Daiches (2nd ed. New York: Ronald Press, 1970).

1201.   Taylor, Walter Fuller. **The Story of American Letters**. Rev. ed. Chicago: H. Regnery Co., 1956. 504p.
First edition appeared under the title *A History of American Letters* (1936). Considered by some to be the best work on this subject. Other works include *The Literature of the American People*, edited by Arthur Hobson Quinn (New York: Appleton-Century-Crofts, 1951), and *American Literature: A World View*, by Willis Wager (New York: New York University Press, 1968).

1202.   Ward, A. C. **Illustrated History of English Literature**. New York: Longmans, 1953-55. 3 vols.

Contents: Vol. I, *Chaucer to Shakespeare*; Vol. II, *Ben Jonson to Samuel Johnson*; Vol. III, *Blake to Shaw*. A one-volume edition (without illustrations) had been issued under the title *English Literature: Chaucer to Bernard Shaw* (New York: Longmans, 1958).

Recommended Collections

1203.   **Best American Short Stories of 1915– , and the Yearbook of the American Short Story**. Boston: Houghton, 1915– . Annual.
Title varies. Each volume contains a selection of short stories and brief yearbook information.

1204.   Emanuel, James A., and Theodore L. Gross. **Dark Symphony: Negro Literature in America**. New York: Free Press, 1968. 604p.
More than simply an anthology. Extensive biographical and bibliographical information as well. *A Galaxy of Black Writing*, edited by R. Baird Shuman (Durham, N.C.: Moore Publishing Co., 1970), should also be considered.

1205.   Hughes, Langston, and Arna Bontemps. **The Poetry of the Negro, 1746-1970**. Rev. ed. Garden City, N.Y.: Doubleday, 1970. 645p.

1206.   James, Charles L. **From the Roots: Short Stories by Black Americans**. New York: Dodd, 1970. 370p.

1207.   **Oxford Book of American Verse**. 2nd ed. New York: Oxford University Press, 1950. 1132p.

1208.   **The Oxford Book of Canadian Verse, in English and French**. Chosen by A. J. M. Smith. New York: Oxford University Press, 1960. 445p.

1209.   **Oxford Book of English Verse, 1250-1918**. New York: Oxford University Press, 1939. 1171p.

1210.   **Oxford Book of Modern Verse, 1892-1935**. New York: Oxford University Press, 1936. 454p.

1211.   Stevenson, Burton E. **Home Book of Verse**. 9th ed. New York: Holt, 1953. 2 vols.
Complementary coverage is found in Stevenson's *Home Book of Modern Verse* (2nd ed. New York: Holt, 1953).

1212.   Untermeyer, Louis. **Treasury of Great Poems**. New York: Simon & Schuster, 1955. 1286p.
Another excellent collection is Untermeyer's *Modern American Poetry and Modern British Poetry* (Combined new and enl. ed. New York; Harcourt, Brace and World, 1962).

1213.   Woods, Ralph. **A Treasury of the Familiar**. New York: Macmillan, 1942. 751p.
Three indexes: 1) Titles; 2) Familiar lines; 3) Authors. A useful sequel is *A Second Treasury of the Familiar* (New York: Macmillan, 1950). The major reference value of these two books lies in their attention to lines of poetry other than first lines.

Poetry

Introductory Works and Bibliographic Guides

1214.   Haviland, Virginia, and William Jay Smith, comps. **Children and Poetry: A Selective, Annotated Bibliography**. Washington, D.C.: Library of Congress, 1969. 67p.
Illustrations and examples of poetry are also included.

1215.   Scholes, Robert Edward. **Elements of Poetry**. New York: Oxford University Press, 1969. 86p.

Bibliographies

1216.   **The Bibliography of Contemporary Poets**. London: Regency Press, 1970. 191p.
Arranged alphabetically by surnames. Gives information on birthdates, pseudonyms, occupations, and other interests. Publications of each author are given full bibliographical descriptions. There are cross references from pseudonyms, and real names are provided where needed.

1217.   Brower, Gary L., and David William Foster. **Haiku in Western Languages: An Annotated Bibliography (with Some Reference to Senryu)**. Metuchen, N.J.: Scarecrow Press, 1972. 133p.
Selective coverage of both books and articles.

1218.   Case, Arthur Ellicott. **A Bibliography of English Poetical Miscellanies, 1521-1750**. Oxford: Printed for the Bibliographical Society by the University Press, 1935. 386p.
Works which contain poems by three or more British authors are arranged chronologically by dates of earliest known editions.

1219.   Deodene, Frank, and William P. French. **Black American Poetry since 1944: A Preliminary Checklist**. Chatham, N.J.: The Chatham Bookseller, 1971. 43p.

1220.   Irish, Wynot R. **The Modern American Muse: A Complete Bibliography of American Verse, 1900-1925**. Syracuse, N.Y.: Syracuse University Press, 1950. 259p.
Over 6,900 books, including many that were privately published or that are otherwise difficult to identify. Chronological arrangement by year of publication, subarranged alphabetically by author. No indexes.

1221.   Kuntz, Joseph Marshall. **Poetry Explication: A Checklist of Interpreta-tion since 1925 of British and American Poems Past and Present.** Rev. ed. Denver: Alan Swallow, 1962. 331p.
Indicates sources of explanation of meanings of poems in a selected group of books and periodicals. The second edition covers through 1959.

1222.   Shaw, John Mackay. **Childhood in Poetry: A Catalogue of the Books of English and American Poets in the Library of the Florida State University; with Lists of the Poems That Relate to Childhood and Notes.** Tallahassee: Robert M. Strozier Library, Florida State University, 1962-66. 8 vols. Reprinted Detroit: Gale Research Co., 1968-72.
Alphabetical by author and then chronological by date of publication. Items are annotated. Children's poems are individually identified if part of a larger work.

Indexes, Abstracts, and Current Awareness Services

1223.   American Library Association. **Subject Index to Poetry for Children and Young People.** Comp. by Violet Sell and others. Chicago: American Library Association, 1957. 582p.
Poems from 157 collections for children and young people from kindergarten through senior high school.

1224.   Brewton, John E., and Sara W. Brewton, comps. **Index to Children's Poetry: A Title, Subject, Author, and First-Line Index to Poetry in Collections for Children and Youth.** New York: H. W. Wilson, 1942. 965p. First supp., 1954. 405p. Second supp., 1965. 453p. Third supp., 1964-69, with G. Meredith Blackburn III, 1972. 575p.
Including the three supplements, this work indexes well over 30,000 poems by more than 5,000 authors.

1225.   Brown, Carleton Fairchild, and Rossell Hope Robbins. **The Index of Middle English Verse.** New York: Printed for the Index Society by Columbia University Press, 1943. 785p. Supplement, by Rossell H. Robbins and John L. Cutler. Lexington: University of Kentucky Press, 1965. 551p.
Main work indexes alphabetically by first line some 4,365 poems written before 1500. Subject and title index. Location list of private manuscripts. Supplement follows the same basic arrangement, with corrections and updatings.

1226.   Bruncken, Herbert. **Subject Index to Poetry: Guide for Adult Readers.** Chicago: American Library Association, 1940. 210p.
Purpose of this index to 215 anthologies is defined in the Preface as "(1) the location of poetry on specific subjects, (2) the location of a poem, the topical matter or dominant idea of which is known, but not author, title, or first line, (3) the location of a poem whose author, title, or first line is not known, but a line or fragment of a line of which is known."

1227.   **Chicorel Index to Poetry in Collections in Print, on Discs and Tapes: Poetry on Discs, Tapes and Cassettes.** Ed. by Marietta Chicorel. New York: Chicorel, 1972.
Another of the very useful, computer-produced indexes from this firm.

1228.   Cuthbert, Eleanora Isabel. **Index of Australian and New Zealand Poetry.** New York: Scarecrow Press, 1963. 453p.
About 4,000 entries in three parts: authors, titles, first lines.

1229.   **First-Line Index of English Poetry, 1500-1800: In Manuscripts of the Bodleian Library, Oxford.** Ed. by Margaret Crum. New York: Modern Language Association of America, 1969. 2 vols.
Includes nearly 23,000 poems. Careful bibliographical scholarship. Especially rich in seventeenth century verse.

1230.   Granger, Edith. **Index to Poetry.** 6th ed. New York: Columbia University Press, 1973. 2100p.
Long the pre-eminent work in this field. First edition, 1904. Covers largest selection of standard and popular anthologies and poetry collections. The first, second, and third editions included prose. In the fourth, fifth and sixth editions, title and first-line indexes are combined, followed by an author index and subject index. Because of changes from edition to edition, most large libraries keep older editions for search questions. Sixth edition includes 121 new collections (15 of them anthologies of black poetry) and new subject headings like "Ecology," "Women's Liberation," etc.

1231.   **Index of American Periodical Verse,** 1971– . By Sander W. Zulauf and H. Weiser Irwin. Metuchen, N.J.: Scarecrow Press, 1973– .
To be issued annually. First volume covered 158 American periodicals. Main part alphabetical by poets' surnames. Title index.

Biographies

1232.   Malkoff, Karl. **Crowell's Handbook of Contemporary American Poetry.** New York: Crowell, 1974. 288p.
Concentrates on poets since 1940. Good supplement to older, standard works. Introduction deals with movements, while the main work treats individual poets (in alphabetical order).

1233.   Murphy, Rosalie, ed. **Contemporary Poets of the English Language.** Chicago: St. James Press, 1970. 1243p.
Biographical and bibliographical information plus selective critical evaluations. Attempts worldwide coverage of poets writing in English. Among the 1,000 poets included are many minor figures for whom information might otherwise be difficult to obtain.

History and Criticism

1234.　Courthope, William John. **A History of English Poetry**. New York: Macmillan, 1895-1910. 6 vols.
A standard work covering the period from the Middle Ages to the romantic movement. Each volume includes an analytical table of contents, and there is a cumulative index in Vol. 6.

1235.　Faverty, Frederic Everett, ed. **The Victorian Poets: A Guide to Research**. 2nd ed. Cambridge: Harvard University Press, 1968. 433p.
Covers bibliography, editions, manuscripts, letters, biography, and criticism for each major poet and for groups of minor ones.

1236.　Hamer, Enid Hope Porter. **The Metres of English Poetry**. 4th ed. London: Methuen, 1951. 340p.
A standard handbook for students and others interested in the technical aspects of the subject.

1237.　Raysor, Thomas Middleton, ed. **The English Romantic Poets: A Review of Research**. Rev. ed. New York: Modern Language Association, 1956. 307p.
This handbook for graduate students is a companion volume to *The English Romantic Poets and Essayists*, by C. W. Houtchens and L. H. Houtchens (Rev. ed. New York: Modern Language Association of America, 1964. 395p.).

Fiction

Introductory Works and Bibliographic Guides

1238.　Briney, Robert E. **SF Bibliographies: An Annotated Bibliography of Bibliographical Works on Science Fiction and Fantasy Fiction**. Chicago: Advent, 1972. 49p.
Four sections: magazine indexes; bibliographies of individual authors; general indexes and checklists; foreign language bibliographies.

1239.　Cotton, Gerald Brooks, and Hilda Mary McGill. **Fiction Guides: General, British and American**. London: Clive Bingley, 1967. 126p.
A classified arrangement, with author and title indexes.

1240.　Scholes, Robert Edward. **Elements of Fiction**. New York: Oxford University Press, 1968. 88p.

1241.　Stevenson, Lionel, ed. **Victorian Fiction: A Guide to Research**. Cambridge: Harvard University Press, 1964. 440p.
Chapters are contributed by 13 specialists. Contents: general materials; Disraeli; Bulwer-Lytton; Dickens; Thackeray; Trollope; the Brontes; Gaskell, Kingsley; Collins, Reade; Eliot; Meredith; Hardy; Moore, Gissing. Analytical index.

Bibliographies of Fiction

1241a. Baker, Ernest Albert. **A Guide to Historical Fiction**. New York: Macmillan, 1914. Reprinted New York: Burt Franklin, 1969. 566p.
Covers about 5,000 novels. Entries are arranged by country and then by historical period. Annotations give plots, settings, and characters. Index of authors, titles, historical names, places, events, etc.

1242. Baker, Ernest Albert, and James Packman. **A Guide to the Best Fiction, English and American, Including Translations from Foreign Language**. New and enl. ed. New York: Macmillan, 1932. Reprinted New York: Barnes and Noble, 1967. 634p.
Arranged alphabetically by authors. Good annotations. Index of places, subjects, titles, characters, historical names, etc.

1243. Barzun, Jacques, and Wendell Hertig Taylor. **A Catalogue of Crime: Being a Reader's Guide to the Literature of Mystery, Detection and Related Genres**. New York: Harper & Row, 1971. 704p.
Annotated guide to some 3,476 crime and mystery stories in the English language. A more comprehensive work is *Who Done It? A Guide to Detective, Mystery and Suspense Fiction*, by Ordean A. Hagen (New York: R. R. Bowker, 1969), which covers over 50,000 novels published from 1841 to 1967 and which has three special supplements: mysteries made into films; place names in mysteries; and a list of characters.

1244. Coan, Otis Welton. **America in Fiction: An Annotated List of Novels That Interpret Aspects of Life in the United States, Canada and Mexico**. 5th ed. Palo Alto, Calif.: Pacific Books, 1967. 232p.
Lists novels and collections of short stories by phase or aspect of American life, with brief annotations indicating subject matter and treatment. Recommended titles are starred. Another major work is A. T. Dickinson's *American Historical Fiction* (3rd ed. Metuchen, N.J.: Scarecrow Press, 1971), which covers novels dealing with the entire period from Colonial times to the present, but which concentrates on books published since 1917. More specialized in focus is Jack W. Van Derhoof's *A Bibliography of Novels Related to American Frontier and Colonial History* (Troy, N.Y.: Whitston Publishing Co., 1971).

1245. Gardner, Frank M. **Sequels, Incorporating Aldred and Parker's "Sequel Stories."** 5th ed. London: Association of Assistant Librarians, 1967. 291p.
Covers about 20,000 titles. Part I deals with adult books and Part II with juveniles. *Bibliography of the Sequence Novel*, by Margaret Elizabeth Kerr (Minneapolis: University of Minnesota Press, 1950), is narrower in scope and lists 3,173 titles in 999 sequences.

1246. Logasa, Hannah. **Historical Fiction**. 9th ed. Brooklawn, N.J.: McKinley, 1968. 383p.
Guide for junior and senior high schools as well as for the general reader.

Classified list, with author and title index. *A Guide to Historical Fiction for the Use of Schools, Libraries and the General Reader*, by Leonard Bertram Irwin (10th ed. Brooklawn, N.J.: McKinley, 1971), and *Historical Fiction Guide: Annotated Chronological, Geographical and Topical List of Five Thousand Historical Novels*, by Daniel D. McGarry and Sarah Harriman White (New York: Scarecrow Press, 1963), also give general coverage, while *European Historical Fiction and Biography for Children and Young People*, by Jeanette Hotchkiss (2nd ed. Metuchen, N.J.: Scarecrow Press, 1972), is more specialized.

1247. O'Dell, Sterg. **Chronological List of Prose Fiction in English, Printed in England and Other Countries, 1475-1640**. Cambridge: Massachusetts Institute of Technology, 1954. 147p. Reprinted New York: Kraus Reprint, 1969.

Chronological arrangement is supplemented by author and anonymous title index. Gives locations in 69 libraries. Later coverage is given in the following works: *English Prose Fiction, 1600-1700: A Chronological Checklist*, by Charles Carroll Mish (Charlottesville: Bibliographical Society of Virginia, 1967); *A Check List of English Prose Fiction, 1700-1739*, by William Harlin McBurney (Cambridge: Harvard University Press, 1960); and *The English Novel, 1740-1850: A Catalogue Including Prose Romances, Short Stories, and Translations of Foreign Fiction*, by Andrew Block (2nd ed. Dobbs Ferry, N.Y.: Oceana Publications, 1961).

1248. Rosenberg, Judith K., and Kenyon C. Rosenberg. **Young People's Literature in Series: Fiction; An Annotated Bibliographical Guide**. Littleton, Colo.: Libraries Unlimited, 1972. 176p.

Covers every series for grades 3 through 9 issued since 1955. Main part is alphabetical by author, with each series in chronological order. Series title index and individual title index. Brief, critical annotations.

1249. Sadleir, Michael. **XIX Century Fiction, a Bibliographical Record Based on His Own Collection**. Berkeley: University of California Press, 1951. 2 vols.

Three sections: alphabetical author list; yellow-backs; novelists' libraries; standard novel series; etc. Each volume has an author and title index. Coverage of our own time, on a selective basis, will be found in E. C. Bufkin's *The Twentieth Century Novel in English* (Athens: University of Georgia Press, 1967).

1250. U.S. Library of Congress. **Author Bibliography of English Language Fiction in the Library of Congress through 1950**. Comp. by R. Glenn Wright. Boston: G. K. Hall, 1973. 8 vols.

Arranged by country and then alphabetically by author. Special list of authors whose works have been translated into English, and an index of translators. Index of pseudonym identifications.

1251. Wilson, H. W., Firm, Publishers. **Fiction Catalog: A List of 4,097 Works of Fiction in the English Language, with Annotations**. 7th ed. Ed. by Estelle A. Fidell and Esther V. Flory. New York: H. W. Wilson, 1961. 650p. Supp., 1961-65. 1966. 299p. Annual volumes since 1965.

A standard library tool, first published in 1908. Main part is alphabetical by author. Subject and title index, with a directory of publishers. Recommended items are starred or double-starred.

1252.   Wright, Lyle Henry. **American Fiction, 1774-1850**. 2nd rev. ed. San Marino, Calif.: Huntington Library, 1969. 411p.
First published in 1939 and revised in 1948. The 1969 edition represents another thorough revision. Some 600 titles have been added, for a total of 2,772 entries. Useful chronological index. Lists novels, romances, short stories, fiction, biographies, travels, allegories and tract-like tales written by Americans. Locates copies in 19 libraries and two private collections. Wright has also compiled *American Fiction, 1851-1875* (San Marino, Calif.: Huntington Library, 1965) and *American Fiction, 1876-1900* (San Marino, Calif.: Huntington Library, 1966). Books listed in Wright are being reproduced in microform by University Microfilms.

Bibliographies of Fiction Criticism

1253.   Adelman, Irving, and Rita Dworkin. **The Contemporary Novel: A Checklist of Critical Literature on the British and American Novel since 1945**. Metuchen, N.J.: Scarecrow Press, 1972. 614p.
Covers novelists whose major works or recognition came after 1945. Cites books and scholarly articles in preference to reviews. An extremely useful reference tool. A more specialized focus is found in *Religion in Contemporary Fiction: Criticism from 1945 to the Present*, compiled by George N. Boyd and Lois A. Boyd (San Antonio, Texas: Trinity University Press, 1973).

1254.   Bell, Inglis Freeman, and Donald Baird. **The English Novel, 1578-1956: A Checklist of Twentieth-Century Criticisms**. Denver: Swallow, 1959. 169p.
A select list of twentieth century criticism of English novels from Lyly to 1956, including citations to books and periodicals. Arrangement is alphabetical by novelist's name and then by title of novel. Continued for period from 1957 to 1972 in *English Novel Explication: Criticism to 1972*, by Helen H. Palmer and Anne Jane Dyson (Hamden, Conn.: Archon/Shoestring, 1973).

1255.   Bonheim, Helmut W. **The English Novel before Richardson: A Checklist of Texts and Criticism to 1970**. Metuchen, N.J.: Scarecrow Press, 1971. 145p.

1256.   Clareson, Thomas D. **Science Fiction Criticism: An Annotated Checklist**. Kent, Ohio: Kent State University Press, 1972. 225p.

1257.   Eichelberger, Clayton L., comp. **A Guide to Critical Reviews of United States Fiction, 1870-1910**. Metuchen, N.J.: Scarecrow Press, 1971. 415p.
"Because contemporary reviews of American fiction for the period indicated have not previously been accessible through standard reference works, this

attempt to direct the researcher to just this type of secondary source is welcome. Although it is by no means a comprehensive listing of reviews published during the period, it does cite reviews of several minor authors and of some titles by major authors not previously listed elsewhere. . . ." [review in *College and Research Libraries* 33 (January 1972): 43].

1258.   Gerstenberger, Donna L., and George Hendrick. **The American Novel since 1789: A Checklist of Twentieth Century Criticism**. Denver: Alan Swallow, 1961-70. 2 vols.

Vol. 1 covers criticism published prior to 1959; Vol. 2 covers criticism published from 1960 to 1968. Arranged alphabetically by novelist, with listings of criticism under individual novels. A second section lists general studies of the American novel by century.

1259.   Thurston, Jarvis A. **Short Fiction Criticism: A Checklist of Interpretation since 1925 of Stories and Novelettes (American, British, Continental) 1800-1958**. Denver: Alan Swallow, 1960. 265p.

A listing of critical articles published in books and periodicals (including "little magazines") on stories and novelettes up to 150 pages. Confined to material in English.

1260.   Walker, Warren S. **Twentieth Century Short Story Explication, Interpretations, 1900-1966 Inclusive, of Short Fiction since 1800**. Rev. ed. Hamden, Conn.: Shoestring Press, 1967. 697p. Supplement I, 1967-69. 1970. 262p.

Except for recent items, many references duplicate those in Thurston. The supplement is particularly valuable because of its recency.

Indexes, Abstracts, and Current Awareness Services

1261.   American Library Association. Editorial Committee. **Subject and Title Index to Short Stories for Children**. Chicago: American Library Association, 1955. 333p.

1262.   Cook, Dorothy Elizabeth, and Isabel S. Munro. **Short Story Index: An Index to 60,000 Stories in 4,320 Collections**. New York: H. W. Wilson, 1953. 1553p. Supplements: 1950-54. 1956; 394p. 1955-58. 1960; 341p. 1959-63. 1965; 487p. 1964-68. 1969; 599p.

Together, the main work and supplements index between 95,000 and 100,000 short stories. Author, title, and subject entries in one alphabet.

1263.   **Cumulated Fiction Index, 1945-1960**. London: Association of Assistant Librarians, 1960. 552p.

Covers about 25,000 works of fiction (including short stories) under some 3,000 subject headings.

1264.   Freeman, William. **Dictionary of Fictional Characters**. Boston: The Writer, Inc., 1963. 458p. With author and title indexes by J. M. F. Leaper. Boston: The Writer, Inc., 1965. 529p. Reprinted 1968.

Main work is arranged alphabetically by names of characters—approximately 20,000 from 2,000 books by 500 British, American, and Commonwealth authors in the last 600 years. Covers novels, short stories, poems, and non-musical plays. Index enables one to find names of principal characters when only author or title is known.

1265.   Siemon, Frederick. **Science Fiction Story Index, 1950-1968**. Chicago: American Library Association, 1971. 274p.

Biographies

1266.   Vinson, James, ed. **Contemporary Novelists**. New York: St. Martin's Press, 1973. 1422p.
Covers 600 living novelists. Biographical and directory information, list of publications, and signed critical essay for each writer. Short personal statement from each novelist who chose to make one.

History and Criticism

1267.   Baker, Ernest Albert. **The History of the English Novel**. London: Witherby, 1924-39. Reprinted New York: Barnes and Noble, 1960-67. 11 vols.
Standard work. Beginnings to early twentieth century. Brief bibliographies and index in each volume. Vol. 11, *Yesterday and After*, by Lionel Stevenson, supplements the original 10-volume set by Baker and was published in 1967.

1268.   Bernard, Harry. **Le roman régionaliste aux Etats-Unis, 1913-1940**. Montreal: Fides, 1949. 387p.
A standard work on the regional novel in the United States.

1269.   Bone, Robert A. **The Negro Novel in America**. Rev. ed. New Haven: Yale University Press, 1965. 289p.
A valuable history.

1270.   Forster, Edward Morgan. **Aspects of the Novel**. New York: Harcourt, Brace, 1927. 250p.
A classic source for discussion of such topics as plot, viewpoint, and characterization.

1271.   Leisy, Ernest Erwin. **The American Historical Novel**. Norman: University of Oklahoma Press, 1950. 280p.

Serials

1272.   **American Literary Scholarship**, 1963– . Annual. Duke University Press, Box 6697, College Station, Durham, N.C. 27708.

1273. **American Literature: A Journal of Literary History, Criticism, and Bibliography**, 1929– . Quarterly. Duke University Press, Box 6697. College Station, Durham, N.C. 27708.
Indexed in: *Abstracts of English Studies, Social Sciences and Humanities Index*. Vols. 1-30 also indexed by Thomas F. Marshall in *Analytical Index to American Literature, Volumes I-XXX, March, 1929–January, 1959* (Durham, N.C.: Duke University Press, 1963). Official scholarly publication of the American Literature Group of the Modern Language Association.

1274. **American Quarterly**, 1949– . 4 nos. and one supp. per year. University of Pennsylvania, Box 30, Bennett Hall, Philadelphia, Pa. 19104.
Indexed in: *Social Sciences and Humanities Index*. Tries to do for American studies as a whole what *American Literature* does for literature.

1275. **The Antioch Review**, 1941– . Quarterly. Antioch Press, Box 148, Yellow Springs, Ohio 45387.
Indexed in: *Abstracts of English Studies, Historical Abstracts, Sociological Abstracts, Public Affairs Information Service, Social Sciences and Humanities Index*. Recent issues have become somewhat more general in scope than previous issues.

1276. **Ariel (Canada): A Review of International English Literature**, 1960– . Quarterly. University of Calgary, Calgary, Alberta, Canada.
Indexed in: *British Humanities Index, Social Sciences and Humanities Index*. Formerly entitled *Review of English Literature*.

1277. **Canadian Literature/Littérature Canadienne: A Quarterly of Criticism and Review**, 1959– . Quarterly. University of British Columbia, Vancouver 8, B.C., Canada.

1278. **The Critical Quarterly**, 1959– . Quarterly. Oxford University Press, London, N.W. 10, England.
Indexed in: *British Humanities Index*.

1279. **Criticism: A Quarterly for Literature and the Arts**, 1959– . Quarterly. Wayne State University Press, 5980 Cass Ave., Detroit, Mich. 48202.
Indexed in: *Social Sciences and Humanities Index, Modern Language Abstracts*.

1280. **Critique: Studies in Modern Fiction**, 1957– . 3 per year. University of Minnesota, Box 4063, University Station, Minneapolis, Minn. 55414.

1281. **ELH (English Literary History)**, 1931– . Quarterly. Johns Hopkins Press, Baltimore, Md. 21218.
Indexed in: *Social Science and Humanities Index*.

1282. **English Association: Essays and Studies**, 1910-1946. **New Series**, 1948– . John Murray (Publishers), Ltd., 50 Albemarle St., London, W. 1, England.
Publication was suspended from 1915 through 1919. Title varies.

1283.   **English Studies: A Journal of English Letters and Philology**, 1919– .
Bi-monthly. Swets en Zeitlinger, Publishing Department, 347 Heereweg,
Lisse, Netherlands.
Indexed in: *Language and Language Behavior Abstracts, Social Sciences and
Humanities Index.*

1284.   **Etudes anglaises**, 1937– . Quarterly. Educational Division, Chilton
Books, 401 Walnut St., Philadelphia, Pa. 19106.
Text is in English and French.

1285.   **The Explicator**, 1942– . 10 per year. Virginia Commonwealth University, 901 W. Franklin St., Richmond, Va. 23220.
Vols. 1-20, 1942-62, have been cumulated into *The Explicator Cyclopedia*. Issue
No. 10 (June) is Index and Check List Issue. Three sorts of indexes: 1) list of
authors treated in current volume; 2) list of contributors; 3) list of explications
found in other journals and books. Available in microform.

1286.   **The Hudson Review**, 1948– . Quarterly. Hudson Review, Inc., 65 E.
55th St., New York, N.Y. 10022.
Indexed in: *Social Sciences and Humanities Index.*

1287.   **Modern Fiction Studies: A Critical Quarterly Devoted to Criticism,
Scholarship and Bibliography of American, English and European
Fiction since about 1800**, 1955– . Quarterly. Department of English,
Purdue University, Lafayette, Ind. 47907.
Indexed in: *Social Sciences and Humanities Index, Modern Language Associa-
tion International Bibliography.*

1288.   **Nineteenth Century Fiction**, 1945– . Quarterly. University of Cali-
fornia Press, Berkeley, Calif. 94720.
Indexed in: *Abstracts of English Studies, Modern Language Abstracts, Social
Sciences and Humanities Index.*

1289.   **The Partisan Review**, 1934– . Quarterly. Partisan Review, Inc., 191
College Ave., New Brunswick, N.J. 08903.
Indexed in: *Abstracts of English Studies, Social Sciences and Humanities Index.*

1290.   **Philological Quarterly**, 1922– . Quarterly. Publications Department,
University of Iowa, Iowa City, Iowa 52240.
Indexed in: *Social Sciences and Humanities Index* Primarily concerned with
English literature, especially the eighteenth century.

1291.   **Poetry**, 1912– . Monthly. Poetry, 1228 N. Dearborn Parkway, Chicago,
Ill. 60610.
Indexed in: *Reader's Guide*. Oldest and most important of existing poetry
magazines.

1292.   **Review of English Studies: A Quarterly Journal of English Literature and the English Language**, 1925– . Quarterly. Oxford University Press, Ely House, 37 Dover St., London, W. 1, England.
Indexed in: *British Humanities Index, Social Sciences and Humanities Index.*

1293.   **Sewanee Review**, 1892– . Quarterly. University of the South, Sewanee, Tenn. 37375.
Indexed in: *Abstracts of English Studies, Annual Bibliography of English Language and Literature, Book Review Index, Current Contents, Social Sciences and Humanities Index.*

1294.   **Studies in English Literature, 1500-1900**, 1961– . Quarterly. Rice University, Houston, Texas 77001.
Indexed in: *Social Sciences and Humanities Index.*

1295.   **Studies in Romanticism**, 1961– . Quarterly. Graduate School, Boston University, 236 Bay State Rd., Boston, Mass. 02115.
Indexed in: *Social Sciences and Humanities Index.*

1296.   **University of Toronto Quarterly: A Canadian Journal of the Humanities**, 1930– . Quarterly. University of Toronto Press, Toronto 5, Canada.
Indexed in: *Canadian Periodical Index, Current Index to Journals in Education, Reader's Guide.* A feature since 1935 has been "Letters in Canada," an annual critical survey of Canadian literature and criticism for the preceding year.

1297.   **Victorian Studies: A Journal of the Humanities, Arts and Sciences**, 1957– . Quarterly. Indiana University, Ballantine Hall, Bloomington, Ind. 47401.
Indexed in: *Abstracts of English Studies, Social Sciences and Humanities Index.*
Available in microform.

1298.   **Zeitschrift für Anglistik und Amerikanistik**, 1953– . Quarterly. VEB Verlag Enzyklopädie, Gerichtsweg 26, 701 Leipzig, East Germany.

LITERATURE IN OTHER LANGUAGES

Greek and Latin

1299.   **American Journal of Philology**, 1880– . Quarterly. Johns Hopkins University Press, Baltimore, Md. 21218.
Indexed in: *Social Sciences and Humanities Index.* Scholarly articles dealing with various aspects of classical studies.

1300.   **L'Année philologique: bibliographie critique et analytique de l'antiquité gréco-latine (fondée par J. Marouzeau)**. Paris: Société d'Editions "Les Belles Lettres," 1928– . Annual.

Each volume has two parts. Part I is devoted to authors and their works. Part II is a classified subject bibliography. Four indexes; collections; names in antiquity; humanists; modern authors. Coverage begins with 1924/26.

1301.   **Classical Philology: Devoted to Research in the Languages, Literatures, History and Life of Classical Antiquity**, 1906– . Quarterly. University of Chicago Press, 5750 Ellis Ave., Chicago, Ill. 60637.
Indexed in: *Social Sciences and Humanities Index*.

1302.   **Classical Review**, 1886– . 3 per year. Oxford University Press, Ely House, Dover St., London, W. 1, England.
Indexed in: *British Humanities Index*, *Social Sciences and Humanities Index*.

1303.   Feder, Lillian. **Crowell's Handbook of Classical Literature**. New York: Crowell, 1964. 448p.
An alphabetical dictionary of names, titles, mythological characters, etc. Gives detailed summaries of individual works.

1304.   Gwinup, Thomas, and Fidelia Dickinson. **Greek and Roman Authors: A Checklist of Criticism**. Metuchen, N.J.: Scarecrow Press, 1973. 194p.

1305.   Harvey, Sir Paul. **The Oxford Companion to Classical Literature**. Oxford: Clarendon Press, 1937. 468p.
Frequently reprinted. Alphabetical arrangement of concise articles on classical writers, literary forms and subjects, individual works, names and subjects in Greek and Roman history, institutions, religions, etc.

1306.   **International Guide to Classical Studies: A Quarterly Index to Periodical Literature**, 1961– . American Bibliographic Service, Darien, Conn. 06820.
Section I is alphabetical by author, with full citations and individual item numbers. Section II is an alphabetical subject index (which refers back to the full citations in Section I).

1308.   **The Journal of Hellenic Studies**, 1880– . Annual. Society for the Promotion of Hellenic Studies, 31 Gordon Square, London, W.C. 1, England.
Indexed in: *British Humanities Index*.

1309.   **The Journal of Roman Studies**, 1911– . Annual. Society for the Promotion of Roman Studies, 31-34 Gordon Square, London, W.C. 1, England.
Indexed in: *Social Sciences and Humanities Index*, *British Humanities Index*.

1310.   **Oxford Classical Dictionary**. Ed. by N. G. L. Hammond and H. H. Scullard. 2nd ed. Oxford: Clarendon Press, 1970. 1176p.
Strong in biography, it also covers literature and civilization.

1311.   Parks, George B., and Ruth Z. Temple. **The Greek and Latin Literatures: A Bibliography.** New York: Frederick Ungar, 1968. (The Literatures of the World in English Translation, Vol. 1). 442p.
Covers translations of literature from any period, made between 1645 and 1965. Volume begins with a general bibliography; arrangement is then chronological and, within each period, alphabetical by author. Index of authors at the end, but no index of titles in translation or of Greek and Latin titles that have authors.

1312.   Pauly, A. F. von, and G. Wissowa. **Pauly's Realencyclopädie der Classischen Altertumswissenschaft.** Stuttgart: Metzler, 1894-1919. Supplement, 1903– . 2 reihe (R–Z), 1914– .
Covers whole field of classical literature, history, antiquities, biography, etc. Long, signed articles by specialists with extensive bibliographies. Generally cited as Pauly-Wissowa. In German references, sometimes cited as R. E. Arrangement and alphabetizing are complicated; supplement is geared to main set.

1313.   Pfeiffer, Rudolf. **History of Classical Scholarship.** Oxford: Clarendon Press, 1968– . 3 vols.
Author is Emeritus Professor of Greek, University of Munich. LC catalogs each title separately and does not provide a series entry. Contents: Vol. 1, *From the Beginnings to the End of the Hellenistic Age.*

1314.   Politis, Linus. **A History of Modern Greek Literature.** New York: Oxford University Press, 1973. 338p.
Covers period from eleventh century to the present. Includes chronological tables, Greek texts of citations, and chapter bibliographies.

1315.   Thompson, Lawrence Sidney. **A Bibliography of American Doctoral Dissertations in Classical Studies and Related Fields.** Hamden, Conn.: Shoestring Press, 1968. 250p.
Covers classical studies from the beginnings of graduate work in the United States through 1963, with some entries from 1964 and 1965. Dissertations cover Greece and Rome from earliest times to 500 A.D. Main listing is by author. Good subject index—average of four entries per dissertation. Also, a title entry for each. Briefer indexes of Greek and Latin words of special importance.

Romance Languages

1316.   Boussuat, Robert. **Manuel bibliographique de la littérature française du Moyen Age.** Melun: Librairie d'Argences, 1951. Supp., 1945-53. 1955. 150p. Supp., 1954-60. 1961. 132p.
Over 8.000 books and articles. Gives major editions, translations, adaptations, and criticism. Author and title index. More comprehensive than Vol. 1 of Cabeen.

1317.   Cabeen, David Clark, ed. **Critical Bibliography of French Literature.** Syracuse, N.Y.: Syracuse University Press, 1947– .
Vol. 1, *The Medieval Period*, edited by U. T. Holmes, Jr. (1947; 256p.); Vol. 2,

The Sixteenth Century, edited by A. H. Schutz (1956; 365p.); Vol. 3, *The Seventeenth Century*, edited by N. Edelman (1961; 638p.); Vol. 4, *The Eighteenth Century*, edited by G. R. Havens and D. F. Bond (1951; 411p.); *Supplement*, edited by R. A. Brooks (1968; 283p.). A selective, evaluative, annotated bibliography, prepared by specialists. A tool of prime importance for advanced graduate students and scholars. Arranged by chronological periods, it lists books, periodical articles, and dissertations. Gives citations to reviews. Each volume has a good analytical index.

1318.   Calvet, Jean, ed. **Histoire de la littérature française**. Nouv. éd. Paris: Del Duca, 1955-64. 10 vols.

Vol. 1, *Le Moyen Age*, by R. Bossuat (1955); Vol. 2, *La Renaissance*, by R. Morcay and A. Muller (1960); Vol. 3, *Le préclassicisme, d'après Raoul Morcay*, by P. Sage (1962); Vol. 4, *Les écrivains classiques*, by H. Gaillard de Champris (1960); Vol. 5, *La littérature religieuse de François de Sales à Fénélon*, by J. Calvet (1956); Vol. 6, *De "Télémaque" à "Candide,"* by A. Cherel (1958); Vol. 7, *De "Candide" à "Atala,"* by H. Berthaut (1958); Vol. 8, *Le romantisme*, by P. Moreau (1957); Vol. 9, *Le réalisme et le naturalisme*, by R. Dumesnil (1955); Vol. 10, *Les lettres contemporaines*, by L. Chaigne (1964). These monographs by specialists follow a pattern similar to the *Oxford History of English Literature*.

1319.   Cecci, Emilio, and Natalino Sapegno. **Storia della letteratura italiana**. Milano: Garzanti, 1965– .

A history of Italian literature to be completed in about ten volumes, with coverage from the earliest period into the twentieth century. Following the plan of the *Cambridge History of English Literature*, chapters in each volume are written by specialists and contain bibliographies.

1320.   Chatham, James R., and Enrique Ruiz-Fornells, comps. **Dissertations in Hispanic Languages and Literatures, 1876-1966**. Lexington: University of Kentucky Press, 1969. 208p.

Lists nearly 1,800 doctoral dissertations completed in the United States, Canada, and Puerto Rico. Excludes those that deal with teaching the subject. Classified arrangement, with detailed author and subject index.

1321.   Cioranescu, Alexandre. **Bibliographie de la littérature française du seizième siècle**. Collaboration et préface de V.-L. Saulnier. Paris: Klincksieck, 1959. 745p.

The first part is devoted to general topics; the second (much larger) part is arranged alphabetically by individual authors of the period. Limited index.

1322.   Cioranescu, Alexandre. **Bibliographie de la littérature française du dix-septiéme siècle**. Paris: Editions du Centre National de la Recherche Scientifique, 1965-66. 3 vols.

Over 65,000 entries covering the period from 1601 to 1715. Detailed index of authors and subjects. Contents: Vol. 1, Generalities; Authors A–C; Vol. 2, D–M; Vol. 3, N–Z; Index.

1323. Cioranescu, Alexandre. **Bibliographie de la littérature française du dix-huitième siècle**. Paris: Centre National de la Recherche Scientifique, 1969. 3 vols.
Similar in plan and coverage to the two earlier period bibliographies by Cioranescu. Contents: Vol. 1, Generalities; Authors A–D; Vol. 2, E–Q; Vol. 3, R–Z; Index.

1324. Curley, Dorothy Nyren, and Arthur Curley, comps. **Modern Romance Literatures**. New York: Frederick Ungar, 1967. 510p.
Brief extracts of literary criticism on major twentieth century European writers in the Romance languages. Index of critics. Similar in concept to Moulton's *Library of Literary Criticism* and to the recent efforts to supplement and update it.

1325. Diaz-Plaja, Guillermo. **Historia general de las literaturas hispanicas**. Con une introd. de Ramon Menendez Pidal. Barcelona: Barna, 1949-67. 6 vols. in 7.
Somewhat similar in plan to the *Cambridge History of English Literature*. Includes coverage of Spanish literature in Latin America and the Philippines.

1326. **Dizionario enciclopedico della letteratura italiana**. Roma: Unedi, 1966-70. 6 vols.
An encyclopedia of Italian literature, similar in arrangement to Bompiani. Vol. 6 contains appendices and title and general indexes.

1327. Foster, David W., and Virginia Ramos Foster. **Manual of Hispanic Bibliography**. Seattle: University of Washington Press, 1970. 206p.
Guide to primary and some secondary sources of investigation in the field of Spanish literature.

1328. Foster, David William, and Virginia Ramos Foster. **Research Guide to Argentine Literature**. Metuchen, N.J.: Scarecrow Press, 1970. 146p.
First of its kind. Four main parts: 1) important bibliographies, guides, and general reference works; 2) journals; 3) general works by period and topics; 4) literary figures.

1329. Gay, Paul. **Notre littérature: guide littéraire du Canada français**. Montréal: HMH, 1969. 214p.

1330. Harvey, Sir Paul, and Janet E. Heseltine. **The Oxford Companion to French Literature**. Oxford: Clarendon Press, 1959. 771p.
Covers French literature from the Middle Ages to the start of World War II in 1939. Alphabetical arrangement of: articles on authors, critics, historians, religious writers, scholars, scientists, etc.; 2) articles on individual works, allusions, places, and institutions; 3) general survey articles on phases or aspects of French literary life, movements, etc.

1331.   Lanson, Gustave. **Manuel bibliographique de la littérature française moderne (XVIe, XVIIe, XVIIIe, XIXe siècles)**. Nouv. éd. rév. et corrigée. Paris: Hachette, 1931. 1820p.
Still useful, though the more recent works by Thieme and Cioranescu make it less vital.

1332.   Le Sage, Laurent, and André Yon. **Dictionnaire des critiques littéraires: guide de la critique française du XXe siècle**. University Park: Pennsylvania State University Press, 1969. 218p.
Biographical dictionary and concise introduction to modern French criticism. It includes information on 119 critics, covering aesthetic theory, major writings. General bibliography of further readings.

1333.   Moisés, Massaud. **Bibliografia da literatura portuguesa**. São Paulo: Editora da Universidade de São Paulo, 1968. 383p.
Basic bibliography of Portuguese literature from the days of the troubadours to the present. After a section of general works, arrangement is by literary period, with subsections for genres. Listings for individual authors include both editions of their works and critical studies about them (periodical articles as well as books). Detailed table of contents. Only authors of critical studies are indexed.

1334.   Osburn, Charles B., comp. **The Present State of French Studies: A Collection of Research Reviews**. Metuchen, N.J.: Scarecrow Press, 1971. 995p.
Essays in English, French, German or Italian. "The essays . . . survey research and interpretation in more than forty topics of French literature from the middle ages through the twentieth century" (Preface). Includes bibliographical references.

1335.   Osburn, Charles B. **Research and Reference Guide to French Studies**. Metuchen, N.J.: Scarecrow Press, 1968. 517p.
Intended as basic guide to reference tooks, but it also includes references to articles in 500 journals. Classified arrangement. Main section is devoted to French literature; there are 11 shorter sections on such topics as romance philology and comparative literature. Author and subject indexes.

1336.   Palfrey, Thomas Rossman, Joseph Guerin Fucilla, and William Collar Holbrook. **A Bibliographical Guide to the Romance Languages and Literatures**. 6th ed. Evanston, Ill.: Chandler's, 1966. 122p.
Classified bibliography of 1,824 items selected for their usefulness to graduate students. Detailed table of contents, but no index.

1337.   **Répertoire analytique de littérature française: revue bimestrielle d'information littéraire et bibliographique**. Vol. 1, No. 1– , Jan.-Feb., 1970– . Bordeaux, 1970– .
". . . The editors promise a time lag of only two to three months between publication or distribution of a book or article in France and its listing in RALF, as opposed to one to three years for the major annual literary bibliographies.

The format of *Répertoire* is still changing, but issues have included citations to books, articles, proceedings, essays in collections, both French and foreign, classed by broad subject areas. These listings are also available on cards, grouped by century. Descriptive annotations accompany many of the items; a few books are treated in full-length critical reviews. To date, each number has included at least one bibliography on a special topic . . .

"Despite this abundance of material, the long-term reference value of RALF is unclear. Because of the broadness of the subject classification and the absence of indexes, it is difficult to locate specific authors or topics. In addition, more than a year's accumulation of cards would be very tiresome to sift through. Possibly librarians will want to keep only the most recent issues in the reference collection and scrap the cards after arrival of the annual MLA bibliography for the corresponding period, although a comparison between the coverage of the latter and the *Répertoire* will have to be made . . ." [review in *College and Research Libraries* 33 (January 1972): 43-44].

1338.   Sainz de Robles, Federico Carlos. **Ensayo de un diccionario de la literatura**. 3rd ed. Madrid: Aguilar, 1965– .
Coverage includes Latin America as well as Spain.

1339.   Saisselin, Remy G. **The Rule of Reason and the Ruses of the Heart: A Philosophical Dictionary of Classical French Criticism, Critics, and Aesthetic Issues**. Cleveland: Case Western Reserve University Press, 1970. 308p.
Part I has alphabetically arranged essays on aesthetics and criticism. Part II deals with individual writers. Numerous cross references. Mainly for scholars in this field.

1340.   Simon Diaz, Jose. **Bibliografia de la literatura hispanica**. Madrid: Consejo Superior de Investigaciones Cientificas, Instituto "Miguel de Cervantes" de Filologia Hispanica, 1950– .
Coverage includes Latin America as well as Spain. Volumes in the series are being continuously revised and updated. Many Spanish library locations are noted.

1341.   Talvart, Hector, and Joseph Place. **Bibliographie des auteurs modernes de langue française**. Paris: Editions de la Chronique des Lettres Françaises, 1928– .
Bio-bibliographies of nineteenth and twentieth century authors. Vols. 1-15 (A–Mirbeau) were published between 1928 and 1963. Vols. 16 and 17 (1965, 1967) comprise a title index of works in Vols. 1-15 and an index of names and pseudonyms of authors and collaborators.

1342.   Thieme, Hugo Paul. **Bibliographie de la littérature française de 1800 à 1930**. Paris: Droz, 1933. 3 vols.
Vols. 1 and 2 contain about 2,000 author bibliographies and Vol. 3 covers more general subjects. Supplemented by *Bibliographie de la littérature française, 1930-1939*, by S. Dreher and M. Rolli (Geneva: Droz, 1948/49. 439p.) and

Bibliographie de la littérature française, 1940-1949, by M. L. Drevet (Geneva: Droz, 1955. 644p.).

1343.   Tougas, Gérard. **Histoire de la littérature canadienne-française.** 4e éd. Paris: Presses Universitaires de France, 1967. 312p.
The second edition (Paris, 1964) has been translated into English by Alta Lind Cook, *History of French-Canadian Literature* (Toronto: Ryerson Press, 1966).

1344.   **Zeitschrift für romanische Philologie. Supplement Heft: Bibliographie,** 1875– . Halle, 1878– .
Bibliography of books and periodical articles dealing with the various Romance languages and literatures. Some interruptions and delays during the periods of war.

Germanic Languages

1345.   Albrecht, Gunther, and Gunter Dahlke. **Internationale Bibliographie zur Geschichte der deutschen Literatur von den Anfangen bis zur Gegenwart, erarbeitet von deutschen, sowjetischen, bulgarischen, jugo- slawischen, polnischen, rumanischen, tschechoslowakischen und ungari- schen Wissenschaftlern.** Berlin: Volk und Wissen, 1969-71. 2 vols.
An international bibliography of the history of German literature which brings together the results of research in Germany, the Soviet Union, and other socialist countries of Eastern Europe. Chronological arrangement with comprehensive indexes.

1346.   **Bibliographie der deutschen Sprache- und Literaturwissenschaft.** Bd. 9– , 1969– . Frankfurt am Main: Klostermann, 1970– .
Includes books, articles, reviews and dissertations, arranged by literary period, with author and subject indexes. A continuation of *Bibliographie der deutschen Literaturwissenschaft* (Vols. 1-8, 1945/53. 1968).

1347.   Goedeke, Karl. **Grundriss zur Geschichte der deutschen Dichtung und den Quellen.** 2. ganz neubearb. Aufl. Dresden: Ehlermann, 1884-1959. 14 vols.
The most complete bibliography of German literature. Useful for an exhaustive search in a large library. Each volume has a detailed index but there is no cumulative index for the set.

1348.   **Introductions to German Literature.** London: Cresset Press, 1968– .
Vol. 1, *Literature in Medieval Germany*, by P. Salmon; Vol. 2, *German Literature in the Sixteenth and Seventeenth Centuries*, by R. Pascal (1968; 274p.); Vol. 4, *Twentieth Century German Literature*, by A. Closs (1969; 433p.). LC classifies and catalogs separately, but provides a series added entry.

1349.   **Jahresbericht für deutsche Sprache und Literatur.** Bearb. unter Leitung von Gerhard Marx. Berlin: Akademie-Verlag, 1960– .
Combines two former series in which language and literature were separate.

Comprehensive coverage of books and articles dealing with all periods of German language and literature. Classified arrangement. Extensive indexes.

1350. Kosch, Wilhelm. **Deutsches Literatur-Lexikon: biographisch-bibliographisches Handbuch**. 3., vollig neubearb. Aufl. hrsg. von Bruno Berger und Heinz Rupp. Berne: Francke Verlag, 1968– .
Contains biographical and bibliographical information about German, Austrian, and Swiss authors. To be completed in eight volumes.

1351. Köttelwesch, Clemens. **Bibliographisches Handbuch der deutschen Literaturwissenschaft, 1945-1969**. Frankfurt am Main, Klostermann, 1971– . (In Progress).
A select bibliography of books, articles, theses, etc., on German literature. It will probably run to 10 volumes when complete. Very detailed subject classification. It is relatively easy to find material on specific subjects, even though author and subject indexes will not appear until the final volume. Will both cumulate and supplement *Bibliographie der deutschen Literaturwissenschaft* (Vols. 1-8, 1945/53. 1968).

1352. **Kürschners deutscher Literatur-Kalender**. Berlin: Walter de Gruyter, 1879– . Annual.
Biographical, bibliographical, and directory information on about 10,000 living German, Austrian, Swiss, and other German-language writers.

1353. Robertson, John George. **A History of German Literature**. 5th ed. Rev. and enl. by Edna Purdie, with W. I. Lucas and M. O. C. Walsh. London: Blackwood, 1966. 720p.
First published in 1902 and long regarded as the best work in English, the book consists of six parts (each covering a major historical period) and is supplemented by a chronological table, chapter bibliographies, and an index.

1354. Yale University. Library. Yale Collection of German Literature. **German Baroque Literature: A Catalogue of the Collection in the Yale University Library**. By Curt von Faber du Faur. New Haven: Yale University Press, 1858-69. 2 vols.
Covers some 2,400 original editions from 1575 to 1740. Classified arrangement, with indexes of authors, composers, and illustrators.

Slavonic Languages

1355. Akademiia Nauk SSSR. Institut Russkoi Literatury. **Istoriia russkoi literatury**. Moskva: Izd-vo Akademiia Nauk SSSR, 1941-56. 10 vols.
A comprehensive history of Russian literature from the beginnings until 1917. Somewhat like the *Cambridge History of English Literature* in that individual chapters are written by specialists, but there are no bibliographies.

1356. Carlisle, Olga Andreyev, and Rose Styron, trs. and eds. **Modern Russian Poetry**. New York: Viking Press, 1972. 210p.

An anthology with historical background information. Concentrates on poets of World War II and of the Revolution of 1917. Reviewers have praised both the selections and the quality of the translations.

1357. Foster, Ludmila A. **Bibliography of Russian Emigre Literature, 1918-1968.** Boston: G. K. Hall, 1970. 2 vols.
Covers books and periodical articles, arranged by author and then by form. It is the only comprehensive bibliography of this elusive material, but it is somewhat difficult to use. Originally a doctoral dissertation at Harvard. Supplement planned for 1974.

1358. Harkins, William Edward. **Dictionary of Russian Literature.** London: Allen & Unwin, 1956. 439p.
Covers individual authors, trends, movements, literary criticism, etc. Some articles (e.g., Soviet literature) are lengthy. No bibliographies.

1359. **Kratkaia literaturaia entsiklopedia.** Glav. red. A. A. Surkov. Moskva: Sovetskaia Entsiklopedia, 1962– .
To be completed in six volumes. A general literary encyclopedia, especially valuable for writers from the various nationalities in the Soviet Union.

1360. Lewanski, Richard Casimir. **The Slavic Literatures.** New York: New York Public Library and Frederick Ungar, 1967. 630p. (The Literatures of the World in English Translation, V. 2).
Covers *belles-lettres* up to 1960. Basic arrangement is by language, with a first section devoted to anthologies, followed by an alphabetical author listing. No index to foreign language titles. There is an author-title index with cross references, plus an index of anthologies and their compilers.

1361. Matsuev, Nikolai Ivanovich. **Sovetskaia Khudozhestvennaia literatura i kritika, 1938/48; 1949/50– ; bibliografia.** Moskva: Sovetskii Pisatel, 1952– . Biennial after 1949/51.
A current bibliography of Soviet literature and criticism.

1362. Moscow. Publichnaia Biblioteka. **Velikaia Oktiabr'skaia Sotsialisticheskaia revoliutsia v proizvedeniiakh sovetskikh pisatelei: K istorii sovetskoi literatury. Bibliograficheskii ukazatel' dlia nauchnykh rabotnikov 1917-1966.** Moskva: "Kniga," 1967.
Citations for *belles-lettres* written on the theme of the Russian Revolution from 1917 to 1966. Annotated. Includes both separates and contributions to journals, yearbooks, and anthologies. Excludes children's literature, folk tales, and newspaper articles. Arranged chronologically · by decade (starting with 1917-1920), then by form (poetry, prose, drama, etc.). Very well indexed. Many cross references.

1363. Reeve, Franklin D. **The Russian Novel.** New York: McGraw-Hill, 1966. 397p.
Separate chapters on the major novelists. Begins with Pushkin and ends with Pasternak.

1364.   **Russkie pisateli: biobibliograficheskii slovar.** Moskva: Prosveshchenie, 1971. 728p.
Contains 300 biographies of Russian writers from medieval times to the twentieth century. Signed articles. Those on major figures run to several pages. Bibliographies of works by and about the authors are appended to the articles.

1365.   Strakhovsky, Leonid Ivan, ed. **A Handbook of Slavic Studies.** Cambridge: Harvard University Press, 1949. 753p.
Chapters 18-24 are devoted to various Slavic literatures.

1366.   Struve, Gleb. **Russian Literature under Lenin and Stalin, 1917-1953.** Norman: University of Oklahoma Press, 1971. 454p.
The best book available in English for the literature of this period, both for courses and for reference work. A sequel dealing with the post-Stalin era is planned.

1367.   Tezla, Albert. **Hungarian Authors: A Bibliographical Handbook.** Cambridge, Mass.: Belknap Press of Harvard University Press, 1970. 792p.
A companion volume to Tezla's *Introductory Bibliography to the Study of Hungarian Literature* (Cambridge: Harvard University Press, 1964).

1368.   Zenkovsky, Serge A., and David L. Armbruster. **A Guide to the Bibliographies of Russian Literature.** Nashville: Vanderbilt University Press, 1970. 62p.
Describes some 300 items. Classified arrangement (general, period, literary form), with author index.

Oriental Languages

1369.   Columbia University. Columbia College. **A Guide to Oriental Classics.** Prep. by the staff of the Oriental Studies Program, Columbia College, and ed. by W. T. DeBary and A. T. Embree. New York: Columbia University Press, 1964. 199p.
Sections on Islamic, Indian, Chinese, and Japanese literatures.

1370.   Kravitz, Nathan. **3,000 Years of Hebrew Literature: From the Earliest Times through the Twentieth Century.** Chicago: Swallow Press, 1972. 586p.
"Kravitz is an excellent scholar who writes with verve and authority. His is the only single-volume history of Hebrew literature, and it is excellent" (George Adelman, *Library Journal*, August 1972, p. 2606).

1371.   Lang, David Marshall, ed. **A Guide to Eastern Literatures.** London: Weidenfield and Nicolson, 1971. 501p.
Chapters by specialists. Covers 18 Oriental literatures, giving historical background, major literary trends, individual authors and their works, general bibliography, and English translations. Author, title, and subject index.

1372.   Waxman, Meyer. **A History of Jewish Literature**. New York: T. Yose-
         loff, 1960. 5 vols. in 6.
Major work on this subject in English.

African Languages

1373.   Herdeck, Donald E. **African Authors: A Bibliographical Companion to
         Black African Writing, 1300-1972**. Rockville, Md.: Black Orpheus Press,
         1973. 520p.
Also to be considered are *Black African Literature: An Introduction*, by J. P.
Makouta-Mbaukon (Rockville, Md.: Black Orpheus Press, 1973), *African Writers
Talking*, edited by Dennis Duerden and Cosmo Pieterse (New York: Africana
Publishing Co., 1972), and *Perspectives on African Literature*, edited by
Christopher Heywood (New York: Africana Publishing Co., 1971).

1374.   Jahn, Janheinz. **A Bibliography of Neo-African Literature from Africa,
         America, and the Caribbean**. New York: Praeger, 1965. 359p.
The African section is expanded and updated in *Bibliography of Creative African
Writing*, by Janheinz Jahn and Claus Peter Dressler (Nendeln, Liechtenstein:
Kraus-Thomson, 1971. 446p.).

1375.   Jahn, Janheinz. **Neo-African Literature: A History of Black Writing**. Tr.
         from the German by Oliver Coburn and Ursula Lehrburger. New York:
         Grove Press, 1969. 301p.

1376.   Zell, Hans M., and Helene Silver, comps. **A Reader's Guide to African
         Literature**. New York: Africana Publishing Co., 1971. 218p.
Covers black Africans south of the Sahara who write in English or French. The
bibliographical section has two divisions: English and French. Each is arranged
by country and then by author. Entries give full bibliographical information and
are annotated. The biographical section contains 51 biographical sketches.
Index.

AUTHOR AND TITLE INDEX
TO BIBLIOGRAPHICAL CHAPTERS

Each item (whether book or periodical) that has been given a separate entry has also been given an item number. These numbers run consecutively from the beginning of the first bibliographical chapter (Chapter 5–Principal Information Sources in Philosophy) through the final bibliographical chapter (Chapter 17–Principal Information Sources in Literature). The index refers to item numbers, not to page numbers. Books and serials mentioned in the annotations but not given separate entries are also indexed; the number in each such case is followed by the designation "n."

The list of chapters thus indexed is as follows:

Ch. No.	Short Title	Item Nos.	Paging
5	Philosophy	1– 93	58– 73
8	Religion	94– 257	95–123
11	Visual Arts	258– 527	138–180
14	Performing Arts	528–1013	204–272
17	Literature	1014–1376	289–342

The following guidelines were used in alphabetizing index entries: articles that occur at the beginning of titles have been omitted in the index. Lengthy titles have been shortened where this could be done without ambiguity. Entries have been arranged in accordance with the "word by word" or "nothing before something" method of filing. Names beginning with "Mc" have been filed as though spelled "Mac." Acronyms (e.g., ARLIS) have been treated as regular words rather than abbreviations. Numbers have been arranged as though written in word form. Works by one author alone have been placed before those by two or more joint authors if the surname and initials of the first author are identical with those of the single author.

SUBJECT INDEX

The purpose of this index is to provide access to broad topics that have received more than passing mention. References are to page numbers.